D0583588

THE EARLY NINETIES
A VIEW FROM THE BODLEY HEAD

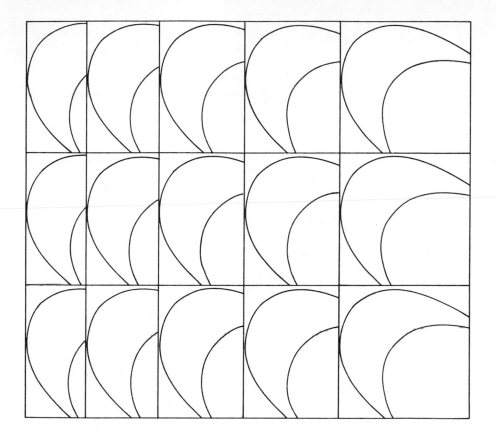

THE EARLY NINETIES

A VIEW FROM THE BODLEY HEAD

JAMES G. NELSON

HARVARD UNIVERSITY PRESS   CAMBRIDGE, MASSACHUSETTS

1971

© Copyright 1971 by the President and Fellows of Harvard College
All rights reserved
Distributed in Great Britain by Oxford University Press, London
Library of Congress Catalog Card Number 70–139718
SBN 674–22225–3
Printed in the United States of America

PREFACE

The climactic years of that remarkable, often bizarre, literary and artistic movement in Britain which at least symbolically ended with the trial of Oscar Wilde in the spring of 1895 coincided with the early years of the Bodley Head, a small bookshop and publishing firm which in so many ways summed up the spirit and ideals of that fascinating aesthetic milieu that produced not only Wilde and Aubrey Beardsley, but Ernest Dowson, Lionel Johnson, Arthur Symons, and W. B. Yeats as well.

A many-sided, often paradoxical period of artistic creativity, the early nineties are difficult to sum up in any comprehensive way. Often presented by historians and devotees as dominated by and in essence the work and personality of a single figure — for instance, Osbert Burdett's *The Beardsley Period* — the era has seldom been brought together in such a way as to highlight its diversities as well as to emphasize its unity of effect.

In an effort to give the reader a sense of the complexities of the literary and aesthetic milieu of the early nineties as well as a knowledge of its distinctive contributions to the permanent realm of art, I have sought to view the seven years 1887–1894 through the eyes of the Bodley Head — its partners, Elkin Mathews and John Lane; its authors and artists; and, of course, its books, which so often in subject matter and especially in format and design express the essence of the period so well.

Although the publication list of the Bodley Head during the early years was not extensive (some hundred or so books) compared with that of the large commercial publishers of the time, my task has, nevertheless, been one of selecting and emphasizing the significant authors and artists and the books that because of their physical makeup or subject matter, or both, seem to me most expressive of the temper of the early nineties and most significant in the light of future developments in both book design and literary trends. While I do not overlook the fact that in both form and content a number of the early Bodley Head books were ordinary and unexciting, I have sought to discuss in far more detail those books that clearly represent a break with the Victorian past and are an anticipation of the future.

The authors and artists of the early Bodley Head were of many different aesthetic persuasions, creators of such a variety of art that from one point of view the genius of the Bodley Head lay in its ability to garner within its ample range almost the whole artistic spectrum of the day. Yet the important contribution of the firm was the design of such books as Wilde's *The Sphinx,* John Addington Symonds' *In the Key of Blue,* and Lord De Tabley's *Poems, Dramatic and Lyrical,* which placed the Bodley Head book within the movement so often associated with the name of William Morris and known as the Revival of Printing, and the content of books like Arthur Symons' *Silhouettes,* John Gray's *Silverpoints,* George Egerton's *Keynotes,* and Wilde's *Salome,* which signaled a definite change in ideas, attitudes, and literary forms.

Within the compass of this book I hope I have been able to afford the reader not only an accurate sense of what I have referred to as the genius of the Bodley Head but also a just and ample knowledge of the literature and the art of the early nineties.

ACKNOWLEDGMENTS

In writing my book I have had the assistance and guidance of many friends and well-wishers, among whom my special thanks must go to Miss Nest Elkin Mathews, daughter of Elkin Mathews, who gave me permission to use the important collection of papers concerning her father and the early Bodley Head, which at the time of my researches was still in her possession; Patricia Hutchins, who not only introduced me to Miss Mathews but gave me the benefit of her extensive knowledge of Elkin Mathews and his friends; Sir Allen Lane, John Lane's nephew, and Mrs. Hans Schmoller, both of Penguin Books, for their help in assisting me in gathering important materials on John Lane; the Directors of the Bodley Head Ltd., especially J. B. Blackley, who along with Miss Susan Carew at my prompting rediscovered and put at my disposal many important data — letters, agreements, and other documents — concerning the early Bodley Head, and John Ryder, who read the manuscript and encouraged me in my venture.

I also take pleasure in acknowledging with gratitude the help and keen interest of P. J. W. Kilpatrick, the grandson of Walter Biggar Blaikie, who opened to me the extensive records of T. and A. Constable, Edinburgh, and helped me interpret them, and to his son, Colin W. Kilpatrick, who for T. and A. Constable Ltd. granted me permission to make use of the firm's records in my book. For giving me the benefit of his expert knowledge of the history of the Bodley Head and the publishing and book trade, I thank Percy Muir, who on several occasions kindly answered my queries and afforded me the hospitality of his home. During my visits to Oxford my researches were aided and expedited by the assistance of Harry Carter and Mrs. L. Thrussell of the Constance Meade Collection, the University Press; R. A. Sayce, Librarian, Worcester College Library; and D. S. Porter of the Bodleian. For permission to go through the Macmillan papers before they were dispersed, I thank Simon Nowell-Smith, whose interest in Sir William Watson and the history of publishing made our conversations most enjoyable, and Mr. T. M. Farmiloe of Macmillan Ltd. Also I must express my gratitude to Miss Gwen Le Gallienne for permission to make use of and publish extracts from the early diary, letters, and other papers of her stepfather, Richard Le Gallienne, and to Mrs. Edgar T. S. Dugdale for her kind hospitality on a number of occasions and for permission to quote from a number of unpublished letters in her possession, including one from Herbert P. Horne.

In addition to those already mentioned, I wish to thank the following persons for permission to quote from unpublished material: Mrs. Nona

Hill, two Arthur Symons letters; the Very Reverend the Prior Provincial, O. P., St. Dominic's Priory, London, three John Gray letters; Lt.-Col. J. L. B. Leicester Warren, various Lord De Tabley letters; Dame Janet Vaughn, a J. A. Symonds letter; Michael B. Yeats and Anne Yeats, a W. B. Yeats letter; Dr. M. Radford, four Ernest Radford letters; Sir Victor Philipse Hill Johnson, three Lionel Johnson letters; Mrs. Menzies Davidson, five John Davidson letters; and Messrs. Riders, Lincoln's Inn, London, a George Meredith letter. Extracts from unpublished letters by Laurence Housman © 1970 by Jonathan Cape Ltd., are reprinted by permission of Jonathan Cape Ltd. and the Huntington Library, San Marino, California.

For permission to publish copyrighted material in print I am grateful to the following: The Bodley Head Ltd. for quotations from J. Lewis May, *John Lane and the Nineties;* Harvard University Press for quotations from *Letters to the New Island,* ed. Horace Mason Reynolds, copyright 1934 by the President and Fellows of Harvard College, 1962 by Horace Mason Reynolds; D. Sturge Moore and Riette Sturge Moore for passages from *A Defence of the Revival of Printing* and *A Bibliography of the Books Issued by Hacon and Ricketts* by Charles Ricketts; John Russell Taylor for passages from *The Art Nouveau Book in Britain* reprinted by permission of A. D. Peters and Company; Peter Green and Messrs. John Murray for quotations from *Kenneth Grahame;* Messrs. Victor Gollancz, Ltd., for passages from *Memories of a Victorian* by Edgar Jepson; Miss Constance Ottley and Clarendon Press, Oxford, for quotations from *Letters of Walter Pater,* ed. Lawrence Evans; Mrs. Eva Reichmann and Granada Publishing Ltd. for extracts from *Letters to Reggie from Max Beerbohm,* ed. Rupert Hart-Davis; Sir John Rothenstein for quotations from *A Pot of Paint, The Artists of the 1890s;* Percy Muir and Messrs. Chatto and Windus for extracts from *Minding My Own Business;* Clarendon Press, Oxford, for quotations from *Letters of Dante Gabriel Rossetti,* ed. Oswald Doughty and John R. Wahl; Brian Reade, Viking Press Inc., and Studio Vista Ltd. for extracts from *Aubrey Beardsley;* Phyllis Grosskurth, Holt, Rinehart and Winston Inc., and Messrs. Longmans Green and Co., Ltd. for passages from *The Woeful Victorian, A Biography of John Addington Symonds;* Michael B. Yeats, Granada Publishing Ltd., and Macmillan Co., New York, for quotations from *The Letters of William Butler Yeats,* ed. Allan Wade; J. Benjamin Townsend and Yale University Press for quotations from *John Davidson, Poet of Armageddon;* Ruari McLean, Messrs. Faber and Faber Ltd., and Oxford University Press, New York, for extracts from *Victorian Book Design and Colour Printing;* Doubleday and Co., Inc., for passages from *The Romantic '90s* by Richard Le Gallienne; Messrs. Cassell and Co., Ltd., and Fairleigh Dickinson University Press for extracts from *The Letters of Ernest Dowson,* ed. Desmond Flower and Henry Maas; Barre Publishing Co. and the Richards Press for passages from *The Quest of the Golden Boy* by Richard Whittington-Egan and Geoffrey Smerdon; Messrs. Jonathan Cape Ltd., for extracts from *Robert Ross, Friend of Friends,* ed. Margery Ross; Messrs. J. W. Arrowsmith, Ltd., and Messrs. John Menzies, Ltd., for extracts from *Young Lives* by Richard Le Gallienne; Messrs. J. M. Dent and Sons Ltd. for passages from *Wales England Wed* by Ernest Rhys; Messrs. Macmillan Ltd. for quotations from *Letters to Macmillan,* ed. Simon Nowell-Smith; the Dial Press and Messrs. Geoffrey Bles Ltd. for extracts from *The Path through the Wood* by J. Lewis May; Macmillan Co., New York, for quotations from *The Autobiography of William Butler Yeats.* Extracts from *The Letters of Oscar Wilde,* ed. Rupert Hart-Davis, © 1962, by Vyvyan Holland, are reprinted by permission of Harcourt Brace Jovanovich, Inc.

For permission to reproduce the following materials used as illustrations in my book, I thank Sir John and Michael Rothenstein for the lithograph of Charles Ricketts and Charles H. Shannon by Will Rothenstein; Miss Nest Elkin Mathews for the drawing of her father, Elkin Mathews; Mrs. Eva Reichmann and Sir Allen Lane for the Max Beerbohm caricature of John Lane; the Library of Congress, Rosenwald Collection, for the photograph of Ernest Dowson; the William Andrews Clark Memorial Library, University of California, Los Angeles, for the photograph of Oscar Wilde and Lord Alfred Douglas; *Punch,* London, for the drawings by E. T. Reed and Linley Sambourne.

For permission to consult various unpublished documents and to quote from them in my book, I thank the trustees and boards of directors of the Huntington Library, San Marino, California; the William Andrews Clark Memorial Library, University of California, Los Angeles; the Poetry Collection, Lockwood Memorial Library, State University of New York at Buffalo; the Academic Center Library, University of Texas; Special Collections, Columbia University Library; the Henry W. and Albert A. Berg Collection of the New York Public Library, Astor, Lenox and Tilden Foundations; the Harvard College Library; Special Collections, Princeton University Library; Department of Manuscripts, the British Museum; Department of Western Manuscripts, Bodleian Library, Oxford; Liverpool City Libraries; City Library, Exeter; the Library, Reading University; and the Provost and Fellows of Worcester College, Oxford.

Portions of my manuscript were read by my fellow student of the aesthetes and decadents, Karl Beckson, whose valuable criticisms I gratefully acknowledge. For the initial idea and for reading and criticizing the entire manuscript I thank my friend and colleague, G. Thomas Tanselle.

For the funds to carry on the research and writing of this book I am grateful to the Dean of the Graduate School and the Research Committee of the Graduate School, University of Wisconsin, for three grants; the American Philosophical Society for a grant from the Johnson Fund; and the John Simon Guggenheim Memorial Foundation for a fellowship, which enabled me to complete my researches in Britain.

James G. Nelson
Madison, Wisconsin
1970

CONTENTS

Abbreviations   xiii

1. The Beginnings of the Bodley Head   1
2. The Bodley Head Book   36
3. Belles-Lettres to Sell   77
4. The Birth of a Book   110
5. The Bodley Head Poets: The Books of the Rhymers' Club   150
6. The Bodley Head Poets: Poisonous Honey and English Blossoms   184
7. The Bodley Head Authors: A Gathering of Playwrights, Essayists, and Fictionists   221
8. The Breakup   266

Appendices

A. Check List of Bodley Head Books, 1887–1894   283
B. The Bodley Head Artists and Illustrators   290
C. The Bodley Head Periodicals   298
D. The Reception of Bodley Head Books in America   306
E. Bodley Head Exports and Imports: England, America, Australia   311
F. Transfers   313
G. Production Costs and Final Inventory   315

Notes   327
Illustration Credits   372
Index   373

ILLUSTRATIONS

	page
Title page by W. B. Blaikie	11
Title page by Walter Crane	42
Title page by Laurence Housman	43
Title page by J. Illingworth Kay	61
Title pages by Selwyn Image and by H. P. Horne	62
Border within a border title page	68
Elkin Mathews, 1895, and caricature of John Lane by Max Beerbohm	93
Statement of limitation and title page of the first Bodley Head book	118
Some bindings for the early Bodley Head: Francis Thompson's *Poems*; Lord De Tabley's *Poems, Dramatic and Lyrical*; J. A. Symonds' *In the Key of Blue*; T. Gordon Hake's *Poems*; Allan Monkhouse's *Books and Plays*	118
Title page by Aubrey Beardsley	127
Title pages by Beardsley for some Keynote series books	164
Frontispiece and title page by Beardsley	165
Design by Beardsley for the Prospectus of the *Yellow Book*	193
Front covers by Beardsley of the first two volumes of the *Yellow Book*	208–209
Title page and first page of text designed by C. S. Ricketts for *The Sphinx*	227
Front and back covers of *The Sphinx* with Ricketts' designs	240–241
Prospectus and order form for F. W. Bourdillon's *A Lost God*	251
Prospectus and order form for Kenneth Grahame's *Pagan Papers*	252
Beardsley's parody of C. S. Ricketts' cover designs for the Bodley Head	257
E. T. Reed's parody of Beardsley's cover designs and illustrations for the Keynotes series	257
Linley Sambourne's drawing of Beardsley pulling the Yellow Book authors	257
Oscar Wilde and Lord Alfred Douglas. Ricketts and Shannon, 1897, by William Rothenstein. Ernest Dowson	269

ABBREVIATIONS

Berg. Letters and other documents relating to the Bodley Head and its authors in the Berg Collection, New York Public Library.

B.H.F. Contracts, letters, and miscellaneous documents relating to the publication of early Bodley Head books in the files of the present Bodley Head publishing firm.

Bodleian. Materials, mainly letters from Lord De Tabley to Mathews and Lane, in the Walpole Nineties collection, Bodleian Library, Oxford.

B.M. Miscellaneous documents relating to the Bodley Head in the Department of Manuscripts, British Museum.

Constable. Letter Books, Day Books, and Ledgers of the printers T. and A. Constable of Edinburgh relating to the Bodley Head, in the archives of the present-day firm.

C.P.R. Chiswick Press records, including the Sold Books, December 15, 1888, to November 12, 1895, in the Department of Manuscripts, British Museum.

C.U.L. Documents relating to the Bodley Head in Special Collections, Columbia University Library.

Diary. A diary kept by Richard Le Gallienne from November 12, 1889, to October 22, 1890, in the Poetry Collection of the Lockwood Memorial Library, State University of New York at Buffalo.

Dugdale. Letters and miscellaneous documents primarily concerning Herbert P. Horne in the possession of Mrs. Edgar T. S. Dugdale.

Dulau. *Books from the Library of John Lane and Other Books of the Eighteen-Nineties,* Catalogue 165, Dulau & Co., Ltd., [London, 1929]. Many of the items in this catalogue are now in the Princeton University Library and the Clark Library, University of California, Los Angeles.

E.M. Letters, manuscripts, and other materials relating to Elkin Mathews and the Bodley Head gathered by his daughter, Miss Nest Elkin Mathews, now in the Library, Reading University.

Hales. A collection of twenty-seven letters from Richard Le Gallienne to Samuel Hales, a Liverpool bookseller who later resided in London, in the Poetry Collection of the Lockwood Memorial Library, State University of New York at Buffalo.

Houghton. Letters, manuscripts, and other documents relating to Walter Crane, Will Rothenstein, and others in the Houghton Library, Harvard University.

Huntington.   Letters of Laurence Housman in the Henry E. Huntington
  Library and Art Gallery, San Marino, California.
Lane.   A collection of letters to John Lane belonging to his nephew, Sir
  Allen Lane, and presently kept at University College Library, London.
Le G.   A large collection of letters written by Richard Le Gallienne, in the
  Picton Library, Central Public Libraries, Liverpool.
Macmillan.   Letter Books and other documents in the files of Macmillan
  & Co. at Basingstoke, England. These materials have since been dis-
  persed to the British Museum and the Library, Reading University.
P.U.L.   Miscellaneous documents relating to the Bodley Head, in the
  manuscript collections of Princeton University Library.
U.C.L.A.   Letters and documents relating to the Bodley Head in the
  "Oscar Wilde and the Nineties Collection" in the William Andrews Clark
  Memorial Library, University of California, Los Angeles.
U.T.L.   Documents relating to the Bodley Head in the Academic Center
  Library, University of Texas.

THE EARLY NINETIES
A VIEW FROM THE BODLEY HEAD

The Bodley Head was established in London in 1887 as a result of the cooperation of two men, Charles Elkin Mathews and John Lane. Yet the history of the Bodley Head should rightly begin with Elkin Mathews because it was his little bookshop in the Cathedral Yard at Exeter which first was associated with the name of Sir Thomas Bodley, the founder of the famed library at Oxford and a native son of Exeter. On the back of a letter written to his sister soon after he opened his book business in the Devonshire county town, Elkin Mathews has drawn up the "fancy title page" of what was to be his first catalogue.[1] That the patron saint of his little shop was to be one of Exeter's most beloved and revered personages is clear from the proposed title: "The Bodley Library Catalogue," which is flanked by the arms of Sir Thomas Bodley. Doubtless the young Mathews was attracted to the memory of one who, like himself, loved old, rare, and curious books. His own patron saint, Izaak Walton, had once written of Exeter as the "city which may justly boast that it was the birthplace of Sir Thomas Bodley."[2] Although Lane implied that the inspiration for the famous name, the Bodley Head, was his,[3] when the bookshop was removed to London in September 1887, without a doubt it carried along its Bodleian associations.

Elkin Mathews was born at Gravesend in 1851, where his family for years had been shipowners and at one time or another had engaged in shipbuilding. Elkin Mathews' father, Thomas George, and his mother, Frances Elkin, were both devoted to books. So foreign to his shy and retiring nature were

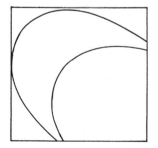 1 THE BEGINNINGS
OF THE
BODLEY HEAD

the sea-oriented occupations of his forefathers that as a rather young man Thomas Mathews retired from the family business and removed himself, his wife, and his children to a serene little village remote from the sea, known as Codford-St. Mary, near the Salisbury Plain in Wiltshire. There in a comfortable house called "The Poplars" the Mathews children were reared — three sons and six daughters — with the generous help of their well-to-do Grandfather Elkin.[4]

Elkin Mathews was largely a self-educated man, whose quiet, unobtrusive nature lent itself to a lifelong preoccupation with books. According to his daughter, Miss Nest Elkin Mathews, the young man left a comfortable and sheltered home — probably in his mid-twenties — and learned accounting in London from his elder brother, Thomas George, before he entered the bookseller's trade. Since he had been a collector of old books and belles-lettres all his life, when the time came for him to choose a vocation, as he once told an interviewer, "it seemed natural that I should turn my hobby to a practical use." [5] And so without ever practicing as an accountant, Elkin Mathews entered the firm of a Mr. Charles John Stewart of King William Street, Strand, who was known as "the last of the learned old booksellers." Later he left London to manage Peach's, a well-known bookshop in Bath, and after two or three years there, returned to London to work for the famous booksellers, the Messrs. Sotheran in Piccadilly.[6]

Mathews, whom J. Lewis May was later to describe as "a neat, dapper, little man, rather fussy and old-maidish in his ways," was during the early years of the Bodley Head a clean-shaven fellow with a bald globular head which May felt to be "much too large for his body." [7] Although he was a quiet, unassuming person, most at home among antiquarian books, he was not without ambition. It was his desire "to become the Edward Moxon" of his time.[8] Despite the fact that it has often been assumed that Elkin Mathews entered publishing only through his partnership with Lane, his stated ambition and the fact that he ventured into publishing in a very small way while still in Exeter prove that his later absorption in the business of publishing was the fulfillment of his early desires.[9]

In the autumn of 1884, with the backing of an uncle,[10] the young bookman, now in his early thirties, went to Exeter and opened a shop at 16 Cathedral Yard (adjoining the Royal Clarence Hotel) under the name of C. Elkin Mathews. According to his later statement, Mathews chose to start his business in the old cathedral city because it lent "itself to the nature of the work upon which I had decided to embark." [11] That he was prepared to offer his customers service in all areas of the book trade is suggested by his stationery, catalogues, and advertisements. He announced himself as an "Ancient and Modern Bookseller" with specialties in books relating to

Devon, Cornwall, and Somerset, as well as scarce and out-of-the-way books and autographs. He also offered to arrange, renovate, and catalogue libraries, and did "bookbinding in the best styles." [12] "An admitted expert by this time of ancient tomes of many periods, Elkin Mathews," according to one report of these early years, "began not only to deal but to publish. The works issued at Exeter were, of course, chiefly of local interest." [13] The titles of the books which bear the imprint of the young publisher certainly bear this out. *We Donkeys on the Devon Coast* by one Miss Maria Susannah Gibbons of Wallingford, Budleigh Salterton, Devon, was published July 23, 1887,[14] and reported the author's spring ramblings via donkey tandem along the byways of rural Devonshire.

Probably Miss Gibbons had her book printed and bound at her own expense, a not unusual occurrence in those days. Since no fewer than five names of booksellers appear as publishers — three from Exeter: Thomas Upward, J. G. Commin, and C. Elkin Mathews; Doidge and Co. of Plymouth, and Simpkin, Marshall and Co. of London — I suspect that they were in fact no more than agents through whom the book was sold.

Soon after his arrival in London in September 1887, Mathews published the *Index* to Dr. Oliver's *Lives of the Bishops of Exeter,* the imminent appearance of which had been advertised at the back of *We Donkeys.* J. S. Attwood, the compiler of the index, was a friend of Mathews and introduced him to a number of local antiquaries in Exeter including C. F. Cooksey, a new cashier at the Wilts and Dorset Bank, who, according to Mathews, was "a jolly fellow, a good herald, geologist and antiquary generally." A letter to his sister suggests that Mathews and Attwood spent many a Sunday enjoying Cooksey's collection of topographical and architectural books, and his vast collection of rare coins, oil paintings, and "celtic curios of all kinds." [15] On November 14, 1887, Mathews in London and James George Commin in Exeter brought out William Crossing's *The Ancient Crosses of Dartmoor* and completed the pre-Bodley Head imprint list of publications with Attwood's *Index* to Dr. Oliver's *Monasticon Dioecesis Exoniensis* early in 1889. None of these publications were in subject matter or form anything like the books which were soon to issue from the bookshop in Vigo Street beginning with Richard Le Gallienne's *Volumes in Folio* of March 1889, the first book to bear the Bodley Head imprint.

Despite the fact that Elkin Mathews went to Exeter prepared to turn his "most cherished possessions" — a sizeable collection of "old, rare, and curious" books — "into cash" since, as he put it, "necessity must now overrule sentiment," [16] indications are that his three years in the Cathedral Close were not profitable ones. In an interview with a reporter some years later, Mathews remarked that on moving to Exeter he soon "found that there was no room for expansion there. A native [probably Commin] was already in possession of the field, and his monopoly of the good book-buyers was not to be assailed. I felt I must seek pastures new, and returned to London." [17]

Although Mathews may have found his Exeter business a bit slow, the immediate cause for his moving to London was John Lane, a young man three years Mathews' junior, who until 1892 held the unromantic position of clerk in the Railway Clearing House at Euston Station, London. The link between the two men seems to have been Elkin Mathews' elder brother, Thomas George, who also worked in the Clearing House. Just when the two future partners became acquainted is not known. Lane had been at the Clearing House since 1868, and, therefore, it is entirely possible that the two met when Elkin Mathews was working in London at Sotherans. Nevertheless, Thomas George Mathews probably introduced them when he found that they had the same passion for old and rare books and items of antiquarian interest.

As one of Lane's friends who knew him in the early days once wrote, "Lane was a born antiquary, and his passion for collecting books, prints, china, glass, samplers, fans, pewter, pictures — in short any and every historical relic that came to his hand — won him a number of friends among persons of similar tastes." [18] Lane, who must have spent much of his spare time making the rounds of London bookshops and auctions, probably supplied Mathews with an occasional rare book and at times drew on Mathews' expert knowledge of the value and authenticity of rare items.

Although there is no proof that the men met until shortly before Mathews returned to London in 1887, it is almost certain that Lane had visited the shop in Exeter and also had seen Mathews when he visited his brother in London. However that may be, some time during the spring of 1887, Elkin Mathews and John Lane decided to bring their stock of books together in a London shop if suitable premises could be found within the next year or so. Correspondence between the two shows that Lane was actively engaged in this matter as early as May 16, 1887.[19]

From all indications, Lane, who had a superb business head, had by this time a considerable knowledge of the book trade. Although it is impossible to tell how large and valuable Lane's collection of books was in 1887, there are indications that it was considerable. R. Pearse Chope, who for a time lived at the residence which Lane shared with Dr. Owen Pritchard at 37 Southwick Street, Hyde Park, remarks that Lane afforded him "the use of his extensive, but peculiar, library." [20] In 1890, before Lane quit the Clearing House and became an open partner in the Bodley Head, Arthur Symons wrote of Lane as "quite a bibliomaniac," who had recently shown him "bewildering loads of Meredith & other first eds., autograph letters, etc." [21]

The letters between Lane and Mathews through the summer of 1887 also suggest that Lane had for some years been buying and selling books on the side and collecting any work which because of its age, its condition, or its bibliographical interest might make it valuable. In May 1887, Lane was tempting Mathews with a copy of Charles Kingsley's *Westward Ho!* And in the same letter, his "tip" to Mathews about buying up first issues of the Mermaid series edition of *Marlowe's Plays* marks him as an alert and knowl· edgeable collector of books, for he had found that the first issue of the plays was withdrawn from the market in consequence of some blasphemous lines and that the second and current issue had only 430 pages, one less than the first.[22]

Just when and how Lane became interested in books cannot readily be established. Nothing in his background would suggest any special reason for his becoming so avid a bibliophile.[23] He was born March 14, 1854, at West Putford, Devon, the only son of Lewis Lane, a farmer, and Mary Grace, the daughter of a miller and grain merchant. When he was three, his parents moved to a nearby farm at Hartland called "Fosfelle," where he lived the life of a farmer's boy and partook of what educational opportuni· ties the locale offered until he left for London at the age of 14.[24] According to J. Lewis May, Lane's mother, with the aid of the Reverend Robert Stephen Hawker, the parson-poet of Morwenstow, "got him a position as boy-clerk in the Railway Clearing House, at a commencing salary of a pound a week." [25] This was in 1868 or early 1869. So some time during the next eighteen or so years, John Lane became enamored of books and prob· ably in time saw that they could be valuable and even, by way of a hobby, profitable.

This interest in rare and beautiful books was surely the only thing that could possibly have brought the partners together. Mathews later said, "finding that we had tastes in common, I took him [Lane] into partnership when I commenced again [after moving from Exeter to London] as a publisher in these offices (that was in 1887), and he continued with me until he set up for himself opposite here in the old office of the *Saturday Review*." [26]

John Lane had come to London in 1869 as a shy, rustic-looking youth who spoke with a strong Devonshire accent, but by 1887 he had largely overcome his awkwardness and boorish manners, and was a very genial, ur· bane man of thirty-three.[27] When J. Lewis May first knew him, Lane was "a little dapper man . . . well groomed, well dressed. His hair, parted and brushed with scrupulous care, was something between auburn and sandy. His beard was trimmed to a point. His eyes were big, bluish, and decidedly expressive." But somehow, according to May, "in spite of his fine clothes and his spruce appearance, he looked like a little farmer, which was natural enough, seeing all his folk were on the land." [28]

When he began to look about for premises in which to settle his and Mathews' collections of books, he knew all the important booksellers in London as well as librarians at the British Museum and other men knowledgeable in art and literature. The letters which passed between Lane and Mathews from May through September 1887 suggest that he was very much in touch with the book market of the day, the shift from one area of London to another of bookselling establishments, and the possibilities of the trade. These letters also show that Lane was most anxious to bring Mathews to London and that it was his initiative that led to the establishment of the Bodley Head sooner rather than later.

Lane no doubt saw in Elkin Mathews his chance to get his toe in the door of a good bookselling business which might easily be expanded into a small publishing firm as well. Mathews not only knew the trade and was willing to venture into publishing, but he also had a good stock of rare books, a bit of ready cash, a desire to come back to London, and an amiable, perhaps easily manageable personality. Since Lane was the man of action, it was incumbent upon him to overcome his friend's reluctance to sever ties and pull up stakes. Seeing at last the possibility of entering an occupation which would free him to exploit his social and professional talents to the full, Lane was not to be deterred. By May 1887, bringing Mathews to London was his primary concern.

"I have seen nothing in the shape of premises at all suitable as yet," he reported to Mathews on May 16. But it is clear that he was looking in earnest, and that both the City and "quiet and out of the way corners" were being considered. "A friend with whom I was dining yesterday thinks that Oxford St. near the circus would be a good sight [sic], Hanover Square end," he writes Mathews. And, as he continues his letter, his eye for business is reflected in the way he takes up the friend's suggestion about advertising, "that we should have a cat. put in a well bound case for the drawing rooms and libraries of the principal hotels . . . and why not clubs in the same way?" [29]

Perhaps the most auspicious sign of Lane's sense of urgency and Mathews' desire perhaps to delay are some cryptic yet humorous lines in several letters in which Lane urges his friend to "be firm in the Fraulein matter." Was Mathews actually in the toils of a Devonshire romance, or was this mysterious Fräulein but a means of restraining a somewhat too impetuous Lane? At the very moment when the terms of the contract for leasing the Vigo Street premises were being negotiated, the fate of the partnership may perhaps have depended upon Mathews' choice between a wife and a London bookshop. Business won out over romance, for the whole affair is last mentioned by Lane in his letter of August 10: "Don't let Fraulein pervert you, *be firm.* You don't mention her in your *letter,* is it all off?" [30]

It was on Wednesday, June 15, 1887, that Lane wrote to Mathews about the premises which in October were to become the Bodley Head. His enthusiasm for the spot and his anxious desire to have Mathews come to town at once to view the quarters is evident in the letter. I write, he says,

. . . to tell you that by the merest chance I think I have found suitable premises at a ⅓ of our contemplated rental viz: — £80. The premises, a shop and W. C. only, are situate[d] in Vigo St: a few doors from Regent St adjoining the R[oyal] G[eographic] Soc:[31] close to Burlington House and the London University etc. indeed it is surrounded by seats of learning, the shop itself is now in the occupancy of my friend Mr. Dunthorne the well known print-seller and fine art publisher, he has removed to larger premises in the same St: store rooms could be had no doubt in the same street, it seems to me that if we had searched London all over that we could not have found any place half so suitable *for a start,* as the risk is nothing and the position is a fine one. I went to Dunthorne's private view on Sat: morn when I asked him in conversation if he knew of suitable premises for a high class bookseller in his street or near, at once he said 'yes'! my own "little box" two doors from here. I must tell you that the shop is small, about the size of your present, but look at the position and the low rental!

Now I hope you will be able to come up on Sat. next [June 18] and stay over Tuesday, so that we may be able to look at the place together on Monday (we get both Monday-Tuesday) of course it will be closed on Tuesday, Dunthorne's customers will [have] *fled* the place I consider: This morn: I met Wilson the deputy superintendent of the B[ritish] M[useum] Reading room, he takes great interest in my, in *our,* venture and we are going down to see the place tomorrow evening, he thinks highly of the position.

Let me have an early line please with your views on the subject.

With my kindest regards,
Yours always
John Lane[32]

According to Lane's not wholly trustworthy introduction to his reprint of *The Life of Sir Thomas Bodley,* Mathews did come up to London upon this summons and "saw and liked the place as much as I did." [33] But before the matter was settled, there was a long, hectic summer for Lane, who, in addition to egging on Mathews, had to be Johnny-on-the-spot when it came to arranging the terms of rental, searching out a storeroom, overseeing the fitting up of the premises, and buying up suitable books for the fall stock. By July 11, Mathews had made formal application for the Vigo Street "cabinet," which was "to be used for the purpose of a high-class old book business — the rent to commence at Michaelmas next." [34]

On August 11, the Royal Geographic Society's finance committee had met and accepted Elkin Mathews as tenant in the place of Dunthorne, but as yet a contract for the Vigo Street "cabinet" had not been signed by Mathews nor had a partnership agreement between Mathews and Lane been drawn up. In fact, according to a letter Mathews drafted early in 1895, shortly after the breakup, he had been forced into the partnership with Lane, having "discovered that through taking some of his books I had practically made him my partner." Although, according to Mathews, he had "at that early stage" not received from Lane "one shilling in cash," Mathews "found there was no choice" but "to submit to a partnership deed being drawn up." [35] Certainly a reluctance to act is suggested by Mathews' draft letter to Lane of Sunday, August 14, which is rife with misgivings about the whole affair. Considerably overwhelmed by all the problems attendant upon moving a book business to London, Mathews wrote:

Dear Lane,

I commenced a letter to you on Friday, but a late post brought amended Draft of Deed of Partnership and the consideration thereof caused me to lose the post. I have an invincible dislike for accounts, and a partnership seems to involve neverending book-keeping. I suppose it will be inevitable. I enclose copy of Nickinson's letter accompanying amended Draft.

I note the insertion of a new clause making it unnecessary to provide a Schedule of specially excepted Books. This no doubt is a good arrangement in one way, but on the otherhand it leaves us in the dark as to the value of our books respectively.

Is it not reasonable to suppose that I must have the greater value? I have now been in business nearly 3 years and have spent in stock . . . about £500 and you know I want to provide a clause to enable me to repay Mr Elkin the sum of £115 (really £125) *when the finances of the business would permit.*

Doubtless if I were to remain down here to the end of my term [of lease] I should be able to do this. As I have now established some position here; but you must see directly the partnership is completed[,] my action is hampered and I am powerless. I have of course sufficient at my Banker's, I think even after I have settled various a/cs, but then your own cash balance would not I am afraid be sufficient to float us.

Unless I look to matters of this kind I don't quite see how the partnership will benefit me — Therefore I am puzzled to know what to say to Mr Nickinson — I think I will delay returning the Deed until I hear from you. . . .

I confess at present I can only wonder how the details will be worked out.[36]

In his reply of August 15, Lane is most agreeable and seems to fall in with all of Mathews' stipulations. "I wish you fully to understand," he begins,

that I agree to take the books on your list at the invoiced prices; with regard to the list of books I just as much as you, object to making one & I dont think one at all necessary; for my part I merely want you to go through my books to mark them off at selling prices, make a total, which we agree to halve in order to ascertain my capital, adding thereto my available cash: The same rule to apply to yours, (excepting the list before named.) With regard to the redemption of your debt to your uncle you can put in any clause or provision you like, only I hope it wont be necessary to draw it out until we have got over the 1st twelve months.

As to the "bookkeeping clause," Lane assures his partner-to-be that he will not be "unreasonable as I have just as much dislike at looking thro' a/c's as you have in keeping them, it will of course be necessary to keep more a/cs than you are now in the habit of keeping, tho' not much I should say." In closing, Lane writes that there is no need to draw up a list of books as "we only want to ascertain *their value* & the agreement had better be left unsigned until then so that the amounts can be filled in." [37]

Meanwhile the rental of the premises was settled upon at £85 per annum, and a storeroom at 13 Buckingham Street, the Strand, was taken at one pound per month. In addition to all these matters, the letters are full of book talk — Mathews in Exeter is preparing a catalogue in an effort to rid himself of his "ordinary stock," while Lane in London is rendering "an account" of his "stewardship," which just happens to include a copy of *Fanny Hill* to be had for thirty shillings. "Shall I give it?" he asks his partner. "I have been buying freely," Lane tells Mathews, "but Oppenheim thinks *very wisely* as he would gladly relieve me of much at a profit." [38]

Lane's letters, dashed off as they so often are during these months of 1887 — usually on the back of Dr. Pritchard's bills or on the Railway Clearing

House stationery — convey very graphically all the haste, excitement, and energy which these various activities demanded of him; yet nothing seems to have missed his care and attention. Late in September, he was already anticipating business and laying plans to capture the attention of the members of the Royal Geographic Society and the Society of Antiquarians who meet nearby: "I think & I fancy they pass our door, we must keep open that night & dress window for them. Let me have your opinion on those suggestions of mine," he urges; "you are silent on the Fanny Hill question." [39]

The first week in October the premises in Vigo Street were all but ready: "I was at the 'Bodley' yesterday morn:" Lane reports,

certainly much progress had been made[;] the bottom cases were in, and I must say they looked fine, they have such a wonderful *polish* on them that I at first thought they were of walnut.

The letter hole is cut, & the first letter to come oddly enough is from the Bodlean[*sic*] which I hold. I meet Pouditch [the carpenter] there tonight at 5 o/c. I hope that you will be able to come up early tomorrow, can't you come per G[reat] W[estern] Railway & so direct to "37" & start on the big case in Pritchards Drawing room? [40]

Mathews, of course, was not so prompt as Lane had hoped, but arrived on Friday, October 7.[41] The shop was stocked and prepared over the week end, and the Bodley Head probably opened for business on Monday morning, October 10, 1887.

It was the opinion of J. Lewis May (who as a stock boy once assisted in the operations of the new establishment) that the move to London "was, on the whole, an ill wind for little Mathews," who was thus caught up and whisked "away from the cloistral calm of the Cathedral Yard in Exeter," and deposited

in the heart of the Metropolis. Not but what Vigo Street was quiet enough in those days. For one thing, there were posts across it then, debarring wheeled traffic from going past the entrance to Albany. There were no motor horns to startle you from your dreams; nothing louder than the trot of a hansom-cab horse and the airy jingle of its bells.[42]

Vigo Street was quiet, but it was certainly not out of the way. Originally called Vigo Lane when it was first planned by the Earl of Burlington in

SIGHT AND SONG WRITTEN BY MICHAEL FIELD

ELKIN MATHEWS
AND JOHN LANE
AT THE SIGN OF
THE BODLEY HEAD
IN VIGO STREET
LONDON 1892

Title page by W. B. Blaikie.

11

1733, the narrow thoroughfare which connects Savile Row with Regent Street was named after the battle of Vigo Bay. And until the Bodley Head made it famous, the most striking event in its history had been a terrible fire which Horace Walpole mentioned in a letter to a friend on April 28, 1761. The quaint little shop, whose sign was soon to rival the library at Oxford in making Sir Thomas Bodley's name known far and wide, was at 6B Vigo Street almost opposite the entrance to Albany, where Lane was later to live and have his shop.[43]

J. Lewis May describes it as "a little bookshop with a brave array of rare editions cunningly displayed to catch the eye of the passing bibliophile." [44] In addition to a large display window, which occupied the whole of the front with the exception of a door, there were large display cabinets extending out from each side of the shop toward the street in such a way that it was next to impossible for a passer-by to divert his gaze from the display of books. May remembers it as "a little box of a place" with books lined "from floor to ceiling. At the far end was a sort of screen, behind which, above a trap-door leading to a cellar, sat the cashier." [45] I am sure Percy Muir is correct when he writes that Aubrey Beardsley's cover design for the prospectus of the *Yellow Book*, volume one, is a fanciful portrayal of the shop window with Mathews as Pierrot.[46]

The Bodley Head sign, which hung outside the shop until Lane took it across the street when the partnership broke up at the end of September 1894, was an oval medallionlike affair with the head (done in terra cotta) inlaid and gilded. The likeness was taken from a portrait of Bodley which Mathews sent up from Exeter in September 1887.[47] From the beginning, it was a beacon to many a booklover and author who was to find within a haven from the mundane pursuits of high-Victorian London. As Ernest Rhys recalled, the Bodley Head became "a west-end Mecca of poets, young and old. A funny little shop, almost the smallest in London, in which there was hardly room to turn round." [48]

For the first few years the Bodley Head prospered under the direction of Elkin Mathews, who appeared to be the sole proprietor of the firm. Lane understandably was reluctant at the outset to give up his position at the Clearing House until the success of the firm was assured and the income was sufficient to support both men. So until January 1892, "Mathews," in the words of Percy Muir, "was in charge, and Lane a comparatively infrequent visitor; only after four o'clock when his office closed. For the time being the business was mostly what Mathews wanted it to be, a metropolitan version of the Exeter business." [49]

Yet if John Lane was a silent partner, he was by no means inactive in the fortunes of the early Bodley Head. There is a good deal to suggest that he exerted considerable influence on Elkin Mathews during these first five years and was able through his extensive contacts with the London literary and artistic world to prepare for the full flowering of the Bodley Head from 1892 through September 1894.

Although there is ample evidence to suggest that Mathews returned to London partly to expand his interest in publishing, there is little to indicate that he alone, without the influence of Lane, would have published the twenty-five books which the firm brought out between 1887 and 1892.

Soon after his arrival in London, Mathews had published Attwood's *Index* to *Lives of the Bishops of Exeter,* and in November 1887, he had brought out (in cooperation with Commin) William Crossing's *The Ancient Crosses of Dartmoor.* Yet no books were published in 1888, and, of the three volumes which appeared with Mathews' imprint in 1889, only one, Attwood's *Index* to *Monasticon Dioecesis Exoniensis,* can be attributed to Mathews' efforts alone. Probably Emily Hickey's *Verse-Tales* and most certainly Le Gallienne's *Volumes in Folio* were the result of Lane's initiative. Of the eleven books included in the firm's list for 1890, such volumes as Ernest Radford's *Chambers Twain,* Cosmo Monkhouse's *Corn and Poppies,* and John Todhunter's *A Sicilian Idyll* were published as a result of Mathews' acquaintance with the authors. But several books published during 1890 and 1891 can be attributed to Lane's efforts — Le Gallienne's *George Meredith,* for example.

And although Elkin Mathews' earliest publishing efforts were more or less unexciting in subject matter, ordinary and uninspired in their appearance, there is no reason to believe that he was opposed to or failed to have his share in the emergence of what — largely through the efforts of Lane and Le Gallienne — soon became the typical Bodley Head book. On the contrary, it was he far more than Lane who was to continue the small, uncommercial atmosphere and tradition of the Bodley Head after the dissolution of the partnership. The fact that Mathews continued to publish belles-lettres such as the poetry of Lionel Johnson, W. B. Yeats, and later, Ezra Pound, in small, artistically designed editions, attests to his commitment to the choice kind of book which during 1889 and 1890 came to be the hallmark of the Bodley Head.

While Mathews was preoccupied with the Bodley Head's antiquarian interests, Lane was busy — largely through social and literary channels — seeking out prospective authors and searching for the type of book which might serve as a model for future publications. So far as the future of the Bodley Head was concerned, Lane's first "find" was the most significant. In Richard Le Gallienne, Lane found not only a promising young author but also a poet who recently had seen through the press a tasteful and attractive little volume entitled *My Ladies' Sonnets.* Privately printed in a limited edition which included fifty large-paper copies numbered and signed by the author, with blue-gray boards and an imitation vellum spine ridged to suggest one of the rare old tomes Le Gallienne loved so well, and fine white handmade paper, rubricated initials and choice type, *My Ladies' Sonnets* was a direct anticipation of *the* Bodley Head book.[50] The fact that it was a "dainty" volume of verse — slight little lyrics about love, world-weariness, the pleasure of old books — further suggests it as the kind of model for which Lane was searching.

John Lane came across Le Gallienne's name in the pages of the well-known London literary journal, the *Academy,* where it appeared a number of times in the spring of 1888. On March 24, the critic James Ashcroft Noble wrote a lengthy, favorable review of *My Ladies' Sonnets,* in which he suggested that Le Gallienne was a very promising young poet with excellent expectations.[51] Le Gallienne's sonnet "Comfort of Dante" appeared signed in the April 7 issue,[52] and his elegy on "Matthew Arnold" was printed along with the *Academy*'s obituary notice of Arnold's death in the April 21 number.[53]

Perhaps more than these, it was the mention of Le Gallienne's "bookish" verse in a review entitled "Some Books about Books" (which appeared in the April 14 issue of the *Academy*) that attracted Lane's attention. As interested in books and book collecting as Lane was, he surely read this article which, among other items, mentioned Andrew Lang's edition of *Ballads of Books.* The reviewer quoted Lang's rendering of a bibliophilic epigram of Martial, and then implicitly criticized Lang for not having taken notice of "the volume of poems published at Liverpool last year by Mr. Le Gallienne, under the title of *My Ladies' Sonnets,* which contains three 'Booklovers' Songs' not inferior, in our opinion, to some of those by contemporaries here included. Or did he think these too long — a fatal fault for an anthology?"[54]

Le Gallienne's connection with the *Academy* dates from September 1887, when, having just published *My Ladies' Sonnets,* he came up to London from his native Liverpool to see whether employment as a writer and reviewer could be found.[55] The *Academy* perhaps was his first hope since his hometown friend J. A. Noble was a regular reviewer for the journal. Noble no doubt armed his youthful protégé with letters of introduction to his London acquaintances and paved the way for Le Gallienne's entree into the world of Fleet Street. That he was at least partially successful in this venture is suggested by the fact that the young writer returned to Liverpool with several books to review for the *Academy.* In addition to being a reader of so important a literary journal, Lane probably numbered many members of the *Academy* staff among his acquaintances. For not only Le Gallienne, but other writers for the *Academy*, such as Gleeson White, Frederick Wedmore, Cosmo Monkhouse, and Noble, were to be among the Bodley Head authors of the near future.

Given the ample evidence provided him in the pages of the *Academy* that Le Gallienne was not only a poet of talent but also the author of "a little volume, the sight and handling of which brings a quick thrill of pleasure to the heart of the booklover," [56] Lane picked up pen and dashed off a note to "Richard Le Gallienne, Esq., Poet, Birkenhead [a Liverpool suburb]." [57] Unfortunately Le Gallienne's fame was not such at this time to afford the post card any chance of reaching him through the mails; so it was returned to Lane, who, then having no doubt inquired of his *Academy* friends Le Gallienne's exact address in Liverpool, dispatched a letter. After some delay on Le Gallienne's part, Lane received a reply, dated May 20, 1888, "From my study, at 85 Oxton Road, Birkenhead."

Always aware of the value of "dainty" volumes of verse in limited editions, Lane had inquired about the availability of copies of *My Ladies' Sonnets* and had urged Mathews to write Le Gallienne concerning the same. I suspect all the bound copies of the book had been sold or distributed and Le Gallienne had to get some more sheets bound since he replied:

I have been living in daily hope of sending you the promised copy of my little book, which the printer was unable to send owing to some accident necessitating rebinding having happened to the remaining copies. These I am told will be in good order & condition early this coming week & then with the least possible delay you shall have your copy. Your friend Mr. Matthews [*sic*] was good enough to write to me as you intimated the likelihood of his doing — & I have replied to him to the same effect as to you.[58]

Having thanked Lane for his "lines on 'First Editions'," Le Gallienne speaks of his forthcoming trip to London during the first week in June, and asks, "Might I hope to see you? I should be glad to make your personal acquaintance; if the feeling is mutual, could it not be arranged?"[59] Evidently Lane was equally anxious to meet Le Gallienne, for in a letter to his old Liverpool "soul companion," Samuel Hales (who now resided in London), Le Gallienne wrote some ten days later: "On Sunday I am full up — at John Lane's (a delightful new bookman acquaintance — made thro' *Academy*) for dinner from 1 to 5 — " [60]

Le Gallienne met Lane for the first time at the home of Dr. Pritchard in Southwick Street early in June — a meeting which must have been thoroughly agreeable to both. Le Gallienne's letter to Lane on July 1, 1888, after returning to Liverpool, suggests that what was to be a long, cordial and fruitful friendship was already well established.

How glad I was to read that, brief & isolated as was our communion that pleasant Sunday afternoon, we did succeed in touching each other.

As you say the meeting for the first time of a friend previously know[n] only thro' correspondence is fraught with no little anxiety, & after the generous frankness of declaration on your part, you must allow me to assure you that tho' the John Lane of pleasant Scriptures is Sweet, John Lane in the flesh is sweeter (if you will not fear the odd smack of cannibalism in the remark).[61]

It is probable that Le Gallienne met Elkin Mathews on the same Sunday afternoon in June 1888. A letter to Mathews dated December 10, 1888, suggests that the three men at first enjoyed London society together. "It is pleasant to think," Le Gallienne remarked,

that I shall be seeing you in the flesh so early as next week — & I am looking forward to our evening together. It will I fear have to be towards the end of the week for the first three nights must be consecrate to Moloch [Le Gallienne's accountancy examinations], while Thursday night I am booked for Oscar Wilde. But Friday & Saturday (I don't know about Sunday) are at yours & Mr. Lane's service. You & Mr. Lane might arrange together for me what will best suit each other's convenience, for whatever it be I know it will be for the delectation of yours sincerely Richard Le Gallienne.[62]

The importance of Le Gallienne's friendship with Lane and Mathews can hardly be overestimated. Not only did he share with the partners a love for and a knowledge of the rare and beautiful books of the past, he — probably more than they — knew something about the production of fine books and certainly was far more a part of the aesthetic milieu of the late 1880s, devoted as he was to Dante Gabriel Rossetti, Walter Pater, and Oscar Wilde and their work.

According to Percy Muir, Le Gallienne's "Liverpool was a distant outpost of the Aesthetic Movement," [63] and although Le Gallienne, young as he was, can hardly be thought of as "its local leader," he made the most of the opportunities its theaters, museums, libraries, and bookshops offered. In the 1860s and '70s, much Pre-Raphaelite art had gone to the great midland towns such as Liverpool and Manchester thanks to the captains of industry who, spurred by Ruskin, attempted to buy culture. Moreover a surprisingly large group of cultured men and women who lived in Liverpool during the 1880s founded literary societies such as Hall Caine's "Notes and Queries" and journals such as James Ashcroft Noble's *Liverpool Argus*. Indications are that there was enough culture in Liverpool to nourish a number of budding poets, novelists, and actors, who later came up to London and made names for themselves. Le Gallienne and William Watson were to win fame as poets and critics while Hall Caine, Holbrook Jackson, Temple Scott, William Tirebuck, and Ashcroft Noble were to find their fortune in various other literary and artistic pursuits. Le Gallienne's close friend Jimmy Welch was to become a London actor of considerable distinction and acclaim. Although Le Gallienne, much against his will, was apprenticed to an accounting firm at the age of sixteen,[64] he found in Liverpool enough direct contact with culture and the cultivated to support his determination to be a writer and to afford him enough outlets for his emergent aesthetic sensibilities to endure his slavery to Mammon.

There is no doubt that Le Gallienne knew Hall Caine and his associates, but he seems to have known James Ashcroft Noble and his coterie a good deal better. And during the last several years of his residence in Liverpool, Le Gallienne took great pleasure in the company of the old litterateur and booklover, Alexander Ireland, who during his later years made his home in the midlands.[65]

Le Gallienne's enthusiasms found their center in the old bookshops of Liverpool, which he frequented day after day during his lunch hour. It was in "a little book-shop . . . owned by a bookseller of the old school" where the noted bibliographer Temple Scott says he first met Le Gallienne. "Almost every day thereafter," Scott recalls, "we would meet in the little book-shop to talk the hours away. . . ." [66]

The shop to which Scott refers was almost certainly that of Samuel Hales, who, judging from the letters that passed between them, was, in the late 1880s, Le Gallienne's most cherished friend and adviser.[67] It was "dear Sammy," who particularly shared and encouraged his love and enthusiasm for old and beautiful books. Largely through Sammy's kindness and generosity, Le Gallienne was able to build up an astonishing collection of rare books while still an impecunious young clerk in Liverpool.[68]

In the autobiographical story *The Book-Bills of Narcissus* Le Gallienne later described those years in which Hales's shop was a welcome refuge. Although Samuel Hales is slightly disguised in *Book-Bills* as Samuel Dale, Le

Gallienne's description of Sammy and his shop is clearly autobiographical. Speaking of "a distinguishing air" about "the unobtrusive shop of Mr. Samuel Dale," Le Gallienne as narrator suggests that the aura came "of a choice bit of old binding, or the quaint title-page of some tuneful Elizabethan. It was an old Crashaw that first drew me inside; and, though for some reason I did not buy it then, I bought it a year after, because to it I owed the friendship of Samuel Dale." [69]

The extent of Le Gallienne's appreciation of this shop and its sympathetic proprietor is revealed in *Book-Bills* when the narrator continues:

And thus for three bright years that little shop came to be, for a daily hour or so, a blessed palm-tree away from the burden and heat of the noon, a holy place whither the money-changers and such as sold doves might never come, let their clamour in the outer courts ring never so loud. There in Samuel's talk did two weary-hearted bond-servants of Egypt [Le Gallienne and Temple Scott?] draw a breath of the Infinite into their lives of the desk; there could they sit awhile by the eternal springs, and feel the beating of the central heart.[70]

For a young aesthete and poet who hated the middle-class world in which he had been reared, the realm of rare books was a world of romance and poetry, a necessary refuge from the business world into whose midst his father had thrust him. The beautiful books in the old-fashioned shops like Hales's stood for the beauty, mystery, and imaginative freedom which were denied him and so largely absent from the work-a-day Liverpool he despised.

Yet the full extent of Le Gallienne's revolt against mammonite Liverpool can best be judged by his devotion to three central figures of the aesthetic movement — Rossetti, Pater and Wilde — a devotion clearly reflected in his passion for books, his pursuit of poetry, and the efforts he made to surround his life with an aesthetic aura, an atmosphere of preciosity and sentiment. It is well known that he liked velvet jackets, long hair, and distinctive dress, and that he affected a romantic appearance. His rooms in Liverpool, both at home and later in Trafford Chambers, also bore the marks of his aestheticism.[71]

His closest friends, too, were chosen for their literary and artistic interests, and Le Gallienne's relationship with them is best revealed in his largely autobiographical novel, *Young Lives,* which through indirection heightens the significance of his aesthetic concerns. The plight of youthful art-lovers at the mercy of materialistic fathers is poignantly represented in an episode in *Young Lives* in which Henry Mesurier (Le Gallienne) having been dismissed from home by an intolerant father goes to room with an aspiring young artist, Ned Hazell. One evening the boys, aroused from sleep, stand by helpless as Ned's drunken father breaks into the room and proceeds to vent his rage against the son's hard-earned *objets d'art* by throwing out into the rain Ned's "pretty editions, his dainty water-colours, his drawers full of letters, his cast of the Venus of Milo." [72]

Henry and Ned discovered Keats together and learned Shakespeare's sonnets by heart,[73] but it was Rossetti's poetry which bound together Henry and his "aesthetic" friend, Myrtilla Williamson (Fanny Corkhill), who lived in "a pretty little house half hidden in its big garden." [74] Myrtilla was very aesthetic in her flowered tea-gowns — a garb in which she was wont to greet her young admirers.[75] She was possessed of "a tiny, sweet-smelling boudoir . . . of which a dainty glimpse, with its books and water-colours and bibelots" fascinated Henry and marked her as one of the sacred few of Sidon (Birkenhead).[76] The influence of Myrtilla is evident in passages of the novel which relate the gratitude Henry and his sister felt toward one

through whom was to come to them the revelation of some minor graces of life, for which they had the instincts, but on which they had lacked instruction. . . . She it was, too, who first handed them the fretted golden key to the enchanted garden of the Pre-Raphaelites, and the striking head of the young Dante in sepia, which had hung in a sort of shrine-recess in Henry's study, had been copied for him from Rossetti's sketch by Myrtilla's own hand.[77]

In the 1880s, Le Gallienne's hero-worship of Oscar Wilde knew no bounds. No other living person so completely fulfilled the young poet's concept of the ideal artist and aesthete as Wilde. Ironically, it was Richard's father (whom Le Gallienne always represented as the arch Philistine) who took him to hear Wilde lecture on "Personal Impressions of America and Her People" at Birkenhead, December 10, 1883.[78] Rupert Hart-Davis conjectures that Le Gallienne paid his first visit to Wilde during his London trip of September 1887.[79] A letter from Wilde to Le Gallienne postmarked October 17, 1887, suggests that Le Gallienne not only sent Wilde a copy of *My Ladies' Sonnets* when it appeared but had previously presented Wilde with a manuscript version which Le Gallienne had had bound. "So I have to thank you again," writes Wilde, "this time for the charming little printed edition of your poems. With its stately brother it shall stand on my shelves, and be a delight to me." [80]

When Le Galliene was in London the following June to meet Lane for the first time, he stayed with Wilde for three days and later wrote ecstatically to Lane about the visit: "But Oscar Wilde, sweet 'Fancy's child', how can I write of him to-night?, of all his dear delightful ways thro' three sweet summer nights & days; suffice it I have never yet more fascinating fellow met, and O! how sweet he was to me is only known to R. Le G." [81] So memorable an occasion did not pass uncommemorated, for Le Gallienne wrote a poem, "With Oscar Wilde, A Summer-day in June '88," which he included in another manuscript volume of poetry which he tendered to his hero the following October.[82]

A letter of March 2, 1889, which Richard sent to his mother, suggests that Wilde was taking a personal interest in his career. "He [Oscar] is very anxious for me to write prose and was very glad to hear of my new book of essays which Mathews is announcing for the autumn under the title of 'Oblivion's Poppy — Studies of the Forgotten'." [83] Shortly after, Le Gallienne, now in London as an assistant to the actor Wilson Barrett, received from Wilde what surely must by then have been a routine note: "I go away for Easter — after that let us meet and make music." [84]

It is perhaps unfortunate that so devoted a friendship should have failed, yet Le Galliennne's enthusiasm for Oscar doubtless waned toward the close of Wilde's career. Wilde was sending his friend tickets to his plays as late as February 1892 — "Dear Poet, here are two stalls for my play. Come, and bring your poem [Mildred, his wife] to sit beside you." [85] But as Le Gallienne's closeness to Lane grew, his devotion to Wilde lessened, for Lane and Wilde heartily disliked each other. Furthermore, Wilde's predilection for contemporary French poetry must have, in time, annoyed Le Gallienne, who became an outspoken critic of the French influence on English art when he published his popular *English Poems* in 1892.

Strong as was the impress of Wilde on Le Gallienne's personality, a deeper and more salutary involvement with the aesthetic movement came to Le Gallienne through his reading of the works of Walter Pater. During the tortuous months through which he labored while writing his first critical study, *George Meredith: Some Characteristics,* Le Gallienne found Pater's newly published essays in criticism, *Appreciations,* an inspiration. His diary entry for November 27, 1889, reveals that he was "Reading Pater's new book of *Appreciations* with all the intellectual & spiritual quickening which his writing always brings to me"; and again two days later: "Reading Pater still with much joy."

Le Gallienne's diary for 1889–1890 is full of perceptive remarks about Pater's writings — comments which suggest that his response to the great mind of the aesthetic movement was no superficial one. Le Gallienne recognized in Pater a kindred spirit whose devotion to the beautiful was an inspiration to his own. On February 22, 1890, he had read aloud to friends "Pater's trans[lation] of the *Cupid & Psyche* of Apuleius," and had gone "to bed haunted by its beauty." The next day he "Started to re-read Marius — feeling at once the power of its clean strong influence." [86]

Le Gallienne undoubtedly possessed "that certain kind of temperament" which Pater calls for in the "Preface" to *The Renaissance,* that "power of being deeply moved in the presence of beautiful objects." His diary entry for November 12, 1889, reads in part: "Read her [Mildred] the 8 pages of *N*[arcissus] & Rossetti's *Jenny* which I had often promised her. How lovely her face is in the presence of Beauty. I cannot imagine one more sensitive to great impressions of the soul. It glows like a flower — I cd. go down on my knees before it." Like Pater's Nicolette in "Two Early French Stories," Le Gallienne's simple little sweetheart was a beautiful object, a work of art to be worshiped.

In December 1889, Le Gallienne writing Lane about his progress on the George Meredith book remarked: "I have learnt much from Walter Pater during the last few months." [87] Indeed, Le Gallienne's own critical principles, which he was to apply as reader for the Bodley Head and as author and critic during the early nineties, were derived primarily from his notion of Pater's impressionistic criticism.

The breadth of Le Gallienne's reading during the years immediately preceding his entry into the Bodley Head is impressive. Not only did he read widely in the older literature of England — Sir Philip Sidney, Shakespeare, Milton, Henry Fielding, and so on — but he also had an avid interest in more recent authors, including Lamb, Thoreau, Keats, and Browning.[88] No less interesting is the varied range of his taste, which enabled him to admire Walt Whitman, find Pierre Loti (no doubt at Wilde's insistence) stimulating, and Whistler's *Gentle Art* "child's play" but the "Ten-O'clock" full of "great illuminating things." [89]

Since neither Mathews nor Lane made any pretense of having read so widely, Le Gallienne's extensive knowledge of literature stood him in good stead when he came to work at the Bodley Head. But even more important was his absorption in the thought and personalities of the aesthetic milieu of the period.

Even though Le Gallienne met Lane and Mathews in June 1888, the time when he would play a major role in the operation of the Bodley Head was still nearly three years off. Like Lane, he was as yet unable to free himself from the uncongenial drudgery of an office job. Not until the spring of 1891 would he find it possible to move to London and devote himself wholly to literature. Meanwhile an opportunity came through the kindness of the famous actor, Wilson Barrett, whom Le Gallienne had come to know through his friend Jimmy Welch. Having been approached by Le Gallienne to "write an account of his life," the actor had informed him that he had, in the past, declined all the many offers of a similar nature; but soon after he wrote Le Gallienne "post-haste" and offered him the position of literary secretary for the spring and summer months of 1889.[90] Despite the fact that Le Gallienne was to take his final examination in accounting in December 1888 and then proceed to open a business with the backing of his father early in 1889,[91] the lure of London and the theatrical world was too much for him. Le Gallienne failed the examination, and in late January made plans to leave the accounting office and join the Barrett entourage in London on February 6, 1889.

It was during this spring that Le Gallienne was able to attend to the publication of his second volume of poetry, *Volumes in Folio*. Filled with bookish verse — or as an announcement termed it, *"Vers de Libricité"* [92] — *Volumes in Folio* was probably in manuscript by the autumn of 1888. "The lovely little book" which Oscar Wilde received in late October of that year is probably the bound manuscript: "Written by your own hand it has the quintessence of grace and beauty." [93]

In almost every way a companion volume to *My Ladies' Sonnets, Volumes in Folio* is in its physical appearance handsome and admirably done. Its "antique boards" covered with blue-gray paper, its imitation vellum ridged spine, its Van Gelder handmade paper, and its tastefully designed title page in black and red made it the perfect setting for the poems within.[94] In its appearance and its subject matter, *Volumes in Folio* is a product of the revival of interest in antiquarian books which in its popular manifestations was largely due to the efforts of Andrew Lang. Beginning with Lang's *The Library* (1881), the Eighties produced a number of books, such as Percy Fitzgerald's *The Book Fancier* and John Burton's *The Book-Hunter,* in which the booklover's appetite for beauty was whetted by discussions of "The Incunables," "Elzevirs and Old Printers," and "Binding and Its Curiosities."

So intense grew the interest in rare books that it gave rise to a vogue for writing "Booklover's Songs" and yielded such collections as Ireland's *The Book-Lover's Enchiridion* (which went through five editions from 1882) and the volume edited by Lang entitled *Ballads of Books* (1887). Le Gallienne's indebtedness to Lang not only for his theme but his title, too, is suggested in the introductory poem, "Ad Lectorem":

Doth the Gentle Reader find
My title dark unto his mind?
Wondering what the Volumes *be*
Which it promiseth from me,
Wondering too how folio
May dwell in duodecimo?
Then 'tis certain he hath ne'er
Read Ballades in Blue China-ware,
Or Proverbs *writ* in Porcelain. . . .[95]

The poems of *Volumes in Folio* such as "Who Has not Loved an Elzevir?" and "A Bookman's Complaint of His Lady" clearly reflect the craze for Elzevirs (which no doubt in part originated in Pater's mention in *The Renaissance* of those "pretty volumes of the *Bibliotheque Elzevirienne*") and the appearance of E. C. Thomas' new translation of Richard de Bury's *Philobiblon* (1888) with its "complaints" of books against the clergy, wars, and so on.

In its "antique" appearance and in its general simplicity of design, *Volumes in Folio* recalls the fine books of the Renaissance which Le Gallienne had come to love. And in its limited editions, especially its large-paper version of fifty copies numbered and signed by the author and its three copies on Japanese handmade paper, the work at once assumed the air of being something rare and precious, an object only for the "few."

Modeled as it was on the earlier *My Ladies' Sonnets,* it is difficult to say how much of the credit for the excellent design and typography of *Volumes in Folio* belongs to Le Gallienne himself. Having spent a good deal of time around the printing shops in Liverpool — especially that of his close friend John Robb — and having seen his first volume through the press, Le Gallienne knew far more than Mathews and Lane about book production at this time. And it is quite possible that Le Gallienne, with the help of Samuel Hales and Robb, designed *My Ladies' Sonnets.* Since Le Gallienne must have felt this format even more appropriate to the contents of *Volumes in Folio,* the general design of this second book of verse should almost certainly be credited to him even though the printing was done at the Chiswick Press.

A number of letters which passed between Le Gallienne and Elkin Mathews during the planning stages of the book show how closely Le Gallienne followed the making of *Volumes in Folio.* On October 30, 1888, Le Gallienne sent Mathews extracts from press notices of *My Ladies' Sonnets* to be used for a prospectus and reluctantly acquiesced in Mathews' view about the initial letters: "I *had* thought of rubricated initials all thro' [as in *My Ladies' Sonnets*] but perhaps the gain would not be commensurate with the cost and trouble so let us leave it as you say — rubricated title only — yes!" As to the title page, Le Gallienne suggested that it bear the quote from *Love's Labour's Lost* from which the title is in part derived, "Assist me, some extemporal god of rhyme . . . for I am for whole volumes in folio!" Although Mathews was desirous of a line or two on Sir Thomas Bodley, Le Gallienne did not get around to penning it.[96] On the tenth of December, Le Gallienne pronounced the proof prospectus "admirable." And "as to the head of Sir Thomas Bodley," Le Gallienne considered that "it looks charmingly quaint in the present position — as to how it will suit the title page we will have to see when the time comes." [97] Other letters indicate that Le Gallienne brought the complete manuscript to London in mid-December, when he returned to take his final accountancy examination, so that it probably reached the printer some time in January 1889.

The birth of *My Ladies' Sonnets* was attended by much excitement. According to Temple Scott, Le Gallienne "behaved himself like a young girl about to dress for her first ball; but we were all palpitating, the solemn bookseller with the rest of us. . . . As the proof-sheets kept coming in new poems took the place of some which were deemed less worthy, much to the printer's disgust." [98] Indeed, the printer suffered so severely from the affair that he "almost died before the book was finally ready for the world's attention." [99] It is doubtful that such furor surrounded the publication of *Volumes in Folio* when it appeared in mid-March 1889, for Le Gallienne was much involved with Barrett and neither Mathews nor Jacobi of the Chiswick Press was likely to have indulged the poet's enthusiasms.

Nevertheless, there was excitement enough, as one of Richard's letters to his mother conveys. It is surely a mark of the time that the poet was clearly more interested in the book's appearance than he was in its contents:

How did you like the look of my little book — for of course (I hope) you have *not bothered to wade through* it, I didn't send it for that — but simply as a symbol of what I trust I need not express. It is *pretty* isn't it? I thought the first one *pretty*, but I am (faithless as ever, you see!) sorely tempted to transfer my allegiance to this new one. I am receiving pleasant compliments all round about it, and it is going off finely at the publishers. The best thing about it yet perhaps is that Scribners of New York have bought 50 copies! [100]

The Chiswick Press records show that the book was printed and off to the bindery by March 7. The total printer's bill of £24.5.2 included the composing and the printing of 250 copies, Royal 16 mo. with handmade paper, the altering of margins and printing a large-paper issue on hand-made paper, and an additional three large-paper copies "on thick Japanese vellum paper." The printer also supplied the binder with the paper used to cover the boards and 300 printed labels for the spines. The composing and printing of 500 prospectuses on handmade paper had cost £1.8.6.[101]

Although on January 9, 1889, Le Gallienne was still sending Mathews lists "of a few more likely folk" who might subscribe to the volume, the announcement of its impending publication which appeared in the *Publishers' Circular* on March 1 stated that "the large-paper copies are all sold." [102] The copies of the ordinary issue were not sold on the day of publication, but the whole edition was soon exhausted and "selling at a premium." Consequently, on April 17, a month after the book was published, Le Gallienne wrote Mathews asking for a check "for my portion of my share in *Volumes in Folio,* the edition being I suppose practically sold out." [103]

Certainly the little book "enjoyed a modest *succès d'estime.*" [104] Le Gallienne's friend J. A. Noble reviewed it for the *Academy,* giving much praise and attention to the book's longest piece, "The Bookman's Avalon." [105] The *Saturday Review* spoke of it as "an ingenious romance of book-lore in the Spenserian stanza. Mr. Le Gallienne," observed the reviewer, "has certainly, too, caught a pleasant echo of the early seventeenth century in his octosyllabics." [106]

In *The Quest of the Golden Boy,* Richard Whittington-Egan and Geoffrey Smerdon characterize the volume as "the first trickle of the torrent of poetry that was to pour from the throats of the nest of singing-birds that Lane and Mathews nourished in Vigo Street," [107] and there can be little doubt that *Volumes in Folio* did in large part set the tone of later Bodley Head books. As a book of poetry whose binding and typography enhanced its subject and made it a work of art, it sounded the keynote of the Bodley Head productions which followed.

In *Young Lives,* Le Gallienne recalls "the peculiar glamour which, almost before he could read," any form of print had for the hero, Mesurier. "While books were still being read to him, there had already come into his mind, unaccountably, as by outside suggestion, that there could be nothing so splendid in the world as to write a book for oneself. To be either a soldier, a sailor, an architect, or an engineer, would doubtless have its fascinations as well; but to make a real printed book, with your name in gilt letters outside, was real romance." [108] That Mesurier's childhood desire to be an author was Le Gallienne's as well is certainly borne out by the numerous proposals for books which emanated from Le Gallienne's ambitious mind once he broke into print.

Shortly after *Volumes in Folio* was published, Le Gallienne on May 22, 1889, signed an agreement with Elkin Mathews to write a critical study of the work of George Meredith.[109] Unable to accompany Barrett to America in the autumn of 1889 because of his asthma, Le Gallienne returned to Liverpool — but not to his parents' home — and took quarters at 29 Trafford Chambers, where, as he explained to himself and to others, he would be able to make the "fullest use of his time; that is by coming down to my dear art as other men to their business — in the same spirit of scorning delights, & thus escaping the many insidious distractions of home." [110]

Le Gallienne's spirits were often low. He wrote peevish letters to Lane, and only with difficulty did he bring himself to work on the Meredith and other projects he had in hand. "Wrote a page, the last of G. M.'s poetry essay with much straining," reads his diary entry for November 12. And again, "Wrote a page & ½ of *Narcissus* with a little bit more ease, but O for those old days when one was like a fountain day & night. Now it is but an occasional feeble jet — after what pumping!" [111]

The year was indeed a kind of trial in the wilderness for Le Gallienne, who, longing to be in London, knew he had to first make his mark with the Meredith book. Meanwhile his main tie with London life was his "dear 'London Partner'," John Lane, who often seemed remiss in his duties.

Many thanks for your letter — but why haven't *you* written before? Who do you think is most in need of letters, you nightly dining in the halls of the great & daily gladdened by precious presentation copies, or I up here sitting alone with something very like Despair at my elbow, & an unfinished book in front of me. I am not going to whine, but I assure you, old man, that the days have been all too many when a word or two from you wd have been precious as gold.[112]

During those trying months of 1889 and 1890, when Le Gallienne labored over the Meredith, he was involved in another friendship quite different from that with Lane. He had met in 1886 a young man who shared his enthusiasm for literature, Robinson Kay Leather, who had edited the undergradute magazine at Liverpool's University College and who wrote verse which was admired among a small circle of acquaintances. Leather's career as a writer, however, was in grave jeopardy because of a progressive paralysis which later caused his death.[113] During late 1889 and 1890, Le Gallienne often enjoyed Leather's company and on several occasions accompanied his friend to the Ben Rhydding Hydro near Leeds, where Le Gallienne took the cure for his asthma and Leather sought relief from his pain.

The extent of their companionship is suggested by the frequency with which Leather's name occurs in Le Gallienne's diary. "Dear old Leather called & cheered me as he always does," he wrote on November 20, 1889. And a week later he noted: "At Leather's for afternoon tea. His sister there & a Miss Sparks. Also a young fellow who played the zither most exquisitely. First time I had ever heard it & it was quite a new experience." Perhaps some of Leather's attraction for Le Gallienne is revealed in the following extract: "R.K.L. called — gloria! The dear old boy *looked* very well — his beard grown to be a great improvement — much struck again, & especially with his beard, with his likeness to Rossetti!" [114]

The best account of the friendship occurs in Le Gallienne's *The Book-Bills of Narcissus*, which contains a whole chapter devoted to Leather under the name of "George Muncaster." Relating how Narcissus and a friend stopped off "one dull September evening" at The Swan Inn at Tewkesbury, Le Gallienne goes on to describe his first meeting with Leather through the good offices of a "Canterbury Series" edition of Walt Whitman's poetry.[115]

One of the fruits of this companionship was *The Student and the Body-Snatcher and Other Trifles*, a volume of short stories, which the Bodley Head published along with the second edition of *George Meredith* in late March 1891.[116] The genesis of this cooperative undertaking is recorded in Le Gallienne's diary for April 14, 1890: "At R.K.L's in afternoon. Suggestion to publish some stories together — R read me his *Student & the Body-snatcher* again & I was more taken than before with its delightful [?] humour." On May Day, Le Gallienne "commenced a little monkish story to go with R.K.Ls — *A Miracle,*" and by May 2 he had finished the story, copied it out, and sent it off to Leather.

In July during another sojourn at Ben Rhydding, Le Gallienne completed the manuscript and forwarded it to Mathews for his consideration. In a letter to Lane the following day, dated July 27, 1890, Le Gallienne, having mentioned that he had just sent Mathews the manuscript, went on to describe Leather as "dangerously ill, it is to be feared fatally." Whether or not his friend's physical condition was as serious as Le Gallienne suggested, he attributed the genesis of the volume to "some inkling" on Leather's part that he was dying and the consequent desire of seeing his work in print before the end. "He is growing almost feverishly anxious," added Le Gallienne, "to publish a few manuscripts he has by him without any delay." [117]

Le Gallienne's usual initiative and great drive are evident in his desire to hasten the project on: "To that end also," he wrote Lane, "I have already obtained an estimate from Robb which is extremely cheap." His usual reliance on Lane to take up his cause and expedite matters with Mathews is evident as he exhorts his "partner" to "press the thing on for me — if only 'for charity's sweet sake'. It is such a pathetic thing to sit & see a young man of such undoubted power as poor Leather slipping inevitably out of the world, as he seems to be doing, & one can well understand how his heart must yearn towards the children of his fancy." [118]

In his letter to Mathews Le Gallienne suggested the book of stories be "a small volume of about a hundred pages, bound in buckram at about *3s.6d.*," [119] and such it turned out to be. The thirteen stories were printed by John Robb at Liverpool and both small-paper and large-paper issues were bound in black buckram with gold lettering on the spine. When it appeared, the *Publishers' Circular* thought it "a miniature volume of great merit." The reviewer observed that "the clever little sketches" were "short and few" and inspired him "with a longing for more." [120]

With the publication of the *George Meredith* in November, Le Gallienne's stay in his native city was drawing rapidly to a close. Although his trip to London in March 1891 was thought to be nothing more than another of those excursion-rate week ends which he had so often taken advantage of, Le Gallienne later referred to the fare as "the very best investment I ever made." [121] When he arrived at 37 Southwick Street, Lane greeted him with the news that Clement Shorter, literary critic for the *Star,* had resigned.[122] Lane was ready to push his friend's candidacy for the post, and Le Gallienne was not one to be bashful.

Since the editor of the *Star*, Ernest Parke, wanted to judge the abilities of several candidates before he made his decision, Le Gallienne was soon at work hastily putting together his first trial column.[123] On April 6, 1891, he thanked Lane for his "various kindnesses" and referred to a note he had received from Shorter as "encouraging." Then he continues, "Have got hold of *News from Nowhere*, & with that & with the items you have given me I *ought* surely to be able to knock out something. I will certainly do my level best." [124] Yet it took some luck as well to win the post from the leading contender, Ernest Radford.[125] On the twenty-eighth of April, Le Gallienne jubilantly wrote Lane that he had just received "a most charming generous letter from Radford — in which believing that the column is of moment to me he finally declines to compete. A modest letter withal." [126] As a consequence of this generous act Le Gallienne got the job.

By June 6, Le Gallienne was residing with his old friend Jimmy Welch at 6 Staple Inn, Holborn, and writing Samuel Hales all about his good fortune. "By this time you have doubtless heard that I have had the luck to succeed Shorter on *The Star* — under the impertinent pseudonym of

'Logroller'." [127] Although the pay was but ten guineas a month, [128] Le Gallienne was ecstatic, poised as he was on the threshold of the best four or five years of his life — that youthful period of achievement which he was later to call "those many coloured energetic years." [129]

His emergence on the literary scene must have been something of an event, for not only did his weekly columns signed "Log-roller" soon establish the *Star* "as the acknowledged organ of the literary world of London," [130] but his "remarkably poetic-looking" appearance, his "fine head of hair and reflective eyes" struck those of the literary and artistic world as mildly romantic.[131]

To Ernest Rhys, he was "the most fantastic figure who appeared in the narrow doorway of the Vigo Street shop" — a "Henry Irving in his black cloak and long black locks." And "Mil-Sweet," Le Gallienne's consumptive little wife — "a most attractive little figure — pathetic too, because her large brown eyes were set in a face that suggested too frail a physique" [132] — must have brought with her something of the aura of Murger's *La Vie de Boheme*.

To J. Lewis May, then the Bodley Head stock boy, Le Gallienne seemed a veritable Shelley.

His pale chiselled features, shadowed by long, wavy, raven-black hair, gave him the air of a Greek god, and it was not easy — at first — to converse with him as with an ordinary mortal; one felt "strained to the height in the colloquy." It seemed strange, moreover, that one so preternaturally beautiful should travel to and from his home — he lived in Brentford — in mundane omnibuses and trains just like any member of the *profanum vulgus,* and still more remarkable that he should have been born on the banks of the Mersey and not on the shores of Hellas. He himself was not, it would seem, altogether unconscious of the godlike attributes of form and feature with which Nature had endowed him, for he affected a style of dress designed as far as possible to indicate his aloofness from the common herd. He wore, like the Scholar Gipsy, a hat of antique shape and a soft abstracted air. His coat was of dark green velvet, his shirt and collar, a la Byron, of some soft grey material, his tie, the hue of willow leaves in the wind, was loosely flowing. Such were his upper garments.

The integuments of the lower, or earthward parts, were a concession to ordinary humanity, a symbol of godlike condescension — he wore trousers! I speak with authority concerning these details, because I was so carried away with admiration for the poet that I went so far as to imitate his sartorial eccentricities. The experiment was hardly a success. My features are, I hope, honest, but few would call them heroic. Moreover, I could not afford velvet. My coat was made of flannel — green flannel.[133]

Le Gallienne's arrival upon the London scene as an established critic brought together at last the three men who made the Bodley Head. By January 1892, when Lane officially came into the firm, the team was assembled and for all intents and purposes already at work. For some time before this event, the influence not only of Lane but of Le Gallienne also on the work of the Bodley Head was clearly evident, and the relations between the members of the trio had been established.

As chief reader for the firm Le Gallienne was to have a great influence on the books which the firm was to accept.[134] Having played a major role in designing the first Bodley Head book, *Volumes in Folio,* and in initiating and carrying through the work on *The Student and the Body-Snatcher,* Le Gallienne was able to make a considerable contribution to the over-all design of what soon was to be known as the Bodley Head book. His familiarity with printing and book production, the many hours he had spent during his spare time at Liverpool poring over the type fonts at John Robb's served him well when he began to publish with the Bodley Head. His superior knowledge and initiative in the business of seeing a book through the press, made him at times a bit contemptuous of his publishers. During the trying days when the *George Meredith* was in the press, Le Gallienne, a bit too prone to belittle Mathews in his letters to Lane, wrote that he was of the opinion that Mathews "knows as much about the *modus operandi* of book production as a suckling pig." [135]

Le Gallienne's willingness, indeed, eagerness to involve himself in Bodley Head activities from the outset is suggested in a letter of 1889 in which he told Lane how glad he was to see the forthcoming Nettleship book on Robert Browning "so nicely announced." And he went on to ask Lane if he was "still disposed" to ask W. and J. Arnold of Liverpool, who printed *My Ladies' Sonnets,* to print the Nettleship. "Anyhow there will be no harm in my getting tentative ideas as to cost of printing from them." [136] The fact that Le Gallienne addressed such a query to Lane indicates not only his interest but also the character of Lane's role in the firm before 1892.

The evidence at hand strongly suggests that practically all the talent represented by the books published at the Bodley Head was enlisted by John Lane. And although before 1892 Elkin Mathews was the executive in that it was he who gave final approval to contracts, signed the checks, and dispatched official letters, Lane made it his business to search out new authors and publicize the firm's activities. Le Gallienne, who himself was one significant fruit of Lane's "passion for everything new under the sun," [137] often remarked in his letters on the new talent Lane's activities were adding to the Bodley Head's list of authors. Referring to Lane's latest acquisition, William Strang, the young artist who in keeping with the Blake-Rossetti pattern was also a poet, Le Gallienne on the twenty-fourth of March 1890 wrote approvingly: "Strang I don't know of, but you are an unexceptionable guide to all manner of *New*dities (god forgive the pun — you won't, I know)." [138]

Le Gallienne's interest in the firm and Lane's aptitude for gathering in promising young writers is apparent even earlier. In the "dear 'London Partner'" letter of December 1889, Le Gallienne had writen Lane: "The new Bodley Head 'announcements' are capital. I congratulate you again. *Corn and Poppies* is a title I like much [;] it is full of suggestion." Then referring to the author of *Corn and Poppies*, the young art critic and poet, Cosmo Monkhouse, Le Gallienne applauded Lane's latest acquisition in a sentence which throws light on his recruiting methods — "I liked him so much that evening at your rooms." [139]

Another early significant find on Lane's part was Arthur Symons. In a letter to J. Dykes Campbell of the *Athenaeum,* dated March 5, 1890, Symons wrote that John Lane had found a publisher for his translation of *Contes Cruels* by Villiers de l'Isle Adam and for his next volume of poems — "Elkin Mathews of Vigo Street, who actually *makes poetry pay!*" [140] Although the *Contes Cruels* was never published by the Bodley Head, the volume of poems — almost certainly *Silhouettes* — was.

Lane's involvement in the firm during the years before he was an acknowledged partner is further indicated by the influence he exerted on Elkin Mathews. Lane was adept at managing people, and Mathews was not immune to his diplomacy. When Le Gallienne wanted the completed chapters of his *George Meredith* set up immediately in print as they were sent in to the Bodley Head, he dared not ask Mathews directly to carry out so unorthodox a request. Instead he wrote Lane: "I haven't suggested it to E. M. but you might, in that sweet way of yours." [141] Certainly if Le Gallienne's remarks in his letters to Lane mean anything at all, Lane was constantly prodding his partner, very cautiously and diplomatically, about one thing or another.

In the eyes of both Lane and Le Gallienne, Mathews was entirely too slow, too cautious, and too unadventurous in expediting the work of the Bodley Head. In addition to the evidence of J. Lewis May and Percy Muir,[142] there is much to affirm the view that Mathews was lacking in the kind of initiative and quick action Lane thought necessary. In a letter of January 1897 to Miss Guiney, Lionel Johnson regrets the delay in the publication of his second volume of poems, and exclaims, "but that maddening miniature of a publisher, Elkin Mathews, delays all things." [143]

Allowing for the foibles and temperament of authors, especially poets, one must conclude that Elkin Mathews' major failing was that often attributed to intellectuals, procrastination, the inability to act decisively. It was this quality more than any other which set him at odds with Lane and Le Gallienne. When Le Gallienne wanted to proceed speedily toward the publication of *The Student and the Body-Snatcher*, he wrote Mathews and begged him to "accelerate his usual rate of progression toward a decision." But he also enlisted Lane's "assistance towards a further hastening on." [144]

Perhaps the best indication of how Mathews' penchant for caution led to serious friction between the key members of the firm is the unpleasantness which occurred when the *George Meredith* was in press during October and November 1890. As the detailed examination of the publication of this volume will bear out,[145] the relationship between the three men was at times seriously strained; and the fact that they continued to work together at all after the ordeal says much for their patience and good sense. Despite the fact that Le Gallienne's seeming inability to complete the book and that the delays and errors of the printer, Le Gallienne's friend John Robb, were at least partially responsible for the delay of publication, it was Mathews' alleged caution and inability to act with decision that were blamed.

A somewhat overwrought Le Gallienne wrote to an equally upset Lane:

if you knew Robb you would know what a d——d silly injustice you do him in your note to me this morning. If there is, & decidedly there *is,* one person to blame in this matter it is that incarnation of all that is vacillating, procrastinating, old-maidish & [?] in human nature, that Elkins Mathews that never answered a letter till it was a month overdue, that attends to no request without the prod of a telegram, that — well, god knows *you* should know him, *you* who in a phrase that will someday be famous when this chapter of our history comes to be written, I have called "the brain in the Bodley Head"; certainly no one should be able to teach *you* anything more of the general weak-mindedness of the great E. M. — though — "but that is another story." [146]

At least once, Le Gallienne wrote Mathews a letter which both Mathews and Lane thought to be insulting and ungentlemanly, a letter which elicited a rebuke from Lane himself. Although Le Gallienne's reply to Lane's charge of indignity shows that he was hurt and somewhat taken aback, it also reveals that the protégé was quite capable of holding his own in altercations with his tutor. With nothing more than a crisp "My dear Lane," Le Gallienne bluntly came to the point: "You & I don't agree on everything, the best of friends never do. We don't, for instance, in your extravagant condemnation of my unfortunate letter to E. M. . . . ." [147]

The unpleasantness over the publication of the *George Meredith*, among other things, doubtless caused a certain coolness to develop between Mathews and Le Gallienne. Whereas Le Gallienne's formal "Dear Mr. Lane" had soon become the familiar "My Dear Johnny," it was not until December 1891 that Le Gallienne dared omit the "Mr." in his salutations to Mathews and suggest, "let us by all means drop all further 'mister-y'." [148] Yet the fact that Le Gallienne seldom acted upon his own suggestion thereafter is proof enough of the distance at which each held the other. Perhaps Mathews found Le Gallienne a bit too forward, a trifle vulgar, and obviously Lane's man. Furthermore, Le Gallienne's letters to Lane are so full of deprecating remarks about Mathews that it is hard to believe his mere politeness toward the elder man effectively masked his real feelings. Surely Mathews was increasingly aware not only of Le Gallienne's insincerity towards him but of Lane's also. "Mathews, poor little man, was really very nice," Le Gallienne wrote the vacationing Lane on September 2, 1892. And with a hint of affection in his tone, he continued: "I saw him this afternoon. Had quite a long talk on old poets with him." [149] Surely it was not conducive to frank and cordial relations between the two partners for Mathews to know that he was less in Lane's confidence than was the reader for the firm.

Although there was no cordial relationship between Le Gallienne and Mathews during the years they worked together at the Bodley Head, their letters maintain a kindly tone which suggests that the serious altercations which occurred caused no open break. Having received from Mathews — presumably for Christmas — a copy of the *Christian Morals*, Le Gallienne on December 26, 1893, expressed his delight in a letter of thanks: "I shall much value it, & shall owe to you many happy moments in its possession." [150] Even as late as October 8, 1896, several years after the dissolution of the partnership, Le Gallienne wrote to inform Mathews that he was "going to call in on" him the next "afternoon about 4. I want your assistance about your patron saint — I. W. [Izaak Walton] Hoping to catch you in. With Kindest Regards,/Yours ever/Richard Le Gallienne." [151]

Although the relations between Le Gallienne and Mathews were not of the best, Le Gallienne and Lane seem to have been most cordial throughout the early years of the Bodley Head. During the two and a half years before he returned to London in 1891, Le Gallienne was often anxious about the genuineness of Lane's loyalty, but there is no reason to believe that his doubts were well founded. As Lane was his only real connection with the London scene, Le Gallienne often chided him for neglecting to write. "Is it that you are ill, sweet friend, — " Richard asked Lane in a letter of June 26, 1889. "Surely I have in no wise offended — or is it that you feel that a man so far from the kingdom of the *Athenaeum* must after all be a poor investment — or what?" [152] Some months later, Le Gallienne's suspicions of

Lane's fickle nature have been allayed by a letter which "quite brisked me up & I worked well on Friday." Then with a touch of anxiety in his voice he added: "I am glad you don't yet desert the sinking ship — I wonder how much longer you will be faithful." [153]

The similarity between Lane and Le Gallienne afforded them an understanding of one another. Both were ambitious, desirous of success, not over-scrupulous in achieving their purposes, effusive in their attentions, capable of flattery, socially adept in a cheap sort of way, sentimental, and somewhat dandified in dress and air. Although altercations occurred and angry accusations were made, the two always seem to have patched them up: "Dear J. L." writes Le Gallienne, "do we still love each other, in spite of all? Surely so,/At least I am/Your affectionate/R. Le G." [154] And despite the fact that hints of jealousy and a bit of petulance show through Le Gallienne's letters at times — "I hope you are not grown too great a man. You were in danger of it last time we met, I think" [155] — both men were remarkably tolerant of one another's foibles and failings.

Although Lane did not become a full-time partner in the Bodley Head until 1892, there can be little doubt that he and Richard Le Gallienne played major roles in the growth and development of the publishing firm long before they began to work side by side with Mathews at the Vigo Street shop. Perhaps the extent of Lane's influence on the Bodley Head before 1892 is best summed up in a statement which Le Gallienne made to Lane in a letter three years earlier: "If Mathews backs you as you deserve to be backed, *The Bodley Head* should soon be fairly launched on prosperous gales. And I, for my poor part, will be faithful." [156]

This declaration of faith in Lane, the belief that his "Johnny" was going somewhere and could take the Bodley Head with it, was no doubt the basis of Le Gallienne's evident joy as on New Year's Eve, 1891, his thoughts strayed toward the image closest to his heart, the Bodley Head. "Do you know," he wrote Lane on January 3, 1892, "at that solemn moment when the clock seems to take a long breath before it strikes the midnight on New Year's Eve, we were kneeling in a church close by here, & as the last stroke fled away I said in my heart — 'at this moment has the spirit of John Lane entered into the Bodley Head' — I wonder if Mathews at that hour quoted 'Thy soul hath drawn my soul,/ This hour,/ A little nearer yet'!" [157] At that moment, the God of the Christian religion had been displaced by another in the form of the Bodley Head, and it is significant and perhaps ominous that Le Gallienne saw his new deity as a "two-headed Janus." [158]

On February 6, 1892, the *Publishers' Circular* listed under "Trade Change" the following announcement: "Mr. Elkin Mathews, of 'The Bodley Head,' Vigo Street, W., has taken into partnership Mr. John Lane, whose recent

'Bibliography of Geo. Meredith' met with much appreciation. The style of the firm will be 'Elkin Mathews and John Lane'." [159] A month later, in the "Announcements for the Season," Messrs. Elkin Mathews and John Lane offered a small but distinguished list of books: *The Earth Fiend*, a ballad made and etched by William Strang in two limited issues on old handmade and Japanese papers, folio; *Sight and Song, Poems on Pictures* by Michael Field; *English Poems* by Richard Le Gallienne; *Silhouettes, a Book of Verses* by Arthur Symons; and *Poems* by Oscar Wilde, with a cover and title page designed by C. H. Ricketts.[160]

When in January 1892 the three principal figures in the Bodley Head came together in their active roles — Mathews and Lane as proprietors and Le Gallienne as chief reader and adviser — the firm's publications already included a number of books which in subject matter, typography, title page, binding, and general design set them apart from the cheap, commonplace books which poured by the thousands from the large commercial publishing houses of Britain. The first book to bear the Bodley Head imprint, Le Gallienne's *Volumes in Folio,* had been printed at the Chiswick Press, and among a number of others which were to bear the distinctive mark of that press's excellent typography and design was *On the Making and Issuing of Books* (1891), by Charles T. Jacobi, the celebrated managing director.

In 1892 the Bodley Head began its very fruitful relationship with another great printing firm of the day, T. and A. Constable of Edinburgh. Michael Field's *Sight and Song,* with its finely designed title page, clearly manifests the excellent work of Walter Biggar Blaikie, Constable's extraordinarily talented manager. Charles Ricketts began his work for the Bodley Head by designing the first book to bear the names of both Elkin Mathews and John Lane, Oscar Wilde's *Poems* (February 1892).

Because Mathews and Lane had the business sense as well as the aesthetic sense to employ such artists as Jacobi, Blaikie, and Ricketts in the making and printing of their books, the Bodley Head was from the outset able to embody in its work the ideals and aims of the Revival of Printing so often

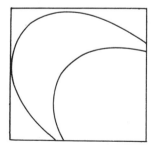

2 THE BODLEY
HEAD
BOOK

associated with the founding of Morris' Kelmscott Press at Hammersmith in 1891. Beginning with *Volumes in Folio* in 1889, the Bodley Head books were a marked departure from the tasteless, often vulgar bindings, design-less title pages, and ugly typography of the books supplied by the large commercial firms. In make-up and in design they anticipated the modern book.

Although Richard Le Gallienne's knowledge of book design and his taste for simplicity were evident in the beauty and distinction of his first books of poetry, *My Ladies' Sonnets* and *Volumes in Folio*, and although John Lane also showed surprising capabilities when it came to book design — Le Gallienne was later to say that he "had a genius for *format*" [1] — the three men who were chiefly responsible for the firm's most beautifully designed books were Blaikie, Jacobi, and Ricketts.

In dedicating his *Lyra Heroica* to Walter Blaikie, William Ernest Henley called him an "artist printer," an epithet which best describes this remarkable man, who began his career as an engineer in India, where he cut roads through the jungles and great forests of Kathiawar and built among other things a palace, a hospital, and a jail.[2] At the age of 31, Blaikie returned with his wife and child to Scotland. In 1878 by chance he met Thomas Constable the printer, son of the famous Archibald, at King's Cross Station in London and rode to Edinburgh with him. Before the journey was over, Blaikie had been talked into joining the printing business in Thistle Street for a six months' trial engagement.[3] He fell in love with the printing of books, rose to be head of the firm, brought T. and A. Constable to an even more prestigious position than it had once enjoyed, and retired in 1922 at the age of 75.[4]

D'Arcy Wentworth Thompson tells us that Blaikie "studied every part and aspect" of the printer's craft, "and brought to it," as someone said later on, "the skill of an engineer, the eye of an artist, and the taste of a scholar." [5] Unsatisfied with the type in use at that time at Constables, Blaikie discovered a font of type which had been cut in 1808 by Miller & Richard, the Edinburgh typefounders. Its possibilities long unrealized, the type was recast and first used in Saintsbury's edition of *The Works of John Dryden*.[6] A compromise between modern and old style, what came to be known as the "Dryden" type suggests Blaikie's desire for simplicity with beauty.

Blaikie had the instinct of a great designer and the patience and versatility which go with it. Whether it was a new operating theater for the Royal Infirmary of Edinburgh or a folding umbrella which could be carried in one's pocket, his designing brought him immense pleasure.[7] Perhaps it was this ability to take infinite pains and spend innumerable hours on a design which made Blaikie's title pages — so simple yet so finely arranged — a standard of excellence in book building. The title page was his special forte.

"All who knew him intimately," says a friend, "will remember the immense pains he took over these, and the hours he would spend in trying one arrangement after another until he had satisfied himself that the best possible design had been reached in balance of colour and form." [8]

As a printer, Blaikie displayed the qualities of sanity, restraint, and good taste. He eschewed extremes of any kind and knew the secret of making a book both readable and quietly beautiful without ostentation. According to Thompson, Blaikie's growing reputation, which reached a peak in the early 1890s, "brought him into some sort of rivalry, or at least comparison, with William Morris," whose Kelmscott Press was established in 1891, "and these two, the skilled tradesman and the great amateur, could never see eye to eye with one another. Morris, who always talked in superlatives, said that Blaikie's type was the ugliest he ever saw; and Blaikie said that Morris's books were just old bric-a-brac." [9] Certainly it was Blaikie's insistence on readability as well as taste which helped make the Bodley Head book a practical yet aesthetically pleasing work which could succeed as a commercial and artistic venture.[10]

In his essay on the books of the 1890s, A. J. A. Symons wrote that the most distinguished books of that decade typographically were done by four printers. "Of these the principal is the firm of T. and A. Constable at Edinburgh. The late W. A. Blaikie, then general manager, was undoubtedly responsible for many of Lane's essays." [11] Certainly this is true. And Blaikie's statement of his ideals and aims as a printer and designer, in an interview which appeared in 1894 under the title "How the Perfect Book is Made," is an excellent means of gauging the fine points of the Bodley Head book. To Blaikie "artistic design and soundness of workmanship" were the bases of fine book production; and although he was an artist who sought to create the ideal book, he never for one moment thought of a book as merely an art object. "You must always remember," he said, "that the first object of a book is to be read, not to become an article of bric-a-brac." Another of his basic beliefs was that a "book must have a character of its own, corresponding to its author's idea." [12]

The author and publisher never needed to fear that Blaikie would produce a book whose elements — binding, type, title page, illustrations — would conflict with or detract from the subject matter. For he always maintained that "the printer's business, if he is an artist, is — and this is the most important thing of all — to give a fitting dress to the writer's thought, to bring out physically the author's abstract idea; in short, to embody the abstract idea in the concrete shape of a book."

Having discussed with his interviewer the various elements which go to the make-up of "the ideal book," Blaikie turned last to what he considered the "crowning glory of a good book," the title page. For him, the title page was the main entrance to the subject matter, and, as such, should set the tone and emphasize briefly but unmistakably the central matter of the book. "The title-page ought to express, clearly and at the first glance," Blaikie stressed, "what the character of the book is. . . . Putting it briefly, I should say that the ideal title-page must be dominated by one chief note, expressing the central feature of the book." Opening a copy of Sir George Reid's drawings of *The River Tweed*, he pointed out that in the midst of "a number of lines the name of the river makes itself seen at the first glance." And to further indicate what he meant, he referred to another book, *Memorials of Crail*, "where 'crail' is the notable object on the title-page."

But much more important in Blaikie's concept of title page design was his notion that the title page "should always have a definite outline of its own. You may notice," he said, "that in all my title-pages I try to introduce this outline, and avoid the two or three lines of type with a great blank in the middle of the page that are yet, as I show you, common enough." Most title pages, according to Blaikie, were either "hysterical," pages on which the lines of type were strung out helter-skelter without seemingly any order or design, or "the common-place title-page, with nothing about it to distinguish one book from another. To hit the individual character of the book, to be dignified and simple is the great virtue of a title-page; but," he added in summary, "it can only be attained by worrying away till it comes right of itself." To Blaikie the title page was the "artistic printer's" greatest challenge. "The surest test of slovenly work," he maintained, is the title page.[13]

Charles Jacobi[14] of the Chiswick Press was a bit more conservative in matters of book production than his counterpart at T. and A. Constable. Much more prone to use the old-face types which had become a hallmark of the Revival of Printing, Jacobi also relished the use of the Chiswick Press wood block page ornaments and decorated initials. Apprenticed in 1868 to Charles Whittingham, the younger, Jacobi later was associated with Edward and Ernest Bell as managing editor of the Chiswick Press before he assumed active and practical control of the press in 1882.[15]

Although, in the opinion of Ruari McLean, "no new ideas in book design came from the Chiswick Press" after the death of William Pickering in 1854 and the retirement of Whittingham, the younger, in 1860, "it continued to function admirably on the supplies of know-how and decorative wood blocks built up in earlier days." [16] Jacobi perhaps added nothing to the printing firm's distinguished production, yet he saw to it that the Chiswick Press's reputation for taste and excellence were maintained. As McLean asserts in his *Victorian Book Design,*

Jacobi was no originator, but he had a strong sense of style in printing and knew how to use the material he had inherited. His sound abilities as a typographer can be seen in the various books he wrote and especially in his ten variants of a title-page, devised for teaching, which are shown in his *Notes on Books,* 1892, and in T. L. De Vinne's *Title-pages as seen by a Printer,* New York, 1901.[17]

Jacobi's collaboration with the artist Walter Crane in producing a book of Crane's own verse, *Renascence,* published by the Bodley Head in 1891, resulted in one of the most beautiful among the Chiswick Press books. This book exemplifies the best work of the Chiswick Press for the Bodley Head. It was set in old-face "Basle Roman" type, its frontispiece and thirty-seven other designs — head and tail pieces in the Chiswick Press manner — were done by Crane himself, and it was printed on fine Van Gelder handmade paper (with an issue of forty on Japanese vellum).

Even more typical of Jacobi, however, is his own book, *On the Making and Issuing of Books,* which was brought out by the Bodley Head on April 6, 1891. Although it shares with *Renascence* the Basle Roman type and the fine handmade paper, its ornaments are drawn from the Chiswick Press supply of wood block head and tail pieces, and Jacobi uses decorative initials and the red lettering he so often preferred on the title page.

Most of Jacobi's ideas on book production and design are contained in this attractive book with its quarter imitation vellum binding and blue handmade paper-covered boards. He was clearly in agreement with the ideals of the Revival of Printing first enunciated by Emery Walker in his lecture before the Arts and Crafts Society in 1888, relegating modern-face type to "newspapers, magazines, school-books, scientific works, pamphlets, and such like," and recommending either old-face or revived old-style type for use in book work of a higher character, belles-lettres, gift books, and so on.[18]

His ideas concerning the margins of books were also in agreement with those of the Revival. "To place the print in the centre of the paper is wrong in principle," he maintained, "and to be deprecated. If we look at a book printed in this fashion, it is apparent to the book-lover that something is amiss"; Jacobi recommended that an aesthetically pleasing page have more margin on the outer than the inner side, and less at the head of the page than at the tail.[19]

His emphasis on fine paper and his predilection for handmade rather than machine-made paper no doubt had much to do with the fact that some of the ordinary issues and all the special and large-paper issues of

Bodley Head books were printed on fine handmade papers. The choicest issues were printed on Japanese handmade vellum in all probability because of Jacobi's liking for its qualities — its strength and what he described as "its beautifully even and smooth surface" which was "capable of receiving the finest impressions." [20]

Although Charles de Sousy Ricketts was only twenty-six when he designed his first book issued by the Bodley Head — Wilde's *Poems* (1892) — he had already collaborated with his lifelong partner, Charles Hazlewood Shannon, in bringing out the first number of the *Dial* (Summer 1889), the most beautiful of the journals of the Aesthetic Movement, and designed several of Oscar Wilde's most famous books.[21] Although Ricketts' best work was not done until after he saw some of William Morris' work from the Kelmscott Press,[22] his early efforts were the work of an extraordinarily gifted artist with a real instinct for book design, a talent which Wilde clearly recognized.

The earliest evidence of Ricketts' interest in book design is a letter which Wilde wrote to Arthur Fish in October 1890: "Ricketts has just done for me a lovely cover for *Dorian Gray* — grey pastel-paper with a white back and tiny gold marigolds. When it appears I will send you a copy." [23] *Dorian*, published in book form in April 1891,[24] by Ward, Lock, & Co. was the first of six books Ricketts designed in that one year, five of which were published by a new firm, Osgood, McIlvaine & Co. Osgood, who had been the London agent since 1886 for Harper and Brothers, established his own house in 1891 and brought out a remarkably interesting group of books designed by Ricketts, including Wilde's *Intentions, Lord Arthur Savile's Crime and Other Stories, A House of Pomegranates,* and Hardy's *Tess of the D'Urbervilles.*[25]

Speaking of the *Tess* designed by Ricketts, Carl Weber remarks that anyone who examines the three volumes must be

struck by the fact that they are different — both in the general attractiveness of the tan (or brownish yellow) bindings with their floral decorations, and in the unusual arrangement of the title-pages — different from almost all previously published books by Thomas Hardy, or, for that matter, by any other author. These books were obviously designed by someone with a genius for artistic lay-out, by someone with taste and originality.[26]

Ricketts met Shannon at an art school at Lambeth in 1884, and the two shared a brown-papered room in Kennington until they went to Paris where they planned to live (as was the custom of the day for young English artists) and study with their favorite French artist, Puvis de Chavanne. At

Title page by Walter Crane.

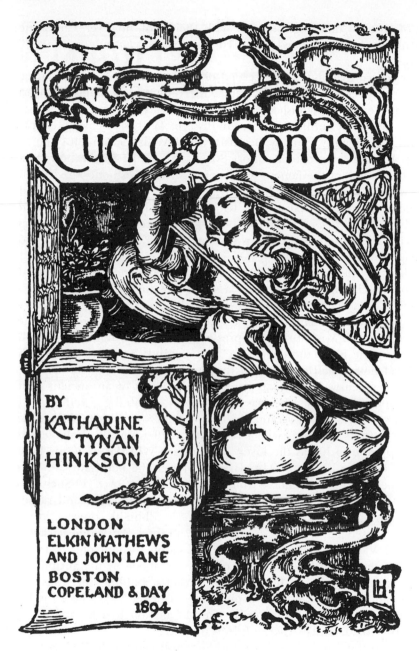

Cuckoo Songs

BY
KATHARINE
TYNAN
HINKSON

LONDON
ELKIN MATHEWS
AND JOHN LANE
BOSTON
COPELAND & DAY
1894

Title page by Laurence Housman.

the close of an early morning interview with their idol, however, Chavanne urged them to return home and dismissed them with *"charmante jeunesse"* on his lips.[27]

On their return to London they settled down in a picturesque old house in the Vale, only recently vacated by James McNeill Whistler, and began to gather about them a distinguished group of artists and writers among whom were Sturge Moore, Camille and Lucien Pissaro, Will Rothenstein, Oscar Wilde, and, occasionally, Aubrey Beardsley, and Whistler himself.[28] Until 1894 when Ricketts moved to Beaufort Street, this house in the now celebrated Vale was one of the famous focal points of the Aesthetic Movement. Not only was the *Dial* born here but also the two beautiful books published by the Bodley Head and designed by Ricketts and Shannon, *Daphnis and Chloe* and *Hero and Leander,* the first book to be printed on paper bearing a V. P. (Vale Press) watermark and a similar monogram on the spine and the page opposite the colophon.

In the late eighties, the Vale was set apart from the noisy King's Road and the commercialism of Chelsea by "a small crossing guarded by an unpretentious wooden gate" situated across from Paulton Square.[29] This very rural-looking portal gave entrance to "a roadway resembling a country lane which," according to Miss Stirling, impressed one as "a veritable oasis from the turmoil of the noisy thorough fare" left behind. The Vale, in which three isolated houses nestled "each in the midst of a spacious garden . . . terminated in greensward and wavy trees, the remains of an ancient deer park." On one side of the lane was "the quaint, rambling dwelling . . . shrouded in creepers, with a veranda front and back," in which William de Morgan, the novelist, and his wife lived until 1910 when the Vale ceased to exist. "Opposite to it was the lovely spot where Whistler grew his larkspurs round a velvet lawn and Alfred Austin [later the poet laureate] was inspired to pen 'Farewell summers from a garden that I love'." [30] Such was the setting for the simple gatherings which — despite the cocoa and rather less than fresh eggs dished up by Shannon after all-night conversations[31] — Wilde immensely enjoyed and extravagantly praised. To Wilde Ricketts' house in the Vale was one of the few in London "where one is never bored." [32] Just how fond Wilde had become of the abode by the autumn of 1889 is indicated by a letter he wrote to Ricketts, bidding the gods "to shower gold and roses on the Vale, or on that part of the Vale where the De Morgans do not live. . . . I must come round," he concluded, "and enjoy the company of the Dialists — *par nobile* as they are." [33]

The *Dial* was the first task Ricketts and Shannon had set themselves after having been sent home from Paris. And the copy of the first number which they sent to Wilde proved irresistible to the great man, who then made the acquaintance of its designers and became for a time their patron. It was probably Wilde, who, with the evidence of the *Dial* before him, suggested to Ricketts that he should design books.[34] At any rate, Ricketts and Shannon became, in the words of Denys Sutton "almost the official artists to Wilde." [35]

Although Ricketts' book designs for Osgood and McIlvaine in 1891 culminated in the Bodley Head production of Wilde's *Poems* in 1892, his best work was done in 1893–1894 and included the now famous Bodley Head productions of John Gray's *Silverpoints,* Lord De Tabley's *Poems, Dramatic and Lyrical,* J. A. Symonds' *In the Key of Blue,* and Wilde's *The Sphinx.* During these years, he and Shannon also issued through the Bodley Head *Daphnis and Chloe* and *Hero and Leander,* two books which in every way anticipated the Vale Press books produced later by Hacon and Ricketts.

Although Ricketts thought of his "earliest experiments in the shaping of books," that done for Messrs. Osgood and McIlvaine in 1891, as "crude and hesitating," he did feel they differed from "ordinary books in the matter of title page, proportion of margin, and in the designs upon their boards." [36] And in *A Defence of the Revival of Printing,* he suggests that his early work would have been much better had he then known such productions of William Morris as *A Tale of the House of the Wolfings* (1888) and *The Roots of the Mountains* (1889), which the Chiswick Press did for him. "These," says Ricketts, "might have initiated me at the time to a better and more severe style." [37]

In addition to the influence of Morris, Ricketts' work for the Bodley Head also bears the impress of the Venetian books of the Renaissance. As Ricketts tells us in *A Defence,* he was by 1891 "utterly won over and fascinated by the sunny pages of the Venetian printers," and it was "one of those rare Aldus italic volumes with its margins uncut" on which the singularly beautiful *Silverpoints* was modeled.[38]

An excellent example of Ricketts' later work for the Bodley Head, which also shows his severer more exotic style, is Wilde's *The Sphinx,* which was published shortly after *Hero and Leander* although, according to the artist, it was finished before it.[39] In his *Defence* Ricketts indicates his duties as designer when he writes, "I built, decorated, and bound 'The Sphinx'," a work which he claims to have been "the first book of the modern revival printed in three colours, red, black, and green." The "peculiar arrangement of the text [long lines of text often filling only the top third or fourth of the page]" was, said Ricketts, necessitated by "the small bulk of the text and unusual length of the lines" of the poem. His printing the entire text of *The Sphinx* in capitals is explained by the designer as "an effort away from the Renaissance towards a book marked by surviving classical traits." [40]

The duties which Wilde accorded Ricketts in connection with the ill-fated *The Portrait of Mr. W. H.* suggest that in his work for the Bodley Head he usually had the task of selecting the type and designing a suitable setting for the books placed under his supervision.[41] As a result, he was able to embody the ideas and aims arrived at through much thought concerning the aesthetic problems of book production.

Certainly Ricketts and Morris during the first years of the 1890s did much to revolutionize English book production and to establish book designing as a profession which demanded great artistic talent. In his youth, says A. J. A. Symons, Ricketts was

a personal anticipation of the modern "typographer" who (in one definition) is a being "concerned exclusively with the designing of printing, the choice of paper, ink, ornament and binding, etc., for the book in hand." These were precisely the tasks to which Ricketts set himself before the establishment of his own press left him free to indulge his preferences without stint or stay; and even when the Vale Press was created, the colophons usually referred to "Charles Ricketts, under whose supervision [this] book has been printed by the Ballantyne Press." [42]

It was those two or three years after he had seen the first Kelmscott books and had begun to study the Venetian book, yet before he had met Llewellyn Hacon (who enabled him to set up the Vale Press in 1896), during which the Bodley Head was privileged to have the services of Charles Ricketts, who in *Silverpoints, In the Key of Blue, Poems, Dramatic and Lyrical,* and *The Sphinx* created the most beautiful and consummately designed trade books of the 1890s.[43]

In the opinion of A. J. A. Symons, Ricketts' books "in many ways, indeed . . . are the most remarkable of all those books" issued in that first great decade of modern book production. "The products of an historically learned mind applied unhistorically," Ricketts' books, Symons concludes, "present a fantastic mixture of archaic pedanticism and revolutionary defiance of precedent." [44]

Like Walter Blaikie, Ricketts shared the current view among the avant-garde that a book must be "a living and corporate whole, the quality of beauty therein is all-pervading; it is not decorated as a modern house is decorated by the upholsterer and the picture dealer; it is conceived harmoniously and made beautifully like any other genuine work of art. Unity, harmony, such are the essentials of fine book building." [45]

That Ricketts was able to achieve his aims and embody his ideals in his

Bodley Head books is suggested by the acclaim they won at the fourth Arts and Crafts Exhibition in 1893. "Among designs for cloth-bindings," reports the critic (probably Gleeson White) for the *Studio,* "the exquisite *Silverpoints,* Oscar Wilde's *Poems,* and Lord de Tabley's *Poems,* after C. S. Ricketts' designs, are a revelation to those who see them here for the first time." [46] The impact of these books not only on the layman but on other artists of the day is suggested in the notes the critic wrote up about the Ricketts and Shannon *Daphnis and Chloe*:

The work of these two artists already has influenced our younger designers to an unusual extent, and if not household words to the outside public, one may doubt if the work of any of their contemporaries is more eagerly studied by their fellow-artists. Even those who do not agree with their ideal pay them the tribute of active hostility, while their admirers look upon the Vale and its *Dial* . . . as a new *Germ* [the early Pre-Raphaelite journal of 1850].[47]

Among the "younger designers" of the day who owed much to Ricketts was Laurence Housman, who during 1893–1894 designed three fine examples of the Bodley Head book, Francis Thompson's first volume entitled *Poems,* John Davidson's *A Random Itinerary,* and Katharine Tynan's *Cuckoo Songs*. Having known Ricketts and Shannon at the Arts and Crafts School and also at Miller's Lane School in South Lambeth, Housman did not come under the influence of Ricketts until in 1889 he attempted to obtain a copy of the first issue of the *Dial,* which brought him an invitation to call at the Vale. "Within a month," Housman later recalled,

Ricketts had dragged me away from my timid preferences for fuzzy chalk-drawing, as a means of concealing my bad draughtsmanship, and had set me to pen-work, with Rossetti and the other pre-Raphaelites as my main guides both in composition and technique. From that time on I felt set — I acquired a new confidence; I had found out at last what I wanted to do.[48]

Again in Housman the Bodley Head engaged the services of an outstanding young artist of the day, one who, in the opinion of A. J. A. Symons, "played a considerable part in the short-lived typographical revival of the eighteen-nineties." [49]

The Revival of Printing, to which Ricketts contributed so much and of which the Bodley Head book is a part, is usually thought of as beginning with the reintroduction of Caslon old-face (old-style) type at the behest of William Pickering in the 1840s.[50] The type employed by the Chiswick Press in George Herbert's *Temple* and *Lady Willoughby's Diary* was introduced in the eighteenth century by England's first great type designer, William Caslon, and bears his name. Whether or not it was revived by Pickering to combat the then universal use of modern-face type, a development of the later eighteenth-century type designers like Baskerville, Bodoni, and Didot, the use of the old-face font became the first means of reacting against the Victorian book which was considered synonymous with the vulgarity and commercialism surrounding middle-class life. Modern-face type had the misfortune of having been in vogue when the introduction of modern press machinery and commercial production methods gave rise to the cheap and mass-produced book; and so any type such as the old-face which recalled a world reminiscent of the craftsman printer and the hand press appealed to the aesthetic sense of authors and book specialists who in the later nineteenth century sought to preserve the artistic integrity of books against the onslaught of commercialism.[51]

Although T. and A. Constable and the Chiswick Press continued to produce finely printed and well-designed books throughout the high Victorian period, book production as a whole in England reached its nadir during mid-Victorian times. According to Ruari McLean, as the nineteenth century progressed, "the quality of book design, as of many other handcrafts, gradually deteriorated as the effect of the Industrial Revolution multiplied." [52] Although good work continued to be done, it was, in McLean's words, "exceptional. The average was low, perhaps lower than it had ever been." In sum, the "typical fault of Victorian book design was feebleness." [53]

But a reaction to commercialism and the ordinary mass-produced book began to manifest itself not only in the interest in type fonts such as Caslon and the Fell type later revived by Dr. Daniel at Oxford but also in the desire on the part of authors and artists to bring all the elements of a book back into some kind of artistic harmony, a unity which would enhance the author's meaning and re-establish the book's claim to being in itself a work of art.

The rediscovery of William Blake in the 1850s by Dante Gabriel Rossetti was the rediscovery of the one man who could best serve the Revival as an ideal. Blake was both a great poet and a great artist who combined both talents in one form, that of the handmade book. In his ability not only to create the text but also to give that text its proper artistic setting, he anticipated the efforts of such Bodley Head works as Walter Crane's *Renascence* and William Strang's *The Earth Fiend*. It was his example which suggested that the ideal book should be the imaginative creation of one mind, and this, in turn, gave impetus to thinking of the book not as a conglomeration of disparate parts — type, paper, text, illustrations, binding — but as a harmonious whole, an aesthetic object. In order to attain such an ideal, then, either the author must be the designer or a designer must be employed who could without violating the text integrate all the elements into a harmonious whole, thereby creating a proper aesthetic setting.

The increasing concern of authors with the design of their books is suggested, for example, by Walter Pater's fear lest the format for his *Studies in the History of the Renaissance*, which appeared in 1873, should be out of keeping with its tone and subject matter. In a letter to Alexander Macmillan of Macmillan & Co., dated September 21, 1872, Pater, having acknowledged receipt of a printed specimen of the essays, regretted that they were not yet "in the form I think most suitable for the book. Some of the essays are so short, and all of them in some ways so slight, that I think the only suitable form would be a small volume, costing about five shillings [which reads as if he had thus early a Bodley Head book in mind]; and I should like to make some suggestions on the binding and some other points." [54] Macmillan, who preferred an octavo volume, was throughout the negotiations for the most part opposed to Pater's attempts to make his book something other than the typical Victorian production Macmillan was in the habit of publishing. On November 2, Pater in a letter to Macmillan said that he liked the page specimen sent him, but he was not satisfied with the paper. And again his taste was surprisingly prescient of Bodley Head books when he told Macmillan of his desires concerning the binding: "It has occurred to me that the old-fashioned binding in pasteboard with paper back and printed label, usual, I think, about thirty years ago, but not yet gone quite out of use, would be an economical and very pretty binding for my book." [55]

What Pater then goes on to write is of special significance as a sign of the aesthetic sensibility later to manifest itself in the makers and buyers of the Bodley Head book in the 1890s. Such old-fashioned paper-covered boards "would, I am sure, be much approved of by many persons of taste, among whom the sale of the book would probably in the first instance be. I have just had in my hands an old book so bound, the pasteboard covers of a greyish blue, and the paper back olive green; nothing could be prettier or more simple. . . ." A further indication of how Pater's sensibility anticipated that of Mathews and Lane is his desire to have "the present paper" — probably a cheap machine-made variety — "changed for paper with rough edges and showing the watermark." [56]

Macmillan's opposition to Pater's attempt to give the *Renaissance* distinction and a setting appropriate to its subject matter is implicit in Pater's reply, dated November 11, 1872:

I was disappointed at the contents of your letter, as the cover I wished for had occurred to me as a way of giving my book the artistic appearance which I am sure is necessary for it, without the expense and trouble of an unusual form of binding. . . . Something not quite in the ordinary way is, I must repeat, very necessary in a volume the contents of which are so unpretending as mine, and which is intended in the first instance for a comparatively small section of readers.

In arguing his case, Pater suggested the problem facing an author who before the Bodley Head was established had to deal with the large commercial publisher. "For a book on art," he pleads, "to be bound quite in the ordinary way is, it seems to me, behind the times; and the difficulty of getting a book bound in cloth so as to be at all artistic, and indeed not quite the other way, is very great." [57]

In Macmillan's reply to Pater, he made it clear that he could not be convinced "that paper covers are more beautiful than cloth" and affirmed that they were "very much less useful." However, Macmillan sent along a book which contained a paper "made to imitate the old wire-wove paper, which can only now be got in this mock rib," [58] which Pater liked and which was, consequently, used in the first edition of *Renaissance*. According to Simon Nowell-Smith, "a compromise was reached. The book appeared, in February, 1873, in a cloth binding of an unusual shade of green of Pater's choosing." [59]

A year or so earlier, Dante Gabriel Rossetti, agonizing over the production and issuance of his belated first volume of poetry, in a lesser way than Pater suggested his concern for the aesthetic setting of his *Poems*. In the tradition of Blake, Rossetti, who often painted pictures to accompany certain of his sonnets and other poems, had designed the binding for this volume. On April 21, 1870, Rossetti, having received from his publisher, Frederick Startridge Ellis, a version of the design, wrote:

Your diagram of the binding appals me, as the *back* is all wrongly arranged, but I hope it may be only your memory that is at fault. [A sketch of the binding design Rossetti wanted follows.]
I suppose the inscription at the back of the rough-bound copy sent is

from the real block. If so, I don't like it. The *O* of *Poems* is monstrously big and makes all crooked. The *O* of *Rossetti* too big also. The gold seems a good colour.[60]

Rossetti's involvement in book production went back to 1866, when he designed the binding and the title page, and illustrated Christina Rossetti's *The Prince's Progress and Other Poems*.[61] The relative simplicity of his binding design is an indication of the growing desire for plainness on the part of those whose work influenced the Revival of Printing, and its curving vinelike motif with just the hint of the honeysuckle blossom done in gold on a dark green cloth is suggestive of *art nouveau* and the Japanese influence. The line and circle motifs which Rossetti often employed are used on the title page, which looks forward to those of Selwyn Image, especially his title page for the Bodley Head production of Ernest Rhys's *A London Rose and Other Poems*. Rossetti's work as a designer of bindings probably influenced William Morris, who in 1873 did a striking design for his own volume *Love Is Enough*. As Paul Thompson points out in *The Work of William Morris,* Rossetti's "remarkably simple bindings with thin spare asymmetrical line decoration" of the 1860s must have influenced Morris' early forays into binding design.[62]

Although William Morris chose the Chiswick Press to do his early volumes, *The Defence of Guenevere* (1858) and *The Life and Death of Jason* (1869), he was not the book-design enthusiast he came to be when, having heard Emery Walker's lecture on printing, he moved to counter the extravagantly bad conditions which obtained throughout the book industry of Britain by designing and producing through the Chiswick Press two notable books from the point of view of typography and make-up, his *A Tale of the House of the Wolfings* (published December 1888) and *The Roots of the Mountains* (published November 1889). In both books Morris employed the Chiswick Press's Basle Roman type although he modified the "e" in the latter volume. These attempts, of course, led to his founding the Kelmscott Press in 1891, the books from which are not on the whole suggestive of the Bodley Head book.

Perhaps the most extraordinary work done in the area of book design before the early nineties was that of Whistler, who in his books and catalogues showed a taste for simplicity yet elegance of design which set the books with which we are concerned so clearly apart from the ordinary ones of the day. The Pennells in their biography of Whistler have told of the great pains and infinite care which the artist took to get his books just right — efforts which had their influence on subsequent book production.[63]

Whistler's *The Gentle Art of Making Enemies,* which appeared in 1890, exemplifies, in the words of A. J. A. Symons, all his "typographical foibles." [64] The title page in every way is a slap in the face of the bourgeois Victorian way of doing things (just as is the subject matter of the book itself), set as it is entirely in italic Caslon capitals which are arranged unequally and, again indicating the Japonesque, out of center. The binding of *The Gentle Art* is described by Symons as being "quite in the modern fashion, composed of brown paper board sides with a mustard yellow cloth back strip, but with a gilt superscription on the front cover which is an enlargement of the half-title." [65]

In his *The Art Nouveau Book in Britain,* John Russell Taylor further indicates the importance of Whistler when he points out that "the most obvious feature of Whistler's book design is his meticulous and wholly idiosyncratic disposition of black and white on the page." This "taste for asymmetrical arrangements," and Whistler's "passion for plenty of white on a page" [66] anticipated Emery Walker's enunciation of the principle in his lecture of November 1888. Whistler wanted "the basic block of print . . . placed not square in the middle of the page (or, strictly speaking, slightly nearer the inner edge) as in a conventional book then and since, but much nearer the inner than the outer edge and noticeably nearer the top than the bottom." [67]

Certainly Whistler's work looks toward the kind of book the Bodley Head produced in that it was done — its effects gained — as Taylor affirms, "by the simplest means" which Whistler found at his disposal. "He required no special types for his books, no virtuoso effects in printing. He had no difficulty," according to Taylor,

in working within the framework of ordinary commercial publishing, using the types normally available in a normal printer's office in the 1880's and the papers on which everyday books were printed, and moreover devising for himself a form of binding (brown paper boards lettered in black; yellow cloth just covering the spine) which was practical, inexpensive, and, when arranged with his own flair for inspired simplicity, both elegant and distinctive.[68]

According to Ruari McLean, Whistler's *The Gentle Art* was "part of a whole new movement in book design, which owed nothing to the Kelmscott Press," [69] and as such was at one with the most characteristic and best of the Bodley Head books. Although McLean sees *The Gentle Art* as owing "a great deal to Oscar Wilde, to ideas on art then effervescing in Paris and in Holland," [70] Wilde, on the whole, owed most to Whistler in his concern for aesthetically satisfying formats for his own writings.[71] That Wilde like Whistler shared the concern of Rossetti and Pater for the total book is suggested in the letter he wrote to John Lane about the binding for *Salome*:

Dear Mr. Lane,/ The cover of *Salome* is quite dreadful. Don't spoil a lovely book. Have simply a folded vellum wrapper with the design in scarlet — much cheaper, and much better. The texture of the present cover is coarse and common: it is quite impossible and spoils the real beauty of the interior. Use up this horrid Irish stuff for stories, etc.: don't inflict it on a work of art like *Salome*. It really will do you a great deal of harm. Everyone will say that it is coarse and inappropriate. I loathe it. So does Beardsley. Truly Yours/ Oscar Wilde[72]

In delineating the aims and ideals of the men primarily responsible for making the Bodley Head book what it was, I have suggested some of the attitudes of mind and aspects of book design which either directly influenced the Bodley Head book or as a common element in the aesthetic milieu manifested themselves therein. Further I have intimated that the Bodley Head book can best be understood in the context of the Revival of Printing, a movement which was primarily a reaction to the mass-produced book, the staple of the large trade publishers of the day. As such, the Revival was but another of the efforts on the part of a few aesthetically oriented men and women who toward the close of the nineteenth century sought by various means to divorce themselves from the commercialism, vulgarity of taste, and debased values rampant in Victorian society.

In its typography, paper, binding, and title pages and in its limited editions, the Bodley Head book was in keeping with the principles enunciated by Emery Walker and later published in a revised form by William Morris in the *Arts and Crafts Essays* of 1893. As a trade book it sought to profit from the Revival of Printing by appealing to the few who desired a book which as a totality was an aesthetically pleasing object.

Entitled simply "Printing" as it appeared in *Arts and Crafts Essays,* the Walker-Morris statement of the Revival's attitude of mind rejected modern-face fonts such as those developed by Baskerville, Bodoni, and Didot as "*positively* ugly." [73] Specifically, modern-face types, they maintained, were "dazzling and unpleasant to the eyes owing to the clumsy thickening and vulgar thinning of the lines." Although not entirely satisfied with old-face types, Walker and Morris felt that "seventeenth-century letters" in contrast to later types were "at least pure and simple in line." [74]

Concerning the arrangement of the type on a page, Walker and Morris were especially critical of ugly, meandering white areas or "rivers." "The general *solidity* of a page is much to be sought for." [75] And far more important was their principle that the unit of a book should be "the two pages forming an opening. The modern printer, in the teeth of the evidence given by his own eyes, considers the single page as the unit, and prints the page in the middle of his paper." As a result, the whole opening of the typical book of the time had "an upside-down look vertically" and "laterally the page looks as if it were being driven off the paper." [76]

Stressing the fact that good paper "would not materially increase the cost in all but the very cheapest books," the essay, which declares that the "paper used for ordinary books is exceedingly bad," pleads for the quality of paper which will enhance the durability and beauty of the book.[77]

In an effort to unify the various elements of a book, Walker and Morris urged "that the ornament, whatever it is, whether picture or pattern-work, should form *part of the page,* should be a part of the whole scheme of the book." If such a principle were followed in book design, the modern practice of disregarding "the relation between the printing and the ornament altogether" would be remedied.[78]

It is the contention of the essay that,

granted well-designed type, due spacing of the lines and words, and proper position of the page on the paper, all books might be at least comely and well-looking: and if to these good qualities were added really beautiful ornament and pictures, printed books might once again illustrate to the full the position of our Society that a work of utility might be also a work of art, if we cared to make it so.[79]

During the seven years between 1887 and 1894, the Bodley Head published a surprisingly wide range of books both in subject matter and in format. There were books on *The Ancient Crosses of Dartmoor* and "sermons" on Dante; lectures such as Beerbohm Tree's pronouncement on *The Imaginative Faculty,* as well as a brief collection of reviews and letters in praise of *Alma Murray as Beatrice Cenci.* In their appearance the books varied from the undistinguished, common cloth binding of Henry Van Dyke's *The Poetry of Tennyson,* with its cheap paper and typography typical of the trade book produced in America,[80] to the elaborately designed and beautifully ornamented books such as Ricketts and Shannon's *Hero and Leander* and *Daphnis and Chloe.*

Although at least one of the most famous of the Bodley Head books, *In the Key of Blue,* is in what Taylor describes as the " 'old-fashioned jam-tart' style of Continental high art nouveau," [81] the Bodley Head book more often achieves its beauty and aura of high quality through simplicity; it is, at its most typical, "at once functional and beautiful," the qualities which Taylor attributes to the *art nouveau* book in Britain.[82] In the *Note on His Aims in Founding the Kelmscott Press,* Morris wrote that he "began printing books with the hope of producing some which would have a definite claim to beauty, while at the same time they should be easy to read and should not dazzle the eye, or trouble the intellect of the reader by eccentricity of form in the letters";[83] yet the Bodley Head book came closer to accomplishing these aims than the Kelmscott Press book.

At its most characteristic the Bodley Head book was simply beautiful, achieving in its format an aesthetic appeal derived oftentimes from the tasteful arrangement of the most economical materials. One of the most accurate appraisals of the Bodley Head book from this point of view appeared in 1892 in the "Books and Book Gossip" section of the *Sunday Sun.* Having just received copies of Le Gallienne's *English Poems* and Arthur Symons' *Silhouettes,* the reviewer only referred to them

to note a fact which they illustrate, and which we have been observing of late, namely, the recovery to a certain extent of good taste in the matter of printing and binding books. These two books which are turned out by Messrs. Elkin Mathews and John Lane are models of artistic publishing, and yet they are simplicity itself, if not cheapness itself. In plain cardboard covers, without any ornament whatsoever, resembling the bindings of the chap-books and horn-books of sixty and seventy years ago, they are the very antithesis of the flamboyant monstrosities in gilding and cloth that used to enshrine the heart-throbs of the minor poets not so long ago; and these cardboard covers must be correspondingly less costly. Yet the whole book, with its excellent printing and its very simplicity, makes a harmony which is satisfying to the artistic sense. Messrs. Elkin Mathews and John Lane deserve credit for this promising innovation.[84]

Although I have suggested that Whistler's books and catalogues were in their simplicity and economy forerunners of the Bodley Head book, the work most striking in this respect before the Bodley Head was established is that of the Rev. C. H. O. Daniel, who began printing minor pieces on an old hand press at his home at Frome. Later at Oxford he revived the Fell types, then long forgotten and lying hidden away at the University Press, and employed them in the creation of a number of small limited editions, primarily of poetry, between 1877 and 1919.[85] In 1883–1884, Robert Bridges, the future poet laureate, designed two of his own books for printing by Daniel "and insisted that they should be plain and without ornament." [86] As Ruari McLean concludes, "the revolt against decoration was already in the air." [87]

Both the Daniel Press and the Rugby Press of George E. Over often achieved through the use of handmade paper, tasteful typography, a simply designed title page, and a paper wrapper a distinctive, tasteful book — witness, for example, the Daniel Press edition of Pater's *An Imaginary Portrait* or Over's little volume of poems by Alfred Hayes, Le Gallienne, and Norman Gale entitled *A Fellowship in Song*, published by the Bodley Head in 1893.[88]

If Taylor is correct in his belief that British *art nouveau* was a reaction against highly ornate decoration and "the elaborately patterned paintings of Burne-Jones or the tapestries and stained glass of Morris and Co. . . . in favour of spareness, elegance and simplicity," [89] the Bodley Head book at its most characteristic can be considered a part of the *art nouveau* milieu in England. Walter Blaikie's "great rule" in book design was "entire plainness and simplicity, with no ornament that is not absolutely required." [90]

The qualities of simplicity and economy expressive of plain beauty can be found in many Bodley Head books such as Cosmo Monkhouse's *Corn and Poppies, The Book of the Rhymers' Club,* John Davidson's *Fleet Street Eclogues,* Frederick Wedmore's *Renunciations,* and Alice Meynell's *Poems.* The other most notable characteristic of the Bodley Head book is what some described as "prettiness," and what Percy Muir referred to as the "exquisite appearance" [91] of some of the volumes which, unlike the very plain books mentioned above and the very elaborate editions such as De Tabley's *Poems, Dramatic and Lyrical,* have about them a charm derived from a touch of ornament, a decorative title page, or perhaps the unusual shape and size of the format.

These books, in particular, expressed the fashion for "pretty volumes," small, sometimes fragile works, which Le Gallienne, Wilde, and others termed "dainty." Certainly the vogue for Bodley Head books such as Ernest Radford's *Chambers Twain,* John Todhunter's *A Sicilian Idyll,* Francis W. Bourdillon's *A Lost God,* Walter Crane's *Renascence,* Michael Field's *Sight and Song,* and Norman Gale's *Orchard Songs* goes back to the mention of "the pretty volumes of the *Bibliotheque Elzevirienne*" in Pater's *Renaissance,* works a desire for which marked one out as among "the elect and peculiar people of the kingdom of sentiment." [92] Those who possessed the Paterian "temperament, the power of being deeply moved by the presence of beautiful objects," [93] sought the kind of book which Lane found in such a forerunner of the Bodley Head book as Andrew Lang's Paterian motivated [94] edition of Apuleius' *The Marriage of Cupid and Psyche*, brought out in 1887 as one of the "dainty" little editions known as the "Bibliotheque de Carabas."

Le Gallienne, in particular, sought in both his verse and in the appearance of his books to achieve this Paterian desideratum. In a letter to his mother, written soon after *My Ladies' Sonnets* appeared, he expressed delight that his first volume was being sought after as if it were a rare and ancient volume. He shared with "Mr. Robert Bridges the distinction, among minor poets, of having his first editions collected by amateurs in this country and America," [95] not only because his work appeared in limited editions but also because it was in format reminiscent of the aesthetically pleasing, dainty books of the past.

When in 1888 Le Gallienne thought seriously of editing a volume of Sir Philip Sidney's poetry, he wrote in a letter to Samuel Hales of his intention of approaching Elkin Mathews about bringing out "a dainty little (say 3 or 4/.) volume edition — Astrophel & Stella is just such a book as book men w[oul]d care for in such form." [96]

Wilde, too, found Pater's term, "dainty," the right one to express his feeling for the aesthetically appealing book, for his enthusiastic response to Herbert Horne's fragile little volume issued from the Bodley Head in 1891 entitled *Diversi Colores* was: "And what dainty delightful verse!" [97] It was verse whose daintiness also was expressed in its carefully designed format. Thinking ahead to the creation of a suitable setting for *Mr. W. H.*, he wrote John Lane that he "should like a book as dainty as John Gray's poems by Ricketts [*Silverpoints*]." [98] These light, fragile little one-volume editions of poems and other belles-lettres which issued from the Bodley Head were the antithesis of the heavy, dull-looking three-volume novels which were so characteristic of Victorian publishing and, as A. J. A. Symons has pointed out, "still persisted" into the 1890s, as witness the publication as late as 1894 of George Meredith's *Lord Ormont and his Aminta*. [99]

Despite the fact that most Bodley Head books are simply ornamented volumes, often small and slender in format, the most talked about, the most remarkable books which appeared with the imprint of the Bodley Head were a comparatively few editions which in their elaborate decoration and superb design are expressive of high *art nouveau* and the aesthete's fondest desire for the rare and exotic in volumes. Such Bodley Head books as the Ricketts-designed *Silverpoints, In the Key of Blue, Poems, Dramatic and*

Lyrical, The Sphinx, and the Ricketts and Shannon productions of *Hero and Leander* and *Daphnis and Chloe,* and Aubrey Beardsley's famous setting for *Salome* are the finest expressions in Britain of that decadent frame of mind which found its ultimate *objet d'art* in that edition of Gautier's *Emaux et Camées* done on Japanese paper and bound in citron-green leather with trellis and pomegranates, owned by Dorian Gray.[100]

Yet the designers and producers of these most elaborate of Bodley Head books never "came dangerously close to making books into mere objects" as Miss Moers suggests was the case with some of the books of the nineties.[101] Without the "expansive, impractical opulence" of Morris' books with their "specially manufactured inks, the imperishable Batchelor paper, the pure vellum bindings," [102] the ultimate in Bodley Head books achieved their exquisite beauty without either demanding the impossible from the printer and publisher or sacrificing the utility and readability of the book. Even in its extremest form — the italics used throughout *Silverpoints* — the type lends itself admirably to the subject matter and tone of Gray's exotic, decadent verse.

The Bodley Head book was not merely a "splendid anachronism," which like the productions of the Arts and Crafts movement *per se* achieved at best "a sterile excellence." [103] Surely the Bodley Head book most acurately fits A. J. A. Symons' description when he writes that

in the use of cloth covers boldly decorated with gold, for instance; in persistent attempt to unify all the factors that go to the make-up of a book; in such seeming affectations as the use of capitals smaller than the body type; in the disposition of the title-page, in the use of unusual shapes and sizes; and in the fitting together of illustrations and text — in a dozen minor ways the books of the "Nineties" are in accord with present practice [in book production], or have influenced it.[104]

In an effort to summarize the general characteristics of the Bodley Head book, the basic principles of the Revival of Printing can best be employed as a standard. Mathews and Lane usually adhered to the Revival's preference for types other than the almost universally used modern-face type. Often, as in Grant Allen's volume of poetry, *The Lower Slopes,* Caslon, an old-face type, was used, and in Crane's *Renascence* another type font introduced in the later nineteenth century by the Chiswick Press, Basle Roman,[105] was employed. Both Caslon and Basle Roman harkened back to pre-Baskerville days and gave an old-fashioned, craftsmanlike appearance to the page which contrasted markedly with a page of modern-face type so closely identified with the rise of commercialism and the mass-produced book.

Sometimes a font of type which effected a compromise between the old-face and modern-face type was used in Bodley Head books such as the Modernized Old Style found in books printed by Ballantyne, Hanson & Co. — *Plays* by John Davidson, for instance — and the Scotch modern-face employed by T. and A. Constable in Le Gallienne's *English Poems,* T. Gordon Hake's *Poems,* and Kenneth Grahame's first book, *Pagan Papers.* Seldom does one find a really exotic, eccentric, or unreadable type in a Bodley Head book. The most extreme in this respect, Gray's *Silverpoints,* with its use of italics throughout, is uncharacteristic.

As to the disposition of type on the page the Bodley Head book is remarkable for its time in its adherence to the principle set forth by Jacobi in his chapter "Of the Margins of Books" in *On the Making and Issuing of Books* and by Emery Walker and William Morris in *Arts and Crafts Essays*; that is, that the two-page opening is to be considered as a unit and that the print should be so disposed as to leave the widest margins at the bottom or tail and outer edge of the book. Jacobi's own Bodley Head book is an excellent example as are also Symonds' essays, *In the Key of Blue,* Wedmore's short stories, *Renunciations,* Davidson's *Plays,* Thompson's *Poems,* and Le Gallienne's *The Religion of a Literary Man* with its unusual pages of text boxed in with glosses. Almost any of the large-paper editions of books issued from the Bodley Head are excellent examples of spacious margins conforming to the preferred arrangement of text. The poorly designed pages with narrow margins found in Le Gallienne's *George Meredith,* Alice Meynell's *The Rhythm of Life and Other Essays,* and the famous *Keynotes* by George Egerton are among the few exceptions.

Like every other aspect of book production the making of paper was revolutionized by the invention of machines which enabled publishers to put cheap books before the public on a mass scale. Once a tedious and time-consuming process, paper-making became a simple, fully mechanized affair through the development in 1804 of the Fourdrinier paper-making machine and in 1809 of John Dickinson's machine, which worked on the cylinder principle. By 1835 all the essential mechanisms for paper production had been developed.[106] As a result the cost of paper-making was greatly reduced, and cheap wood-pulp machine-made papers became the basis of the mass-produced book.

Nevertheless fine handmade papers continued to be made, and the value and aesthetic appeal of many of the Bodley Head books are enhanced by the use of these handmade papers. Almost all of the books bearing the Bodley Head imprint were printed on laid paper and practically all of the large-paper and other special issues were printed on handmade paper. For instance, William Watson's *The Eloping Angels* appeared in a small-paper issue on laid paper, and two large-paper issues, one of 250 copies on Dickinson handmade paper and another of 75 copies on Japanese vellum. Similarly Walter Crane's *Renascence* was published in an ordinary issue on laid paper and two large-paper issues — 100 on the Dutch handmade paper known as Van Gelder and 40 on Japanese vellum, a strong, hard, very smooth paper usually reserved for the finest editions. The special issues of Lord De Tabley's *Poems, Dramatic and Lyrical,* William Strang's *The Earth Fiend,* William Bell Scott's *A Poet's Harvest Home,* and Augusta De Gruchy's *Under the Hawthorn* were printed on Japanese vellum to enhance their aura of rarity and value. Several Bodley Head editions, including the large-paper issue of J. T. Nettleship's *Browning,* were done on the fine Whatman handmade paper. A number of editions, including fifty copies of *In the Key of Blue,* were printed on handmade paper from the Dickinson Mills in Hertfordshire. And Wilde's *The Sphinx* was done on an unbleached Arnold paper. Certainly much of the charm, the special feel of the Bodley Head book, derived from the avoidance of cheap pulp papers and the care with which the paper was chosen.

But the two elements of the Bodley Head book which are most outstanding and play the largest role in helping create its true distinction are the title page and the binding. Walter Blaikie, who played a key role in the creation of the Bodley Head book, prided himself most on his title pages, and other designers like Jacobi, Ricketts, Laurence Housman, Selwyn Image, J. Illingworth Kay, and Aubrey Beardsley were equally aware of the importance of the title page to the success of the book.

If one calls to mind the title pages of earlier eras, their salient feature is a very long title. Although printers like William Bulmer and Thomas Bensley were able to reduce them to some order and preserve the page from the generally cumbersome appearance of most title pages of the time, it was not until after the middle of the nineteenth century that William Pickering created the first really modern title page by simply reducing the number of words to a bare minimum and setting them "in small capitals (the size of the text face employed in the book) carefully letter-spaced, with a simple, openly-engraved device or ornament." [107] Bulmer had used the same formula in his 1804 edition of *Poems by Goldsmith and Parnell,* yet, according to McLean, "in the hands of Pickering it became the basis of the English title-page for a hundred years." [108]

Whether the title page of Victorian books was either cluttered up with various and sundry sizes of type or sparsely printed over with undistin-

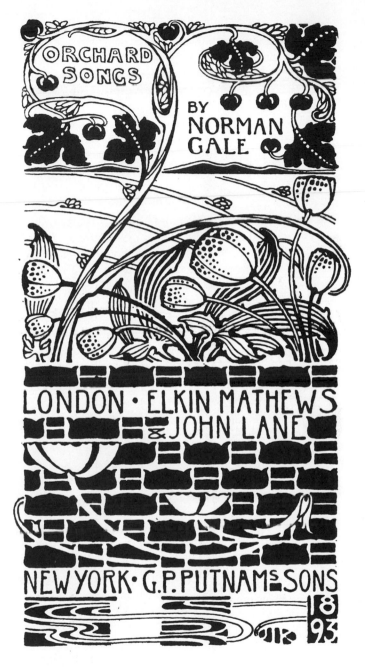

Title page by J. Illingworth Kay.

Title page by Selwyn Image.

Title page by H. P. Horne.

guished type, it was in any case less attractive than its predecessors. Ruari McLean, who has compared "the dismal lack of style of a late nineteenth-century middle-class villa" with many a contemporary title page "set in spidery types, over-widely spaced with unplanned margins," complains that the Victorian title pages were not just actively ugly, "they are worse, for they are negative." [109]

In his appraisal of the title page of the first edition of Thomas Hardy's *The Trumpet-Major,* McLean points out that it "fails because it was produced, not in bad taste, but in no taste. There is no sign of any thoughtful intention at all in the arrangement of the type. It sprawls without coherence or plan: it could be moved up or down without spoiling the effect." [110]

In keeping with the general effect of simplicity, the Bodley Head book most often displays a title page carefully and sometimes subtly ordered, with a minimum of words to achieve its purpose. In many ways the most attractive are the most simple — the title pages designed by Walter Blaikie. By employing only eleven words and his hallmark, a vine leaf device, he achieved in Alice Meynell's *Poems* his ultimate essay in simplicity. By the subtle choice of size and style of type and by arranging the words on the page one above the other to give a slender horizontal effect, Blaikie created a title page which in its unobtrusive appearance is in keeping with the quiet humility with which Mrs. Meynell's poems were tendered to the public.[111]

Although often very like the style evolved by William Pickering, Blaikie's work can at times compete with the most imaginative of the Bodley Head title pages. The best of Blaikie title pages was designed for Michael Field's attractive little volume, *Sight and Song.* Strikingly asymmetrical in its disposition of type, the page is centered by a round device of blossoms, berries, and leaves printed in an orange-red tone. The title and the name of the author are run across the entire width of the top of the page with the publisher's name and the place and date of publication printed in a tight block which suggests a period and brings the page to a close. This playing off of three geometric forms — rectangle, circle, and square — against one another gives the whole a sense of variety and vitality.

That Blaikie could still achieve a handsome, well-proportioned title page even when exigencies demanded the use of longer titles, is evidenced by his title page for George A. Greene's *Italian Lyrists of To-day,* in which his substitution of a more elaborate oval device for his usual vine leaf design subtly reflects the Italianate character of the book.

Blaikie seldom ventured to experiment so boldly as he did with the title page of *Sight and Song,* relying primarily on the Pickering style or slight variations thereof. Yet the title pages of Bodley Head books are most often thought of as remarkable experiments, and their designers as highly imaginative innovators within the form. Among these artists is Laurence Housman, who began as a disciple of Charles Ricketts and entered the field of book design almost simultaneously with him. In reviewing Housman's work in *The Art Nouveau Book in Britain,* Taylor speaks of his "varied and unconventional handlings of the title-page," and goes on to remark about his "series of ingenious and elaborate off-center designs." [112]

The first work Housman did for the Bodley Head was Francis Thompson's *Poems,* which was in every way a triumph of imaginative book design. The off-center title page is an excellent example of the new aesthetic attitude not only in its arrangement and integration of the decorative design and the type, but in its use of an off-red (Taylor terms it yellow-ochre) [113] color. The design, which features three stylized flowers in the midst of elaborately intertwining vines, and the title, publishers' name, place, and date form a very compact block of exotic color set off-center so as to create enormous margins at the fore-edge and tail of the page.

Housman submitted this design along with a letter to Lane on September 1, 1893, with directions to "have a good strong type that will give about the same coloring as the design, and," he further suggested, "it may be well to set the lines closer together than I have indicated, in order to keep the lettering solid and also I think improve the shape for the page." [114] Housman apparently did a good deal of worrying over the title page as is indicated by his directions to Lane and the printer. "I am inclined to suggest an experiment proof *all* in red ink," he tells Lane. "If the type were of good strength I think it would tell sufficiently." Then he went on to give further instructions about the type: "I have put the date a little too far to the right, please have this corrected." And in a P.S. he cautioned: "Don't take my lettering of 'POEMS' as a standard. I should prefer something lower and broader. Anything that will take off the height consistent with good lettering will be an improvement." [115]

By September 6, Housman had received a proof of the title page which was anything but satisfactory. Having "put it right" as to the type and arrangement of the design, he wrote Lane that if Folkard and Son, the printers, "can only hit a decent red, of which I have sent them a sample, red I should prefer it to be." After discussing some points about the frontispiece which inadvertently had been printed also in red, Housman suggested that "if the *red* title page turns out hideous, you will, on your own responsibility revert to black? and I will be content and waste no more time, but I have sent them a very *yellow* sample which I hope will draw them away sufficiently from their fatal love of pink." Voicing the designer's familiar complaint against printers struggling with the unusual and extraordinary, Housman concluded, "They do not seem to be accurate copiers of what is set before them in the way of arrangement, so it would be well for you to ask to see my corrections before passing their final proof." [116]

On September 9, Housman had seen more proofs and was willing to allow the title page to "go for exhibition" at the Arts and Crafts Society show, "but if it has not been already printed for the book I should like the upper set of type to be dropped to within $\frac{1}{10}$th of an inch of the top of the design, and for the three lines not to have more than $\frac{1}{10}$th inch of leading between them: — Poems and Francis not to have more space between them than Francis and Thompson." Then and only then was Housman ready to venture, "I think it will be quite right." [117]

Housman's title page for Davidson's *A Random Itinerary* is very similar in that the design and type are placed off-center toward the upper left side of the page and are printed in the exact same yellow-ochre color.[118] Less compact and tightly ordered, the Davidson title page exhibits a rather simple, abstract design of interrelated curves or coils suggestive of snail shells or *art nouveau* curls of hair, a design Housman must have liked, for he employed it again, this time upside-down, on his title page for Allan Monkhouse's *Books and Plays,* another interesting variation on the Thompson title page.

In Katharine Tynan's *Cuckoo Songs,* Housman combined frontispiece and title page in a fine example of the *art nouveau* variety — a woman with flowing robe and headpiece sitting before the casement of open windows playing a lute. The whole is framed by a treelike vine whose fantastically curving tendrils clasp the stonework of the house. The lettering of the title, drawn by Housman, is included in the main design, whereas the names of the author, publishers, place, and date are inscribed upon a kind of scroll-like rectangle worked loosely into the lower left corner of the design.

Some of the best *art nouveau* title pages are those elaborately designed by an artist whose reputation has not survived his time, J. Illingworth Kay. Ingenious works of art, Kay's title pages (and half-title designs) for Norman Gale's *Orchard Songs,* Richard Garnett's *Poems,* Grant Allen's *The Lower Slopes,* and W. P. James's *Romantic Professions* are good examples of lettering carefully incorporated into an elaborate design. *Orchard Songs,* bound in a yellow-green linen with the half-title design printed on the front cover in brown, is a mediocre little book of verse about glow-worms, nightingales, first kisses, budding orchards and babies. The aura of it all is caught in Kay's title page, with its patterns of brick wall, pool and flowers, fruit and leaves woven together by sinuous tendrils and branches.

Unlike Kay's work, Walter Crane's decorated title pages, with their evocation of the Middle Ages and the realms of romance, are more in the Pre-Raphaelite manner. Crane was a master at integrating into a harmonious whole his finely drawn lettering and the pictorial design. The most beautiful of his efforts in this direction is the title page to Ernest Radford's book of verse, *Chambers Twain,* which is illustrative of the title poem. Openly symbolic like most of Crane's work, the title page contains a heart-shaped window divided in the gothic manner by a slender column, enshrining two draped figures, a youth representing joy, awakening with the sun and looking out toward the future, and an aged man representing pain, waiting for death. Crane's beautiful lettering in this work as well as in Augusta De Gruchy's *Under the Hawthorn,* Effie Johnson's *In the Fire and Other Fancies,* and Todhunter's *Sicilian Idyll* is indicative of his belief that "the lettering should be the chief ornamental feature of the title page." [119]

Crane's own book of verse, *Renascence,* is prefaced by a title page which expresses his concept of symbolic illustration — here a nude female figure intertwined with her hair, and flights of doves rising with the dawn of a new day. As a backdrop, the curves of the artist's palette are played off against a rectangular mass of white upon which the lettering in black is imposed. As in the other works mentioned, lettering and design are framed, the whole suggestive of the "secret of the book." [120]

Another distinctive designer of title pages for the Bodley Head was Selwyn Image. Image, Herbert P. Horne, and the architect, Arthur Mackmurdo, were founders of the Century Guild, a group dedicated to the rehabilitation of the arts. When the *Hobby Horse,* the beautifully produced journal of the Guild, appeared in 1886, it was one of the first expressions of a revival of interest in fine printing. Some of Image's title pages are rather simple, involving, for instance, in Laurence Binyon's *Lyric Poems,* merely the use of a form of his graceful, distinctive lettering and a rustic design composed of two branches with leaves and berries which form a kind of wreath. Others, such as the title page he designed for Ernest Rhys's *A London Rose,* are composed of elongated rectangles which Taylor attributes to the influence of Dutch brick architecture on members of the Century Guild.[121] The title page for *A London Rose* — Rhys later wrote that it was "exactly what a title-page to a poetry book should be" [122] — exhibits a variation of the drawn lettering found in Binyon's *Lyric Poems,* a distinctly modern lettering in its slender, slightly rounded sans-serif appearance. This is contained in one elongated rectangle enclosed in another, which serves as a decorative border of checkered patterns separated by a yet smaller version of the elongated rectangle filled with wild roses. Other examples of Image's title page designs among Bodley Head books are Michael Field's *Stephania* and Elizabeth Chapman's *A Little Child's Wreath,* mentioned by A. J. A. Symons as an important example of Image's "mixture of lettering and ornament." [123]

The most distinctive Bodley Head title pages are the work of the two artists who played the key roles in the *art nouveau* book, Aubrey Beardsley and Charles Ricketts.[124] Beardsley's work for the Bodley Head dates from the latter part of 1893,[125] the year in which he suddenly rose to fame as the featured artist in the first number of the *Studio* (April 1893) and as illustrator of J. M. Dent's edition of *Le Morte Darthur.* His first assignment was to do a title page and cover design for a small volume of short stories by George Egerton. This was the now famous *Keynotes,* which in its first issue appeared in December 1893, a book whose immediate success initiated a whole series of books by that title.

The title page for *Keynotes* shows the artist at home within the limits of the line-block process, a photomechanical method of reproducing art work which had lately found acceptance as the cheapest and easiest means of book illustration. Unlike Walter Crane and Ricketts, who preferred to work with the hand-engraved wood block, Beardsley seemed made for the modern process and turned its chief disadvantage — its inability to reproduce intermediate half-tones — into an artistic triumph.

A. J. A. Symons attributes to the title page of *Keynotes* what he calls "a successful reversal of the Morris convention, which had the authority of centuries. Instead of placing the type area of the title-page in a border of which the inner margin is the narrower, the lettering panel is shifted boldly to the right-hand side, though it is comprised within a design placed upon the page in a normal manner." [126] This variation of the off-center design was employed even more strikingly in another Keynotes series book of 1894, Florence Farr's *The Dancing Faun,* in which the lettering panel is set apart from and placed parallel with the design. Beardsley's design for *The Dancing Faun,* which features Whistler as faun, is simplicity itself, the antithesis of his early Burne-Jones style. In its two-dimensional effect and its display of large areas of white played off against solid black areas, it suggests the influence of the Japanese print on Beardsley's work at this time.

Even more notable is Beardsley's title page for the third book of the Keynotes series, Dostoevski's *Poor Folk.* Depicting a prim young woman sitting on the roof of a house, the page is, like that of *The Dancing Faun,* divided into two parallel panels, a picture panel on the left and a lettering panel on the right. Brian Reade suggests that "the girl's white silhouette was probably a new version in contemporary clothes of the mediaeval-looking maiden in the heading of Chapter VI, Book XV (p. 749 of vol. II) in *Le Morte Darthur.* . . . This panel, with the stately drainpipe and beauti-

The Religion of
a Literary Man
(Religio Scriptoris) by
Richard Le Gallienne

London: *Elkin Mathews*
and John Lane, Vigo Street
New York: *G. P. Putnam's*
Sons: 1894

Border within a border title page.

fully planned lines and masses, is," in Reade's opinion, "one of the best of Beardsley's smaller designs." [127]

In his title page for Kenneth Grahame's *Pagan Papers,* Beardsley placed the lettering panel at the top, enclosed by a thin border of leaves emerging upward from the design which encompasses the lower third of the page. The paganism and latent evil reflected in the faun and horned figure in this design is elaborated and fully activated in the bizarre and highly wrought title design for Wilde's *Salome.* Placing the lettering panel to the upper right-hand side of the page, Beardsley paralleled it with a strange pedestaled figure with horns, fully developed breasts, and phallus (in the suppressed version only), flanked by two tall candlesticks. A winged boy — also desexed in the published version — in an attitude of worship and an exotic butterfly complete the design. The title design and the ten drawings which illustrate *Salome* were all reproduced by the line-block craftsman Carl Hentschel.

Although Beardsley's title page for Davidson's *Plays* is more conventional, it is carefully designed, with the printed titles of the plays placed in a triangle or inverted pyramid form at the top of the page, with the figure of Harlequin forming the apex at the center. Not only does the lettering point to him as the center of attention, but the full-page frontispiece opposite displays six figures in costume — Oscar Wilde and Henry Harland among them — glancing in Harlequin's direction.

The Bodley Head title page owes much to Whistler: his desire to reduce it to its utmost simplicity, even bareness, and his practice of setting the type and design off center. Taylor's appraisal of Whistler's mode, "the luxurious elegance of dropping a small, compact body of text in the middle of a sea of white paper" [128] applies equally well to Ricketts' title page for *Silverpoints.* Whistlerian technique is quite evident in Ricketts' placing the two small blocks of type to the extreme left side of the page, leaving enormous margins of white at the outer edge and tail. Devoid of decorative design of any kind, the page's restrained simplicity is in keeping with the over-all effect of elegance achieved through a conscious effort at simplicity and restraint.

Ricketts used this same approach in Symonds' volume of essays, *In the Key of Blue.* The title page displays two rectangular blocks of type, one extending across the top of the page and the other across the bottom. Here the margins are not so broad as in *Silverpoints*; but since there is no design or decorative effect between the two blocks, the contrast of black and white is boldly achieved. The over-all aesthetic appeal of the page is enhanced by printing the places of publication, London and New York, in red. More extensive use of red lettering is found in Ricketts' title page for De Tabley's

Poems, Dramatic and Lyrical. Again using geometric patterns of type which reflect his delight in the sobriety and discretion of the Renaissance title page, Ricketts sets the type in a solid block, except for the date in roman numerals, which is set into the wide margin at the tail of the page.

Ricketts' most startling innovations in title page design appear in his exotic setting for Wilde's *The Sphinx* (1894). Here the title page is placed on the left, opposite the first lines of the poem, which begin with an intricately woven initial letter in green. That Ricketts was moving toward doing away with the title page altogether is suggested by the fact that the page is almost totally usurped by an elaborate design done in a rust-colored red which creates the effect of a frontispiece. The title and author's name appear at the top of the design in black while Ricketts relegates his own name and that of the publishers to three lines of small type in green at the bottom.

Ricketts' revival of the use of the colophon in *Hero and Leander* and the variations just noticed in his title page to *The Sphinx* suggest his desire to return to the practice of early book builders, who set apart a special page for the title of the work alone, relegating the name of the printer and the place and date of publication to the colophon. His use of geometrically patterned blocks of type printed in black and red and Beardsley's use of the inverted triangle of type in Davidson's *Plays* conform to the practice of early makers of books as set forth in Alfred Pollard's essay "On Some Old Title-Pages, with a Sketch of Their Origin, and Some Suggestions for the Improvement of Modern Ones" published in the *Hobby Horse* in 1888.[129] In his exposition of the beauties of early title pages, Pollard stressed among other things "the massive arrangement" of types "either in rectangles like those now used in this magazine, or triangles," "the skilful use of red ink" and "the restriction of the number of types to a minimum, which usually allowed only one, and seldom more than two." [130]

On the whole, the same men and much the same aesthetic ideas which made the Bodley Head title page what it was must be credited with the distinctive features of the binding, which was in its own way very different from the highly colored bindings, heavily decorated in gold, so much in vogue during the Victorian age.

Although specially made cloth for covering books became available about 1825,[131] the ornate decorated cloth binding did not degenerate into a tasteless hodgepodge of celtic strapwork borders, grotesque "cinquecento" ornaments, and meaningless abstraction until the 1840s and '50s. For a time, Ruari McLean tells us, the "source for the decoration of cloth bindings was obviously the designs on leather bindings, . . . then there are designs which appear to have been built up from printers' flowers; and others based on the baroque designs in old pattern-books, or other engraved originals." But as time went on, "the dignity and taste of designs deteriorated, as recollections of Georgian restraint grew fainter." [132]

The most prolific designer of bindings during the Victorian period was John Leighton (who often used the pseudonym of "Luke Limner"), whom Sybille Pantazzi describes as "an exceptionally active and versatile commercial artist." [133] Some of his most notable work was designing covers for the large square octavo gift and table books of the 1850s and '60s, heavy and ornate in format. An excellent example of his work is Falconer's *Shipwreck*, which appeared in 1858. "Full of delightful details," the cover, as described by Miss Pantazzi, is composed of "alternate shells and heart-shaped festoons of rope in the border, dolphins on a background of algae in the corners, and in the oval centre, a mast with sail and pennant, stars, a chain and a portrait medallion" — all this in addition to the lettering.[134]

Along with the reaction against the Victorian book in the 1880s there was also a revival of interest in bookbinding, due in part to the increased interest in antiquarian books and the growing emphasis on book building as an art and craft which had been sadly neglected since the rise of commercialism. For instance, Alexander Ireland's *Enchiridion or Booklovers Manual* [135] awakened a number of persons to the beauties of old and rare books bound for the most part in leather and stamped elegantly in gold or, if unbound, in simple paper boards usually adorned with nothing more than a printed paper label for the spine.

Richard Le Gallienne's books reflect his interest in the 1880s in fine old books, the bindings of which must have been a revelation to one brought up on the usual trade bindings of the day. Le Gallienne's preference for the relative simplicity of the book bound before Victorian times says much for his taste. Certainly most of the pleasure his earliest books of verse afford us today comes from their external appearance, which derives from the pre-Victorian book. For example, the large-paper issue of *Volumes in Folio* is cased in quarter imitation vellum with the attractive blue-gray paper-covered boards which adorn a number of Bodley Head books as well as some of the Kelmscott Press productions. The spine is artificially ridged with bands (the cords upon which in old volumes the sections were sewn), and it bears a paper label printed in black. The rare Japanese paper issue is cased in quarter vellum and marbled paper boards.

Le Gallienne was much attracted to the very inexpensive and extremely simple temporary bindings which were placed on books manufactured before the advent of publishers' cloth,[136] for he used a similar, but permanent, covering for his *English Poems* of 1892. Bound in boards covered by plain cream-colored paper and adorned with nothing more than paper labels on the spine, *English Poems* is an excellent example of the way the

Bodley Head book often achieved distinction in a most economical way. Other examples are the bindings for the famous *Book of the Rhymers' Club* and for Herbert Beerbohm Tree's little book on *The Imaginative Faculty*.

Other Bodley Head books which in their pseudo-antiquarian dress must have struck the Victorians as old-fashioned but are apt to appeal to us as more in keeping with our own taste in binding are Le Gallienne's edition of William Hazlitt's *Liber Amoris* and his edition of *The Poems of A. H. Hallam*. The bindings, which are very similar to *Volumes in Folio*, are, in their use of white imitation vellum paper and cream-colored paper boards, the result of Le Gallienne's taste in pre-Victorian bindings. Hazlitt's *Liber Amoris* and the Hallam are very attractive little volumes much enhanced by the ridged spines and paper labels reminiscent of the 1820s and '30s.

The new interest in the binding of books was evidenced among the members of the Arts and Crafts Society by T. J. Cobden-Sanderson, who lectured on the subject in November 1888 and contributed to the volume of *Arts and Crafts Essays* of 1893. Although Oscar Wilde in his review of the lecture for the *Pall Mall Gazette* felt that Cobden-Sanderson was going too far "in treating bookbinding as an imaginative, expressive human art," he was very appreciative of the lecturer's efforts to raise the craft to a just esteem in the eyes of the public. Wilde's own feelings on the matter were that bookbinding was an "impressive" rather than "expressive" art. "If a man has any message for the world," Wilde remarked, "he will not deliver it in a material that always suggests and always conditions its own decoration. The beauty of bookbinding is abstract decorative beauty." [137]

Wilde's interest in the subject is further suggested by the fact that he saw to it that advertisements for his books contained a statement about the binding. As one contemporary newspaper noticed,

In the case of new books, details of the binding are now very frequently advertised along with the particulars as to size, price, &c, usually given. This is an innovation for which Mr. Oscar Wilde is mainly responsible. Announcements of his fairy tales, dialogues, and poems invariably include interesting bits of information as to "moss-green end-papers," special designs of "lilies in heliotrope and gold," &c. In fact the taste for piquant covers bids fair to develop an excess of preciousness. Take the following extracts from the list of a well-known firm of publishers of *belles-lettres* [Mathews and Lane]: — "Ornaments for binding designed by Selwyn Image." "Cover (bluebells and laurel) designed by C. S. Ricketts." [138]

Wilde's desire to see his works given an aesthetically appropriate setting led to his efforts to have artists like Ricketts, Shannon, and Beardsley design his books; consequently, at least some of the sensation his volumes created is due to their often beautiful yet bizarre bindings. For instance, Beardsley designed the binding for the English version of *Salome,* which in its ordinary issue appeared in a coarse-grained canvas dyed an odd greenish blue hue and in the de luxe issue was cased in a green silk. Imposed upon these exotic backgrounds was a weird design in gold, the neat symmetry of which is interrupted "by the placing of the roses and the inner leaves," an artistic stratagem which Brian Reade considers characteristic of Beardsley.[139] This relatively simple binding design was substituted for a far more elaborate full-cover design which Beardsley first drew. A bold display of serpentine peacock feathers growing out of what Reade describes as "a 'Japonesque' ground," the all-over pattern first devised by Beardsley was most "evocative of the late Aesthetic or *fin de siècle* period."[140]

Full vellum-covered boards were chosen for *The Sphinx,* Wilde's last published work before his imprisonment; and Leighton Son and Hodge of London did the binding.[141] Both the front and back covers are decorated with Ricketts' bizarre designs stamped in gold. On a kind of architectural backdrop suggested by a series of simple structural lines accented by small circular devices reminiscent of Rossetti, Ricketts placed four strangely beautiful figures including two of a weird female sphinx.

For his plays, Wilde chose C. H. Shannon to design the binding. *Lady Windermere's Fan* is sparingly but attractively done in a mauve-colored cloth stamped with three small flamelike designs in gold on the front and back covers and the lettering on the spine accentuated by two small flower devices also in gold.

Ricketts, Shannon, and Housman were influenced by the binding designs of Dante Gabriel Rossetti.[142] Setting to work in the 1860s, when Victorian binding styles were the rage, Rossetti designed a binding for Christina Rossetti's *Goblin Market* (1862) which was in complete contrast to the cloth bindings issuing from press after press on every hand. "A severe design of straight lines with tiny circles blocked in gold on blue cloth,"[143] Rossetti's cover reflected his recent introduction to things Japanese by James McNeill Whistler.[144] This penchant for achieving his effects through hardly more than a hint of design is again apparent in his binding for Swinburne's *Atalanta in Calydon* (1865), consisting of four simple gold roundels on white buckram.[145]

"Highly idiosyncratic and effective"[146] is an apt description of Rossetti's binding design for his own *Poems* of 1870. Treating the two covers and spine as a whole, Rossetti created a more elaborate effect than usual. Although the basic unit of his design is a curious little semicircle within a circle, once combined into a kind of diaper pattern, it creates the effect of an intricate lattice work upon which Rossetti imposed a flower with stem and leaves.

This technique of employing a geometrical pattern as a lattice or backdrop for a more solid design and thereby creating a kind of aesthetic counterpoint is evident in some of Ricketts' best binding effects. It is seen, for instance, in its subtlest and most exquisite form in his binding design for *Silverpoints*. And few would deny that Ricketts ever did better. For his choice of wavy gold lines upon which he placed thirty-three flamelike willow leaves with blossom was a triumph of imaginative design. Since Gray mentioned plants in every poem except one and in several wrote about the processes of growth ("The Vines," "Song of the Seedling"), the greenness of the background and the leaves of the design are an attractive extension of the poetry.[147] Moreover, Gray's love of artifice, which his poems convey, and the poet's eager acquiescence in the aesthetic notion that art is superior to nature, are caught to perfection by Ricketts, who in his binding design allowed the gold *art nouveau* pattern to dominate the green field upon which it is imposed.

In what Ricketts referred to as its Persian saddle book form,[148] the binding of *Silverpoints* and its "build" in general owe much to the designer's interest in books of the Italian Renaissance. A Bodley Head catalogue of 1893 refers to *Silverpoints* as having been "founded" throughout "on the Aldine Italic Books," and Symons speaks of its aura as being "at once intensely personal and reminiscent of the Renaissance." [149] Certainly Ricketts' use of a single motif — that of the flamelike leaf — stamped into the binding in staggered rows brings to mind those books in the library of Lorenzo the Magnificent bound in full Florentine leather, embossed with the Florentine lily as a repeat motif.

A similar use of the repeat motif is tastefully employed by Ricketts — this time without a background pattern of any kind — in his binding for De Tabley's *Poems, Dramatic and Lyrical*. Like all the Bodley Head books designed by Ricketts, it was bound by Leighton Son and Hodge; both covers are decorated with a curious motif which when repeated in rows running diagonally across the cover suggests gilt rose petals parachuting to earth in a windless sky. Broken only by the intrusion of an angel within a heart design set in the upper right corner of the covers, the repeat motif is a perfect example of the Renaissance book design with an *art nouveau* aura.

Among his Bodley Head books Ricketts' cover for *In the Key of Blue* is his most bizarre excursion into the elaborate realm of *art nouveau* design. The extremely curvacious but graceful pattern of laurel and hyacinths was stamped in gold on a blue cloth in the trial issue, but the regular edition was bound in a rich cream color when the designer protested that critics would otherwise be tempted to refer to the binding as "Ricketts blue." [150]

Another Bodley Head book whose binding design goes back primarily to Rossetti is Thompson's *Poems*. Laurence Housman's employment of a circle within a circle motif is reminiscent of Rossetti's variation on a circle, and Housman's use of a cluster of circles along the spine surrounding the lettering is a direct imitation of Rossetti's decoration on the spine of his *Poems*. That Housman's conception of what a book should be was very much in keeping with the aesthetic ideas of the Bodley Head group is further suggested by his choice of an odd shape — almost square (Pott 4to) — for *Poems* and his care in specifying paper-covered boards of a most unusual color. On September 20, 1893, he wrote Lane and enclosed the design for the cover. Although he had worked with a dummy copy supplied him by the printers, R. Folkard & Son, Housman expressed some uncertainty about his correctly reckoning the thickness of the spine. If the design is too thick, he told Lane, "that part of the design must be reduced." (Could Housman have known about the trouble Rossetti had with his *Poems?* When the book was bound it was discovered, much to Rossetti's horror, that the decorative panel on the spine was too wide. As a result, the text had to be padded out with a number of blank pages at the end.)[151] Then he went on to make more precise his desires concerning the matter:

The brown paper I want is rather grey-brown, I suppose you could send me samples. The second colour — brown, for which I send an extra drawing, might be made by some colourless stain, if such a thing is ever done; I made it on the sample cover I showed you merely by applying shell-lac [*sic*] varnish to the brown papers, and its gummy consistency gave the darker tone. If such a thing can be printed with, I think that is certainly the way to get the colour best. But of course your binders will know all about that.[152]

In its binding the Bodley Head book was very different from the gaudy decorated cloth books of the day; the only book bound in the Victorian fashion is the second issue of William Watson's *The Prince's Quest*, which was taken over — binding and all — from Kegan Paul and Trench in 1892. It is interesting to compare the binding and title page of this issue with that of the second edition, published by the Bodley Head a year later with the excellent title page which Blaikie had designed complemented by an extremely simple binding of tan buckram with lettering in gold on the spine.

Although full vellum was used at times to bind special editions of Bodley

Head books like *Silverpoints,* Watson's *The Eloping Angels,* De Tabley's *Poems, Dramatic and Lyrical,* Gale's *Orchard Songs,* as well as *The Sphinx* and *Hero and Leander,* some Bodley Head books gained their attractiveness and distinctly modern look from the use of colored linen cloth-covered boards stamped with a simple design and lettering in a contrasting tone. For example, Ernest Rhys's *A London Rose* is bound in a tan almost khaki-colored linen with lettering accented by three leaves stamped in rose-colored ink in the upper right corner of the front cover. The lettering on the spine is also in rose. Similarly, the ordinary issue of *Orchard Songs* is bound in a greenish yellow version of the same cloth. J. Illingworth Kay's half-title design of fruit, leaves, and lettering is stamped in brown on the cover with the lettering on the spine also in brown. And Laurence Housman went so far as to suggest the use of a dress material as binding for Davidson's *A Random Itinerary.* Having enclosed the frontispiece in a letter to Lane, Housman went on to ask about the cover. "You were to let me know whether that 'dress material' would take gold," he remarked.[153] Whether or not the rather coarse-grained rust-colored material in which the book is actually bound is the "dress material" Housman desired, is anybody's guess.

With its odd shapes and sizes, its array of binding materials in an assortment of solid colors, the Bodley Head book was a distinct departure from Victorian book practice. Its employment of artists who sought to combine all the physical elements of the book into a harmonious and aesthetically proper expression of the subject matter and tone put the Bodley Head in the forefront of commercial publishers whose work anticipated in a very real way the modern book. Generally in accord with the principles of the Arts and Crafts Movement so far as book design was concerned, it strove to achieve these ideals within the scope of modern commercial practice. To explain how it was possible to create such tasteful, aesthetically appealing books, so well printed, so expertly designed, and yet sell them at low enough prices to achieve a commercial success, is the purpose of the following chapter.

During the early years of the Bodley Head Elkin Mathews and John Lane published volumes of poetry primarily but also literary essays, a number of plays, including some of Wilde's most important, several notable critical studies of literary figures, some fiction — mainly volumes of short stories — and a series of portraits drawn by Will Rothenstein, his early *Oxford Characters*. The firm's specializing in belles-lettres was to a large extent the result of calculation. In fact, one could go so far as to say it was a calculated risk.

Toward the close of the 1880s there were signs which suggested that there was a relatively large group of persons who were willing to buy not only rare and exotic volumes from the antiquarian bookseller but also choice limited editions of contemporary authors. Percy Muir in *Minding My Own Business* has said that Lane "saw that there was a public for daintily produced books"[1] and therefore decided to appeal to the current interest in beautiful books and the taste on the part of a few for bizarre and unusual collector's items; his contention is easily documented.

I have already shown that in the 1880s there was an increasing interest in antiquarian books. Auction records and sale catalogues amply indicate the fact that prices for book rarities were rising rapidly because of a surprisingly widespread demand. Anyone who dealt in the rare book market would have been aware of this fact. Lane's letters to Mathews during the summer of 1887 clearly show that both men, but especially Lane, were fully

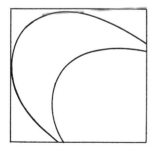

3 BELLES-LETTRES
TO SELL

cognizant of these developments in the book business. Lane's interest in such items as *Fanny Hill* and the first issue of the Mermaid series edition of Marlowe's *Plays* has been noticed. And Lane was most anxious to get out a catalogue of first editions soon after the opening of the Vigo Street premises. As early as May 16, 1887, he was expressing his view that it would "be better for both of us" if he were to hold on to editions such as Kingsley's *Westward Ho!* and "fit together as many other rare books in such exceptional states as I can during the next 6 to 12 months. I believe that a cat. of 1st editions of such books would create a sensation." [2]

That Lane was fully aware of the market is further suggested by these remarks to Mathews concerning a Browning volume. "The item you mention," he wrote, must have been listed in "a very old cat. The last cat. I saw it in was Pearson's at £5.5.0, but Wheeler 8 or 9 months ago told me that mine was worth more, it being a better copy; I don't suppose there is a copy in the whole of London for sale." In the same letter Lane asked Mathews to advise him what prices he should pay "for two copies of the Sporting Novels by Surtees *1st Editions in cloth & half bound*." [3]

Of more significance to us is the recognition on the part of Lane that something approaching a craze for first editions was creating a market for new books by contemporary authors, especially books of belles-lettres issued in tastefully designed limited editions. Among his speculations in books during 1887 was Andrew Lang's edition of *The Marriage of Cupid and Psyche*, published by David Nutt, in the Strand, a firm which anticipated the Bodley Head's policy of publishing choice books of belles-lettres in limited editions.[4] In a letter to Mathews, dated September 11, 1887, Lane remarked that although Lang's little book had been published so recently as June or July in an edition of only 500 copies at 3/ or 3/6, "I looked all round for a copy, but in vain, until Friday week when I happened to be in Denny's[?] shop & saw one. They asked me 6/– for it, but allowed me to take three for 16/6." Then he questioned, "Do you think I should get a few more copies at 5/6 or 6/–? It is a charming book to look at & *to read*." [5]

The interest in rare books, especially first editions, led in time to an eager desire for small, limited editions of modern books. One observer of the book market complained in a *Fortnightly Review* article in 1894 that "the first editions of Dickens and Thackeray are no longer the rage of the collecting public," yet "every ephemeral and often rubbishy tract by living authors" is now eagerly sought after.[6] Richard Le Gallienne's first volume of poetry, *My Ladies' Sonnets* of 1887, sold out almost at once and made a profit of some thirty pounds for its author.[7] And scarcely two years later, he was able to report in a letter to his sister that he had "just heard a pleasing thing from one of the chief librarians here [the British Museum] to whom Lane introduced me — that the Museum has just recently bought a copy of *My Ladies' Sonnets,* small paper too, for 15/–. The little book is becoming sought after he said — all which is encouraging isn't it?" [8]

All of this speculation was not lost on Lane and Le Gallienne, who were largely responsible for establishing the publishing policy of the Bodley Head. Their belief that limited editions of belles-lettres tastefully done would sell was fully borne out by the success of the first Bodley Head book, *Volumes in Folio.* Not only did both small- and large-paper issues sell out quickly, but Scribners of New York bought fifty copies to satisfy their American clientele's demand for such examples of belles-lettres.[9]

So certain was the Bodley Head of its ability to sell these books that it was later to buy up the remainders of books which, having been published in the early 1880s and therefore lacking the advantage of a vogue, did not find sufficient buyers. For instance, the attractive little volume of poems by three Balliol students who later gained fame, H. C. Beeching, J. W. Mackail, and J. B. B. Nichol, entitled *Love in Idleness,* which appeared in 1883 under the auspices of Kegan Paul and Trench, was in every way a forerunner of the Bodley Head book, which just ten years later found a more numerous and enthusiastic group of purchasers. Bound in quarter imitation vellum with pink paper-covered boards and a vignette on its title page by William Bell Scott, *Love in Idleness* — both in subject matter and design — appealed much more to the aesthetic milieu of the early nineties than that of the early eighties. Since Kegan Paul and Trench seem to have been in financial trouble at this time,[10] the Bodley Head also bought from them the remainders of Watson's *The Prince's Quest,* Frances Wynne's *Whisper!,* and Colonel Ian Hamilton's *The Ballad of Hádji* which they reintroduced with a cancel title page and a frontispiece by William Strang.

Wilde's *Poems* is the signal example of the Bodley Head practice of having transferred to its current lists the unsold copies of belles-lettres moldering in the storerooms since the early eighties. Wilde's first volume of poetry had been published by the house of Bogue and Company in 1881. When the firm went bankrupt, there were about 220 copies in unsold sheets remaining.[11] Mathews and Lane bought up these sheets, engaged Ricketts to design a new title page, half-title, and cover and published the new issue of *Poems* on May 26, 1892, at 15/– a copy, each signed by Wilde.[12] Within days the entire issue was sold out.

That the Bodley Head in the early nineties was taking advantage of a real mania for limited edition of belles–lettres is witnessed to by the attention the press gave the craze. The *Publishers' Circular* for July 29, 1893, took notice of it with an article entiled, "The Demand for First Editions," in which it was pointed out that the hue and cry was mainly for editions of modern authors such as Andrew Lang, Robert Louis Stevenson, and Austin Dobson.

The early things of Locker (now Locker-Lampson) are also very scarce. Here, for instance, is a charming copy of his "Selections," published as far back as 1868. It contains Richard Doyle's illustrations, and is worth a great deal more than its original price. William Morris's first editions always find a market, and there is a considerable demand for William Watson's.[13]

W. Roberts, in his article entitled "The First Edition Mania," took a rather jaundiced view of the situation, declaring that the craze for first editions has "now reached its extremest form of childishness." What especially struck him as completely irrational was the fact that "now, every little volume of drivelling verse becomes an object of more or less hazardous speculation, and the book market itself a Stock Exchange in miniature." [14] Unable to understand why the book-buying public of the day aspired to possess first editions of "essentially ephemeral" volumes by contemporary authors, Roberts cited the case of a local firm of booksellers who made "a parade of no less than forty first editions of Mr. Lang's publications, which are offered at a total sum of nearly £30." And pointing to a specific book, he stated that Lang's *The Library* was selling "at seven shillings, six pence, or about double its original price." [15]

Lang notwithstanding, it was one of the Bodley Head poets, Norman Gale, who served Roberts as the most notorious example of an author whose works were giving impetus to the craze.

Mr. Gale's books of rhymes began to appear in 1885, and at the present time a complete set of the first editions of his booklets, about twenty volumes on large and small paper, is catalogued at £100 — the published price of many of which did not exceed three shillings and sixpence.[16]

The Bodley Head took full advantage of this mounting demand for books which from the outset were collectors' items. Seldom did Mathews and Lane issue a book which in its first edition exceeded 500 copies. To make the Bodley Head book even more attractive to the buyer, a statement of limitation was often included along with the author's or publisher's signature. Then for those who were willing to pay more for even rarer and more luxurious formats, 46 Bodley Head books were published in large-paper issues of from 25 to 250 copies, sometimes bound in vellum. Occasionally the edition would include a special issue of from 3 to 40 copies on Japanese handmade paper.

Another indication that the Bodley Head book was designed to meet the demands of a particular group of booklovers is the kind of statement included in the advertisements which appeared bound in the back of most Bodley Head books and in journals such as the *Publishers' Circular,* the *Academy,* the *Athenaeum,* the *Spectator,* and *St. James's Budget.* The number of copies was almost always indicated along with a description of the paper and the mention of any features which would enhance the book's rarity and value. When Cosmo Monkhouse's little volume of poems, *Corn and Poppies,* appeared in 1890, it was described in advertisements as having been "finely printed by R. and R. Clark, of Edinburgh, on handmade paper, in an edition of 350 copies fcap. 8vo, at 6s. net, and 50 numbered and signed copies, with proofs of an etching by William Strang as Frontispiece, crown 4to, large paper, at 15s. net." [17] The advertisement for Robert Bridges' *The Growth of Love* was obviously calculated to attract the collector, for Mathews and Lane carefully chose to include: "choicely printed in Fell's Old English type on Whatman's handmade paper, by Mr. Daniel, at his Private Press; limited to 100 copies." [18]

There were many charges in the press that a considerable amount of calculation and, to a certain extent, manipulation of the book market was being indulged in by the Bodley Head and a growing number of smaller publishers during the nineties. In his *Fortnightly* article, Roberts stated that in his opinion a good deal of the speculation was "the direct outcome of the artful machinations of a few of the trade." [19] And the success of the Bodley Head to both satisfy and give impetus to the vogue for choice volumes of belles-lettres can be judged to some extent by the fact that the practice of issuing limited editions aroused a controversy of considerable proportions.

Neither the idea of limited editions nor of large-paper editions was new to the book world of the nineties. As to issuing large-paper copies, the practice can be traced back to Aldus, who used sometimes to print a few copies of his books on blue paper of a larger size than normal. Then there was the practice in the seventeenth century of publishing "fine paper" copies at a time when the general quality of paper used by printers was inferior. In the eighteenth century books like Pope's *Homer* were published on large paper as well as small; Sterne's *A Sentimental Journey* is an example of the fairly common practice of printing subscribers' copies on a larger page. The Foulis Press of Glasgow regularly issued large-paper copies, and quite a few of the big color-plate books of the late eighteenth and early nineteenth centuries provide further examples. Sir Walter Scott's *Border Antiquities of England and Scotland* of 1814 appeared in an enormous two-volume large-paper edition, which on India paper sold for £26.15.0, and John Martin's famous illustrations to Milton's *Paradise Lost* appeared in 1827 in a two-volume edition of the epic on large paper. According to John Carter, the practice of issuing large-paper editions was much less common in the middle quarters of the nineteenth century, though it survived with some of the more self-conscious printers. However, a revival of interest in the large-paper copy was signaled by such books as Robert Bridges' first volume of poems in 1873.[20]

The practice had been and was a legitimate one. Large-paper editions were aesthetically appealing and, indeed, were a joy for those habitually subjected to the niggardly margins and cramped pages of most Victorian books. There were certainly the few who shared Whistler's aesthetic sensibility and "had a passion for plenty of white on a page." Despite the fact that to some frugal minds a neat dark block of print islanded in an ocean of white handmade paper was offensive, to others it was aesthetically satisfying.

However that may be, the Bodley Head was confronted with serious charges, which amounted to an accusation of unethical business practices. Roberts had asserted that "the only two motives which have operated in the making of these books are the getting of the smallest amount of text into the widest size of page, and the skill which can spread over the greatest amount of space the smallest quantity of original thought." [21]

Addressing himself to the question of who actually bought these "books of which only two or three hundred copies are struck off," Roberts answered that it was by and large "the booksellers who, learning that the number to be printed is limited, buy up in the anticipation of a rise." [22] The accuracy of his supposition is largely borne out by subscription lists such as that for Ricketts and Shannon's *Daphnis and Chloe*, issued from the Bodley Head in 1892. Those who subscribed for the largest number of copies were invariably booksellers, including J. and E. Bumpus, Hatchards, Truslove and Hanson, and Sotherans of London; Blackwell of Oxford and Deighton, Bell at Cambridge; and the American firms of Scribners and Copeland and Day.[23] Rendering a judgment his essay had often implied, Roberts concluded that "this trafficking in limited editions, and the first edition craze generally, is nothing more or less than barefaced gambling from beginning to end." [24]

The most implacable foe of the limited edition was the *Pall Mall Gazette,* which during July and August of 1893 provoked the Bodley Head to defend itself. In its "Literary Notes" column for July 1, the journal broached the subject by way of a comment on Norman Gale (who had actually in some instances destroyed almost the whole edition of some of his books), and went on to make reference to the "bibliolunatic" who is lured into buying a book not because of any intrinsic merit its subject matter may have but because of its scarcity.[25]

The major attack occurred in the "Literary Notes" column for July 29, when after noticing with displeasure Macmillan's new policy of making the number of large-paper copies of any book depend on the number of advance orders, the spokesman for the journal flatly declared: "Now, there is no excuse for large-paper copies. They are ugly, clumsy, and uncomfortable to hold. . . . No one who cares for an appropriate arrangement of type and margin, no one who cares for literature, has any desire to possess them. They belong entirely to the province of the speculative bookbuyer." Then coming perilously close to slander the writer singled out Messrs. Mathews and Lane as publishers who "issue nearly all their books on the principle that rarity, not excellence, involves a speedy rise in price." [26]

Mathews and Lane's rejoinder, which appeared as a letter to the editor, was a flat denial of the accusation. "The commercial value" of the Bodley Head book "after the edition has been exhausted never enters into our calculations," the partners asserted; and, they continued,

to your writer's taunt that "rarity, not excellence," is our motto, we give an unqualified denial, and as a proof of our confidence in their "excellence" . . . we may mention that of every book we have issued since February, 1892 . . . we have taken the entire risk. We have made one other rule — namely, if we accept an author's MS, it is always with the distinct understanding that the author receives a royalty.

As to why the Bodley Head issued limited editions, the partners declared that the practice was based entirely on "the probable demand for the book. As a fair proportion of our books are by young or unknown writers," Mathews and Lane explained, "they have not a large public. There are about 500 people who care sufficiently for poetry to purchase it in this country, and it is for these that we seek to cater." Then with a voice tinged with contempt, the writers continued, "perhaps your paragraphist would like us to yield to the immorality of printing 1,000 copies of a book instead of the 350, of which we know we can dispose, because 1,000 cost comparatively very little more to produce. Such reckless publishing, however, has done much to ruin the book trade in this country." [27]

The Bodley Head's ability to meet the demand for belles-lettres and at the same time make an edition of 350 copies pay was the result of several conditions which obtained at the time. Although today it is an extremely expensive — almost prohibitive — affair to print fine editions of belles-lettres in very small quantities, the cost of book production in the early nineties was so low that the Bodley Head not only printed editions of 350 copies and made a profit but charged on the average no more than five shillings net per copy.

According to Marjorie Plant, who in *The English Book Trade* has explained why the cost of book production in the nineteenth century generally declined, "savings in the cost of composition were effected on the one hand by the introduction of composing-machines and on the other by the taking of stereotype moulds in readiness for a new impression." [28] In addition, she points out that the use of casing in place of the hand-worked binding "not only reduced the cost of covering a book to a few pence but also made it possible for the binder to keep pace with the accelerated output of the printing-press." [29] Although illustrations were once "too dear . . . to be included in any but expensive volumes," they were by the late nineteenth century "available for all types of publications." [30] Fortunately, the Bodley Head flourished some years before the first World War. "From 1914 to 1936 production costs more than doubled." [31]

Another factor in the matter of costs was, of course, the payment of authors. And here again the Bodley Head found itself operating at a most opportune time. Poets in general and minor poets in particular found it very difficult indeed to survive during the late nineteenth century. As a result, a publisher was not constrained to pay top prices for the poet's services. As Le Gallienne says in *The Romantic '90s,* it "soon became known of Lane and the Bodley Head . . . that he was strangely desirous of publishing poetry, was willing even to pay for it, and, moreover, was able to sell it. Till then the 'minor poet' had been a figure for newspaper mockery." [32] And Le Gallienne's opinion is upheld by Ernest Rhys in *Wales England Wed* when he recalls that the Bodley Head "was probably the only firm that ever made poetry 'pay,' but John Lane was a shrewd business man." [33]

One need not go to memoirs for assertions of the Bodley Head's business magic. Katharine Tynan, soon to be a Bodley Head poet herself, writing in the *Irish Daily Independent* during the early nineties remarked how fortunate a young gentleman Le Gallienne was. "I don't know by what legerdemain he and his publishers work, but here, in an age as stony to poetry as the ages of Chatterton and Richard Savage, we find the full edition of his book sold before publication. How is it done?" she queries Messrs. Elkin

Mathews and John Lane. "For," she continues, "without depreciating Mr. Le Gallienne's sweetness and charm, I doubt that the marvel would have been wrought under another publisher." [34] That her response to the Bodley Head book was considerably different from that of the *Pall Mall Gazette* is indicated by her remark that "these publishers, indeed, produce books so delightfully, that it must give an added pleasure to the hoarding of first editions." [35]

Not only was the poet a reasonable author to pay, poetry itself was often less costly than other kinds of literature to print. Because of its aesthetic nature, its form and line, poetry seldom fills a page as fully as prose. Although most volumes of poetry before or since the Bodley Head book can be viewed as an attempt on the publisher's part to get "the smallest amount of text into the widest size of page," [36] the charge is largely specious. R. D. Brown has shown in "The Bodley Head Press: Some Bibliographical Extrapolations" that Mathews and Lane consistently used "large type sizes and large leading between the lines of type" in their books of verses.[37] No doubt such practices can be seen as a clever means of expanding "a few poems into a respectable though slender volume of verse." [38] Yet it was not the practice of the day to produce clumsy editions of poetry in which the verse was fully packed upon the page. Moreover, the Bodley Head can hardly be said to have created the modern-day practice of issuing small volumes of poems printed in ten- or eleven-point type with six-point leads between the lines such as, for instance, the first editions of T. S. Eliot, Robert Frost, Wallace Stevens, or to mention a more recent book, Kathleen Raine's *The Hollow Hill.*

By consulting Ellic Howe's *The London Compositor*,[39] one can readily see why some Bodley Head volumes of poetry were more economical to produce than books of prose. In 1891 the cost of typesetting was based on 1,000 ems and the ten-point size of type. Since it was easier and speedier for the printer to work with larger type sizes, type sizes above ten-point were discounted at the rate of $\frac{1}{4}$ d. a point per 1,000 ems. Sizes below ten-point were increasingly costly. For instance, T. and A. Constable's bill for printing William Watson's *The Prince's Quest* bears this further charge: "Extra for small type on 8 pp. advts. 14s." [40] Similarly discounts of $\frac{3}{4}$ d. per 1,000 ems were allowed for printing separated by six-point leads and more.[41] "At these less-than-a-penny deductions per 1,000 ems, Lane's savings would at first glance not appear large," observes R. D. Brown, but he goes on to point out that "1,000 ems of poetry, leaded and in large type, will cover quite a few pages — and Lane specialized in small books. Obviously, in this stretching out of the text lay the chief savings in composition costs." [42]

During the early years, the Bodley Head employed a number of printers, beginning with the Chiswick Press in 1889. Besides Le Gallienne's *Volumes in Folio,* eight other Bodley Head books were printed there through November 1891, when the two firms ceased business transactions. The most costly by far was Walter Crane's *Renascence,* the bill for which totaled £126.2.4, including binding.[43] The 500 small-paper copies cost £44.17.0 for the handmade paper, composing the type and printing; the cost for binding was £16.13.4. Altering the margins and printing 100 large-paper copies amounted to £14.19.0; the binding cost was £5. A large-paper issue of forty-four copies on Japanese vellum was also printed at a cost of £17.5.0; binding cost was £7.14.0. In addition, the total sum included the cost of duplicating Crane's eleven designs by electrotyping and the printing of 1,000 prospectuses.[44]

Among the Chiswick Press books were two curious little volumes printed for H. Buxton Forman: *Three Essays by John Keats* and *The Backslider and Other Poems* by Antaeus (W. J. Ibbett). That Forman had only fifty copies of the essays printed and went to the expense of handmade paper, a frontispiece, and a gray handmade envelope for a wrapper, suggests that he thought of the work largely as a privately printed affair. Yet at the price charged per copy, ten shillings and sixpence, he probably made a profit after the Chiswick Press bill of £3.3.6 was paid.[45] Of the hundred copies of Ibbett's poems which were printed, only fifty were actually folded and stitched into their gray handmade wrappers. Selling at seven shillings and sixpence, Forman or Ibbett — whichever had to pay the printer's bill of £10.0.6 — possibly made a small sum after paying a commission to the Bodley Head.[46]

Although Todhunter's *A Sicilian Idyll* and Ernest Radford's *Chambers Twain* were printed in editions of 250 small-paper and 50 large-paper copies, the difference in the printer's bills amounted to £15.12.2. Despite the fact that Todhunter's play seems to have called for more type (since Radford's poems — one to a page — are seldom more than eight lines in length), composing and printing the 300 copies amounted to £21.11.10 while Radford's poems came to £37.4.0. The fact that *Chambers Twain,* imposed as 16mo, required the use of $7\frac{1}{2}$ half-sheets of Imperial handmade paper whereas *A Sicilian Idyll* called for only $3\frac{3}{4}$ half-sheets of the same paper seems to have been the major factor in the costs.[47]

Just why no more Chiswick Press books were published by the Bodley Head after F. W. Bourdillon's *A Lost God* appeared at the close of 1891 is not known. Perhaps it had something to do with the fact that John Lane came into active partnership in the firm early in 1892. There is every indication that he became chiefly responsible for the publishing interests of the

Bodley Head while Elkin Mathews continued to oversee the antiquarian book interests of the firm. Lane immediately instituted the policy of paying a royalty to the author of any book he accepted for publication, and this suggests that he was unwilling any longer to publish books simply on a commission basis. Of the nine Chiswick Press books published by the Bodley Head, only two, Le Gallienne's *Volumes in Folio* and Todhunter's *A Sicilian Idyll,* were actually contracted for by Mathews. The others were all paid for by the authors.

Lane turned to Scotland for his printers, in particular to Edinburgh's most outstanding printing establishment, T. and A. Constable. Although R. and R. Clark had done the English edition of Van Dyke's *The Poetry of Tennyson* and Monkhouse's *Corn and Poppies* in 1890 and J. Miller and Son had printed several Bodley Head books including J. T. Nettleship's *Robert Browning* and Philip Bourke Marston's *A Last Harvest,* Mathews had never employed T. and A. Constable. One of Lane's first acts in 1892 was to journey to Edinburgh[48] to see Walter Blaikie, the director of the firm, whose growing reputation as an "artist printer" was doubtless known to Lane. William Ernest Henley's *A Book of Verses,* printed by Blaikie in 1888 for David Nutt, was just the kind of pretty little volume which would have attracted Lane's eye.

Fortunately for those interested in a more detailed account of printing costs, the records of Constables' transactions with Mathews and Lane still exist. Between January 1892 and September 1894, Constables printed some twenty-nine separate titles for the Bodley Head, including Le Gallienne's *English Poems,* Alice Meynell's *Poems,* De Tabley's *Poems, Dramatic and Lyrical,* Norman Gale's *Orchard Songs,* Wilde's *Salome* and *Lady Windermere's Fan,* Kenneth Grahame's *Pagan Papers,* George Egerton's *Keynotes,* and Lionel Johnson's *The Art of Thomas Hardy.*

The first Bodley Head manuscript to reach T. and A. Constable was Michael Field's *Sight and Song.* Since, according to Blaikie, the publisher generally settled the size of book he wanted and gave the printer an idea of the kind of format he preferred, Lane specified that the book of verse be done in the same style as the popular Grahame R. Tomson's *A Summer Night,*[49] an attractive little volume of poems published by Methuen and Company in 1891. Bound in blue paper-covered boards with a moon and stars design in gold in the lower left corner of the cover, the book is a good example of the kind of volume Lane was interested in. Although the quality of paper and other materials in *A Summer Night* make it a less attractive and obviously inferior book to *Sight and Song,* the format, size, and type are the same.

Once the printer had the manuscript and Lane's instructions in hand, it was only four days before Constables had "the pleasure" of sending the Bodley Head an estimate for printing the book.[50] The cost for the paper, composing the type, and printing 400 copies was £16.10.9, to which was added six shillings for printing the design on the title page in red, and a further sum of £6.1.0 for alterations and proofs. Constables' bill for the printing totaled £22.17.9 or about one shilling and twopence per copy.[51]

The production of Le Gallienne's *English Poems* resulted in a more complex transaction. Again, as in the case of *Sight and Song*, Mathews and Lane suggested the book be done in the style of Henley's *Lyra Heroica*, which had just appeared in an edition of 100 copies on Van Gelder paper in addition to the small-paper issue. Blaikie seems not to have agreed, for he wrote Mathews and Lane on May 2, 1892, to say that he thought the style of *The Song of the Sword* just out would better suit Le Gallienne's poems. Then on second thought, he suggested, "How would it do to make this volume uniform with 'Sight and Song' in Elzevir type, instead of using the Pickering type of Henley's volumes." [52]

The Letter Book entry for May 6, 1892, indicates that Blaikie's first suggestion was followed and *English Poems* was composed in the same type as *The Song of the Sword* [53] in an edition of 800 small-paper, 150 large-paper, and 30 on Japanese vellum. Total costs, which included "alterations, proofs and altering margins for Japanese paper and handmade paper copies," plus electrotyping and mounting the title for red and black printing came to £51.18.6.[54]

The least costly of the Bodley Head books so far as the printing at Constables was concerned was William Strang's beautifully illustrated *The Earth Fiend*, which cost only £7.14.0 for composing the type and printing 175 small-paper and 55 large-paper copies. Strang, an artist who wrote his poem largely as an excuse for illustrating it, had the paper supplied to the printer, which lessened the sum. Since Strang's poem was not long, there was comparatively little print to set in type.[55]

Printing costs at Constables, which often included the paper, ran up to £130.16.9 for the 3,000 small-paper and 260 large-paper copies of Le Gallienne's *The Religion of a Literary Man*. Included in the total cost was £1.7.0 for printing red on the title pages, £9.18.0 for electrotyping the 132 pages, and £6.17.6 for making a set of electro shells to be supplied the American publisher, G. P. Putnam's Sons of New York.[56]

Although averages mean little when such factors as quality of materials, number of copies, and amount of text vary so greatly from book to book, and although a number of the volumes printed for the Bodley Head ran into the thousands of copies, a book of prose such as Kenneth Grahame's

Pagan Papers and a book of poetry like Richard Garnett's *Poems* may be taken as typical Bodley Head productions so far as printing costs are concerned.

Printed by T. and A. Constable, both books were published on November 30, 1893. The composing, printing, and paper for Garnett's *Poems* cost £2.7.0 per edition-sheet of 16 pages (octavo) while the cost for *Pagan Papers* came to only £2.1.0 per edition-sheet of 16 pages. Since each copy of *Poems* required the use of 11¾ sheets, the cost of 550 copies totaled £27.12.3,[57] whereas the 550 copies of *Pagan Papers,* each of which required only 11 sheets, cost £22.11.0.[58]

These facts suggest that either the paper for *Poems* was more expensive than the paper for *Pagan Papers* or that the printer charged more for setting the type for the poetry than for the prose, or both. Since the paper employed in both books was a machine-made laid paper, the cost of composing may very well have made the difference. This could have resulted from the fact that the printer either charged more for setting up the poetry with its stanzas and special arrangement of type on the page or for the use of a particular type font.

In addition to the printing costs, the production of a book involved the purchase of paper, the quality of which had much to do with the value and aesthetic appeal of the book. At the time Emery Walker gave his lecture on printing before the Arts and Crafts Exhibition Society in 1888, the paper used for ordinary books in England and America was, he said, "exceedingly bad." [59] When the Bodley Head book was being produced, there were two classes of paper available to the publisher in both "laid" and "wove" varieties — handmade and machine-made. And although connoisseurs of books despised machine-made paper, there were many varieties, some of which were quite good and durable. Jacobi is typical of the good printer of the day in recognizing the very great varieties, "not only in shade of colour, but in style and quality" of machine-made paper, yet recommending, when durability and quality were sought for in a fine book, a handmade paper, "its texture being stronger and of more lasting properties." [60] Similarly Walter Blaikie asserted that "many machine papers are quite as durable as handmade. Still, many books look handsomer on the latter." [61]

The Bodley Head consistently used good quality paper in its books. Although most ordinary issues were printed on machine-made paper of the laid variety, all nine of the Chiswick Press books, both small-paper and large-paper issues, were done on handmade paper. And fine handmade papers, including Japanese vellum, were used in the many large-paper and special issues of Bodley Head books.

Although good paper was available during the late nineteenth century, it was seldom used "except for very expensive books," [62] which suggests that good paper was very expensive. Yet in his essay on printing Walker expresses the opinion that the use of high quality paper actually "would not materially increase the cost in all but the very cheapest" books.[63]

Jacobi, in his discussion of the cost of paper in *On the Making and Issuing of Books,* said that "the relative difference in value of a good machine-made as compared with a hand-made paper may be roughly estimated as one-third. Whatman paper is a little dearer, and may be reckoned as four times the value of a machine paper." Yet he went on to point out that "in limited editions of a work, the question of price is not so much to be considered, as the total amount of paper absorbed is not great. For this reason, it is advisable to use the best." [64]

Since most Bodley Head books were limited editions, it cannot be assumed that the use of good and fine quality paper in these books greatly increased production costs. Because the printer usually supplied the paper once the publisher stated a price limit, the records available almost invariably include the cost of paper with the composition and the printing costs, a practice which makes it difficult to estimate the exact cost of the paper per book. Yet some idea of the price of paper can be gained from occasional printer's entries which list the supply of paper separately.

For instance, both Grant Allen's volume of poems, *The Lower Slopes,* and Lionel Johnson's *The Art of Thomas Hardy* were printed on a Double Crown (a paper size measuring 30" x 20") machine-made laid paper, which cost twelve shillings, threepence per ream.[65] Since it required 5⅘ reams to print the 800 copies of Allen's book, the total paper cost amounted to only £3.11.1,[66] while the 1,500 copies of *The Art of Thomas Hardy* took 36½ reams and came to £22.7.2.[67]

Some idea of the wide range in the cost of good papers can be indicated by observing that the rather thick machine-made laid paper with its deckle edges (in imitation of handmade paper) used in the small-paper issue of Watson's *The Eloping Angels* cost twenty-five shillings per ream, almost double that of the paper used in the Allen and Johnson books. As a result, the 6⅗ reams of Royal machine-made laid paper which the ordinary edition of 2,000 copies required cost £8.5.0, or £3.3.0 *more* than the cost of composing and printing the edition — £5.2.0.[68] That the cost of paper for *The Eloping Angels* was way out of proportion to the total production costs is indicated by the fact that the paper for *The Lower Slopes* amounted to only about a fifth of the total production cost (exclusive of binding) of £15.6.1.[69] Watson's *The Eloping Angels* was also published in a large-paper issue of 250 copies on Imperial (30" x 22") handmade paper, the printing and paper for which cost £3.12.0, while the Japanese vellum paper alone for 100 copies of an additional large-paper issue amounted to an even £4.[70]

The information on the cost of binding Bodley Head books provided here comes largely from the firm's Inventory Sheets,[71] drawn up when Mathews and Lane dissolved their partnership at the close of September 1894, and from the Chiswick Press records, which occasionally include the binding costs. It is very difficult to single out the binderies which did the actual work, but, in various ways, I have come to the conclusion that Leighton Son and Hodge of London and Orrock and Son of Edinburgh bound a number of the Bodley Head books. Orrock was the official bindery for T. and A. Constable during the nineties and letters from Blaikie to Mathews and Lane often mention Bodley Head books (for example, Alice Meynell's *The Rhythm of Life,* Michael Field's *Sight and Song,* Le Gallienne's *English Poems,* and G. S. Street's *The Autobiography of a Boy*) as having been sent to Orrock for binding. Unfortunately, the records of the firm were destroyed by fire during the second World War.

Leighton Son and Hodge's work is less easy to identify even though several of the most beautifully bound Bodley Head books like *In the Key of Blue, Poems, Dramatic and Lyrical,* and *The Sphinx* bear the initials of the firm on the bindings. T. and A. Constable's records also indicate that they sent *The Eloping Angels* and *Keynotes* to Leighton Son and Hodge to be bound. Again no records remain, but the Inventory Sheets indicate that binding the ordinary issues of Bodley Head books cost anywhere from 3¾ d. per copy for the ribbed ("T") cloth binding of Wicksteed's *Dante: Six Sermons* and the moiré fine ribbed ("AA") cloth binding of Street's *The Autobiography of a Boy* to 11 d. per copy for the elaborately designed bindings for *Poems, Dramatic and Lyrical* and *In the Key of Blue.* Le Gallienne's *English Poems* bound in paper-covered boards cost 3¾ d. per copy, whereas the buckram binding for Meynell's *Poems* and *The Rhythm of Life* cost 7½ d. per copy.

A statement dated February 5, 1892, received by the Bodley Head from Leighton Son and Hodge concerning the binding costs for Oscar Wilde's *Poems,* indicates that the cost was at the rate of sixty shillings per hundred copies. When it was decided to gild the tops of the pages, the price rose six shillings to sixty-six shillings[72] or roughly £7 for binding the 230 copies in Iris Cloth blocked in gold on back and side. The total cost, including £2.12.6 for the engraving blocks, was therefore about £9.12.6.[73]

Chiswick Press records reveal that the 500 copies of the ordinary issue of *Renascence* bound in blue handmade paper-covered boards and vegetable (imitation) parchment spines cost £16.13.4, or nearly 8 d. per copy. The binding in paper-covered boards of 100 large-paper copies with real parchment spines totaled £5. The de luxe issue of *Renascence* printed on Japanese vellum and bound in portfolio cases with real parchment spines lettered in gold and tied with a white silk riband amounted to £7.14.0 for the forty-four copies.[74] The binding costs for Eugene Benson's *From the Asolan Hills* bound in paper boards with vegetable parchment back and label pasted on cost £7.10.0 for the edition of 300, or 6 d. per copy.[75]

The other major cost factor which needs to be considered in connection with the Bodley Head book is the payment to authors. During the early nineties there were generally three methods by which an author and publisher could reach an agreement. According to Jacobi, the author often would part with his copyright for a lump sum and perhaps receive a royalty on all copies sold, the publisher undertaking all risk. Another method was referred to as the "half-profit" system, in which the profits were equally divided between author and publisher after the expenses of production and distribution had been paid. A third method was known as "publishing on commission," the author paying all expenses of production and advertising, and allowing the publisher a commission on all copies sold; the publisher accounting to the author at the trade price, and copies, 13 as 12 or 25 as 24, according to the value of the book, less review and presentation copies.[76]

On the basis of the legal agreements or contracts I have found for Bodley Head books (principally in the files of the present Bodley Head publishing firm) it is possible to form an accurate notion not only of the way in which Mathews and Lane went about paying their authors but also of the royalties paid. Before Lane took active charge of publishing in 1892, a number of the Bodley Head books were published on commission. Such was the case with F. W. Bourdillon's *A Lost God* and Crane's *Renascence,* but from 1892 through September 1894, Bodley Head authors were paid either a lump sum for the copyright, a royalty on the number of copies sold, or a half-share in the profits.

Only the most popular authors, who demanded the most, were extended an offer of a half-share in the profits. For instance, Le Gallienne in 1889 was paid a lump sum of £20 on the day of publication for his *George Meredith: Some Characteristics;* but in June 1894, when his popularity was at its peak, he was given half the profits accruing from both *Prose Fancies* and *The Religion of a Literary Man.* Likewise Norman Gale, whose dainty little limited editions of poetry were the rage in the early nineties, was no doubt lured away from David Nutt by an offer of half the proceeds from the 2,270 copies of his *Orchard Songs.* One of the most popular of all the Bodley Head

Caricature of John Lane by Max Beerbohm.   Elkin Mathews, 1895.

poets, William Watson, received half the profits from both *The Prince's Quest* and *The Eloping Angels*. But the most common agreement between Mathews and Lane and an author called for the payment of royalties.

Early agreements such as those drawn up for Le Gallienne's *George Meredith* and J. T. Nettleship's *Robert Browning* were very formal looking affairs, written out on legal-sized paper in fully legal terminology; but, later, contracts were rather simple documents, consisting of the terms briefly written out on a piece of Bodley Head stationery, to which was affixed a six-penny stamp across which the author signed his name.

Since many of the contracts were essentially the same, it might be useful at the outset to make some generalizations based on a number of these agreements. When Mathews and Lane agreed to publish a book at their own risk, they agreed to pay for the printing, the binding, paper, distribution, and advertising, and any art work, such as a frontispiece, decided upon. The royalties granted an author were usually either ten or twenty per cent of the published price; that is, if a copy sold for five shillings net, the author received either sixpence or a shilling per copy. If a Bodley Head book was also brought out in America through the agency of a firm such as Stone and Kimball or Roberts Brothers, the royalties received on those books were half the amount paid on English editions. Royalties were usually paid to the author within the first month after the first quarter day subsequent to the publication of a book, and the author was usually allowed from six to twelve free copies of his book.

When a single payment or lump sum was made for the right to publish, the amount paid ranged from the £15 accorded Nettleship for his *Robert Browning* to the sum of £25 paid to James Ashcroft Noble for *The Sonnet in England and Other Essays* and to Lena Milman for her translation of Dostoevski's *Poor Folk*. The average payment, which Le Gallienne received for the *Meredith* and John Davidson for *A Random Itinerary*, was £20.

A typical example of a contract calling for a royalty to be paid is that agreed upon by Mathews and Lane and Kenneth Grahame, whose *Pagan Papers* was published on November 30, 1893. The contract, on Bodley Head stationery, is dated September 20, 1893, and reads as follows:

Dear Sir/ *Pagan Papers*/ We undertake the publication of this book defraying ourselves the entire cost of paper, printing, binding, advertising and distributing, and agree to allow you a royalty of 10% on the published price payable quarterly reckoning from one month after the first quarter day subsequent to publication. The first edition will consist of 450 copies at

5/– net and we shall forward you six gratuitous copies and supply any additional ones you may require at the ordinary trade price.

Yours faithfully
Elkin Mathews & John Lane [signed]

To Kenneth Graham [sic], Esq.

I agree to the terms of the above
Kenneth Grahame [signed]
Kensington, 20 September 1893.[77]

A similar contract was finally arrived at for John Gray's famous *Silverpoints,* which appeared in March 1893. Gray was an almost unknown writer when his friend Oscar Wilde proposed to Mathews and Lane that they publish a volume of his poems at Wilde's expense. A contract now in the Princeton University Library was actually drawn up to this effect on June 17, 1892. But the volume which was supposed to appear in the autumn of 1892 was put off until the spring of the following year, and, in the meantime, Charles Ricketts was employed to design the book, which Mathews and Lane agreed to publish at their own risk. Thus the real contract for the published *Silverpoints* was drawn up on January 4, 1893, and reveals a Mathews and Lane "prepared to issue" *Silverpoints* on the following terms:

To print on hand-made paper, bind, publish, and advertise 275 copies [250 @ 7/6; 25 @ 21–] at our cost, allowing you a royalty of 20% on the net receipts. Of course we leave you to settle with Mr. Ricketts. We further agree to give you 12 ordinary copies & 3 of the special edition and in consideration of the help we have received in this matter from Mr. Oscar Wilde we present him with a copy of each edition and to Mr. Ricketts — alike for his aid — one special edition and three ordinary copies. Any further copies you require will be supplied at the usual trade terms.[78]

When it came to contracts, Wilde was one of the more difficult of the Bodley Head authors. Unlike most of the writers Mathews and Lane had to deal with, Wilde was very knowledgeable about business matters and insisted on carefully drawn-up contracts embodying various stipulations designed to protect his interests fully. The agreement for Wilde's *Poems,* dated October 24, 1891, consists of a letter to Wilde from Elkin Mathews, who undertook to issue the volume on the following terms:

To instruct printer to supply Title-page with my imprint for 230 copies on receipt of Artist's Design for cover at cost of £5.5.0[.] Block to be prepared from same the cost of which as well as that of Title-page[,] Binding and Advertising to be first charges on the amount received for copies sold.

The cost of Advertising not to exceed £5.5.0[.]

For my commission I agree to take 20% on the net published price, it being agreed that the book shall be brought out as a net one, the price to be fixed when bound[.]

After the above charges have been met the Balance to be remitted quarterly, the first Balance to be struck Six Months after date of publication[.]

I am, Yours faithfully
Elkin Mathews [signed]

Oscar Wilde Esq.[79]

Drawn up by the legal firm of Markby, Wilde, and Johnson of 9 Lincoln's Inn, the contract for Wilde's *The Sphinx* is a far more elaborate contract. The formal agreement — bearing Wilde's deletions of the word "author," which throughout is changed to "poet" — is signed by Wilde, Ricketts, Shannon, Mathews, and Lane, and includes among the witnesses' signatures that of Edward Shelley, the Bodley Head stock boy who was to figure prominently in Wilde's trial.

Mathews and Lane agreed to purchase the rights to *The Sphinx,* and Ricketts agreed to illustrate the book on the following terms:

(1) The publishers shall pay the poet a royalty of 10% on the gross sum received on the sales rendering accounts every six months.

(2) The publishers shall determine all details respecting the publication, the price at which copies are to be sold and the number of copies for publication in this country, America and elsewhere.

(3) The artist will before the 1st day of October 1892 submit to the publishers for their approval ten designs for decorating[,] colouring and fully illustrating the Poem also specimens of paper or other material and binding.

(4) The artist will execute and see to the reproduction of the designs when approved and prepare for and superintend through the press the said work and will make arrangements for the supply of all materials and labour for printing[,] issuing and binding the first and other editions thereof according to his own judgment but at the expense of the publishers with the stipulation that their total expenditure exclusive of advertisements[,] sales and fees paid to the author and artist shall not exceed £150 for an edition of 300 copies or less and £50 per 100 for any larger number which they may decide to produce.

(5) The publishers shall pay to the artist the sum of £45 which shall be paid as follows[:] £10 [£30 marked out by John Lane and £10 inserted] on the 18th of July 1892 and £10 on the eighteenth of each month until the total amount shall have been paid.

(6) The copyright of the work and of the illustrations and designs and of all future editions thereof shall belong absolutely to the publishers [Wilde has written in here: "personally." In the margin by (6) Wilde has written: "the publishers are not to have the right to sell the copyright of the poem, without the poet's sanction."] [80]

Two of Wilde's most famous plays, *Salome* and *Lady Windermere's Fan,* were included with other works in an agreement signed on August 3, 1893.[81] In addition to paying Aubrey Beardsley for the ten full-page illustrations for *Salome,* Mathews and Lane agreed to furnish Wilde "with clichés to be used only for an edition to be issued in Paris." Moreover, "for translating and royalty," Wilde was to be paid the sum of one shilling per copy on the small-paper and three shillings per copy on the large-paper issue of the play; and there was a stipulation on the part of the Bodley Head that "the royalties agreed upon in the foregoing shall only become payable as the books are sold." *Lady Windermere's Fan* was to be published in the same format as Wilde's *The Duchess of Padua* and *A Woman of No Importance* and, like them, was to have a binding design by Charles H. Shannon. The royalties agreed upon for each of the volumes was twenty per cent of the published price of all copies sold.[82]

An even more difficult author was William Watson, who, at the time Mathews and Lane were negotiating to bring out a second edition of his *The Prince's Quest* and two new works, *The Eloping Angels* and *Excursions in Criticism,* was in an asylum recovering from a serious mental breakdown which had occurred on December 11, 1892, when the author charged the carriage of the Duke of Edinburgh which was proceeding down the park at Windsor.[83] In January 1893, Watson, still very ill and excitable, was planning to leave for Switzerland under the care of his brother, Robinson, who served as go-between with the Bodley Head.

In a letter dated January 6, 1893, Robinson assured Lane that Watson was "perfectly competent to enter into any business arrangements regarding his work," but, he hastened to say, "it will be best to have all matters settled with the smallest possible amount of discussion, as there is a tendency in him to undue excitement." [84] Several days later, on the eve of his trip to the Continent, Watson was found to be "distinctly less clear mentally than he was a few days" before,[85] but Lane somehow was able to get a contract covering the three books signed.

Rather unusual in some of its provisions, the contract committed the Bodley Head to publish *The Prince's Quest* as a reprint and to issue in a separate and suitable form Watson's new poem, *The Eloping Angels.* Although Lane clearly had wished to publish the two poems together in one volume, he was willing to accede to Watson's demands for separate books provided Watson cancel the agreement made and signed by him on November 15, 1892 (which precluded the Bodley Head from publishing the poem for five months after date of contract) "in favour of this authority for us to print it at our will." The agreement also empowered Mathews and Lane "to make the best arrangements possible, under the circumstances, for America. . . . In consideration of the aforesaid rights," the contract read, "we agree to advance you the sum of twenty five guineas, making together with the five guineas advanced on November 15th 1892, a total of thirty guineas on account of your share in the profits of the two above mentioned books." After having defrayed the costs of paper, printing, binding, and advertising, "and after allowing for the thirty guineas already advanced," the contract continued, "the residue, or in other words profits, shall be divided equally between the author and publishers." Perhaps the most unusual clause in the agreement was one very much in keeping with Watson's character, that is, his demand "that the books of the firm, so far as relates to your [Watson's] publications, shall be open to your inspection, or that of any one person acting on your behalf." [86]

Notable departures from the usual Bodley Head agreement were the contracts for Herbert Beerbohm Tree's *The Imaginative Faculty* and Ricketts and Shannon's edition of *Hero and Leander.* Tree, the half-brother of Max Beerbohm and a leading actor and producer of the London stage, was, in accordance with an agreement signed on June 8, 1893, to be given 250 copies of his little book in lieu of royalties, that is, if he bought 150 additional copies at the ordinary trade price. Since 1,000 copies were published, this left 600 copies at the disposal of the Bodley Head.[87]

Hero and Leander, like *Daphnis and Chloe,* which had been issued earlier from the Bodley Head, was designed by Ricketts and Shannon and was printed at the Ballantyne Press. Having already begun to garner subscribers for the book, Ricketts and Shannon decided to offer it to the Bodley Head. After preliminary negotiations, Mathews and Lane drew up an agreement, dated February 5, 1894, in which the partners stated they were "prepared to take 200 copies of this book [*Hero and Leander*] at 20/10 per copy being the same proportion of the published price as we paid you for the copies of *Daphnis and Chloe* which we purchased." Mathews and Lane further agreed to advertise and subscribe the book at their own cost and as they deemed fit, subject to the following regulations:

i That you hand over to us the names of all existing subscribers
ii That our imprint shall appear on the titlepage as in the colophon as in *Daphnis and Chloe*
iii That 14 extra copies be conceded for the following purposes: six for public libraries as prescribed by act of parliament[88] and one each for review in the following papers

Athenaeum	Academy
Spectator	Speaker
Times	Daily Chronicle

and one each to the publishers (as kindly suggested by yourselves)
iv That half the money be paid on March 1st provided the books have been delivered, or on date of delivery of books if such date be later than March 1st, and the remainder of the money within four months of the date of the first payment.
v That 1000 prospectuses of the book with our imprint be supplied to us with the least possible delay
vi That no reissue of this work with the illustrations shall appear within the space of five years.[89]

Although in the case of *Silverpoints,* John Gray was left "to settle with Mr. Ricketts," the Bodley Head was usually responsible for paying the artists and designers. The contract for *The Sphinx* called upon the publishers to pay the artist, Charles Ricketts, £45 for his part in overseeing the production. And as large a sum as this seems to have been, the Bodley Head paid Beardsley even more, 50 guineas, for his ten illustrations for *Salome.*[90]

The only book of art work per se published by the early Bodley Head was Will Rothenstein's *Oxford Characters,* a series of lithographed portraits of well-known Oxford men. Each of the twelve parts, which began to appear in June 1893, was made up of two portraits and was to sell for five shillings per part (small-paper) and ten shillings and sixpence per large-paper copy. According to the agreement, which was drawn up on December 20, 1893, long after the first part had appeared, the publishers paid Rothenstein "five pounds for each drawing done for this series on the day of publication," with each portrait becoming the property of the Bodley Head; and Mathews and Lane reserved "the right to reject any portrait executed without previous consultation with ourselves or any drawing the fidelity of which is objected to as a portrait." The agreement also precluded the artist "from issuing privately or publishing from any other source the portrait of any well known Oxford character, without our permission." [91]

Among other payments which Bodley Head contracts called for were those to persons serving as editors, which usually meant little more than that a writer provided a preface to the work of another, as in the case of Alice Meynell, who received five guineas for selecting the poems and providing a preface for *The Poems of Thomas Gordon Hake*.[92] George Moore probably did little more than that in connection with Lena Milman's translation of Dostoevski's *Poor Folk,* although the contract, which awarded him ten pounds, called upon him to revise the translation as well as to furnish a preface.[93]

A much more interesting example of a contract specifying an editor and assigning a fee for his services is that of the publication of William Hazlitt's *Liber Amoris* (1894 version), in which the author's grandson W. Carew Hazlitt, a noted author in his own right, "is hereinafter called the Editor." In June of 1893, the Bodley Head had published a reprint of the rare 1823 *Liber Amoris* with a facsimile of the original title page, various appendices with documents relating to the work, and a long "scholarly" introduction by Richard Le Gallienne, who served as the editor. Soon after publication, W. C. Hazlitt, a barrister at law of Barnes Common, Surrey, turned up the original manuscript of the work or decided to allow it to come to light. On August 9, 1893, he signed the contract with Mathews and Lane in which he was dubbed "editor" of a second Bodley Head *Liber Amoris*,[94] this time one based on the original manuscript of the work and containing eleven letters from William Hazlitt to P. G. Patmore upon the subject, a letter from Sarah Walker to Hazlitt, the Diary of Mrs. Hazlitt in Scotland (1822), and five letters from Mrs. Hazlitt to her son and sister-in-law written between 1824 and 1831. According to the terms of the agreement, W. C. Hazlitt was to "grant to the publishers, all such copyright, and control as he, as representative of the respective writers possesses in and over the following M.S.S. [There follows a list of the documents mentioned above.]" In return for £54.13.9, Hazlitt was to see the volume "thro' the press, adding such preface and notes, as may appear to the editor necessary." Although the copyright went to the publishers, the manuscripts remained as before the private property of the editor. Curiously, it was stipulated in the contract that "the name of the Editor shall not appear in any form in the said volume." [95]

Under certain conditions, a number of the Bodley Head contracts provided for an adjustment of royalties. One example is George Egerton's book of short stories, *Keynotes*. Signed on August 26, 1893, the agreement awarded the author a royalty of sixpence for each of the first 5,000 copies sold; it then stipulated that "if this number should be exceeded," the publishers "will increase the royalty on all copies issued at the same published price in excess of 5,000 copies to eight pence per copy."

Another type of adjustment of royalties is provided for further on in the contract where it reads: "If it becomes necessary to lower the price of the book after it has been a certain time in the market, the royalties shall be lowered in the same proportion as the price, or proportionately raised should the price become higher." Provision for yet a third kind of adjustment is also written into the *Keynotes* contract if and when Mathews and Lane succeed in arranging for the issue of the book in America. "On all copies supplied for that market, royalties at $\frac{1}{2}$ the rate we agree upon for English edition" will be paid.[96]

Keynotes was brought out in America by Roberts Brothers of Boston, a publishing firm which also issued another of the Keynotes series books which appeared before the dissolution of the partnership, Florence Farr's *The Dancing Faun,* the contract for which, dated May 24, 1894, contained the statement that arrangements had already been made for publishing the book abroad. The matter of royalty payments for the American edition was largely the same as for *Keynotes,* the contract reading that the Bodley Head agreed to pay Miss Farr "one half of the profits remitted to us by the American house which will issue it." [97]

A surprisingly large number of Bodley Head books were brought out in the United States. Although the Bodley Head had no agency of its own in America until after Lane made his first trip to this country in the spring of 1895,[98] the firm carried on an extensive business in the United States. Although Lane's boast that he had placed an American edition of every book he had published [99] is not quite true, the vogue and influence of the Bodley Head in America was largely due to his efforts. Nine publishing houses brought out some thirty-eight separate titles bearing the imprint of Mathews and Lane between 1889 and 1894.

Since the number of Bodley Head books exported increased sharply after 1892, Lane was no doubt the liaison man for the firm. Even before he became an active partner, he seems to have taken the initiative in arranging with Macmillan to bring out one of the earliest books to be exported to America from the Bodley Head, Crane's *Renascence.* From the contents of a letter from Crane to Lane dated January 23, 1891, it is clear that some months before the book appeared Lane was determined to find an American outlet for the volume. Crane, anxious to get his book out about Easter, wanted to make a final decision about how many copies of each issue of *Renascence* needed to be printed. "You said something about an arrangement with an American house, and that a larger edition than we first thought of might be advisable." [100] Matters seem to have progressed well, for two days later Crane wrote to Lane, "with regard to the American supply[,] I would accept the terms you offer if a good number is taken." [101]

As late as April 23, 1891, Crane had heard nothing more and wrote

Mathews that the "Messrs Whittingham tell me they ought to know whether any copies for America are to be printed before they proceed with the printing of my book." Crane expressed his hope that the matter could "be settled at once as I do not wish to delay the printing." [102] Two days later, Crane again wrote Mathews to say that since Lane's negotiations concerning an American edition had apparently fallen through he wished to proceed with printing the book "unless the offer is taken up at once." [103] Whether Lane's efforts in behalf of the book finally paid off or whether Mathews approached Macmillan on his own, by April 29, 1891, Mathews was able to write Crane informing him that he had seen Frederick Macmillan, who had "agreed to take the 200 copies of *Renascence* for the American market upon the terms I submitted to you and which you approved." [104] The terms were that Macmillan would purchase 150 copies of the small-paper issue at 3/6 in quires, 35 large-paper copies at 8/6 in quires and 15 Japanese vellum copies at 17/6 also in quires. According to Mathews' letter, "the cost of binding is to be added and the copies delivered complete when ready." [105]

By May 14, 1891, the delays and negotiations were near an end, and Frederick Macmillan wrote Mathews: "if you can deliver our copies of 'Crane's Renaissance' [*sic*] on Monday the 25th inst. we shall have no objection to its being published on Friday or Saturday of the same week." [106] Perhaps because of the long-drawn-out uncertainty concerning the matter, the title page of *Renascence* bears only the imprint of the Bodley Head, although each of the three issues is supplied with a statement of limitation listing the number of copies printed for both England and America. By May 29, Crane was able to write Mathews saying that he had "just heard from the Chiswick Press that they have delivered the 150 copies for America to you with a few copies for the press. The large paper," he continued, are expected "to be ready early next week & the Jap: vellum a few days later." [107]

Macmillan seems to have been the preferred agent for Bodley Head books abroad, at least at first, perhaps because there was an American branch with which arrangements could be made through a London office. Between 1891 and 1894, Macmillan published eight Bodley Head books in the United States and refused the offer of several more. Among those published in America was Symonds' *In the Key of Blue*, some large-paper copies of which Macmillan refused in November 1892 only to turn around and request ten copies for export the following month. [108]

During that same winter an exchange was arranged by the Bodley Head and Macmillan which had to do with unsold copies of the American editions of *Renascence* and the soon to be published *Excursions in Criticism* by William Watson. On November 7, 1892, Macmillan wrote Mathews and Lane to say they would be "happy to accept proposal that we take some copies of Watson's *Excursions* @ 2/6 in exchange for the remaining copies of Walter Crane's vol. of poems, which we presume you will credit to us at the price paid for them." [109] Macmillan's inventory suggests that Crane's book had not done well in America. As of June 1, 1892 — a year after publication — Macmillan in New York still had on hand 68 small-paper, 26 large-paper and 13 Japanese vellum copies.[110]

Although Macmillan usually agreed to purchase Bodley Head books for export at the rate of half the English published price, Frederick Macmillan could not see his "way clear to take any of Hallam's *Poems*" at that price when the day of publication drew near in April 1893. However, he offered a counterproposal which suggested: "If you can supply the book @ 2^s/– in cloth (the published price being 5^s/–) we will take 200 copies, but we cannot pay more than that. I return the proof sheets herewith." [111] Despite the reduced margin of profit, Mathews and Lane must have accepted the offer, for on April 17, the Bodley Head was informed that Macmillan preferred to have their copies of Hallam "bound in the same style as those that are issued to the English trade." [112]

In November 1893 Frederick Macmillan was willing to take 225 copies of Edmund Gosse's edition of *The Letters of Thomas Lovell Beddoes* in cloth at half price and, in addition, ready to export 100 copies of W. P. James's *Romantic Professions* at 2/6 per copy, but he refused to act as agent in America for the most popular of the early Bodley Head books, *Keynotes,* and he refused Lane's offer of the *Yellow Book.* On September 21, 1893, Macmillan in a brief but revealing letter to John Lane wrote: "I regret that I cannot share your enthusiasm for the stories by George Egerton which you kindly left with me. I return the proof sheets herewith." [113] The book was then offered to Roberts Brothers, who published most of the books in the Keynotes series in America. Copeland and Day became the publisher of the *Yellow Book* in the United States after Macmillan had declined. "After communicating with Mr. Brett [the manager for Macmillan in New York]," Frederick Macmillan wrote Lane on March 20, 1894, "I regret to say that we do not see our way to take up the 'Yellow Book' for the United States. I return the sheets herewith and thank you for giving us the refusal of the magazine." [114]

The informal and seemingly off-hand arrangements for importing and exporting books can be seen in the abortive attempt on the part of the famous American poet and literary celebrity on both sides of the Atlantic, Louise Chandler Moulton, to get the *Collected Poems of Philip Bourke Marston* published. Marston, a blind poet and son of the painter, Westland Marston, was beloved by many of the literary figures of the day. After his death in 1887, Marston's work enjoyed quite a vogue, which brought forth no less than three separate volumes of both unpublished and previously published poems in addition to a book of short stories. The chief perpetuator of his memory was Mrs. Moulton, who had made it an important part of her year to go to England in the summer and to stay well into the autumn, holding court for all the literary and artistic personages of the day. Mrs. Moulton, who had known Philip since 1867, was a close friend of the Marstons and shared and probably relished all the calamities that befell that distinguished clan and its intimates over the years.[115]

In 1887 Marston's *Garden Secrets* was brought out in Boston by Mrs. Moulton's own publishers, Roberts Brothers. In 1891, Elkin Mathews published the poems of Marston's last years in a volume compiled by Mrs. Moulton entitled *A Last Harvest*. At the same time, Mrs. Moulton was preparing for publication in America — again through Roberts Brothers — *The Collected Poems,* using largely the material she had prefaced to *A Last Harvest.*

In a letter from London, dated August 26, [1892,] to Mr. Niles, the director of Roberts Brothers, Mrs. Moulton told him that Elkin Mathews had called on her the day before "and wished me to offer you, in his behalf, 2/5 per unbound copy of Marston's Collected Poems — *for one hundred copies* — with the imprint of Elkin Mathews and John Lane on title page — Please take notice that there is only one t. in Mathews." Then she went on to say that she was "half inclined to think this is the *best* chance for the book"; and she held out to her American publisher the further possibility that Mathews might order more, "but that he would like to *begin* with 100 copies — as *you* began with 100 of 'A Last Harvest'." [116] Despite Mrs. Moulton's good offices and her interest in the Bodley Head, Mathews' offer fell through, for it was the London firm of Ward, Lock, Bowden and Co. which published *The Collected Poems* in Britain in 1892.

It was the general practice of the Bodley Head to make arrangements with an American publisher before a book went to press so that if the publisher desired, as he usually did, the title page could bear the joint imprint of the two firms. On occasion the publisher in the United States bought "stereos" or "shells" in lieu of the printed sheets or bound copies. Stereos and shells were casts of pages of type made in metal, either by a plaster or paper process.[117] Once a book's pages were stereotyped, the printer could distribute the type; and if another printing was called for, the stereos could be used; or if an American edition was desired, the molds could be shipped abroad and an edition run off there.

Such was the case with Le Gallienne's *Prose Fancies* and *The Religion of a Literary Man,* both published in the United States by G. P. Putnam's Sons of New York. These very popular books were printed at T. and A. Constable in May 1894. A letter to the Bodley Head mentions the fact that Constables has "been instructed today by your Mr. Lane" not only to print 1,100 copies of *Prose Fancies* and 115 large-paper copies of *The Religion of a Literary Man,* but to send "a set of shells . . . to Messrs. Putnam, Bedford Street," and charge them to the Bodley Head.[118] The imprint was, according to the instructions, "to bear the names of your firm and Messrs. Putnam in usual way. American shells to have no reference to portrait." [119]

That the shells were not a satisfactory means of reprinting a book for an American edition is indicated by the serious complaints which arose over the molds shipped to Putnams. On July 26, 1894, T. and A. Constable acknowledged a letter from Mathews and Lane which had conveyed the complaint of the Messrs. Putnam about "the electro shells of Mr. Le Gallienne's 'Prose Fancies'." "We regret exceedingly that this mistake has occurred, yet we cannot accept any responsibility for the error, nor can we explain it." [120] Pointing out that there was "no mistake in the English edition for which we are responsible," Constables suggested that the fault lay with the readers and revisers of the American firm whose duty it was "to check any error that may creep in. The press reviser should have checked the very obvious error on page 63, with on one side the chapter heading 'Irreverent People' and on the other, the heading 'The Devils on the Needle'." Moving on to a consideration of "the larger question of plates," Constables felt "naturally a delicacy in touching the question; yet the shells are exactly the same as we use ourselves, and we do not know that you have had cause to complain of our printing of them."

In Constables' opinion, shells being half finished work "should not be sent out of any office" as "different establishments have different ways of working." That other firms had, however, experienced similar problems with the shells is evidenced by the fact that T. and A. Constable concluded the letter with a reference to R. and R. Clark, another large Edinburgh printing firm, which received so many complaints that it was obliged to replace the use of shells with finished plates.[121]

Despite this one reversal, the fortunes of the Bodley Head book in America seem to have been quite acceptable. Although the number of copies sent abroad varied from as few as 25 to as many as 500 or more,[122] an average of 150 to 200 copies of a book were published abroad. These copies sold at considerably higher prices than those on sale in England. For instance, Oscar Wilde's *The Sphinx,* which Copeland and Day sold for twelve dollars in its ordinary edition and thirty dollars in its de luxe binding in the United States,[123] sold for two guineas (about $9.60) and five guineas (about $24.00), respectively, in Britain. Similarly Copeland and Day priced the ordinary edition of *Salome* at three dollars and seventy-five cents,[124] whereas it sold for fifteen shillings (about $3.60) in England. Seldom, however, did a Bodley Head book sell for more than two dollars in the United States, one dollar fifty cents being the usual price.[125]

Although the books exported to America far outnumbered those imported by the Bodley Head, five imports at one time or another were included among Bodley Head lists. One such book purchased from Scribners, Henry Van Dyke's *The Poetry of Tennyson,* ran through three editions before 1895. Scribners also provided two other books, Richard Henry Stoddard's *The Lion's Cub with Other Verse* and Dr. Philipp Schaff's *Literature and Poetry.* The first import from Stone and Kimball was *O'Shaughnessy, His Life and Work,*[126] edited by Mrs. Moulton, and from Lippincott came Charles Abbott's *Travels in a Tree Top.*

Mathews and Lane's success as publishers of belles-lettres cannot be denied. The Paterian few were numerous enough to support the kind of venture the Bodley Head book represented. Judged in the light of the large commercial publishing business, the successes of the early Bodley Head were modest. Whereas the Victorian publisher usually issued a first edition of from 750 to 1,000 copies at a minimum, the Bodley Head book seldom was published in more than 550 copies. But that a publishing house could devote itself to volumes of minor poetry, plays, and essays and almost totally ignore fiction, especially the novel, and succeed is remarkable. Add to that the fact that the Bodley Head book was in many cases a work of art in itself, beautifully bound, well printed on high quality paper and finely designed, and the feat becomes even more wondrous.

The costs of materials and labor were very low, and authors asked very little in the way of payment so that the average price of the Bodley Head book was a very competitive five shillings — often three shillings and sixpence, as in the case of the Keynotes series books. These factors plus a literary and artistic milieu which fostered an interest in belles-lettres and a desire for beautiful things were the grounds for success.

When the breakup of the partnership occurred at the close of September 1894, the Bodley Head was not only financially very sound but riding the crest of two new and impressive successes: George Egerton's *Keynotes,* in its fourth printing, and the *Yellow Book,* the talk of the town. Both partners were to continue the publishing business in their own separate ways. Mathews, continuing the early Bodley Head tradition of a small publisher dealing exclusively in choice volumes of belles-lettres, would make a very comfortable living throughout his life. Lane would make an astounding success and a fortune as a publisher of quality books of a generally popular variety.

To sell their books, Mathews and Lane during the early years relied primarily on subscriptions and a moderate amount of advertising. It was standard practice at the Bodley Head to issue a prospectus of 1,000 copies two or three months before a book was to be published. Often a very attractive pamphlet, the prospectus was made up of a page devoted to describing the book and stating the price of its various "editions," sometimes offering, as in the case of Bourdillon's *A Lost God,* a prepublication price advantageous to the subscriber. Another page contained an order form which the subscriber could fill in and return to the publisher. Sometimes a more elaborate four-page document was issued with excerpts from reviews of the author's earlier works. The prospectuses, which usually cost about £1.2.6 per thousand, enabled the publishers to gauge the interest in the book in question before committing themselves to printing. When, as in the case of Laurence Binyon's *Lyric Poems,* only 107 copies were subscribed, an edition of only 356 copies was printed. But when the prospectus for Gale's *Orchard Songs* enlisted over 1,400 subscribers, a first edition of nearly 2,500 copies was printed.[127]

Although Bodley Head advertising never approached the coverage larger publishers sought, modest advertisements did appear, especially at the opening of the spring and autumn seasons, in a number of carefully selected journals and newspapers. In addition, it was standard practice to insert a current list of books in the back of most Bodley Head volumes. As I will show later, however, the best advertising was that which came from the attention reviewers in both England and America gave the Bodley Head book.

Although the number of copies of a Bodley Head book usually sold was small, the firm did have some notable successes which were the envy of much larger houses. Le Gallienne's *The Religion of a Literary Man* ran into its "fourth thousand" soon after publication, and the first edition of Lord De Tabley's *Poems, Dramatic and Lyrical* was entirely sold out before the day of publication. Watson, who vied with Le Gallienne as a best-selling author, was so popular during the early nineties that both his *Eloping Angels* and *Excursions in Criticism* were sold out within a week of publication.[128] Two big Bodley Head successes were Wicksteed's *Dante: Six Sermons,* which had first appeared under the auspices of another publisher, Kegan Paul, in 1879, and Van Dyke's *The Poetry of Tennyson.*

A total of twenty Bodley Head titles went into further printings before the breakup in 1894: eleven titles required second printings, six required three printings, and three — Francis Thompson's *Poems,* Le Gallienne's *The Religion of a Literary Man* and George Egerton's *Keynotes* — required fourth printings. *Keynotes,* which appeared in December 1893 was the biggest seller — some 6,071 copies were in print at the time of the breakup,[129] and among the periodicals which issued from the Bodley Head, the only one actually published by the firm, the *Yellow Book*, was by far the most popular. Of the two numbers which appeared before October 1894, 7,000 copies of the first and 5,000 of the second were printed.[130]

The most accurate estimate of how well the volumes sold can be gathered from the last list of Bodley Head books which appeared in May 1894 and the Inventory Sheets of the firm drawn up probably in late August or early September 1894. Of the 107 separate titles (including books transferred from other publishers) issued from the Bodley Head, the advertisements as of May 1894 listed 77 titles as still in print. Yet the Inventory Sheets list only forty-four titles as remaining in print, which suggests that during the last six months of the partnership either thirty-three additional titles sold out in the normal course of business or most of these titles were removed from the firm's inventory by special sales such as that conducted by Sotheby, Wilkinson & Hodge whose *Catalogue of the Stock of Books of Messrs. Elkin Mathews & John Lane, of Vigo Street, who have dissolved partnership,* netted a total of £399.1.0.[131]

However this may be, the Inventory Sheets show that most of the 107 Bodley Head titles did sell out. Of the forty-four titles remaining in print, twenty-one had been published in the preceding six months, that is, since January 1, 1894; and of the seventeen titles first published in 1893, seven were in second, third, or fourth printings. Of those six titles remaining from 1892, only Michael Field's *Sight and Song* and Greene's *Italian Lyrists* remained in the original printings. Six hundred and thirty-three copies of the first number of the *Yellow Book* were unsold, and 1,030 copies of the second number.[132]

In view of the fact that the Aldine Poets published by William Pickering between 1830 and 1853 sold at five shillings per volume bound in cloth with paper labels, it is remarkable that the Bodley Head book often sold for no more.[133] It is astonishing that the Keynotes series books sold for only three shillings and sixpence when the price is compared with that of various series of reprints issued earlier in the century, for example, Bentley's Standard Novels, begun in February 1831 at six shillings per copy and only later reduced to three shillings and sixpence.[134]

A few of the finest Bodley Head books did sell for considerable sums. Wilde's *The Sphinx* was the most expensive: two guineas for the small-paper issue and five guineas for the large. The Ricketts and Shannon books, *Daphnis and Chloe* and *Hero and Leander,* sold for two guineas and thirty-five shillings, respectively. Yet *Silverpoints* was priced at a very reasonable seven shillings and sixpence for the ordinary issue and one guinea for the vellum-bound copies. Although Wilde's *Salome* sold for fifteen shillings and thirty shillings per copy for the ordinary and de luxe issues, respectively, Wicksteed's *Dante* and *Alma Murray as Beatrice Cenci* only cost the buyer two shillings, and Beerbohm Tree's *The Imaginative Faculty* sold for two shillings and sixpence.

The Bodley Head's margin of profit can best be indicated by analyzing the cost plus royalties required to publish a typical book of 550 copies such as A. C. Benson's *Poems*. The printer's records show that the cost of composition, printing and the paper for the *Poems* totaled £32.7.6,[135] and Bodley Head records indicate that the author was paid £17.5.7 in royalties.[136] The binding can be estimated (on the basis of similar books for which the binding costs are known) at about £10. If the cost for advertising and distributing the books is roughly set at £5, the total cost to the Bodley Head was about £64.13.1. Since the book sold retail at five shillings net per copy and probably (on the basis of other five-shilling books for which trade prices are available) sold to booksellers at four shillings, twopence, income accruing from the 550 sold copies was about £126.0.10. This amount less the total cost indicates a margin of profit on the volume of approximately £61.7.9.

The profit for A. C. Benson's *Poems* is small, however, when compared with that which Wilde's *Salome* yielded. Of the 755 small-paper copies printed, 605 had already been sold at the time of the breakup. Since the ordinary issue sold at fifteen shillings per copy retail and twelve shillings and sixpence to the trade, income from this issue totaled about £415.17.0. Out of 125 large-paper copies, 115 were sold at thirty shillings per copy, which yielded £172.10.0. The total income, therefore, from the two issues can be estimated at £588.7.0. Wilde was paid a royalty of one shilling per small-paper copy sold and three shillings per large-paper copy sold, which totals £47.10.0. The total printing bill for both issues, paper included, amounted to £25.14.0.[137] If ten pounds is added for advertising and distributing and twenty pounds for binding plus £52.10.0 paid to Beardsley, the total cost of *Salome* was roughly £155.14.0. Deduct this from the total income, and a profit margin of some £432.13.0 for the Bodley Head is indicated.

There is reason to believe that when the early Bodley Head came to an end, the partners, who had started out together in 1887 with a good collection of rare books but little or no capital, had made enough money during those seven years that when the assets of the firm were split Lane was still able to move across the street into Albany and establish himself almost immediately as a major publisher.

The relations between author and publisher at that most crucial period of a book's inception when in an agony of anxiety and indecision the principals worry over the final contents and shape of the book are seldom chronicled in any detail, for rarely are those letters and other mementos which pass between author and publisher — often in temper, at times in despair — preserved. Although little or nothing of worth remains concerning the prepublication history of most early Bodley Head books, a considerable run of documents does survive for some of Mathews and Lane's most interesting volumes. Loath to leave out of consideration so important a part of the firm's publishing history, I hope by describing for the reader the trials and tribulations which preceded the published success of Richard Le Gallienne's critical study *George Meredith: Some Characteristics* and Lord De Tabley's *Poems, Dramatic and Lyrical* to throw some light on an aspect of publishing history often ignored.

In less than a year after Le Gallienne, an almost unknown, impecunious young provincial, met Mathews and Lane in June 1888, he had been miraculously released from "the cavernous defiles of the Mammonite Country" [1] — Liverpool, where he had been an apprentice accountant — had joined the famed actor, Wilson Barrett, as his literary secretary and had published a second volume of poems, *Volumes in Folio.* Such rapid improvement in his position brought an excess of energy which enabled Le Gallienne to serve

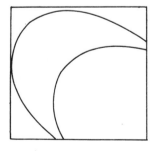

4 THE BIRTH
OF A BOOK

Barrett, compose poetry, write reviews for the *Academy*, and lead a busy social life as well as conceive of and set to work on at least four books: an autobiographical account of his developing aesthetic sensibilities, *The Book-Bills of Narcissus*; a volume of short stories, some by him and some by Robinson K. Leather, entitled *The Student and The Body-Snatcher*; a critical study of George Meredith's works; and a volume of essays to be known as *Oblivion's Poppies: Studies in the Forgotten*. Of the last, only the title remains, but the other three projected books became realities.

No sooner had Le Gallienne seen *Volumes in Folio* through the press in March 1889 than he set about drawing up a plan for the book on Meredith. By May 22, 1889, he had signed an agreement with Mathews to complete satisfactorily at least four chapters by October 1 and all eight chapters by New Year's Day, 1890.[2]

Undaunted by the demands of the agreement that he deliver in less than seven months a manuscript productive of at least 240 pages of printed text, Le Gallienne set to work on his first sustained critical effort in late May while on holiday at Salisbury. Writing to Lane on May 30, he was full of Meredith: "You must blame *Sandra Belloni* 'sundries,' " he abruptly began,

for having kept me silent when you charmed so sweetly. For your first letter
I owe you a real debt of gratitude, which I have been trying to repay
in the way you would best care for I am sure, assiduity on G. M. Not so
much on the poems as I am not feeling very well yet, not quite up to
poetry like G. M.'s, but on the before-mentioned novel which I have nearly
finished — after [?] many delighted hours.[3]

Having received a "very encouraging" letter from Meredith himself, Le Gallienne was all admiration and enthusiasm,[4] which survived another two weeks and his next letter to Lane, who had undertaken the task of providing the book with a detailed bibliography. Buoyantly proclaiming their togetherness in the project, Le Gallienne wrote: "Yes, dear Lane, as we parted even still are we one in the spirit — 'Meredith!' 'Meredith!' All thro' the day have our two hearts been beating, I'll swear, like two waterbury watches." [5]

The fact he had just finished reading *Rhonda Fleming* and was attempting "to make up deficiencies," doubtless in his knowledge of the English novel, by reading *Middlemarch*, suggests that Le Gallienne was planning to write his chapter on Meredith's novels shortly. Yet he went on to tell Lane that after completing his reading of George Eliot's novel he would "fall hard on the poetry & write the article at once — I am anxious to get that done ere I leave here." [6]

Just how Le Gallienne came to be an admirer of George Meredith's work is not known. The closest one can come to pinpointing the genesis of his enthusiasm is the statement of his friend Temple Scott, who shared Le Gallienne's noontime reveries in old Liverpool bookshops and the fellowship of Samuel Hales. Having described the celebrations surrounding the publication of *My Ladies' Sonnets* in 1887, Temple Scott recalled "that it was during this period that my poet [Le Gallienne] was introduced to Meredith's novel, 'The Egoist' — probably by the gently satirical bookseller [Hales] — and the introduction sent him on the gallant adventure of reading all the novelist's writings." [7]

From Le Gallienne's letters and diary entries beginning with his return to Liverpool in October 1889, it is clear that his enthusiasm for his subject hardly outlasted the first flush of discovery, a visit to Meredith at Flint Cottage, and the stimulation that comes from being among congenial people and exciting surroundings. High though his spirits had been in the summer, the autumn found Le Gallienne depressed and forlorn. The asthma which had plagued his eight-months' sojourn in London had prevented him from accompanying Barrett on a tour of America. His support gone, October found him fitting up a garret in Liverpool which he glorified with the name of Trafford Chambers,[8] hoping to write the Meredith and his *Book-Bills* in time to win fame and re-establish himself in London the following year.

As early as July 24, 1889, a Le Gallienne letter foreshadows the coming disenchantment. "I have been trying to get on with my Meredith work," he wrote Hales, "& that & the weariness of wretched health have seemed to make my days full." [9] But the start of a provincial tour with Barrett broke in and interrupted his writing. It was not until he was faced with the daily routine of Meredith and nothing but Meredith that enthusiasm turned to distaste. While in Liverpool during his holiday in June, Le Gallienne had longed to be settled there, free to pursue his work for "the next three months — I w^d move mountains," he wrote Lane.[10] But once he found himself isolated there for the next nine months, his strength failed him.

The first of October had come round, and he had not one, much less four, chapters to show Elkin Mathews. His reneging on the terms of his agreement with the Bodley Head did not go unchallenged, for late in October Le Gallienne was harassed enough to write Mathews a letter which Lane and no doubt Mathews himself thought "ungentlemanly" — a letter which must have grown out of an altercation with Mathews over his failure to live up to the terms of the contract or to explain satisfactorily his failure to do so. Referring to "my unfortunate letter to E. M." in a letter to Lane dated

October 26, Le Gallienne seemed stunned by his friend's "extravagant condemnation." Rebutting Lane's charges of bad form and a lack of dignity,
Le Gallienne averred that athough his "Inner teaching of natural gentleness" was not that of the etiquette books, it hadn't, on the whole, given
"folk a bad impression." [11] Whether he was referring to Lane or Mathews
or both, Le Gallienne rounded out his defense with a jibe at "the modern
young man" who affects "a pompous seriousness" and accounts anything less
a lack of dignity.[12]

Having asked Lane's forgiveness for having "wounded" him in his previous letter, Le Gallienne in his next word to Lane told of having sent off
the first Meredith chapter to be completed, "George Meredith and His
Critics," to Frank Harris of the *Fortnightly Review*.[13] Hopeful of its acceptance, he went on to say that whether or not it was taken, "the writing of it
will not be lost time, for I shall be able to use nearly the whole of it in
the book — & it certainly contains some of the best critical writing I have
done — at least in my own opinion & that of two or three friends here
whose opinion I value." [14]

With the very first entry in his diary begun on November 12, 1889, Le
Gallienne's struggle to grind out his Meredith chapters one after the other
had begun. "Wrote a page, the last of G.M.'s poetry essay with much straining," he recorded. And on November 26 he noted: "Finally finished G.M.'s
poetry essay. Great Heaven what a time a trifle takes me these days!" [15]
Allowing a good deal for this diarist's conscious efforts to dramatize his situation for posterity, one must believe that Le Gallienne's efforts at pushing
on with his critical study were doubtless painful. Le Gallienne had begun
to realize that for a novice to read through, digest and compose a study of
Meredith's *oeuvre* within a space of scarcely a year was a bit more than
even a genius like himself should undertake.

Nevertheless, his burden was lightened and his critical study immeasurably
enriched by his reading of Walter Pater's new book, *Appreciations*, which
Le Gallienne perused at this time "with all the intellectual & spiritual
quickening which his writing always" brought to him.[16] From this work,
Le Gallienne learned his critical approach to Meredith: an impressionistic
appreciation which best suited one who lacked the requisites to treat his
subject from a learned, scholarly point of view.

It is likely that Mathews and Lane wanted the Meredith book to be a
critical account typical of the times, with a chapter indicating Meredith's
place in the development of the English novel and his debt to the great
writers of the immediate past — Dickens, Thackeray, and Eliot. But Le
Gallienne's inability to carry through with his work was, no doubt, due in
part to his growing awareness of his very serious limitations as a scholar.

As a result, Pater's new essays in criticism must have been a revelation to him. It was no longer necessary for him to approach Meredith through his antecedents, comparing his style, themes, characters, and plots with those of a whole host of other English writers. A critic's own personal impression of how Meredith's work affected him was enough.

That at last all the elements of the Meredith had coalesced in his mind is evident in his "My Dear 'London Partner' " letter of December 22, 1889. Detailing for Lane the contents of a letter he had recently dispatched to Elkin Mathews, Le Gallienne indicated his desire to "depart a little from the lines originally suggested by you & agreed upon between us — of course it was quite impossible till one had thoroughly read G. M. to say finally how he could best be treated." [17]

Aware that any deviation from the original plan of eight chapters listed in the agreement of May 22 might bring another and perhaps fatal confrontation with Mathews, Le Gallienne was most careful to play down the changes in emphasis he proposed. "The deviations will be very slight," he assured Lane, "& will practically be confined as regards omission to the chapter on his *Originals,* one that would necessitate a 'behind the scenes' knowledge of society which only old men of the world are likely to possess." [18]

Having freed himself from the difficult and dangerous job of identifying Meredith's characters with their originals in real life, Le Gallienne went on to extricate himself from another obstacle in the path of his new concept of the Meredith study. "To merely trace his [Meredith's] debt to Dickens and Thackeray," he reasoned, "would be little profitable and not particularly gracious — do you think?" Recalling the fact that he and Lane had earlier agreed "that the introductory review of contemporary fiction could be spared," Le Gallienne went on to say that he was now "more than ever convinced" it should be so:

for such a review with its inevitable "placing" of G.M. would be at variance with the whole spirit of my study, which in its way will be a modest protest against the comparative method of criticism — a method which is for ever telling one what a man's work is *like,* quarrelling with it for what it is not, but invariably shirking the effort of looking patiently at it, & telling us what it *is.* The very reverse is my aim in regard to G.M. — viz. to give in a brief space a positive impression of his essential qualities & describing them as they appear to me.[19]

In keeping with his new understanding of his subject, Le Gallienne went on to suggest that " 'A point of view' will best & modestly express my attitude — 'George Meredith, Novelist & Poet. A Point of View'." Then he continued:

My first chapter will be on 'Style & general characteristics', & will be probably the most important in the book as of course G. M.'s style is the most significant thing about his work (as it always is about any work) & *means everything*. Get to know the *reason* of a man's individual style & you have really got to know *why* he writes, what artistic message he came to bring — & that, of course, is the main thing to know about him.[20]

As to the other chapters, Meredith's own phrase "The Comic Muse" struck Le Gallienne "as a good title for the comedy chapter, & probably 'The Pilgrim's Scrip' for the 'wit and wisdom' chapter."[21]

Le Gallienne's critical approach to his subject detailed in this letter also fits in well with the bias of the first chapter to be completed, "George Meredith and His Critics." This essay was largely an immediate response to William Watson's widely discussed statement on Meredith which had appeared in Henley's *National Review* in October 1889. Watson's "Fiction — Plethoric and Anaemic" was a spirited and cutting attack on the society novel of the day in general and on the brilliantly mannered world of Meredith's *Diana of the Crossways* and *The Egoist* in particular. Watson declared *The Egoist* to be "the most entirely wearisome book purporting to be a novel that I ever toiled through in my life."[22]

Le Gallienne had had high hopes of drawing some publicity and perhaps bringing about a literary controversy with Watson when he mailed off his essay to the *Fortnightly* early in November. Unfortunately, it was declined,[23] a reversal which Le Gallienne attributed to the fact "that Watson, whose article of course it mainly attacked, is 'in' with [Frank] Harris," the editor.[24] Consequently, Le Gallienne planned to tone down the controversial elements in his essay before printing it in the Meredith volume. "I shall, of course," he wrote Lane,

miss out all merely temporary allusions, & take care not to seem to attach too great an importance to the article [Watson's] (really a very superficial one) but simply take it as a type of the philistine criticism of G.M. — or as I have expressed it — "the British public's long insensitive disregard of Mr. Meredith finding voice & endeavoring to justify itself, graceless & unrepentant."[25]

Once Le Gallienne had established the method of his critical study, his spirits soared somewhat and the old confidence in his ability to move a mountain came upon him, for on the very threshold of Christmas he could "confidently look forward to getting the whole thing out of hand by the end of January," and dared to ask Lane " — who are the printers, by the way? W & J. A[rnold]? I am much exercised," he went on to say, "ab^t the form. We must have a neat tasteful volume." [26] By way of conclusion, Le Gallienne turned to thoughts concerning the dedication of the book. "I have been thinking it would look odd to dedicate studies in a living man's work to anyone but the subject there of, so how would it be for you & I jointly to 'offer' our labours to G. M. as a little tribute of appreciation etc. etc. you know." [27]

On New Year's Eve Le Gallienne sent the poetry essay off to Mathews and planned to post the chapter on style and the one on Meredith's critics by the following week end. In an effort to facilitate matters, Le Gallienne suggested that these three chapters be sent on to the printers as soon as possible. "The sight of proofsheets would give me a fillip in finishing the other chapters." [28] It never occurred to him that such a move would cause considerable trouble later. Still misjudging the rapidity with which he could complete the book and the time it would take to print it, Le Gallienne looked forward to publication at an early date. And so, apparently, did others. For his diary entries for January 13 and 14 of the new year, 1890, mention "unexpected" notices of Le Gallienne and his "G. M. work in *The Porcupine* [Liverpool]" and the *Speaker*.

Some idea of why the book was further and further delayed beyond the original deadline of January 1 can be gained from a letter to Lane dated January 3, 1890, in which Le Gallienne wrote that he was sending off the chapter on *The Egoist* and *Richard Feverel* the next day,[29] yet the chapter was not actually dispatched until February 4. Because of his continuing to revise it, the chapter on "George Meredith and His Critics" was not sent off until February 5. And although he fully expected "to complete *The Comic Muse* this next week [the second week of January]," it was "still dragging" as of March 5, 1890.[30] The "Pilgrim's Scrip" chapter, which he mentioned in the January 3 letter to Lane as the chapter "in which I intend dealing with all his wit & phrase-making," was not finished until October — some ten months later.

Nevertheless, his diary entries for January and February suggest that Le Gallienne was working well enough and in rising spirits. His chapter on Meredith's women was off his hands by January 23, and soon after he was able to record that his chapter on *The Egoist* and the novels generally, dispatched to Mathews on February 4, was "the result of the best week's work I have yet done." [31]

Once Elkin Mathews had four chapters to peruse, he sent them to a reader, S. T. Whiteford, who found them acceptable. The diary for February 7 records the receipt of a letter from Lane which carried the good news that "the G.M. essays had been read by Whiteford for Mathews — & that all were highly satisfied with them!" To celebrate, Le Gallienne boarded the train at 10:45 P.M. on Sunday evening the ninth "for 10/– worth of London." [32] The next two days not only "passed very pleasantly" but also gave him "many assurances that, whatever clouds there may be about, my fortunes are decidedly in the ascendant." Most important, the budding young critic found "Mathews in a very satisfactory attitude." [33]

Until April there is every sign that Le Gallienne, Lane, and the publisher, Elkin Mathews, had every intention of going through with the publication of the Meredith some time that spring. From the contents of a letter of February 18, 1890, it can be gathered that such advanced activities as feeling out reviewers and considering estimates for printing were under way.[34] Well aware of the importance of the critical opinion of the press to the success of the book, Le Gallienne, relying largely on Lane, was attempting to line up enough key critics to insure the *Meredith* a good press. That it was something of a touchy, uncertain business is suggested by Le Gallienne's comments to Lane concerning Theodore Watts, who as a major reviewer for the *Athenaeum* was one whose good opinion needed to be courted. "It was good of you to write so to Watts," wrote Le Gallienne, who then ventured: "I think he is interested in me — but then he is rather an intermittent person, given to fitful enthusiasms. However, we will hope." In order to further the matter, Le Gallienne went on to say that when he is next "in town, I shall take him at his word in a former letter to me & call again at *The Pines*." [35]

About the critic and future Bodley Head poet, Arthur Symons, Le Gallienne felt more secure. "Arthur Symons, good too," he remarked to Lane. Then he continued: "I should think we are pretty safe in his hands, for he is a great friend of Mrs. Alexander Ireland who has often expressed a wish to introduce me to him." [36]

That the matter of securing a printer was going forward is suggested in the letter when Le Gallienne mentioned to Lane that John Robb's estimate for printing the *Meredith* had been sent to Mathews, "who can tell you all about it & save repetition here. I hope it will seem reasonable, as it does to me," he went on to say, "for the work could not be better done than by him & it will save so much time & trouble having it done here." [37]

John Robb was a Liverpool printer who had been instrumental in getting

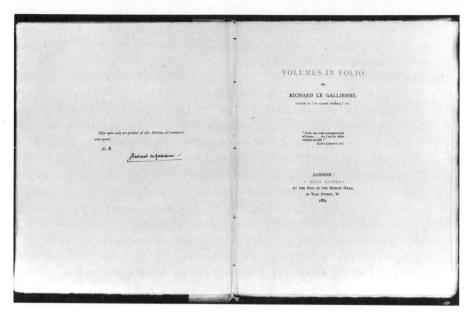

Statement of limitation and title page of the first Bodley Head book.

Some bindings for the early Bodley Head: Francis Thompson's *Poems*; Lord De Tabley's *Poems, Dramatic and Lyrical*; J.A. Symonds' *In the Key of Blue*; T. Gordon Hake's *Poems*; Allan Monkhouse's *Books and Plays*.

Le Gallienne's *My Ladies' Sonnets* published in 1887. If his fictionalized account of Robb's part in that production is anywhere near the truth, Le Gallienne's devotion to Robb and his desire to throw work his way can be fully understood. In chapter XXVII of *Young Lives*, Le Gallienne described the publication of his first book, a volume of poems entitled *The Book of Angelica* in the fictional account. Robb in the guise "of a little Scotch printer, who had a great love for poetry and some taste in it," called Mr. Leith, was a friend of Angelica's parents. One evening when Le Gallienne as the young Henry Mesurier was visiting his sweetheart's family, Leith was present. In the course of the evening, Angelica (Mildred) produced her manuscript copy of Henry's poems. Having read a few, Leith exclaimed, " 'The Man's a genius . . . his poems must be printed.' " Proposing that if Henry could "provide him with a list of a certain number of friends he could rely on for subscriptions," Leith agreed to "take the risk of printing an edition, and give Henry half the profits." [38]

A good-hearted, honest laborer of a convivial nature, Robb struggled along as a printer on what seem to have been very limited resources. Le Gallienne had great confidence in him as a capable and trustworthy man. Unable to forget Robb's kindness easily, Le Gallienne suggested to Mathews that his old benefactor and barroom crony print his *George Meredith*.[39] If Robb were employed, Le Gallienne not only would be helping a friend but would also have the printing under his direct surveillance at all times. Since Robb's estimate was doubtless a very reasonable one, with Le Gallienne's assurances of the printer's reliability, Mathews awarded him the contract.

By February 18, Le Gallienne had written his prefatory note and was working on the "Comic Muse" chapter, and by March 5, he had found a "specimen page from Robb very satisfactory." [40] At this point, Le Gallienne's feelings for his study were not of the fondest. "O when will this d——d book be done with," he recorded in his Diary. "I think I would consent to let it drop into limbo at once, so it should be out of the way." [41]

But Le Gallienne continued to struggle with his chapters — the "Comic Muse" was posted to Mathews on March 11 — and to concern himself with details about the format of the book. "Robb has promised to send me a proof of Fullerton's note[42] tomorrow," Le Gallienne reported to Lane on March 15. "He is now going ahead, four chapters are in type & the rest soon will be." As if the book were practically completed, he told Lane that he had "written to Mathews about the binding — egg him on, will you? And by the way, about the illustrations — are they underway?" [43]

Lane's reply to this letter can be largely reconstructed from Le Gallienne's next, dated March 24. Lane had made arrangements with Fullerton to publish a short essay on Meredith's reputation in the United States as a kind of appendix to Le Gallienne's study. He had also acquired a pen and ink sketch of Meredith's chalet at Box Hill, drawn by Meredith's son Maxse; the sketch and a drawing of the novelist were to be used as illustrations.[44] Having approved of Lane's efforts, Le Gallienne went on to say: "Robb is getting on with the setting-up. I have some proof this morning — but what about the paper? Will you stir Mathews up? & don't forget to insit on a good paper." [45]

The remainder of Le Gallienne's letter to March 24 is given over largely to response to Lane's criticisms of the "Meredith and His Critics" chapter, which had appeared as an essay in *Time* on March 1. It can be surmised from what Le Gallienne wrote that Lane was very alarmed about his friend's pugnacious attacks in the article and elsewhere — perhaps reviews — on important literary figures of the day such as William Sharp (Fiona MacLeod) and William Watson, who in revenge could very easily cause a bad press for the *Meredith* when it appeared. The letter also cautioned Le Gallienne that while he had few friends in the world of literature, he had all too many enemies. "I thought I had rather a goodly number of literary acquaintances . . . . & I certainly never dreamed that I was important enough to have enemies, as your underlining seems rather to imply — except, O yes! it be poor Century Guild Horne!" [46] Then twitting Lane, he continued:

Forgive me if I say that your opinion of my Time article amuses me. Have you read it? or do you quote? And seeing that on your confession to me you have read one other of my chapters, don't you think it is a little rash to be so off hand in so absolute & dreadful a condemnation? Follow the advice given in the said article — & avoid the superlative. You don't know how *bad* I may be in those other essays — & having used "worst," it is inelegant to have to say worst-est, don't you think? [47]

This bantering tone, which bordered on the sarcastic and ironic at times, broke through the generally jovial and cordial tone of letters Le Gallienne sent to Lane at this time. Perhaps it resulted from Le Gallienne's sense of having been exiled to Liverpool to sit "alone with something very like Despair at my elbow, & an unfinished book in front of me," [48] while Lane lived it up in London and hoped to get equal billing with Le Gallienne on the title page of the *Meredith*. Le Gallienne very well may have resented — and later did resist — Lane's efforts to play along at making a bibliography as a means of sharing half the honors of the Meredith study with his friend. While Le Gallienne was suffering through all of Meredith's works and making painful efforts at comprehending them, Lane was mainly relying on others to provide him with the titles of essays, books, and articles which he would include in his bibliography. "Have you read any of G. M.'s novels yet?" Le Gallienne once ventured to inquire of Lane. Then with something more than a mere semblance of seriousness, he continued: "Forgive my banter, but you are such a d——d fraud, you know!" [49]

Although the April 2 entry in Le Gallienne's diary indicates that he was "correcting proof of G.M.," the absence of any mention of what Le Gallienne had come to refer to as that "d——d book" for the next few months suggests that the *Meredith* was shelved until the following autumn. By April, the chapter on Meredith's style was still unfinished and the chapter to be entitled "The Pilgrim's Scrip" was not even begun. Since the book had originally been scheduled to appear for the spring 1890 season, Le Gallienne's failure to keep his part in the bargain must have precipitated the decision to postpone publication in hopes of bringing out the book during the fall and winter season of 1890. Even if Le Gallienne had been ready to publish in April or even May, it is very uncertain that Lane would have had his bibliography ready. The only reference to Lane's part of the bargain occurs in a letter of March 15 in which Le Gallienne mentioned that a minor matter concerning the text "need not delay your bibliography which you can send as soon as you like." [50]

The notion of doing a bibliography to accompany Le Gallienne's study of Meredith was probably the result of what John Carter has spoken of as the new interest in collecting modern authors and an even more recent development, "the use of the author-bibliography." [51] Buxton Forman's *A Shelley Library*, published by the Shelley Society in 1886, had given rise to the kind of fully developed bibliography issued during the nineties and later by Forman's disciple, T. J. Wise.[52]

Lane, no doubt, saw the Meredith bibliography as a chance to establish himself as a literary figure and with comparatively little effort to get his name attached to a book. In addition to spending some time with Le Gallienne at the British Museum, his efforts at research seem to have been directed toward making contact through the mails with the literary great of the recent past as well as the present — a task Lane would have enjoyed. His letters aimed at eliciting bibliographical information from essayists and reviewers of George Meredith's work are to be found in the Berg Collection of the New York Public Library, at Princeton, and at various other libraries in large quantities. For the most part, his inquiries seem to have met with success, and much to Le Gallienne's surprise, Lane received a reply from the great and unapproachable Swinburne. "You are lucky," Le Gallienne told Lane in February, "to have got a letter from A. C. S. for he writes but rarely. What it is to be great!" [53]

One of the earliest correspondents in connection with the bibliography was Meredith, himself, who first replied to Lane from Box Hill, Dorking, on May 5, 1889 — soon after the Meredith volume was conceived. "I have to thank you — & I do so from the heart — for the compliment you propose offering to my books," he wrote.

I would not withhold my consent, but when I read your expressions of feeling for the works, & hear that a young & enterprizing publisher is bent on running risks to bring out a bibliography, I cannot think that you have taken the right measure of my popularity. I am afflicted with the thought that he would lose his money & you your time, for which I should be sorry in any case; but to know myself the cause would add a sting of remorse. Therefore be warned, meditate on it & make inquiries. I am all but certain that the public would have no taste for such a book. — As to my first vol. of verse, I have not a copy & have not seen one for years — I have no wish that it should be heard of. The dreadful "Olive Branch" appeared in "Household Words." In the Revue des deux Mondes, there were compressed *renderings* in 3 Numbers apiece, of *Richard Feverel* & *Sandra Belloni*: not direct translations. I know of no others.

Very truly yours
George Meredith [signed] [54]

In addition to various letters from Meredith himself, Lane was aided in his researches by such notables as Henley, Watts-Dunton, William Sharp, Robert Louis Stevenson, and Andrew Lang, whose reply was a bit more witty than most: "I do not think I ever reviewed any novel of Mr. Meredith's," he wrote, "and certainly I was entirely unable to work my way through The Egotist [*sic*]. I only remember much wit about a man's legs." [55]

The decision to delay publication of the Meredith volume must have been made early in April, for after that date neither Le Gallienne's diary nor his correspondence mentions it. During the late spring and summer, Le Gallienne's chief preoccupation was his autobiographical *Book-Bills of Narcissus*, which he completed and sent off to Frank Murray, the publisher, on June 26, 1890.[56] In addition, he was composing a few poems, including a sonnet to Dante's Beatrice and a sonnet on Paolo and Francesca, and writing an occasional review. "Slaughtered half-a-dozen 'innocents' for *The Academy* & sent off," reads his diary entry for July 1.

In the summer of 1890, Le Gallienne found himself involved in a series of unhappy disagreements and misunderstandings with his fiancée, Mildred, who seems to have come close to destroying a relationship which was in time to lead to marriage. "Long serious talk with Mil," he recorded in his diary on June 30, "which I must hope may help her. For my part I think I must go away." Perhaps it was his experiences with a jealous sweetheart that formed the basis for a story he began to write in September, entitled "The Way of a Man with a Maid." The diary also records his involvement with Robinson Kay Leather, either accompanying him to the Hydro at Ben Rhydding or reading and talking with him in Liverpool.

However he spent his summer, it is evident that he did little or nothing on the *Meredith*; September found him in much the same position he had been in in April. Not until September 11 is the diary's silence on the subject of Meredith broken: "Had hoped to get at last chapter of G.M. but alas hopeless today!" Only when it was decided some time in September that the book was "to be rushed out at last," [57] did the work of proof correcting and the writing of the chapter entitled "The Pilgrim's Scrip" get under way in earnest.[58] Although on October 20 Le Gallienne was still "straining at G.M.," [59] he was able to record in his diary the following day that he had "finished same at last, thank god, preface & all." [60]

That Elkin Mathews, too, was at work once again on the *Meredith* is suggested by Le Gallienne's reply to his letter, which reached the author in late September. "The title-page is, of course, not at all satisfactory," Le Gallienne agreed, but, he told Mathews, "I will attend to it. As to the binding," he continued, "it seems odd but certainly no samples have ever reached me, or you should have heard by return. If Dent can give us the same cloth as the *Appreciations*, I should say, with you, we cannot do better so let it be." As to the touchy question of whether or not Lane's name was to appear on the spine, Le Gallienne was frank and forthright with Mathews:

As to lettering on back, I don't think Mr. Lane's name ought to appear, unless it be stated also what part of the book is his because to link our names together as you suggest is misleading — seeming to imply that the whole book is joint, essay, & all — I certainly do not think it would be usual. Mr. Lane will I know agree with me in that. This is how I would prefer it. [A sketch bearing the title and Le Gallienne's name alone follows.] I don't think it would improve appearance to have your name at bottom — as it would interfere with plainness of effect. Nor do I want a label line — This in great haste, yours sincerely,
Richard Le Gallienne [signed]
P.S. Thanks for the V. [olumes] in F. [olio] safe to hand.
P.S. I have seen Robb this afternoon. He is going ahead with bibliography.

I am writing Mr. Lane — his bibliography seems to me a very sound piece
of work. It must have represented no small time & patience.[61]

    Lane evidently was unhappy with Le Gallienne's desire to leave his name
off the spine of the *Meredith* and told his friend so in a letter whose contents can largely be gathered from Le Gallienne's reply of October 6, 1890.
Suggesting that the bibliography was the most valuable part of the book
and that Le Gallienne should count it a privilege to have his name linked
so prominently with Lane's own, he supported his demand for equal billing with parallel cases and the opinions of the senior members of Lane's
pet Ye Sette of Odd Volumes society, which Le Gallienne turned aside as
ludicrous.
    While attempting to view the matter reasonably and to placate Lane,
Le Gallienne stood firm in his opinion. "My dear Lane," he wrote,

I am sorry we don't agree on that little matter of the label, for I am put
in a very unpleasant position thereby &, if you *will* misunderstand me,
must I am afraid be made to seem somewhat mean. However, if you are a
true friend you will not, for real friendship should be able to bear a
difference of opinion & a little plain speaking.
    Now lookhere, don't think I forget all your hard work on this G. M.
book, or underrate your bibliography. Probably the latter *is* actually the
most valuable part of the book, but be that as it may, it is not ostensibly
so; ostensibly it is an adjunct to my studies, for, as you yourself wrote
me sometime ago, the book is *mine*. It is not joint, in any sense of
half-&-half (& in connection with that word "joint" remember that the
suggestion of a joint dedication was *mine*).
    Therefore, I say, it is out of all proportion to have your name linked
with mine on the back in the way you propose. If not, it ought to be in
the same type on the title-page. It would convey a totally wrong
impression, & imply a joint authorship in the studies — tho' truly it
would give me a right to share in the honours of the bibliography.[62]

Loath to be adamant and totally inflexible, Le Gallienne then proceeded
to propose one or two compromises:

Let me hasten to say that I should be really glad of your name on the
back — placed there in a proportionate manner. I don't know whether or
not your talk of "fame" with me is sarcasm, but anyhow the idea of
association with you is very pleasant to me.

Here is suggestion No. 1 [There follows a sketch of the title page, which is composed of a shortened title: "George Meredith" followed by Le Gallienne's name. Toward the bottom of the page is inserted: "with a bibliography by John Lane."] This seems to me the best way to settle it — properly spaced & with proportionate type it would not look at all too long — I am sure.

Failing that I suggest the omission of both our names & letting it read thus. [The sketch which follows reinstates the full title: "George Meredith Some Characteristics" followed by the phrase "with a bibliography" and concluded with the initials "E. M."]

Or failing both how w[oul]d you like [there follow a sketch of the title page bearing a short title, John Lane's name as author, and concluding with a large question mark.] [63]

Although Elkin Mathews' advertisement in the *Publishers' Circular* for September 1, 1890, announced that Le Gallienne's *George Meredith* would be "ready at last week of September," [64] the "Books and Rumours of Books" section of the same issue stated that "Elkin Mathews will publish next month" the Le Gallienne study.[65] Was the book scheduled for publication about October 1 only to be postponed indefinitely again? Perhaps Lane thought so, especially when the close of October drew near. Only a frantic letter from his friend surely could have called forth this Le Gallienne salutation: "My Dear J. L. — I beseech you — think of your trousers! There is really no necessity to —— yourself. At least, I think not. Robb is working hard, & I can see no reason why the whole thing should not be in bales by the weekend." [66]

A few days later, on October 28, Le Gallienne was able to report to Lane that with certainty the book would be "in binders hands by Saturday. *Every sheet,* saving the title-page, contents etc. *is printed off* — they were printing the portrait this afternoon when I called, & will do the title page etc. tomorrow." [67] But no sooner had the printing been substantially completed than a serious new problem arose. Advance orders for *George Meredith* soared beyond expectations as the date of publication approached, so much so that Mathews' order to Robb to print a first edition of 750 copies had to be revised upward. On October 28, a letter from Mathews reached Robb which, along with a check, asked Robb to increase the number of copies to 1,000.[68] Reporting this news to Lane, Le Gallienne was much perturbed:

Does he [Mathews] really imagine then that the book has *yet to be printed?* It would seem so. Whereas, of course, as I say, Robb has according to instructions, printed an edition of 750 copies, almost the whole of which lies in bales for the binder. Moreover Mathews never gave any order for stereos & the consequence is that my portion is distributed — tho' the bibliography still remains in type.[69]

Rising orders for the book on the eve of publication and the fact that no ready means were available to print off another 250 copies meant, in Le Gallienne's opinion, that Robb should be commissioned "to print another edition, & then we would be able to advertise a second in a week or two after the first — an advertisement which, as you know, not unfrequently sets a book going for one or two more." [70]

News that the type already had been distributed must have come as a shock to both Mathews and Lane. Their reaction to the news can be gauged — again indirectly — from Le Gallienne's reply, dated October 30, to a very angry Lane letter. Lane's fury seems to have been directed toward Robb, who appears to have disregarded Elkin Mathews' request of several weeks earlier to hold the type for the *Meredith* in readiness for the possible printing of additional copies. Yet Le Gallienne sought to defend Robb and cast all the blame for the present difficulties on Mathews. "True it is," he wrote,

that barely three weeks ago, E.M. asked Robb to keep the G.M. in type, but then a good half of it had been printed off; & quite apart from that[,] E.M. was thus asking an impossibility, for Robb has not unlimited type & he had one or two other jobs running on at the same time that needed the G.M. type as soon as done with. Moreover, E.M. had no right to expect Robb to stand still "to his order." What he should have done was to order stereotypes at first, it would only have been another £5 or so — he was reminded of it at the time, but with his usual good sense he preferred to go on hesitating in his foolish nervous fashion & — well, the result.

Of course, it is quite immaterial to me where Mathews prints. *I* personally should have saved countless time if the book had gone to Clark's in Chiswick, but, of course, Mathews consulted his own pocket in going to Robb, who, moreover, to my mind, is a good honest fellow, & an exceptionally good workman, who I would be glad to assist, & who in my opinion deserves support.[71]

That Mathews was angry enough to threaten taking the *Meredith* out of Robb's hands is clear from Le Gallienne's further remarks which also sug-

Title page by Aubrey Beardsley.

gest his opposition to such a move. "If M. decides to take the thing from him," he wrote, "it will simply be a loss of temper, which will mean loss of money." [72]

Le Gallienne was probably justified in defending Robb, but instead of blaming Mathews he should have charged himself. For the real cause of the whole trouble doubtless dated back to December 31, 1889, when he first suggested that his chapters be sent off to the printers and set up in type as soon as possible.[73] Since no one knew better than Le Gallienne how limited Robb's small shop was, he should have recognized what a burden such a course of action would place upon the printer if the completion of the Meredith study was delayed for some time. By October 1890, Robb's resources must have been strained beyond the point of toleration, so he ignored Mathews' order to keep the *Meredith* in type.

Le Gallienne's letter of October 30 was his second defense of Robb in as many days. The day before he had had to appease the wrath of Lane, who seems to have found the proofs of his bibliography inordinately full of errors. "I have seen Robb in accordance with your sensational letter," wrote Le Gallienne on the twenty-ninth, "& I must say that it seems to me that you have been rather unjust in your hasty wrath. Why! there are but *two* actual errors in the whole thing (according to the proof sent by you to R. this m[ornin]g)," the rest, he explained, "are simply the omissions of the new matter which is quite 'decently and in order' disposed of in the postscript." [74]

Le Gallienne suggested that Lane should be "indebted to Robb for extra carefulness than otherwise, for," he wrote, "I have seen a good score of undetected errors on your returned proof which would have [?] been passed but for Robb." [75] Lane's anger towards Robb was indeed unjustified if, as Le Gallienne contends, "the corrections you did make, — not to speak of the original M.S. — were in many cases so undecipherable & involved that I do not wonder that there should be 2 mistakes, but rather am surprised that there are not 20." [76] Apparently the close of October brought with it an end to all the tensions and difficulties arising from the publication of *George Meredith,* for in his letter of October 30 Le Gallienne asks: "Dear J.L. do we still love each other, in spite of all? Surely so." [77] Even in the letters of late October in which he was hard-pressed to placate his friend and defend himself and Robb, there were signs of a returning joviality called forth by more pleasant tasks attendant upon publishing a book: "I sign the American copies either this evening or first thing in the morning," he wrote Lane, and lightheartedly joked, "offers for the distinguished nib used in the solemn function will be entertained up till noon tomorrow, application to be by telegram." [78]

George Meredith: Some Characteristics was, according to copyright records, published on November 21, although Le Gallienne stated some days before that the book was to be out on the nineteenth.[79] As far back as October 22, Lane had asked Le Gallienne to come up to London and be his guest at 37 Southwick Street and partake in the festivities he was planning for the occasion. "Many thank yous for your kind invitation to town. I will come first week Nov., as suggested," was Le Gallienne's reply. Then — probably in jest — he asked: "Must I go to the O[dde] V[olume]'s? & what am I that I dare face the great Pollock?" [80] But acquiescing in Lane's plans, Le Gallienne continued, "never dream I undervalue your kindness — Therefore 'I have written to Brown' — as ran the title of a dead farce." [81]

Apparently, Le Gallienne was received at a dinner of the Sette of Odd Volumes at one of their Friday nights early in November. In a letter to his mother, the author spoke of the evening as "a very pleasant success, my book, of which Lane had procured a bound copy, being made one of the chief features of the evening, and your boy being referred to in an introductory speech in most encouraging terms."

The book looks charming as it stands complete and I long to send you a copy, but there were but two more bound, and these we have thought well to send to Theodore Watts, and the great man himself — whose acknowledgement we are naturally awaiting with some anxiety.[82]

Doubtless something of the "whirl" he found himself in during these November days[83] was due to Le Gallienne's hopes and fears about the reviews to follow fast upon the publication of his book. Lane and Le Gallienne had been attempting to maneuver the book into safe hands on publication as far back as the previous February. The daily reviews were, indeed, most favorable and gratifying to Le Gallienne and Lane. The *Globe* for November 26, 1890, declared that "It is such books as this — the product of an enthusiast — that gradually bring to a writer readers. It is difficult to resist the buoyant connection which pulses through these pages. George Meredith must surely be the literary divinity that he is pictured!" [84] Despite the feeling on the part of the *Times* that Le Gallienne "seems determined to follow his idol's example in the matter of zaribas," with a choice passage or two quoted to prove the point, they ventured to suggest that "the many admirers of Mr. Meredith's works will, however, be glad to have their attention directed to this handsome little book in his honour." [85]

The *St. James Gazette* notice of December 4 was entirely another matter. "Mr. Le Gallienne has much more zeal than discretion. He is out of date.

He is unnecessary. His advocacy produces no sense of novelty, or of vision, or of discrimination. He labours painfully with critical tares, which have long ago withered under the scythe of time." Sensing the attitude of an aesthete, the reviewer remarked with a touch of scorn: "He talks of entrenching himself with a choice minority behind the poems, now that the vulgar public has found out the novels." [86] The following day Le Gallienne wrote Lane: "I dare say you will be anxious to know whether I have survived the St. James' broadside. Really as they say at certain interesting seasons, I am 'doing wonderfully well under the circumstances'." [87]

One of the most favorable reviews appeared in the *Pall Mall Gazette* on December 5. Written, according to a Le Gallienne letter, by Arthur Symons,[88] it found the *Meredith* "a most interesting and irritating book." Mr. Le Gallienne, it said, "knows his Meredith thoroughly, he possesses the requisite enthusiasm, the indispensable insight," but, unfortunately, he was unable "to say what he had to say in a single, straightforward, concise manner" [89] — which seems to have been the most persistent accusation leveled at the author. After recommending the study "to those who already know and love the work," as a "sympathetic and intelligent" appreciation, the reviewer called attention to "an invaluable Bibliography of seventy pages, in which Mr. Lane has had the happy thought of including the principal reviews." [90] To Le Gallienne, this notice coming on the heels of the *St. James* blast was, indeed, "a great cheerer — &," he continued in a letter to Lane, "*The Athenaeum* let me down much more lightly than I feared — making the one important admission of 'critical faculty.' I don't think we need fear much now, do you?" [91]

Perhaps Le Gallienne was a bit premature in his feeling that the worst was over, for in mid-January 1891, Henley of the *National Observer* launched one of the most devastating attacks against Le Gallienne's critical stance. "Le Gallienne has a poor opinion of the 'comparative method' of criticism which has, he says, sadly overgrown its uses," wrote the reviewer, yet "his idea of criticism is to produce a perpetual splutter of superlatives, a lather of metaphors." [92]

The book received its share of severe criticism, but it profited not only from the fact that the majority of notices were favorable but also from the widespread attention it received. Of all the personal messages Le Gallienne was showered with, the one from Meredith himself was most rewarding. "Yes! this letter from 'the Master' was worth waiting for," he exclaimed as he began to relate the news to Lane. "I would we were together to give it the Bacchanalian honours. I will try to believe in myself after this," he concluded.[93]

Another encomium which Le Gallienne thought "quite kind," was a letter from Oscar Wilde, who asked, "I want so much to see you: when can that be? Friendship and love like ours need not meetings but they are delightful." Then continuing with sentiments which struck Le Gallienne as having "quite the sincerest ring about" them,[94] he concluded, "I hope the laurels are not too thick across your brow for me to kiss your eyelids." [95]

No sooner had the first edition appeared than the "Books and Rumours of Books" column of the *Publishers' Circular* carried the following announcement on December 1: "Mr. Richard Le Gallienne's book of critical essays, 'George Meredith: Some Characteristics,' only published on November 22, is already out of print. Mr. Elkin Mathews has a second edition in the press." [96] As soon as Le Gallienne got back to Liverpool from London, he went to see Robb who, as Le Gallienne reported to Lane, "seems to be 'shaping' satisfactorily — 'clothed and in his right mind' for the time being. Sundry embarrassments having been lifted from his shoulders." [97] By December 8, Robb was back on the job, working away at the second edition.[98] In his letter to Lane of December 12, Le Gallienne asked, "what about the bibliography? Robb is more than ready for it. Don't give him an excuse for delay." [99]

Unfortunately, Lane did just that. In his preface to his bibliography, "George Meredith and His Reviewers, 1850–1890," Lane had, in admitting the incompleteness of his work, announced his intention to enlarge his work in future editions and called on those with a special knowledge of the subject to communicate with him.[100] As a result, he was inundated by information concerning materials he had omitted from the first edition, and it took him some time to rearrange and enlarge his work for the second edition. Indeed, so numerous were the additional entries to the bibliography that the second edition of *George Meredith* contained sixteen more pages than the first.

By January 1891 the main body of the text had been reset, but Lane's delay and Robb's inability to move rapidly enough with the bibliography once he had received it caused Le Gallienne untold agony. Consequently, on January 20, Le Gallienne had to write Elkin Mathews to say, "in pursuance of my promise to look after Robb — I am, reluctantly enough, returning you the copy of the bibliography by tonight's post — because I can quite see that if it be left to him we will not have the Second Edition out in another month." According to Le Gallienne, "another lock in his affairs seems to have come upon him & consequently one of those unmanageable moods we have spoken of." [101] Explaining that Robb was quite agreeable to his sending Mathews the bibliography, Le Gallienne assured Mathews that Robb was willing to make the publisher "the fair allowance for his not printing it. With this & the gain in time," Le Gallienne pointed out, "I am quite sure it will cost you very little more than the origial estimate — for it is certain, I think, that we are losing sales by this delay." [102]

That this final intransigence on Robb's part was the last straw for Le Gallienne is apparent in his letter to Lane, which suggests that even his friend's honesty had at length been called in question. "Tho' I still believe in Robb's *honesty,* I don't think I shall be eager for any further business relations with him. The time & annoyance this attempt to assist him has cost me is more than I can afford." [103] Le Gallienne's belief that a second printing announced soon after the first "not infrequently sets a book going for one or two more" [104] was in time fully realized, for a third was called for in 1893.

Lord De Tabley's Poems, Dramatic and Lyrical

Lord De Tabley's *Poems, Dramatic and Lyrical,* 1893, was one of a number of Bodley Head books whose appearance caused a considerable stir in literary circles. A gathering of poems written over a lifetime, the book was an immediate and surprising success which, near the end of De Tabley's life, brought him a measure of the fame hitherto denied him. A remarkable man in many ways — a scholar who had published learned treatises on such diverse subjects as numismatics and the brambles of Europe — Lord De Tabley owed his belated recognition to the artistic and literary milieu of the early nineties.

When he published his pioneering work, *A Guide to the Study of Book-Plates,* in 1880, it "fell flat on the market, and," according to one of his biographers, "for many years not a single copy was sold." [105] But when in 1892 the Bodley Head reissued it at the height of an interest in rare books and curious forms of art, the *Guide* sold out immediately and gave rise to a fad which was attended by a whole rash of books on the subject. Commenting in 1894 on the vogue which his *Guide* had so unexpectedly created, De Tabley wrote his sister that he found "the fashion" for book-plates "really very tiresome." Always reluctant to accept any favor of fate as such, he went on to remark: "It is like the irony of life that the only thing I should have succeeded in, is what I look upon as a complete trifle." Indicating something of the proportions of the vogue which he had created, he peevishly exclaimed, "I can't shake off my connection with the subject, and I have letters every day and all the papers are full of Egerton Castle Hardy and the other men who are now carrying on the subject." [106]

Seemingly unaware of the change in sensibility which was the obvious explanation of the book's ultimate success, De Tabley recalled that when he began collecting book-plates, "C—— came into the room and said she hoped I would keep it dark, for people would suppose me to be mad! The curious thing was that for ten years after my book came out, it remained perfectly dead. Then, all of a sudden every copy went and I could have sold three or four editions with the greatest ease." [107] In a pessimistic, self-deprecatory vein very typical of his letters to Mathews and Lane during the year in which his *Poems, Dramatic and Lyrical* was in preparation, he concluded:

I have failed in literature[,] I have failed in politics, I have failed in such a miserable thing as being a landlord, which any fool can manage. Nothing remains except those contemptible book-plates! It is like poor Lear, whose pictures are all wrong, whose serious writing is all wrong, but who made his one hit with a book of nonsense. [108]

Like Wordsworth's Lucy, Lord De Tabley had lived, according to Max Beerbohm, "among untrodden ways." [109] After some early unsuccessful efforts in the spheres of politics and literature, he had withdrawn into himself only to emerge once again into the social and literary world of London during the last two or three years of his life. Something of a surprise among what Le Gallienne referred to as *"cette galere,"* [110] De Tabley shared with his younger Bodley Head brothers the distinction of being virtually unknown when his book of poems appeared in 1893. Since his first poetic success, "Casimir and Zelinda, or Love and Chloroform," had been performed with great acclaim at Tabley House during the Christmas holidays of 1847 when he was twelve,[111] De Tabley had published several volumes of poetry including an interesting blank verse drama, *Philoctetes.*[112] But after a long blank verse play entitled *The Soldier of Fortune* had received an exceptionally cold reception when it appeared in 1876, De Tabley lapsed into silence, only to come before the public in 1891 when, through no efforts of his own, Alfred H. Miles included a judicious selection of his poems in the influential *The Poets and the Poetry of the Century.*[113]

Miles's warmly appreciative preface to the poems and the aesthetic appeal of their classical mode and Virgilian tone of *lacrimae rerum sunt* caused a stir in literary circles which led several of his friends to suggest that he publish again. "On finding that the public would listen to him," wrote Theodore Watts,

I urged him to bring out a volume of selected pieces from all his works, an idea which for some time he contested with his usual pessimistic vigour. Having, however, set my heart upon it, I spoke upon the subject to Mr.

John Lane, who at once saw his way to bring out such a volume at his own risk.[114]

With the reception of Miles's selections in mind and the fact that the Bodley Head itself had successfully brought the name of the poet before the public again with the reissued *A Guide to the Study of Book-Plates,* Lane doubtless thought a selection of De Tabley's poetry was a good risk. Thus was the genesis of what came to be one of the early Bodley Head's most dramatic successes. At the very end of his life, De Tabley, whose poetry had in the sixties and seventies fallen on deaf ears, became literally overnight a poet of considerable acclaim, a man mentioned by Swinburne and Morris to succeed Tennyson as Poet Laureate, an author addressed by Oxford undergraduates and Winchester boys with letters of passionate admiration. On the publication of *Poems,* Gladstone, long one of De Tabley's few admirers, wrote the author that he rejoiced to find his old belief justified at last.[115]

In his reminiscences of the nineties, Richard Le Gallienne, who played an important part in the creation of *Poems, Dramatic and Lyrical,* tells how the work of producing the book began. Aware that De Tabley's friends were "endeavouring to arouse his ambition," Le Gallienne ventured to second them in their efforts by proposing to De Tabley that he "make a selection from his poems of what he considered best worth preserving." [116] According to Le Gallienne,

the idea seemed at once to please and alarm him. But he was such a poor judge of his own work, he said, and couldn't trust himself to know the good from the bad. Then, with an indescribable shyness, and as though he were asking me a preposterous favour, instead of, as I naturally felt, doing me a charming honour, he surprised me by saying that he would undertake it, if I would help him make the selections. Of course, I readily agreed, and thus I came to enjoy a measure of intimacy with him and gain some insight into his lonely nature, so full of charming simplicity and friendly humanity beneath its melancholy reserve.[117]

The work on the selections was no quick and easy matter. As Le Gallienne tells it, there were "many meetings, and more letters" between the two men who "would take volume by volume" of the poetry, "each make our independent selections, and then compare them. There was also a quantity of new work to go through." According to Le Gallienne, De Tabley had an odd "way of dividing his tentative lists of selections into what he called 'dustbins,' labeling them, according to his idea of their relative excellence, as *Dustbin I* and *Dustbin II*." [118]

In the words of his friend Watts, De Tabley, "had a strong dash of the sensitive, not to say the morbid, in his nature." [119] And it was this quirk that set the tone for his extended dialogue with the Bodley Head concerning the publication of *Poems*. His share of the correspondence with Lane and Mathews, which is largely preserved in the Berg Collection of the New York Public Library and the Walpole Nineties Collection at the Bodleian, reveals a man whose confidence in himself had perhaps too easily been broken by a series of what De Tabley considered fate-bedeviled attempts to win recognition as a poet. Of a highly suspicious nature, De Tabley submitted almost every incident in his life to an analysis which led him more often than not to see the incident in the worst possible light. The most transparent statement, the kindest remark of a friend or an acquaintance, was anatomized lest some irony or subtle slight go undetected.

Believing that he had been misunderstood by society and thwarted at every turn by a malicious fate, De Tabley was by 1892 the temperamental artist *par excellence*. Although he was terrified of being hurt and rejected again by the world, De Tabley, despite a painfully defensive attitude, was tempted once again to risk humiliation in a last desperate effort to win recognition. The lure of fame and the pathetic desire to win the approbation and acclaim of his fellows brought him to this last task of embodying in *Poems, Dramatic and Lyrical* the quintessence of the poetry of a lifetime.

De Tabley's defensive attitude, his need to pave the way with excuses and pessimistic, self-deprecatory statements is revealed in some of his earliest letters to Le Gallienne. "I have been so out of touch for many years with modern verse-writing that it would have been imprudent for me in the highest degree to have meditated a reprint without having a younger mind to consult." [120] On another occasion he confessed to Le Gallienne:

You have seen so many of my failures that it will not make things worse if you see some more. And if by any happy accident any of the 5 could just scrape over the admission level, it would be most acceptable just now. It is rather a forlorn hope I know whether any of these 5 unpublished pieces would do. Still *One* might, though I don't expect it.[121]

During the summer of 1892, with Le Gallienne's advice De Tabley was hard at work choosing enough poems old and new to fill a book of about

200 pages. By mid-August he seems to have been ready to decide on an arrangement of the poems and to paste them up so as to estimate their length. "Kindly endeavour to procure me either by advertising or sending round," he asked Elkin Mathews, "a copy of 'Rehearsals,' published by Strahan and 'Searching the Net,' published by Isbister." De Tabley needed copies of his early poems "merely for paste and scissor purposes." [122]

Nearly a month later, the poet, spending the summer at Ryde in the Isle of Wight, had "practically got into fair order to go to press, a volume of slightly over 200 pages" [123] before the first real bit of temperament showed itself. De Tabley almost from the first sought to insure his having his own way and forestalled any pressure from his publishers to do otherwise by feigning a loss of inspiration or affecting a desire to throw the whole thing up as a hopeless, tiresome venture doomed to come to nothing.

De Tabley's letter to Lane of September 10 is an excellent example of the poet's strategy. Desirous of getting the material in the form he had arranged it to the printer without leaving the publishers ample time to examine it and perhaps suggest changes, De Tabley commenced his letter to Lane with a tale of woe: "About a week ago very serious bothers began connected with some property of mine which have worried me extremely and knocked every grain of poetry out of my head. And if things don't [get better] I shall be able to do nothing more to the MS. For when I stop dead short like this, I am very seldom able to go again." Assuring Lane that he would "be very much interested to receive Mr. Le Gallienne's kind notes," he, nevertheless, went on to warn that "if his notes suggest any considerable rearrangement of my own scheme, as is quite possible, I fear that with the best will in the world, I shall hardly be able to carry it out now." Consequently, De Tabley put forth the following suggestion. "To get the MS to you as I have arranged it, by about the middle of this month — say the 16 or 17th and then let Mr. Le Gallienne have a general look through it, just as it is going to press." [124]

For a publisher, whose risks are always high, De Tabley's pessimistic analysis of everything must have been a trial. "I may tell you," he wrote in September,

That I do not think above 120 pages of the 200 [pages of poetry] are up to the level which make them worth reprinting. 80 pages seem to me under that level. But you are quite right that a book of 120 pages would be but a skimpy affair and therefore I may also tell you that the longer pieces have worked out rather worse than I expected. I had forgotten so much of these that I was able to judge of them much as if they had been written by somebody else. The smaller lyrical pieces have worked

out rather better than I expected but public and critics never judge a
book by these; but entirely by the longer ones.[125]

As to whether or not any of the new poems should be included, De
Tabley was "most anxious to hear Mr. Le Gallienne's opinion. . . . I fully
expect [them]," he told Lane, "to be much worse than the old [ones] and
if this is the case, it is really questionable whether to have any of [them]." [126]

Back in Bournemouth, where he spent his winters, De Tabley, on October
4, addressed his publishers in a mood which suggested that he was ready to
throw up the whole project peremptorily: "The M.S. is ready, whenever
and supposing your wish to send for it but if there is any hitch, I am more
ready than ever to drop the whole business." [127] Perhaps attempting to
anticipate criticism and elicit praise, De Tabley went on to say that he had
sent Le Gallienne "a few additional pieces (which have never been published)" for his inspection. "These were, however, all condemned by me
without hesitation, as not up to the level for publication some two months
ago. Therefore," he concluded,

the chance of his finding anything in them, is very slight and not worth
waiting for, supposing you mean to go on with the book. I only sent
them to Mr. Le Gallienne at the very last, as my original material had
proved so bad that it struck me these could not be much worse.

Supposing you wish for the M. S. kindly indicate the safest way for me
to send it to you — Book post, parcel delivery or what? And I suppose
registered? It will be no great loss if it went astray. But it is annoying
losing anything, quite irrespective of the value of the thing lost.[128]

That De Tabley had every intention of going on with the work is suggested
by a reference to Charles Ricketts, who by October had been chosen to do
the cover design and illustrations for the volume.

De Tabley evidently wanted the frontispiece to be illustrative of the initial
poem, "A Hymn to Astarte," but the frontispiece of the published volume
was based on another poem, "The Defeat of Glory." Inquiring of Mathews
and Lane, "Did you send on the first draft of the first piece in the volume
to Ricketts," De Tabley in a postscript went on to a consideration of what
he called "the paper difficulty."

I suppose that in books got up with any choiceness, the plates must always be printed on the same paper as the text though of course in cheap popular books the plates are on quite different paper from the text. It will be as you say difficult in this case to find a paper suitable.[129]

De Tabley seems not to have welcomed Charles Ricketts as the designer. Whether he feared the highly original and successful Ricketts as an artist whose illustrations would detract from his poetry or whether he dreaded a striking cover design is not known. Nevertheless, he was often critical of Ricketts during the prepublication phase of *Poems* and at times spoke slightingly of him.

Having gotten the go-ahead to send the manuscript, De Tabley turned his attention at once to a consideration of the book's format. "As to size of page," he wrote Lane, "if I had no illustrator to think of, I should say, copy *Rehearsals* both as to size and type." [130] This book of verse, which De Tabley had published in 1870, was a small volume cased in dark blue cloth-covered boards, stamped in black and gold, typical of its time. De Tabley's suggestion that it serve as a model for *Poems* indicates his fear of showiness and display of any kind, his desire to appear before the public once again in a way least likely to tempt fate. That when it actually appeared *Poems, Dramatic and Lyrical* was in its format and design anything but unobtrusive may have been a cause of extreme anxiety to De Tabley.

Recalling that Le Gallienne's recently published *English Poems* was an inch taller than *Rehearsals* though of the same breadth, De Tabley went on to suggest that Lane "consult Ricketts as to the *smallest* page, above the *Rehearsals* size, which is calculated to give his plates proper room & proper margin." Since De Tabley had based his estimates on the page and type size of *Rehearsals,* he told Lane that he would be in "a great fix if the size of the page requires more 'copy' than the *Rehearsals* pages did." [131]

In his letter dispatched to Mathews and Lane on October 7, the day he sent off the manuscript of *Poems,* De Tabley was still much exercised about the length of the book. "As I want to make 200 pages, I suppose there is no objection to my filling up at the end the amount by which I run short. I expect this to be from 6 to 8 pages," a lack which, he told his publishers, could easily be supplemented by "old materials passed by Mr. Le Gallienne, (but not used as yet in the M.S. as it goes to you)." [132]

The manuscript of *Poems, Dramatic and Lyrical* probably went to T. and A. Constable about mid-October. For on the twenty-first, Blaikie wrote to Lane enclosing the estimate for printing the book and a specimen page which the printer begged Lane not to show to De Tabley. "I have only had it set to form an estimate from," he emphasized. Blaikie's chief problem was, of course, to make what he called a "good & suitable & homogeneous book" out of the material sent him. In order to do his best, Blaikie reminded Lane, "it is well for us to see the illustrations & to try & adjust a suitable type & page for them. In all book making there is always a tendency to leave such grouping to chance." Begging Lane to send him by return mail any of Ricketts' drawings or even a single rough proof, Blaikie concluded: "*Then* I can try & do something suitable. It will probably not affect the financial aspect of the estimate but I will try & give some character to the page." [133]

Ricketts probably had not begun work on the designs for De Tabley's poems, for Lane was not able to comply with Blaikie's request. Consequently the printer went ahead as best he could. On November 7, he sent Mathews and Lane two specimen pages — one page of stanzaic verse and one of long lines. It was Blaikie's opinion "that a book printed along with Mr. Ricketts' drawings must be in very strong firm type. We would have preferred," he reiterated,

seeing one of his drawings, but as that evidently can't be got at present we assume that they will be strong & bold. We have accordingly put a strong line round the page which strengthens & consolidates the page & will give the volume great character throughout & help to harmonize with the illustrations. We have taken the pencil sketch you sent as the proper size to make the border lines.[134]

Amplifying his concept of the page somewhat, Blaikie went on to explain that "with the broken lines of poetry of different metres it is impossible without the rules to get a good strong homogeneous page — as you may get a very dainty one." [135]

Although as late as October 16 Lord De Tabley had still been insisting that Lane send along to Constables a copy of *Rehearsals* as a model for the type and page content of the new book,[136] Lane and Ricketts, not to mention the printer, seem not to have agreed. Instead, probably at the behest of Ricketts, Lane dispatched a copy of Hélène Vacaresco's *The Bard of Dimbovitza*, the cover design and title page of which Ricketts had recently done for Osgood & McIlvaine.[137]

As it turned out, Blaikie had already decided on a somewhat stronger and blacker Caslon old-style type for *Poems, Dramatic and Lyrical* than that used in *Rehearsals,* a type and size identical with the type Ricketts had employed in *The Bard.*[138] Although the page of *Poems* is not so large as that of *The Bard,* it accommodates almost precisely the same amount of type. Whether because of Lane, Mathews, or Ricketts or all three, Blaikie's idea to enclose the page in rules was vetoed. On November 10, Constables received the order to "compose in type [Lord De Tabley's *Poems*] as last specimen, but without border lines." [139]

Another matter of serious consideration was the title for *Poems.* Lord De Tabley first broached the subject on October 8, when he announced abruptly, "It will be a very difficult question to find an appropriate title for the book." Expressing "a strong objection to using the word 'Poems' in any form or mixture whatever," he went on to set forth his reasons.

I think that would claim a higher level for the reprint than I ought to give it. The title must be Verse or Verses in some form or other — unless I go into a fancy title, such as I have given to all my previous attempts. The awkwardness about a fancy title is that the outer public don't know whether the book is prose or verse, unless you tag on a second explanatory line.[140]

On October 19, in a postscript, De Tabley asked Lane what he thought about "Occasional Verses for a general title for the volume. This was common enough before the close of the last century but it has not I think been revived lately." [141]

Although he and Le Gallienne seem to have agreed in an exchange of letters on simply calling the volume "Poems by Lord De Tabley," [142] Lane evidently was the first to propose *Poems, Dramatic and Lyrical,* a title which immediately reminded De Tabley of Tennyson's *Poems, Chiefly Lyrical;* for on October 31, De Tabley wrote Lane to say that he was afraid "that the likeness between your proposed title and that of Tennyson's first book is, notwithstanding what you kindly say sufficient for the ill natured critic to call attention to it." [143] Since Tennyson had died on October 6, De Tabley, overcautious as usual, was of the opinion that

just now a microscopic light is being concentrated upon all Tennyson's beginnings and it is sure to strike somebody. And if it does strike any critic on an influential paper, the book will be simply done with through a slip in the title before anyone opens its pages.[144]

Just how important this matter of a title seems to have been to De Tabley is further suggested in a letter to Lane of November 3, in which he sought to give a resumé of the situation. Having received a letter from Le Gallienne concerning the title that morning, De Tabley agreed to Le Gallienne's consulting *"one more* literary friend. And if he sees no objection to *'Poems Dramatic and Lyrical,'* let that be the title and no further reference to myself is necessary. If the literary friend has hesitations as I have, I am quite willing that the title should be *Astarte and Other Poems,* or *Poems New and Old.* But I prefer Astarte though I will accept either." [145] Although De Tabley objected to the published title because it was reminiscent of Tennyson, I suspect that is why Lane suggested it. No doubt he believed that to link a new book of poetry with Tennyson's name at a time when the loss of the Laureate was most felt, was good business.

Ricketts' famous cover design for *Poems, Dramatic and Lyrical* must have been ready by late October, for in his letter to Lane of October 24, De Tabley, having left it up to Lane whether to print a large-paper issue or a Japanese-paper issue, went on to mention the cover design rather cryptically. "As regards the cover the Rose petals, is my sisters suggestion and I should be glad on her account, if Mr. Ricketts would kindly adopt it, as I know she wishes to have a hand in our venture. But we had better not call it Rose-Petals, as that design will go just as well with any other name." [146]

Does this suggest that Ricketts' design was a purely abstract one and that for purposes of advertising, the publishers wanted a descriptive name for it? However this may be, De Tabley seems to have had the dubious honor of naming the design. And although he withdrew his suggestion when it occurred to him that "that design will go just as well with any other name" (I have always seen it as seeds parachuting to earth), the advertisements of *Poems* often included a statement to the effect that there were "6 Illustrations, and Covers of Rose Petals designed by C.S. Ricketts." [147] A statement of De Tabley's shortly after suggests that his response to the whole cover design was something less than enthusiastic. "Is it worth your suggesting to Ricketts," he ventured to remark to Lane, "that a dewdrop or two, here and there, would improve the Rose petals of his cover?" [148]

As the actual business of printing got under way in December, De Tabley's temper seems to have become even more pessimistic. Not having received on time the proofs Constables had evidently promised him, he dispatched a letter, dated December 21, to Mathews, in which he declared that the printing firm was "quite hopeless. If they don't mean to send, they should say so. But saying they will send on a definite day[,] another not doing so, is quite too bad. I have employed numerous printers, but I have never been treated in this way yet." [149]

The delay in receiving proof could possibly have been caused by an order from Mathews and Lane to either slow down or stop work entirely on De

Tabley's *Poems*. Soon after, De Tabley's letters to Lane and Mathews suggest that because of fewer subscriptions than had been anticipated the Bodley Head was contemplating a postponement and possibly cancellation of the book. Consequently, during December, De Tabley seems to have thought his book would never appear. Writing to a friend from Poole, near Bournemouth, he declared:

I have entirely ceased to think about my book. The publishers, I expect, have quite dropped it. Its failure would vex one a little, mainly because I have wasted the whole valuable summer upon it, in a year after influenza. Life is all a matter of luck. Some have it, and others have it not.[150]

De Tabley's belief that his book had been rejected was probably due to the fact that Lane, who had been very ill with influenza earlier in December, had been less attentive to De Tabley than usual, and possibly to a delay on Mathews and Lane's part in making a decision in the matter and promptly informing the author. Having received no word about his publishers' intentions, De Tabley, anxious and no doubt mystified, wrote Lane on the last day of the year:

You mentioned, when you wrote on the 15th inst: that you hoped to be about again in a fortnight. That period has now elapsed and two days beyond it, and as tomorrow is the New Year, and it is very important for me to know what course you mean to take about the publication of my book, I trust that you will, if you are well enough, give me a brief line to enlighten me on this point; always remembering that if you wish to give the book up you are at liberty to do so.[151]

Lane's immediate reply must have increased De Tabley's anxiety, for not only did he then by return mail inform Lane that there was "a good deal" in his letter "which I cannot assent to and upon which I should like to have my say," but went on to propose two courses of action:

that you have *now* the option of giving up the Book on the basis of my paying Constable's bills, £5. each for the designs and a sum, not exceeding £20. for transferring these, printing them, etc. On this basis, I could at once settle up with your partner without troubling you further in the matter and receiving of course the Book in Quires as my property.[152]

Since the Bodley Head had agreed to assume all risks and pay all costs in connection with the volume with the exception of the plates, and had agreed to pay De Tabley a royalty of 10% on all receipts over and above the production costs,[153] De Tabley's first option was an extremely considerate and generous one. As to the second option, De Tabley's letter continued: "If such an arrangement is not palatable to you, I trust I may receive within a few days, an assurance from your partner and yourself, that you will both do your utmost to bring out the Book without fail, on or before April 3rd 1893, Easter Sunday." [154]

Clearly De Tabley was wholly unwilling for the Bodley Head to lose money on the venture, whatever the terms of the contract might have been:

Suppose that three weeks before that date, you find that not half the Edition is subscribed for; then don't again put off publication. But come to me stating what you stand to lose, and let me by taking a greater risk than at present, minimise the chance of your suffering any. I do not think I am unduly sanguine about my work. But as I sold 300 copies of "Rehearsals" with next to nothing done for that Book by the Publisher and at a time when people read poetry much less than they read it now, surely, I may expect to sell 300 copies now, quite apart from those which you get upon the market by personal application. And if you manage to get a quarter of the Edition subscribed and I sell 300 more, that would only leave you with 150 copies on your hands, as I learn from your Catalogue you publish an Edition of 600. . . . But if all you say about the difficulty of getting subscriptions means that you now think the Book is bad, or what comes to the same thing in poetry, neutral, then for Heavens sake, let us honestly face the situation and give up the Book now altogether. It is unfair, keeping me in suspense, if this is how things are to end.[155]

With perhaps a touch of sarcasm, he concluded, "Most of the young gentlemen who come to you have nothing to do but to rhyme. But I alas, have a great deal else to do." [156]

It is doubtful that the publishers intended to go so far as to give the book up when it was already in print. I suspect that once Mathews and Lane realized that subscriptions for *Poems* were lagging and that the book would not be bound and ready for the Christmas season, they decided to wait and publish the book at the height of the spring season of 1893. De Tabley himself had suggested such a course earlier, when he heard about Tennyson's death. "Don't you think a *postponement* of my small book until, say, Easter in the next year might now be advisable," he asked Lane on October 11. "The public will read & attend to nothing this side of Xmas except Tennyson, and that very rightly." [157]

If Lane and Mathews were still undecided about the disposition of *Poems,* De Tabley's strong letter of January no doubt called forth a firm decision which was immediately communicated to the poet. From his letter to Lane of January 4, it is clear that it placated the disturbed De Tabley and reassured him in the matter.

Thanks for your letter of the 3rd inst. which is quite satisfactory. I am obliged to you and your partner for having given me a definite assurance that you will publish the Book not later than April 3rd. I am also grateful to you both for still feeling some confidence in the quality of the volume. And I only hope this may not prove misplaced. But I am never satisfied or anything like satisfied with any work of mine and just now I am unwell and have a number of business troubles which make me take rather a gloomy view. And as I took this view myself I thought it just possible that you might share my doubts and that in such a case, it would have been best for us to wind up. But as you assure me that it is not so, I will dismiss any such idea from my mind.[158]

Then turning to unfinished business, De Tabley returned to the subject of the title page for *Poems* which had some days before led him into a serious altercation with Mathews and indirectly with Ricketts. On December 22, having completed his work on the proofs. De Tabley had returned them to Mathews along with a concluding note and a prefatory one, the table of contents and the title page as he wished it to appear. De Tabley's suggested title page, in addition to a lengthy title and the facts of publication, contained his full name, John Leicester Warren, followed by his title, Lord De Tabley, and his degrees, and gave "the late W. B. Scott" and his engraving equal billing with the illustrator, C. S. Ricketts.[159]

Obviously this shapeless, overcrowded title page design would not do. De Tabley's page was a typically Victorian one with short and long lines of type strung out down the page; the actual title page by Ricketts is, in its placing of the type so as to give a block or rectangular effect, its antithesis. Not only is Ricketts' title page strikingly modern in appearance but there is no mention of W. B. Scott and his engraving, which De Tabley had insisted on including in the volume.

De Tabley was in no mood to be crossed in the matter of the title page. On January 3, 1893, he fired off a letter to Mathews. "Dear Sir," he began, "after your handsome letter of the 1st I will at once dismiss from my mind, the matter of the title-page. I have not been unreasonable," he pointed out,

in accepting corrections from his [Lane's] reader [presumably Le Gallienne] and from Mr. Lane during the preparation of this volume. Even when I could not agree that such were advisable. But Mr. Ricketts has given so much and such unnecessary trouble that I could not accept *his* alterations or interference.[160]

However, having received Lane's letter of January 3 which reassured him about the publication of *Poems,* De Tabley was much more reasonable concerning the title page the following day. Of the opinion that "the title page question had better be settled forthwith," he proposed that the publishers send him "such a title page as *you can each pass* and approve of. And I will either adopt it, or alter it very slightly." [161]

The Bodley Head's objections to De Tabley's draft title page can be surmised from what the poet went on to say. Agreeing to "give way about taking old Scott off the title page," De Tabley turned to the next bone of contention: "You say my title page is too much burdened with text, therefore, you can simply say 'Poems, Dramatic and Lyrical by Lord De Tabley.' My own description was made perhaps too long as confusion has arisen already in consequence of my late name and my present one." Although he had included the letters "M.A." and "F.S.A." "to show I'd had some education which many writers start upon verses without," he was agreeable, under the circumstances, to have them out as well. "I will leave you," he concluded, "to describe Ricketts' part of the title page. But as I have thrown over all my superfluous baggage, I trust you will describe that worthy [Ricketts] at no particular length either." [162]

In accordance with De Tabley's suggestion in his letter of the fourth that everything connected with the book be finished up "with all reasonable speed," T. and A. Constable completed the letterpress by January 27, 1893. On that date Blaikie wrote Mathews and Lane to say that he was sending them "a set of printed sheets of Lord de Tabley's Poems which are now complete and await your instructions." [163]

Blaikie then went on to say, "We hope you will like this volume. It has been printed with extraordinary care & we think the actual workmanship could not be surpassed." Apparently Ricketts' designs for the book were still not forthcoming from the engravers, Dawsons,[164] for Blaikie expressed his fear lest "the illustrations (which we have never seen) may kill the letterpress & we hope there will not be a frontispiece facing the title." [165]

The composition, printing and paper for 750 copies of the ordinary issue of *Poems* and 100 copies on Japanese paper amounted to £57.1.11, and an additional £7.5.6. was charged for the red printing on the title page, alterations and proofs and printing eight pages of cancels.[166] Mathews and Lane's initial order of 850 copies of *Poems* and a belated attempt to raise the number to 800 ordinary and 110 Japanese paper copies[167] suggest that the pre-publication demand for the book was not so small as Lane had led De Tabley to believe. In October, the poet had written Lane that he couldn't "help thinking that if you print more than 500 copies, you will be left with a huge lot, undisposed of." Apprising the publisher of the fact that his "most successful poetry book never sold above 200 or 300 copies," De Tabley, nevertheless, felt that "unless a dead set is made against the Book by Gosse and Henley," *Poems* ought to sell 500 copies.[168] Since the Bodley Head was not averse to publishing only 300 copies of a book of poetry, Mathews and Lane must have had some idea on December 17, when their order to Constables went off, that De Tabley's *Poems* would sell unusually well.

Ricketts' work was the last to be completed. Having succeeded very well in keeping the printer and the author in the dark about his illustrations, Ricketts unveiled them engraved and ready for the printer in February just in time to have them inserted in the book before it went off to the binders in mid-March. Whether this was a consciously planned stratagem or whether he was very busy and pressed for time is not known. Nevertheless, he did seem to have a free rein in the matter, having chosen the poems he would illustrate without any consultation with the author. When De Tabley arranged the poems in sequence for publication, he was still unaware which poems were to be illustrated. Consequently, when the letterpress and illustrations were finally gotten together, it was found that three of the five engravings came close together at the end of the volume. "This occurred," according to De Tabley, "because Mr. Ricketts didn't think it necessary to tell me what he meant to illustrate and what he did not mean to illustrate." [169] The mix-up was partially remedied by using one of the designs, "The Defeat of Glory," as the frontispiece. Although De Tabley was somewhat dubious about the nature of Ricketts' cover design, once he received the binding specimen of the cover, his reaction was enthusiastic: "I think it is successful, striking and I quite approve of the same." [170]

In accordance with De Tabley's demand of January, *Poems, Dramatic and Lyrical* appeared at the beginning of April. In fact the book was being circulated toward the end of March as Lord De Tabley learned from a letter from Lane dated March 28, 1893.[171] To Lane's request for De Tabley's views of the book, the poet, pessimistic to the end, wrote back: "It will be a failure most assuredly. All the surroundings and antecedents guarantee that. My only doubt is whether it will be a moderate failure or a resounding one." [172] When, a few days later, every copy had been sold and a second printing had been ordered, De Tabley was stunned. In a letter to his sister on April 7 he compared the surprise to having had a fortune left him. "Not one word have I heard from the publishers one way or other about the book, and I made sure the thing was done for. When this morning I see it stated in three different newspapers that every copy of the first edition has been sold." Since the English edition was 600 copies, he pointed out, "I am literally astounded, if this be true. I expected to sell about fifty or a hundred at most, and I really cannot believe it." [173]

So certain had been De Tabley that the book would be a disaster, he had even asked Lane, before publication, not to send a copy to his close friend Theodore Watts for review in the *Athenaeum*. "It will do no good — rather the reverse. I hope you are sending out no copies to private individuals? In the case of a Book of more than doubtful merit, doing this, seems to me a great mistake. I have given up any idea of sending any copies myself to my private friends. It merely inflicts upon them the trouble of writing a letter which is seldom sincere & which is written unwillingly." [174] It was not long before De Tabley was bestirring himself with unwonted vigor to get copies of *Poems* to the reviewer and his friends.

"I hear that the Times people have got no copy of my Book," he complained to Elkin Mathews on April 14. "And I also hear of another influential paper to which nothing has been sent. I also have been told in two places from people who wish to order the Book, that they cannot get their orders for copies attended to." [175] Now that *Poems* was selling, De Tabley was in a frenzy to meet the demand lest the interest should suddenly subside. "Unless you are going to throw up the Book altogether," he informed Mathews, booksellers' demands must be met without delay. "This is the most critical time and a fortnight hence the Book will be forgotten and no one will touch a copy." [176]

While he spurred on Mathews to get the remaining sheets of *Poems* bound and distributed, De Tabley worried and fretted about the forthcoming reviews. Again expecting the worst, he was pleasantly surprised. Watts's essay, which was the lead item in the April 22 *Athenaeum*, was enthusiastic. A full two pages, the *Athenaeum* review was a major factor in the continuing success of *Poems*; coming early as it did, it helped establish the very favorable reception the book received in the periodical press. Quoting liberal portions from the dramatic monologue "Jael," Watts, noticing the evidences of "a true imagination at work — an imagination of a high order — " and the high artistry involved in the handling of form and structure, declared, "this poem alone gives Lord De Tabley a high place among contemporary poets." [177]

Fully appreciative of De Tabley's lyrical gifts, Watts nevertheless dwelled upon the poet's "real knowledge of nature" as "one of the strongest points displayed" in the lyrics. Aware of De Tabley's "thorough knowledge of botany," the critic was of the opinion that "not even Tennyson's nomenclature of natural objects is more invariably accurate." As to the book's art work, Watts was less kind. "Mr. Ricketts's illustrations are striking, but of very unequal merit," he observed.

While the illustration to "The Two Old Kings" is (save for the fantastic drawing of the hands) as good as it can be and full of the deepest mediaeval sentiment, an incongruous introduction of modern objects in a mediaeval composition, like that which often made the designs of the late W. Bell Scott so grotesque, will sometimes spoil the finest work of Mr. Ricketts. At his best, however, he is full of the Gothic feeling, and imagination is never lacking in his designs.[178]

Of course, it was Watts's remark about Ricketts' drawing of the hands which De Tabley latched on to. "You see he notices Ricketts's bad hands," he observed to Lane. "Perhaps that worthy will now believe us. This defect is really quite obvious." [179]

Edmund Gosse's notice in the *Saturady Review* was also most generous in its praise of De Tabley. "Poetry so full and scholarly as his, so tempered in its magnificence, so excellently furnished and adorned, cannot but command the suffrages of a considerable audience." [180] And although De Tabley was "rather afraid we shall get no review or a bad one, in the Spectator," R. H. Hutton, the editor, who De Tabley thought was "so strange a fellow and so full of crochets," [181] wrote, on the whole, a very favorable review of *Poems*. Persuaded that De Tabley was not a poet of the first rank, Hutton nevertheless thought him "certainly entitled to a high place" among the minor ones. "His work is marked by an individuality and refinement that raise him above the crowd of obscure singers." [182]

What with all these favorable reviews and Le Gallienne's "logrolling" effort in the *Nineteenth Century*,[183] *Poems, Dramatic and Lyrical* was an unqualified success. By April 11, Mathews had already instructed T. and A. Constable to print a second edition of 500 copies.[184] So pleased was Elkin Mathews with the sales that on June 7, 1893, he not only sent De Tabley his first royalty check of £7.5.0 but also offered to adjust the royalties upward in favor of the poet — a most extraordinary move on the part of a publisher.

I have this morning gone very thoroughly into the costs of production of the volume and I am prepared to adjust my original offer on the following lines:
To allow you a royalty of 1/– per copy on the first edition of 600 copies for England= £30. 0.0

Royalty of 6^d per copy
on American edition of 150= £ 3.15.0
Royalty of 2/– per copy
on 100 Japanese copies £10. 0.0
£43.15.0

With regard to the second edition we will pay Dawson for the plates (£27.16.9) and allow you a royalty of 1/– per copy. You may remember that the old plan of publication was for us to take the risk of the volume & allow you a royalty of 10% on the net receipts which would amount to 7^d per copy.[185]

Since the original agreement had called for De Tabley to pay the cost of engraving the plates, which came to £40.6.0, the new proposal, according to Mathews, was in part designed to enable De Tabley "to recoup" his "expenditure on the production of the plates."[186]

After much work, anxiety, loss of temper, exasperation, pessimism, and many misgivings on the part of both author and publisher, the saga of *Poems, Dramatic and Lyrical* can be said to have come to a happy ending for all on February 4, 1894, when, writing from Poole, De Tabley acknowledged receipt of the latest statement and royalty check from his book. With a remainder of 200 copies of the second printing yet unsold, De Tabley, of the opinion that the sale had by that time ceased, chose the opportunity to thank Mathews and Lane "for bringing out this book of mine to begin with, and for all the trouble which that has brought [?] upon your firm."[187]

Although the early Bodley Head was a haven for the poets and artists of the English *fin de siècle,* it was never the express purpose of the firm to espouse a particular artistic or literary cause or to promote single-mindedly the aesthetic and decadent ideas of the period. Mathews had little sympathy with the Decadents and their work, and Le Gallienne in his poetry and criticism was a major opponent of their view of life and art.[1] Of the three, Lane alone was attentive to or in any way sympathetic toward the work of the Decadents. Yet, despite Lane's interest in "curious works of art," as Wilde expressed it,[2] his willingness to consider and even publish literature and art which struck others as scandalous,[3] his tastes, like Mathews', were actually very ordinary and somewhat old-fashioned. It is difficult to see how Lane, who was moved to tears by the sentiments and commonplace message expressed in William Watson's sonnet, "Life is still life, not yet the hearth is cold," [4] could have been aesthetically much involved in the work of Oscar Wilde or Arthur Symons. Yet as a business man, Lane, more than his partner, was willing to publish work which did not greatly appeal to his own particular tastes — a point which should remind us that the Bodley Head was founded as a business and remained as such. Despite their delight in rare books and other *objets d'art* and their natural inclination toward cultivated, aesthetically oriented artists and intellectuals, Mathews and Lane were business men whose primary interest was in achieving success.

It is true that the Bodley Head was a gathering place for the poets and

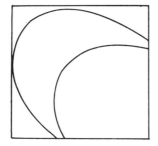

5 THE BODLEY HEAD POETS:
THE BOOKS OF THE RHYMERS' CLUB

artists of the early nineties. The quaint eighteenth-century atmosphere of the shop, its uncommercial aura, its touch of *haute* Bohemia, indeed, drew to it the artists who, having been offended by the Philistines, the materialistic middle class, turned to the Bodley Head as a place of refuge where the few who appreciated beauty and a more comely way of life could be met with. But these men and women were of many different aesthetic persuasions, creators of such a variety of art that the genius of the Bodley Head lay in its ability to garner almost the whole range of artistic production of the early nineties. The Bodley Head was the mouthpiece for many of the significant voices of art.

Even in its ability to bring within its sphere widely divergent views of art, the Bodley Head was, in an odd sort of way, suggestive of the times. Despite the distinct difference between the poetry of Arthur Symons and John Gray and that of William Watson and Alice Meynell, for example, neither the Bodley Head nor such journals as the *Yellow Book* and the *Savoy* scrupled to publish them side by side. The capacity for the literary or pseudoliterary and artistic groups of the time to tolerate a wide spectrum of aesthetic views on the part of its members is amazing. Although the Rhymers' Club was composed of a number of exponents of the Celtic Movement, from a literary point of view it included Arthur Symons, whose French symbolist-oriented poetry was the antithesis of that written by his fellow Rhymer, John Davidson, who espoused an antidecadent, strenuously masculine artistic credo.

Similarly, the Century Guild, out of which the Rhymers probably grew, mingled among its mildly Pre-Raphaelite, Ruskin-Morrisian, arts-and-crafts-oriented leaders, H. P. Horne, Selwyn Image, and Arthur Mackmurdo, such literary and artistic notables as Wilde, Ernest Rhys, Walter Crane, Will Rothenstein, Laurence Binyon, Lionel Johnson, John Gray, and Arthur Galton. Generally speaking, anyone who was interested in art and sought companionship with others dedicated to opposing the forces of a rampant materialism was welcome.

Like the Century Guild, the Vale group included Wilde and, on occasion, Beardsley and Whistler, men whose work was far closer to a perverse and uncompromising decadence than anything Ricketts and Shannon, its leaders, were willing to create. The very fact that those who attended the evenings at the Fitzroy settlement often appeared at the Vale, the Cheshire Cheese, or Lane's particular pet, Ye Sette of Odd Volumes,[5] suggests the tie that binds was something more than a devotion to a particular and narrow creed such as decadence, naturalism, Pre-Raphaelitism, Celticism, realism, traditionalism, or what have you.[6]

Tired of the dogmatism and didacticism of Victorian literature, it was enough for the aesthetic critics of the nineties if a poem, a play, or a picture could, in their opinion, merit the epithet, "a work of art" — a phrase which disarmed all criticism and gave dignity to even the most questionable literary or artistic effort. No longer willing to judge a work of art by its message, the critics most representative of the literary and artistic milieu of the early nineties were far more concerned that the object of their consideration be simply good art. In his "Editorial Note" to the first number of the *Savoy*, Arthur Symons, himself a product of the early Bodley Head, wrote:

To present Literature in the shape of its letterpress, Art in the form of its illustrations, will be its aim. For the attainment of that aim we can but rely on our best endeavours and on the logic of our belief that good writers and artists will care to see their work in company with the work of good writers and artists. . . . All we ask from our contributors is good work, and good work is all we offer our readers. This we offer with some confidence. We have no formulas, and we desire no false unity of form or matter. We have not invented a new point of view. We are not Realists, or Romanticists, or Decadents. For us, all art is good which is good art.[7]

A year or so later, Symons was even more specific in his rejection of narrow aesthetic points of view as a basis for critical judgment. In his prefatory letter to George Moore in *Studies in Two Literatures,* Symons wrote:

Has either of us ever doubted that the work of art has but one reason for existence, that it should be a work of art, a moment of the eternity of beauty? . . . Yet, here they undoubtedly are, critics to whom art means a theory, a belief, a science; the Ibsenites, the Realists, the Romanticists; people who, when you offer them a rose, say, yes, but it is not a violet. Frankly, I do not understand this limiting of oneself to a school, a doctrine, a costume. I have, and I keep for myself, my own way of seeing things, my own way of trying to say them; you have your own vision of the world, and your own technique. But to you, as to me, whatever has been beautifully wrought, by whatever craftsman, and in whatever manner of working, if only he has been true to himself, to his own way of realizing the things he sees, that, to you as to me, is a work of art.[8]

Under the influence of Pater's dictum that *"all art constantly aspires towards the condition of music,"* [9] the close relationship, the similarity, the essential unity of the arts were stressed and the differences minimized. In the face of an increasingly hostile world, artists of all persuasions tended to make common cause with one another; aesthetic points of view were submerged beneath a common front based on mutual respect and admiration. Rather than quibble over a doctrinal difference, critics tended to stress the experimental, distinctively new elements which set a poet apart from the great Victorians. [10]

In his essays, "The Decadent Movement in Literature" and "Modernity in Verse," Symons praised the "decadent" or "modern" elements in William Ernest Henley's verse while he ignored the poet's counter-decadent point of view. Annihilating all barriers between what was commonly thought of as decadent and counter-decadent verse, Symons suggested "Verlaine's definition of his own theory of poetical writing — 'sincerity, and the impression of the moment followed to the letter' " — as Henley's. [11] "In *A Book of Verses* and *The Song of the Sword*," Henley, in the opinion of Symons, had "brought into the traditional conventionalities of modern English verse the note of a new personality, the touch of a new method. The poetry of Impressionism can go no further, in one direction, than that series of rhymes and rhythms named *In Hospital*." [12] Tracing the sources of Henley's inspiration in these sonnets to Meredith, Patmore, and Whitman, Symons also found "something of the exquisitely disarticulated style of Verlaine." [13] Henley's use of musical techniques — the symphonic structure of his *London Voluntaries* — and his genuine appreciation for Whistler's impressionistic art were further points of contact with the Decadents. [14]

Under such circumstances, it was difficult to dogmatize and philosophize. In speaking of the Rhymers' Club, Yeats would sometimes say, recalling the early nineties,

"We had such and such ideas, such and such a quarrel with the great Victorians, we set before us such and such aims," as though we had many philosophical ideas. I say this because I am ashamed to admit that I had these ideas and that whenever I began to talk of them a gloomy silence fell upon the room. [15]

The "one conviction shared by all the younger men, but principally by Johnson and Horne, who imposed their personalities upon us," Yeats went on to point out, was an opposition to all ideas, all generalisations that can be explained and debated. Symons fresh from Paris would sometimes say—"We are concerned with nothing but impressions," but that itself was a generalisation and met but stony silence. Conversation constantly dwindled into "Do you like so and so's last book?" "No, I prefer the book before it. . . ." [16]

The philosophy of the Bodley Head — largely unwritten and to some extent unconscious — was perfectly consonant with these attitudes towards art. Mathews, Lane, and Le Gallienne, who as chief reader was in an excellent position to influence the choice of books, sought to gain distinction for the Bodley Head by publishing books which they considered, in Symons' phrase, "simply good art." Mathews and Lane offered their clientele whatever was original, inventive, and new in the way of poetry, illustration, and book design, irrespective of its particular aesthetic point of view.

Le Gallienne seems to have been the only one of the major figures in the firm to attempt to articulate or evolve a philosophy of the Bodley Head. His letters to Mathews and Lane reveal his readiness to think in terms of a philosophy, and there is evidence that the partners looked to him as apologist for the Bodley Head in the essay "The Philosophy of 'Limited Editions'," which was called forth by attacks in the newspapers and journals on the firm's policy of issuing small, numbered editions.[17]

As early as December 1891, Le Gallienne's letters to Mathews reveal his efforts to inculcate in the senior partner a philosophy grounded upon quality and distinction. Rather than accept for publication the kind of poetry which in its mediocrity and sameness was pouring forth from the larger commercial publishing houses, Le Gallienne sought to maintain and enhance the Bodley Head's reputation for quality by looking for works which in their style and idiom were fresh and different. "In regard to Mr. Wyrille[?] Holmes' verses," Le Gallienne wrote Mathews,

they are, I am afraid, soon disposed of, for they have none of the qualities of poetry save that fatal fluidity which flows like a great river thro' the door of Kegan Paul. They are quite without distinction of any kind & I certainly would not advise you to publish them on any terms. Such merely negative books can only blunt the reputation for taste which the Bodley Head has undoubtedly achieved: the aim being, I conceive, to have each book in your list, so to say, "sensitive," individual. Such verses as Mr Holmes' mean nothing but mediocrity. They came with no sense of freshness, & are quite devoid of charm.[18]

From numerous reader's reports it is clear that quality, or what Le Gallienne considered to be quality, was the criterion uppermost in his mind when he read a manuscript for the Bodley Head. On April 1, 1893 Le Gallienne informed Lane that he had

sent a round dozen MSS. back to Bodley . . . including Brett — thin gentlemanly stuff — & Crockett — not bad at all but hardly of sufficient strength or distinction for you to publish, & therefore, I surmised not good enough for your imprint at any price. Isn't that your philosophy? It is a philosophy you must resist all temptation to break.[19]

Similarly, in his report on John Davidson's *A Random Itinerary*, Le Gallienne, admitting to having been "a little severe," attributed his strictures to "a wish that is ever before me — to keep 'The Bodley' publications as near to the level of literature as I know how." [20]

The Bodley Head rejected much poetry which later found its way into print under the auspices of another and, according to Le Gallienne, less discriminating publisher. In another reader's report to Mathews, he asked:

I wonder if you noticed Mr. Unwin's list [of publications] this week — "The Songs of William Renton"!! You remember? that Lake Poet who grew so irate abt. his MS. What an ass Unwin is to take on all such rubbish. I daresay everyone of the rejected eleven [manuscripts] herewith will eventually appear either in his, Stock's or Kegan Paul's list.

The Bodley Head must beware more & more of such a policy — & now in the hour of your success will begin the temptation, so well avoided all along.

Preserve your distinction at all costs.[21]

Although Le Gallienne's philosophy of quality and distinction was not proof against much that was mediocre and commonplace, as even a glance at the books of Bodley Head poetry will reveal, it did make the firm receptive to some of the more experimental, avant-garde writers who, in an effort to break away from the poetic voices and modes of the Victorian era, sought to avail themselves of distinctly different models and more modern modes of expression. Some of these new currents of poetry found a voice, for instance, between the covers of the now famous books of the Rhymers' Club, which, strikingly heterogeneous in nature, were typical products of the day. As Le Gallienne pointed out in a review of *The Book of the Rhymers' Club* (1892):

[This] first concerted attack of the "Bodley Head Poets" on the British public . . . was not conceived as such and had no prevailing tone. It had no purpose beyond bringing together in friendly association, after the manner of such old miscellanies as *England's Helicon* or Davidson's *Poetical Rhapsody,* examples of the work of twelve poets, most of them young, and recently arrived in London.[22]

Similarly, Yeats, in his letter of April 1892 to "the New Island" concerning the Rhymers' Club, cautioned his audience against conceiving of the Rhymers as

a school of poets in the French sense, for the writers who belong to it resemble each other in but one thing: they all believe that the deluge of triolets and rondeaus has passed away, and that we must look once more upon the world with serious eyes and set to music — each according to his lights — the deep soul of humanity.[23]

By distinguishing between the dilettantism of the English Parnassians[24] and the more serious intentions of the Rhymers, Yeats clearly recognized the poetry of his generation, and, in particular, that of the Rhymers as the latest of those recent efforts in verse to set a course away from poetic forms and preoccupations of the great Victorians. The Rhymers' "search for new subject matter, new emotions" clearly, for Yeats, signaled what he termed "the reaction from that search for new forms merely, which distinguished the generation now going." [25]

This search for new subject matter and new emotions, Yeats discerned, for instance, in the poetry of two of the Rhymers, Arthur Symons and John Davidson. And although their search often led them to a common subject matter — the music hall was his example — Yeats observed: "No two attitudes towards the world and literature could be more different, and despite the community of subject no two styles could be more dissimilar." [26] Recognizing the work of both poets as "interesting signs of the times," Yeats, in his essay on the Rhymers, distinguished one further characteristic of the new poetry.

Not merely are they [Symons and Davidson] examples of that desire for new subject matter of which I have spoken, but of the reaction from the superrefinement of much recent life and poetry. The cultivated man has begun a somewhat hectic search for the common pleasures of common men and for the rough accidents of life. The typical young poet of our day is an aesthete with a surfeit, searching sadly for his lost Philistinism, his heart full of an unsatisfied hunger for the commonplace. He is an Alastor tired of his woods and longing for beer and skittles.[27]

The first of two books of poetry compiled by the Rhymers appeared in February 1892, two years after Yeats and Ernest Rhys brought them together under the appellation of the Rhymesters' Club. Until recently it was generally held that the club was founded in 1891 [28] and was a rather short-lived affair — it "lasted two or three years, and then 'ceased upon the midnight with no pain'," according to J. Lewis May.[29] But, thanks to Karl Beckson,[30] documents have come to light which show that the club was meeting early in 1890 — probably by January or February — and a post card addressed to Elkin Mathews from G. A. Greene, the Rhymers' secretary, found among the Elkin Mathews papers, indicates the group was still dining together as late as June 1895.[31]

In the *Autobiography* Yeats tells of the founding of the club.

I had already met most of the poets of my generation. I had said, soon after the publication of *The Wanderings of Usheen,* to the editor [Ernest Rhys] of a series of shilling reprints [the Camelot Classics], who had set me to compile tales of the Irish fairies, "I am growing jealous of other poets and we will all grow jealous of each other unless we know each other and so feel a share in each other's triumph." He was a Welshman, lately a mining engineer, Ernest Rhys, a writer of Welsh translations and original poems, that have often moved me greatly though I can think of no one else who has read them. He was perhaps a dozen years older than myself and through his work as editor knew everybody who would compile a book for seven or eight pounds. Between us we founded The Rhymers' Club, which for some years was to meet every night in an upper room with a sanded floor in an ancient eating-house in the Strand called The Cheshire Cheese. Lionel Johnson, Ernest Dowson, Victor Plarr, Ernest Radford, John Davidson, Richard Le Gallienne, T. W. Rolleston, Selwyn Image, Edwin Ellis, and John Todhunter came constantly for a time, Arthur Symons and Herbert Horne, less constantly, while William Watson joined but never came and Francis Thompson came once but never joined; and sometimes if we met in a private house, which we did occasionally, Oscar Wilde came.[32]

Soon after the initial meeting, Rhys, in a letter to the American poet and critic Edmund Clarence Stedman, dated May 21, 1890, wrote in closing: "I wanted to tell you of a 'Rhymester's Club' lately formed here, but must leave this & other things till next time." [33] The next time was on July 9, 1890, when Rhys's enthusiasm for the new club overflowed into several pages of description.

You ask about our "Rhymester's Club." We had a very jolly meeting last Friday, — a sort of Marlowe night, as that afternoon a benefit performance for the Marlowe Memorial had been given at the "Shaftesbury." John Davidson — author of "Scaramouch in Naxos" & ot[her] most original Plays, lately much discussed; Willie Yeats, a young Irish poet; T. W. Rolleston, another Irish poet, or rhymester, to use the Club term; Nettleship, the painter, O'Leary, the old Irish rebel; & two or three others less notable were there. Not a large gathering, you see; but a right jovial & friendly one.[34]

It was at this meeting that Rhys, having failed to compose and bring along a quatrain in honor of Marlowe, was "exiled," as he reported it to Stedman, "to a far corner with a glass of crystal fluid at his elbow, & bidden compose a quatrain there & then, or — die!" [35] Taking revenge on his fellow rhymesters for behaving in so tyrannous a manner, Rhys composed the quatrain on Marlowe that was to appear a year and a half later in *The Book of the Rhymers' Club*:

> *With wine, & blood, & reckless deviltry,*
> *He sped the flames, new-fired our English verse:*
> *Bethink ye, rhymesters! what your praise shall be,*
> *Who in smug suburbs put the Muse to nurse?* [36]

Although the meetings often are described as having been tame if not downright dull, Rhys's description of the "Marlowe night" suggests that the "more or less chief feature in the programme," the reading of each other's verse, was carried out "to a Bacchanalian accompaniment of whiskey," which, said Rhys, "kept the fun going merrily." In fact on this occasion the reading of his slyly satirical lines "led to an uproarious scene, in the midst of which" Rhys, "feeling his life in danger, escaped incontinently into the rain without, & so home!"

Continuing his exuberant account of the Rhymesters, Rhys went on to inform Stedman that the meeting had been held "at that most perfect of old Fleet St. Taverns, — the 'Old Cheshire Cheese'," and then mentioned that at a previous meeting the American who was later to be editor of the *Yellow Book*, Henry Harland, had attended. In concluding his account of the club, Rhys quoted what he termed "the R's Club ballad," Rhys's own verses which under the title of "The Toast" were to open *The Book of the Rhymers' Club* when it appeared in 1892.[37]

A means by which "latterday rhymesters beguile the tedium of everyday London a little," [38] the meetings of the club have since been chronicled by many of the notables who attended. Having been prefaced to the volume as a whole, Rhys's stanzas from "The Toast," I suppose, must be taken as the keynote of the whole adventure:

> As once Rare Ben and Herrick
>   Set older Fleet Street mad,
> With wit not esoteric,
> And laughter that was lyric,
>   And roystering rhymes and glad:
>
> As they, we drink defiance
>   To-night to all but Rhyme,
> And most of all to Science,
> And all such skins of lions
>   That hide the ass of time.[39]

Despite the accounts of the sanguine Rhys, the meetings seldom lived up to the wit and boisterous jollity of the past. In his memoir of the times, *Naphtali,* C. Lewis Hind tells of attending a meeting held "in the drawing-room of the highly respectable house of Dr. John Todhunter," the Irish poet and playwright, who lived near Elkin Mathews and the Yeats family in Bedford Park. According to Hind, Todhunter

was a kind of sedate father of the Rhymers' Club, and that meeting in his house, at any rate, was dull and decorous.[40] Most of the poets talked most of the time with articulated precision about quantitative equivalents, and, with the exception of courteous Dr. Todhunter, no one seemed to notice the guest of the evening — Francis Thompson. We — that is, Vernon Blackburn and I — had brought him there by special request. I wish the meeting had been held at that "pub between two stage-doors" [the Cock near Leicester Square?]. Bedford Park seemed to awe those tame young poets. Francis Thompson sat next to Ernest Dowson, but I did not see them speak to one another. The 'Nineties poets were often like that — remote, shy, aloof.[41]

Although the Cheshire Cheese was the usual place of meeting, doubtless because of its literary past and its central location, meetings were held not only at Todhunter's but also at the homes of other members. A popular setting for the gatherings was the house in Fitzroy Street where the Century Guild had its headquarters and where the Rhymers H. P. Horne and Lionel Johnson lived for a while with Arthur Mackmurdo and at times Selwyn Image.

One of the most celebrated meetings of the Rhymers was held there on the last Thursday of January 1891, at which time a whole host of luminaries appeared, in the words of Lionel Johnson, to inflict "their poems on each other." [42] Yeats seems to have been in charge of the arrangements for this gathering,[43] for in mid-January he wrote Horne "that next Thursday week would suit the Rhymers very well for their next meeting & that they would be very glad to accept your suggested invitation to 20 Fitzroy St." [44] Ernest Dowson has recorded his response to the evening: "Thursday at Horne's . . . very entertaining: a most queer assembly of 'Rhymers'; and a quaint collection of rhymes." Running through the names of some of the performers, Dowson gave his opinion of their verse.

Crane (Walter) read a ballad: dull! one Ernest Radford, some triolets & rondels of merit: "Dorian" Gray[45] some very beautiful & obscure versicles in the latest manner of French Symbolism; and the tedious Todhunter was tedious after his kind. Plarr and Johnson also read verses of great excellence; and the latter, also, read for me my "Amor Umbratilis": And Oscar arrived late looking more like his Whistlerian name,[46] in his voluminous dress clothes, than I have ever seen him. — [47]

Lionel Johnson's reaction to the same meeting appears in a letter to Campbell Dodgson on February 5: "We entertained the other night eighteen minor poets of our acquaintance: from Oscar Wilde to Walter Crane, with Arthur Symons and Willie Yeats between." All, he concluded abruptly, "were inimitably tedious, except dear Oscar." [48]

Herbert Horne's report to Ernest Rhys on Wilde's effect on the temper of the meetings was hardly exaggerated. Referring to one of the earliest meetings, February 9, 1890, Horne wrote: "I asked the Rhymers here the other evening. Oscar came in at the end, after the rhymes were all over, and smiled like a Neronian Apollo upon us all. A kind of enthusiasm or inspiration followed." [49] At least one meeting took place at the home of Edwin J. Ellis late in 1891. The guest of honor on that evening was Miss Maud Gonne who was, according to Yeats, on her way to Paris.[50]

Although the atmosphere was different, the meetings at the Cheshire Cheese were much the same as those held at home. Edgar Jepson, in his *Memories of a Victorian,* tells us that the Rhymers' Club gathering

was a meeting of poets, rather in the English and Johnsonian tradition, in a gloomy, ill-lit, panelled room at the Cheshire Cheese. I do not know that wine was forbidden, but to each poet was his pot of beer and churchwarden pipe, and perhaps to drink wine would have been an ostentation. It was at one of those meetings that I first met Mr. W. B. Yeats, wearing in those days the air of a Byronic hero, long-haired and gaunt, and delivering his poems in a harsh and high and chanting voice. . . . Those gatherings at the Cheshire Cheese were of a profound solemnity. I never heard a Rhymer laugh; their smiles were rare and constrained. For besides Dowson and Yeats and Johnson and Plarr there were some of the most serious English poets I have ever met, at least three of them bearded. There was Dr. John Todhunter, a son of the arithmetic and algebra which were my curse at school, an aged man with one of those flowing beards, and G. A. Greene, with a trimmed beard, whom Plarr called *Il Greno,* because he had so seriously soaked himself in Italy, and Hillier and Rolleston, all seething with the stern sense of their poetic mission, and all of them, except Yeats, read their verses in hushed voices. I was never a Rhymer myself, but when I went to their meetings I read my verse — in a hushed voice.[51]

One of the more lively meetings must have been the evening when John Davidson, who according to Yeats had accused the Rhymers of lacking "blood and guts," appeared on the scene with four Scotsmen whom he there and then proposed as members. To impress the Rhymers with their literary prowess, "one read out a poem upon the Life Boat, evidently intended for a recitation; another described how, when gold-digging in Australia, he had fought and knocked down another miner for doubting the rotundity of the earth." Doubtless intimidated by so bald a show of force, the Rhymers complied with Davidson's wishes although, Yeats later recalled, they all "secretly resolved never to meet again." Fortunately the club survived this most perilous of crises but only at the expense of seven hours of work on the part of Yeats, who, having succeeded in convening another meeting, made it possible for the members to gather and to vote the Scotsmen out.[52]

Although much of the poetry read on these evenings must have been a bore, the meetings surely had their great moments what with Yeats chanting his "Lake Isle of Innisfree" and Lionel Johnson, solemn and austere, reading his own and Dowson's poems. "I shall . . . remember all my life," wrote Yeats in *The Trembling of the Veil,*

that evening when Lionel Johnson read or spoke aloud in his musical monotone, where meaning and cadence found the most precise elocution, his poem suggested "by the Statue of King Charles at Charing Cross." It was as though I listened to a great speech. Nor will that poem be to me again what it was that first night.[53]

It was the impact of such readings which prompted Yeats a year or so after the Rhymesters came together to suggest that the members compile an anthology of their verse. "For long I only knew Dowson's *O Mors . . .* and his *Villanelle of Sunset* from his reading," Yeats remarked, "and it was because of the desire to hold them in my hand that I suggested the first *Book of The Rhymers' Club.*"[54] Plans for the volume were probably laid during the late spring or early summer of 1891, and an editorial committee which included Greene, Johnson, Le Gallienne, Todhunter, and Dowson was formed.[55] In June 1891, Yeats, who seemed very optimistic about the rapidity with which such a book could be compiled and published, wrote Katharine Tynan, " 'The Rhymers' Club' will publish a book of verse almost at once. You might take it as a subject of one article. It will give you a chance of saying much about the younger writers — Le Gallienne, A. Symons and so forth."[56]

It was no easy job to contact all the members and gather from them suitable poems for the volume. Even though the committee was busy soliciting manuscripts by early summer, Elkin Mathews was not approached until November. In his capacity "as an official exponent of the sentiments of the 'Rhymers' at their last meeting," Ernest Dowson wrote Victor Plarr (about June 9, 1891) asking if he could be counted on "as a contributor to 'The Book of the Rhymers Club' which it is proposed to issue, in an inexpensive manner in the autumn." [57] At that time Yeats, Greene, Johnson, Radford, Le Gallienne, Ellis, Todhunter, and Dowson had promised to join in the scheme while Manmohan Ghose,[58] Symons, Rolleston, and Rhys had not yet definitely committed themselves to the venture.[59]

In elucidating the club's plans for publication, Dowson assured Plarr that the expense would "be *very small,* as it will be distributed amongst all in proportion to the pages given to each; and in view of their number, and the fact that the maximum of space allowed to any Rhymer is 6 pieces: it could not very well be any thing than inconsiderable; profits of course, if any, on the same scale." [60]

Assuming that Plarr would join his fellows, Dowson then went on to describe the procedure decided on at the last meeting. Lionel Johnson who intended to be in London all summer had been chosen to serve as the "receiver of all the verses, although," as Dowson observed,

the selection is either to be made by the whole Club in council (wh. seems to me impracticable) or by a committee of 3 to be subsequently selected: 2nd that the maximum of pieces is to be 6 & the minimum 3 (probably). 3rd that each rhymer is exhorted to send in *double* the number of pieces he wishes inserted — say 12 for 6. 10 for 5 etc & that he may mark them in the preferential order he gives to them himself: & must state, where & when, if at all, they have been published. 4th. that the verses should be sent if possible to Johnson before the 26th inst: in order that they may be put before the House at the next meeting of the Rhymers & the book be got under way *quam celerrime.*[61]

Whether the summer of 1891 proved — what with holidays and a general exodus from town — to be a bad time to gather an anthology together or whether the task of choosing the selections proved tedious and time-consuming or both, it was autumn before the material for the book was substantially arranged. Then on November 12, Yeats wrote to Elkin Mathews to say that "Lionel Johnson, George Greene and myself, three members of the Rhymers' Club, wish to see you about the publishing of 'The Book of the Rhymers' Club' (a volume of poems by the members) and propose to call on you next Monday about 3 o'clock." [62]

It is doubtful that any other publisher was approached by the club. By the fall of 1891, the Bodley Head already had established itself as the pub-

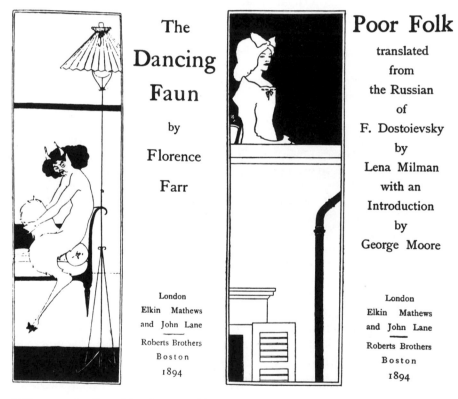

The
Dancing
Faun

by

Florence

Farr

London
Elkin   Mathews
and John Lane
———
Roberts Brothers
Boston
1894

Poor Folk

translated
from
the Russian
of
F. Dostoievsky
by
Lena Milman
with an
Introduction
by
George Moore

London
Elkin   Mathews
and John Lane
———
Roberts Brothers
Boston
1894

Title pages by Beardsley for some Keynotes series books.

Frontispiece and title page by Beardsley.

lishing house of choice so far as the younger and more promising of the poets were concerned. Moreover, Le Gallienne, Ernest Radford, John Todhunter, and Walter Crane were among the Rhymers who were by this time Bodley Head authors. Then, too, Mathews must have been fairly well known to the group since he lived in Bedford Park next door to the Yeats family and not far from the Todhunters' residence.[63] It is also very possible that Mathews had been something of a permanent guest of the club for some time. In a letter to the publisher dated January 13, 1891, Ernest Radford, requesting Mathews to forward to Cosmo Monkhouse an invitation to a Rhymers' Club meeting, went on to issue one to Mathews himself. "I believe," he wrote in a postscript, "you do not rhyme but I shall be very glad if you will join us." [64]

However that may be, the meeting between Elkin Mathews and the Rhymers was held and an agreement was worked out. On November 23, Greene, the secretary of the club, received Mathews' proposal, and he immediately set about the business of communicating the matter to Yeats and Lionel Johnson. In acknowledging the publisher's letter, Greene expressed his desire to see the matter "settled without delay. I may say that, for myself," he concluded, "your proposal appears to me to be a fair one." [65]

On December 2, 1891, Yeats wrote Katharine Tynan, "*The Book of the Rhymers' Club* has been taken by Elkin Mathews and will appear about Xmas. It is a very fine work and will give you material for an article or two." [66] Although it hardly came in time to be a Christmas present for the Rhymers, as Yeats and Johnson expected,[67] the book was in proof by late December and appeared in February 1892. Hailed by one columnist during the week of publication as "a kind of modern English 'Whistle-Binkie'," [68] *The Book of the Rhymers' Club* was offered to the public in a small-paper issue of 450 copies of which 350 were for sale at five shillings each and a large-paper issue of 50 numbered copies for sale at ten shillings, sixpence each. The small-paper issue was covered in an unusual yellowish orange cloth with a white paper label printed in black attached to the spine. The large-paper issue was published in blue boards with a white parchment spine lettered in gold. It was further enhanced by a yellow silk marker attached to the headband. Printed by J. Miller and Son of Edinburgh, *The Book of the Rhymers' Club* is almost square (advertised "16mo") in its appearance and, on the whole, not remarkable in its physical features, though well printed. Very inexpensively made (remainders of various papers were probably used),[69] the volume, whether or not a conscious effort was made in that direction, struck reviewers as "a recurrence to the excellent fashion of the Elizabethan age." [70]

Much to the joy of all concerned, *The Book of the Rhymers' Club* sold out almost at once. Writing to Arthur Moore on March 2, 1892, Dowson remarked apropos the volume, "The edition is now absolutely épuisé, which is charming." He then went on to speculate about the possibility of "a reprint & if so whether it will mean any personal profit. I wonder!" [71]

By late February the reviews of the book were beginning to appear. Replying to Plarr's query as to whether or not he had come across any as yet, Dowson wrote that he had seen none "save only logrollers, which quoted L.[ionel] J.[ohnson] and Rhys at some length, and Symons! — damning the rest of us with but the faintest praise." [72] On March 2, Dowson had been reading "the D.[aily] C.[hronicle], Lang, Image, & the Black & White on the Rhymers." [73] Although the reviewers generally were mildly pleased — and some amused — with the anthology, Andrew Lang's remark in a *Daily News* review to the effect that "a ransom of five shillings seems rather exorbitant for their [the Rhymers'] combined effort" [74] was resented by the members and later labeled "very uncivil indeed" by Yeats.[75]

In his review, Lang took the small number of copies issued as a sign of the age's unsympathetic attitude toward poetry and pictured the Rhymers as minor poets whose feeble efforts were hardly enough to make the Philistines listen. Condescending and irreverent in his attitude toward the pieces he singled out for comment, Lang did manage to express a sense of admiration for a group of poets who dared "to disregard public indifference." [76]

The review by Selwyn Image mentioned by Dowson appeared oddly enough in the *Church Reformer*. Attempting to refute Lang's contention, Image viewed the small number of copies printed as a mark of "the modest temper of the Club." Image, who praised the Rhymers and defended them against the strictures of the pernicious Lang, felt the expenditure of five shillings on the volume was altogether worthwhile. "Those of us, who are wise and have a nice taste in literature, and who have five shillings (I think it is) in our pocket to spend, will do well to lay out this sum in adding so dainty a volume to our libraries." [77]

To some reviewers the existence of such a group as the Rhymers' Club in so unpoetical an age came as a complete surprise and the issuance of *The Book of the Rhymers' Club* — at least to one critic — something of an offense. Yet on consideration this critic decided that since the book extended to "94 small pages only," the fact of its existence could not "be very strongly resented, even by those who least like the growing bard. This is but an *opuscule,* after all; and, if an offence, it is 'only a little one'." Of the opinion that the Rhymers must first "learn how to rhyme," the reviewer was much gratified to see that these gentlemen, who, according to one of their number, "put the Muse to nurse" in "smug suburbs," have not forgotten to sing of the London in which they dwell. "By the Statue of King Charles the First at Charing-cross," "At Citoyenne Tussaud's," "Chatterton in Holborn," "Freedom in a Suburb," "Sunset in the City," "Plato in London" — these (and the "Cheshire Cheese" ballade) are all metropolitan in topic and in tone and, moreover, they are among the pick of the pleasantly-filled basket.[78]

Although it is impossible to find historians of the Rhymers' Club who agree on the membership, it is undeniably incorrect to assume that the twelve who contributed to the first volume were the only members. In addition to Dowson, Ellis, Greene, Johnson, Le Gallienne, Plarr, Radford, Rhys, Rolleston, Symons, Todhunter, and Yeats, Allan Wade lists Selwyn Image, John Davidson, William Watson and Francis Thompson.[79] Even this list omits Herbert Horne, at whose house some of the Rhymers' Club meetings were held, and Norman Gale, who was asked to contribute to the first volume but did not.[80] One of the problems involved in determining membership arises from the fact that there seems to have been very little difference between the term "member" and the phrase "permanent guest." Among those generally listed as permanent guests were an American-born poet and actor by the name of William Theodore Peters; the Bodley Head authors Oscar Wilde, John Gray and J. T. Nettleship; and Edward Rose, Morley Roberts,[81] A. B. Chamberlain, and Edward Garnett.[82] It is likely that Elkin Mathews was also accorded this status by the Club.

When *The Second Book of the Rhymers' Club* appeared in June 1894, Arthur C. Hillier made a baker's dozen of the cenacle's twelve who had published verse in the first book. And although a third book was contemplated, nothing remains to suggest what poets planned to participate. The call for contributions to *The Second Book* probably was issued by G. A. Greene as early as the spring of 1893 — or so I gather from the fact that in mid-August of that year Dowson wrote Plarr:

I have had a prolonged epistolary paralysis or I would have afflicted you with a letter before. In fact I have only just reminded myself to-day that Greene's letter demanding rhymes [for *The Second Book*] is still unanswered & likely to remain so. But I am trying to hunt up the necessary half dozen & will dispatch them: though I should think the Star Chamber will have decided by this time to dispense with me.[83]

Fortunately, as we know, the so-called Star Chamber did not decide to blackball the tardy Dowson, for the most famous poem in *The Second Book* is the haunting "Cynara." Although he thought it unlikely, Dowson did bestir himself despite the heats of August and soon — with "a thousand apologies for the unconscionable delay" — dispatched a letter and eight lyrics to Greene. With the excuse that he had put off answering the Rhymers' secretary "until I could select some versicles to send with it," Dowson pointed out that he was sending

a few more pieces than the required number in order that you may select: but I have marked them in the order in which I should wish personally to have them published. I suppose there is no likelihood of any Cheshire Cheese gathering before the Autumn?

Once more please forgive my epistolary short-comings. Yours vy sincerely   Ernest Dowson

List of Verses
1. "Cynara"
2. "To One in Bedlam"
3. "You would have understood me"
4. "Ad Manus"
5. "Benedictio Domini" [later withdrawn]
6. "Love heeds no more" * [i.e. "The Garden of Shadow"]
   Extras
Growth
Dead Child
* I will send you a title for this   ED.[84]

Other Rhymers seem to have been even more remiss in their duties toward the second volume for, according to Karl Beckson, the selections for *The Second Book* were not finally made until early 1894. Having received proofs in the spring, the contributing members awaited publication, which occurred in late June 1894.[85]

The Second Book of the Rhymers' Club appeared in its ordinary issue as a squarish volume covered in a sturdy brown buckram casing, lettered in gold on the spine. The large-paper issue, in blue paper boards, was enhanced not only by a parchment spine to which a paper label printed in black was attached, but also by an orange silk marker stitched to the headband. Since the first book had fared so well with the public, *The Second Book* was published by Elkin Mathews and John Lane in London and by

Dodd, Mead and Co. in New York. Of the ordinary issue there were 500 copies for England (400 of which were for sale) and 150 copies for America. There were fifty large-paper copies for England and twenty for the United States.

Although there were numerous reviews,[86] Yeats's remarks in a letter to John O'Leary, dated June 26, [1894,] are the most noteworthy:

> I send you *The Second Book of the Rhymers' Club* in which everybody is tolerably good except the Trinity College men, Rolleston, Hillier, Todhunter and Greene, who are intolerably bad as was to be expected — Todhunter is of course skilful enough with more matter of fact themes and quite admits the dreadful burden of the T[rinity] C[ollege] D[ublin] tradition — and some are exceedingly good, notably Plarr, Dowson, Johnson and Le Gallienne.[87]

These two books of the Rhymers brought together examples of verse encompassing almost the whole range of the poetical voice of the early nineties. Often distinguished by their sense of world-weariness and a nostalgia for the past, the poets of the Rhymers' Club were for the most part alienated from and hostile to life as it was lived in a great materialistic industrial society. While some sought escape into a realm of faerie, a primitive past of legendary heroes and magic-filled romance, others — pursuing a passion or predilection for strange, bizarre manifestations of the beautiful around them — lost themselves in the exotic, often sinister beauty uncovered in the seamy, out-of-the-way backwaters of city life, remote from the main stream of Victorian middle-class culture — a beauty even more compelling and intoxicating because it was not pure but bound up with the ugly, the hideous elements of life and therefore symbolic of the experience of a race grown old in sin and sated with forbidden pleasures.

Not only were the tone and the themes of these volumes typical of the time, but the form in which these sentiments took shape was likewise a reflection of the aesthetic point of view. The verse which fills the pages of the two Rhymers' books is, for the most part, brief and lyrical — there are no long poems. In part reacting to the long didactic poem beloved of the Victorians — especially the often uncontrolled and excessively heavy-handed effusions perpetrated by the "Spasmodics" [88] — later nineteenth-century critics stressed the aesthetic value of the work of art in which the matter and form were indistinguishable and pointed to the lyric as the ultimate form of poetic expression. Speaking of the tendency of the various forms of art to aspire *"towards the condition of music,"* Pater had said that the ideal types of poetry are those in which this distinction [between matter and form] is reduced to its *minimum;* so that lyrical poetry, precisely because in it we are least able to detach the matter from the form, without a deduction of something from that matter itself, is, at least artistically, the highest and most complete form of poetry.[89]

As a result of this emphasis on the part of the most perceptive and influential critics, the most typical and indeed the best poems of the early nineties tended to be both lyric and symbolic.

Although a number of Rhymers (Ernest Dowson, Arthur Symons and Lionel Johnson) attained the stature of accomplished minor poets, of those who contributed to the Rhymers' Club books, Yeats is the only one who was to rise to the front rank of poetical genius. A long way from being the poet who was later to win the Nobel Prize, the Yeats of the Rhymers' Club was a painfully shy, introspective young provincial who had come to London with his family in 1887 only to be repelled by the city,[90] which contrasted markedly with the remote and misty Sligo, the place in the world he loved most.

Like so many of his artist-contemporaries, Yeats felt a strong sense of alienation, and a feeling of "isolation from ordinary men and women," an isolation which, as he later observed, was

increased by an asceticism destructive of mind and body, combined with an adoration of physical beauty that made it meaningless. Sometimes the barrier between myself and other people filled me with terror; an unfinished poem, and the first and never-finished version of *The Shadowy Waters* had this terror for their theme. I had in an extreme degree the shyness — I know no better word — that keeps a man from speaking his own thought.[91]

Continuing his description of his early verse, Yeats went on to say: "burning with adoration and hatred I wrote verse that expressed emotions common to every sentimental boy and girl, and that may be the reason why the poems upon which my popularity has depended until a few years ago were written before I was twenty-seven." [92]

What distinguishes Yeats's Rhymers' Club verse above all else is his absorption in Irish legendary matter and a disenchantment with the world of present-day realities. Of the twelve poems he contributed to the two volumes, none were political and almost all attest to his deep commitment to the legends and stories of Ireland's past. In the midst of Mammon's kingdom, Yeats spent his days in the British Museum compiling an anthology of Irish fairy tales, an activity which, as he later wrote, kept "my mind upon what I knew must be the subject-matter of my poetry." [93] Of the opinion that Shelley and Morris would have written more affecting poetry had they solidly set their works "upon some Welsh or Scottish rock," [94] Yeats during his early years as a Rhymer strove to create poetry which drew its power from a specific locale — the misty landscapes of old Eire. "Careful to use a traditional manner and matter," Yeats sought to create that "sensuous, musical vocabulary" which would complement and heighten the lore which so moved him.[95]

Desirous of being lifted out of what Shelley called "the trance of real life" by beautiful and strange surroundings, Yeats lost himself in the folk tales and romances of his nation's remote past. The poems of the Rhymers' volumes clearly show how Yeats was beginning to use Irish lore for the matter of his work. Always insistent upon authenticity, he rejected such compilations as William Allingham's *Irish Songs and Poems* ("these poems are not national," he wrote) in favor of those like John Todhunter's *The Banshee and Other Poems,* which captured the authenticity, the true flavor of the Irish past unadulterated by an overweening artifice.[96] Yeats's review of Todhunter's book indicates the effect these Irish legends had on his imagination at the time he was composing his Rhymers' Club poems. Todhunter's "legends," he wrote with enthusiasm, "belong to those mythic and haunted ages of the Tuatha De Danaan that preceded the heroic cycle, ages full of mystery, where demons and gods battle in the twilight. Between us and them Cuchulain, Conall Carnach, Conary, Ferdiad and the heroes move as before [a] gloomy arras." [97]

That these legends were to Yeats a good deal more than just a means of involving himself in the cause of Irish nationalism is suggested by the fascination with which this material held him. Not only were these fairy stories and this folklore nourishing to an imagination starved by the cold, loveless world of the immediate present, but they were also expressive of his own situation. For, after all, there is very little difference between Father Gilligan, whose weary struggle with the grim reality of life and death was relieved only by the momentary respite from heaven,[98] and the Yeats who standing "on the roadway or on the pavements gray" of London suddenly heard "in the deep heart's core" the "lake water lapping" on the shores of Innisfree.[99] Nor is the predicament of the man who dreamed of fairyland much different from that of the young aesthete who buried himself in dreams and in books while the exigencies of life beat ominously and peremptorily at the doors of his consciousness.[100] Although the young dreamer of Rhymers' Club days had not yet gone so far as to call down upon himself the terrible doom which was visited on the man who "might have known at last unhaunted sleep" or that which overtook O'Driscoll in "The Folk of the Air," there is every indication in the common theme of these poems that the situation was fraught with the possibility of tragedy not only for Yeats himself but for his whole generation.

What the magical groves of Irish fairy tale were to the young Yeats, an ideal of lost youth and beauty were to his fellow Rhymer, Ernest Dowson. Although his major theme was the poignant, powerful emotion of Rossetti's poetry, Dowson's poetic response to life was essentially Paterian. Few if any of Yeats's tragic generation expressed more perfectly than Dowson the attitude of mind and the aesthetic sensibility so movingly set forth in "The Conclusion" to *The Renaissance.* Desperately aware of the "awful brevity" of life and the sense of impending doom — "They are not long, the days of wine and roses" — Dowson sought to stay despair and assuage the thirst for an unattainable ideal not only by losing himself at brief intervals in "art and song" but ever more disastrously giving himself up to the search for sensations.[101] No one, not even Yeats himself, was so successful in realizing in the verse of the early nineties that artistic ideal — the union of form and matter — to which Pater was so devoted.

Dowson had come up to London in March 1888 from Oxford. When he joined the Rhymers, he was neither the seedy habitué of what Symons was later to call "those charming supper-houses, open all night through, the cabmen's shelters," nor the despairing vagrant whose "curious love of the sordid" [102] was to drag him down to an early and pathetic end. He was rather, according to his friend Edgar Jepson, in danger of becoming a fashionable poet who dressed well, attended the *salons* of Sir John and Lady Simon of Kensington Square and Sir Joseph and Lady Prestwich, and was in constant demand by the elite of London society.[103] Although his *Verses* was not published until 1896, Dowson's poems had begun to appear in the *Century Guild Hobby Horse* as early as 1891, and his contributions to the books of the Rhymers' Club were written when Dowson was, for a brief span of years, at the height of his artistic powers.

As early as 1886, Dowson had written a sonnet, "Of a Little Girl," [104] in which he had expressed his adoration of innocence, a theme which became a central preoccupation of his later poetry. In "Ad Domnulam Suam," the poet's reluctance to see the "little lady" of his heart become a woman is poignantly expressed. "Little lady of my heart," he pleads,

> Just a little longer,
> Be a child; then, we will part,
> Ere this love grow stronger.

Written before he had met Adelaide Foltinowitz, the daughter of a Polish restaurant owner,[105] the poem suggests how powerfully Dowson had come to realize what was, so far as one can determine, a purely imaginative creation. Probably in part an expression of Dowson's role in what Edgar Jepson refers to as a cult of little girls at Oxford during the eighties,[106] the imaginary "little lady" was perhaps a kind of Jungian *anima*, the embodiment of the poet's own youth and innocence, or perhaps the poetic self which was destined to be destroyed by maturity on its contact with reality.

Although the child who was "loved long ago in lily-time" in the poem "Growth" can "readily be identified with the poet's attachment for Adelaide . . . for it was written apparently when he was most deeply in love," [107] there is no perceptible difference between the poetic idealization of this child and that of his earlier, pre-Adelaide verses — a situation which reminds one of Pater's Leonardo, whose image of the Mona Lisa had been "defining itself on the fabric of his dreams" since childhood. "But for express historical testimony," Pater wrote, "we might fancy that this [the portrait of the Lady Lisa] was but his ideal Lady, embodied and beheld at last." [108]

If Symons is correct in his evaluation of Adelaide's effect upon Dowson, the relationship — at least so far as his poetry was concerned — was a most efficacious one. Reminding Symons of Verlaine's "girl-wife," Adelaide

had the gift of evoking, and, in its [*sic*] way, of retaining, all that was most delicate, sensitive, shy, typically poetic, in a nature which I can only compare to a weedy garden, its grass trodden down by many feet, but with one small, carefully-tended flower-bed, luminous with lilies.[109]

Although Dowson had planned to marry Adelaide when she was of age, he was never to know her as a real woman. As his poetry suggests, the real child, Adelaide, was to merge with the imagined one. Dowson idealized her beyond recognition into a symbol, not of eternal, but of evanescent youth — an innocence, virtue, and beauty he thought of in terms of white flowers, usually the lily, or other objects associated with a cold, virginal whiteness such as the moon or snow. In his "Villanelle of Sunset" the child whom the poet addresses as his "white bird" is expressive of Dowson's obsession with this ideal of youthful beauty and his desire to sink into oblivion with his "tired flower" upon his breast.

Just as in "Ad Domnulam Suam" so in "Growth," Dowson, anticipating the loss of the child, laments her change from innocence to maturity.[110] Although in the poem's second and final stanza, the poet's doubts are dispelled, and he hastens "to adore/ The glory of her waking maidenhood," in actuality, the poet's ideal of innocence and beauty was lost and he hastened in life to forget and drown his despair in a feverish search for sensations symbolized by the color red — in particular, the red rose.

In his most famous poem, the *"Non sum qualis eram bonae sub regno Cynarae,"* all of Dowson's most characteristic poetic motifs are gathered up in what has come to be for many the essence of decadent poetry. Dismissed by the New Critics as a sentimental, self-pitying expression of late Romanticism,[111] "Cynara" has, nevertheless, remained through the years a favorite anthology piece since it appeared for the first time as such in *The Second Book of the Rhymers' Club* in 1894. Although from one point of view Dowson can be taken to task for not developing the paradox inherent in the recurring refrain, "I have been faithful to thee, Cynara! in my fashion" and for not expanding the thought and situation expressed in the first stanza, the poet judged on his own terms wrought well indeed.

"Cynara" is an imaginative creation of a mood of despair which one is invited to savor as one savors the fragrance of roses or as one should linger over any aesthetic experience, pleasurable or otherwise.[112] Dowson's aim is to create a situation in which his desolate mood can be most exquisitely realized and then to sustain that mood briefly through the use of appropriate words, images, and rhythms. This Dowson succeeds in doing in the three opening lines of alexandrines by subtly manipulating the rhythm and the choice of sounds so as to create a hovering sense, a savoring of the bitter mood of loss and despair. For example, the long drawn-out "ah" of the first line is picked up in the final syllable of the name Cynara, and, as the dominant tone, is echoed again and again throughout the poem.

For a lyric moment, the remaining three stanzas serve to sustain the aesthetic experience created in the first stanza — to sustain and intensify it. Only "between the kisses and the wine," the "red" passion symbolized by the roses, can the white passion for the cold, virginal ideal which Cynara is be most powerfully and poignantly experienced. As the intensity of the situation mounts through the "flung roses" and the "dancing," the desolation and the sickness of the old passion, too, intensifies. As her erstwhile lover cries for "madder music and for stronger wine," his erotic and sensual "feast is finished and the lamps expire"; yet the mood of desolation and despair rises to a more intense hunger, a spiritual hunger which displaces the fleshly, sensual experience. As the light of sense goes out,

Then falls thy shadow, Cynara! the night is thine;
And I am desolate and sick of an old passion,

Yea hungry for the lips of my desire:
I have been faithful to thee, Cynara! in my fashion.

Though he flung riotously the roses, emblems of vice, to deck the path of sin; though through the "bought red mouths," the "madder music" and the "stronger wine" Cynara's lover put the "pale, lost lilies," symbols of Cynara's innocence and cold purity, "out of mind," the debauch has served only to intensify the terrible awareness of Cynara's unforgettableness. The ultimate impression, that of despair, is epitomized in the lines "When I awoke and found the dawn was gray." The past, once brightened by a beautiful ideal, gives way to a barren and hopeless present — a life of haunting memories, drugged forgetfulness and bought love.

Although the situation in "Cynara" which sustains the poet's mood of despair is a symbolic one, the mood of disillusion and depression is very real, just as it is in what has been called "the saddest and most exquisite of all his poems," [113] *"Ah, dans ces mornes sejours."* According to Flower and Maas, in September 1891 Dowson thought his innocent relationship with Adelaide was at an end because he had come to believe that a widely reported case of the abduction of a sixteen-year-old girl named Lucy Pearson and her terrible mistreatment at the hands of her captor reflected upon the holiness of his relations with his thirteen-year-old Adelaide.[114]

Once again, as in "Cynara," channeling his feelings through his favorite vehicle of emotion — a lover agonizing over the loss or impending loss of his innocent and virtuous lady — in the opening lines of *"Ah, dans,"* a man stands above the grave of his beloved and recalls the past marred by disagreements, reproaches, and misunderstandings. Sad and lonely, the desolate lover finds, ironically, that

> *. . . now death discloses*
> *Love that in life was not to be our part:*
> *On your low lying mound between the roses,*
> *   Sadly I cast my heart.*
> *I would not waken you: nay! this is fitter;*
> *   Death and the darkness give you unto me.*

Then with a touch of wry irony, he concludes:

> *Here we who loved so, were so cold and bitter,*
> *   Hardly can disagree.*

It was under the impact of this terrible sense of having been misunderstood and the consequent sense that all was over between him and Adelaide that he finally decided to follow his friends Charles Sayle and Lionel Johnson into the Roman Catholic church.[115] Since John Henry Newman, the Catholic church had been identified in the minds of a few as a realm set apart by belief and circumstance from the disturbing course of modern life, and it increasingly appealed to those who sought escape from what they conceived as the crass materialism and hideous vulgarity typical of Protestant Victorian England. The exclusiveness of the Roman church, its beauty, its yet undisturbed aura of mystical medievalism, its ordered, unchanging ways, even its dogmatism were to those repelled by a world hostile to beauty and contemptuous of the artist's vision, a serene if sombre abode.[116]

During the months before he was received into the Catholic church, Dowson wrote his poem about the Carmelite nuns (which was later to appear in *The Book of the Rhymers' Club* as "Nuns of the Perpetual Adoration"). Along with "Flos Lunae" and "Amor Umbratilis," it had been grouped in the *Century Guild Hobby Horse* for October 1891 under the general title "In Praise of Solitude." Clearly a reflection of Dowson's thoughts on the eve of his conversion, "Nuns of the Perpetual Adoration" suggests the strength of the appeal the Catholic church had for him.

There is a sharp contrast between Dowson's response to the life of the cloister and Matthew Arnold's response forty years before. In his "Stanzas from the Grande Chartreuse," Arnold had described his visit to the monastery in the French Alps on Sunday, September 7, 1851. It was a stormy, dark evening when Arnold, newly married, arrived with his young wife. Melancholy and sick with a sense of being out of tune with the world of the present, the poet recognized a kinship between himself and the ghostly monks which he expressed in the famous lines:

Wandering between two worlds, one dead,
The other powerless to be born,
With nowhere yet to rest my head,
Like these, on earth I wait forlorn.
Their faith, my tears, the world deride —
I come to shed them at their side.

But despite a strong sense of identity, Arnold could not share the faith of the monks which was now, he knew, "but a dead time's exploded dream."

And although their existence was, as Dowson later observed, "Calm, sad, secure," it moved Arnold to ask himself, *"What dost thou in this living tomb?"*

Unlike Arnold, however, Dowson did not resist the call to come in. The "high convent walls" were a welcome refuge from the "wild and passionate" world outside. Like his nuns who had seen "the glory of the world displayed; . . . the bitter of it, and the sweet," Dowson, too, had come to know only too well that "the roses of the world would fade,/ And be trod under by the hurrying feet." Therefore, he observed,

> *. . . they rather put away desire,*
> *And crossed their hands and came to sanctuary;*
> *And veiled their heads and put on coarse attire:*
> *Because their comeliness was vanity.*
> *And there they rest; they have serene insight*
> *Of the illuminating dawn to be:*
> *Mary's sweet Star dispels for them the night,*
> *The proper darkness of humanity.*
> *Calm, sad, secure; with faces worn and wild:*
> *Surely their choice of vigil is the best?*
> *Yea! for our roses fade, the world is wild;*
> *But there, beside the altar, there, is rest.*

That Dowson was not alone among the Rhymers in his response to the Catholic church is borne out by several of Lionel Johnson's poems which appeared in the two Rhymers' Club volumes, "A Burden of Easter Vigil," "To a Passionist," and "The Dark Angel." Having preceded his friend and fellow Rhymer into the Roman fold, Johnson was more of an ascetic than Dowson or any of the other Rhymers. Although his early inclination toward the priesthood did not fulfill itself, after proceeding through Winchester school and New College, Oxford, where he came under the influence of Pater, Johnson went up to London in 1890 with what he gave out as Newman's greeting to him on his lips: "I have always considered the profession of a man of letters a third order of the priesthood!" [117]

In appearance, a delicate, handsome boy of fifteen,[118] Johnson shied away from what seemed to him the crass and feverish world of his day, losing himself in books, a group of literary friends, and his dreams of more comely ages — the Athens of Plato, the world of the medieval church, the reign of Charles I. In answer to Yeats's question of why he kept aloof from men and women, Johnson replied, "In my library I have all the knowledge of the world that I need." [119] The hustle and bustle of the daylight hours was not for him. When the streets of London were noisy with the voices of men and women going about the routine business of getting and spending, Johnson was sleeping. He came alive only when the hush of evening fell across the gray pavements and the starry order of the skies cast a spell of peace over the city. Calling on Johnson one afternoon about five, Yeats, much to his surprise, was told that his new friend was not up. "He is always up for dinner at seven" the manservant added by way of encouragement. [120]

Shut away from the world in his room, whose doors and windows were hung with gray corduroy curtains as a further means of closing out the light and sounds of a hateful London, Johnson existed in a realm apart — a calm, serene atmosphere befitting one who entertained of a night such revered personages as Plato. Fearful not only of the world but also of his own weaknesses, Johnson created for his edification images of order and strength, proof against the assaults of whatever made for disorder and imperfection. Like Arnold, he idolized the great men of the past who in the midst of a world frightening and disheartening in its turmoil and disharmony remained calm and serene in their steadiness of purpose.

In his poem, "Plato in London," the poet invited Plato into the cloistered atmosphere of his own room. Like a priest ministering before the altar, Johnson invoked the philosopher divine:

The pure flame of one taper fall
Over the old and comely page:
No harsher light disturb at all
This converse with a treasured sage.
Seemly, and fair, and of the best,
  If Plato be our guest,
  Should things befall.

Essentially a poem in which the poet plays off London, a modern Sodom and Gomorrah, against images of order — Athens, Plato's "own city of high things," and "the calm stars, in their living skies" — and reason — Plato who "shows to us, and brings,/ Truth of fine gold" — "Plato in London" expresses Johnson's sense of an order inherent in the universe which denies the "noise and glare" of the world. His sense of reverence for Plato reflects his devotion to those who, unlike himself, were able to "possess their souls" (as Arnold expressed it) and create for themselves a reasonable, serene and comely life.

His communion with Plato having provided him with a brief respite from the death-in-life of modern existence, the poet sternly commands:

Lean from the window to the air:
Hear London's voice upon the night!
Thou hast held converse with things rare:
Look now upon another sight!
The calm stars, in their living skies:
    And then, these surging cries,
      This restless glare!

That starry music, starry fire,
High above all our noise and glare:
The image of our long desire,
The beauty, and the strength, are there.
And Plato's thought lives, true and clear,
    In as august a sphere:
    Perchance, far higher.

That Johnson found comfort and joy in such images, whether they were men of the past like Plato or men of the present like Newman and Pater, is further borne out by his portrait of Charles I in his most famous poem, "By the Statue of King Charles at Charing Cross." [121] Left alone with his thoughts and night, the poet meditates upon the martyred king who had come to be revered as a saint by Johnson and the ardent advocates of the Anglo-Catholic movement. An alienated artist figure who, like Rossetti's James I,[122] was thrust into a life of action against his will, Johnson's Charles is a forerunner of those moderns who found the aesthetic temperament a torment in a world made for action. Alone and aloof, "the fair and fatal king" rides on through "London's gloom," bringing grace to those who faint from weariness, "vexed in the world's employ." Through "the splendid silence" of the night, "the saddest of all kings/ Crowned, and again discrowned," Charles becomes the very image of the "passionate tragedy" of those who in the cause of art, beauty and high-mindedness are martyred by the world.

Arnoldian in its elegiac tone, "By the Statue of King Charles" represents Johnson at his best. Like the face of Charles, his verse is often "stern/ With sweet austerity." Life which to him was a weary, dispiriting affair at best, impressed itself on his poems in sombre, stately measures, traditional metaphors, and a chaste and careful choice of words. Employing the classic image of a ship reaching a calm and secure harbor as the vehicle of his basic poetic device — a contrast between a safe haven and a perilous realm without — Johnson in the poem, "In Falmouth Harbor," once again recreated his favorite setting of stars, night and perfect stillness.

> *The large, calm harbour lies below*
> *Long, terraced lines of circling light:*
> *Without, the deep sea currents flow:*
>   *And here are stars, and night.*

Safe within the charm of the silent bay, the voyager's memories of the desperate journey through the desolate wastes beyond only serve to deepen the sense of peace.

> *Far off, Saint David's crags descend*
> *On seas of desolate storm: and far*
> *From this pure rest, the Land's drear End,*
>   *And ruining waters, are.*

> *Well was it worth to have each hour*
> *Of high and perilous blowing wind:*
> *For here, for now, deep peace hath power*
>   *To conquer the worn mind.*

Although the sailors, symbols of the active life, "cast/ Their ropes, and watch for morn," Johnson, the sea-tossed wanderer, unwilling to face "the annulling light" of yet another "pitiless dawn," calms himself with the thought:

> *Thou art alone with ancient night:*
>   *And all the stars are clear.*

> *Only the night air, and the dream;*
> *Only the far, sweet smelling wave;*
> *The stilly sounds, the circling gleam,*
>   *Are thine: and thine the grave.*

In his use of the harbor as "Death's dreamland," Johnson reverses the symbolic pattern of Tennyson's "Crossing the Bar," a poem in which the great Victorian even at the end of a long and full life envisions death as a venturing forth from the serene haven of old age upon a voyage over unknown seas.[123]

It is doubtful at best that Johnson believed his moments of calm would at length fade into a dreamland of death, for at times a sense of being doomed to a frustrating and unnatural life and an early, terrible, unhallowed end surfaces in his poems — a sense which the powers of the Roman church were unable to dispel. Attempting through the masquerade of a historical setting to cloak the personal element,[124] in "Mystic and Cavalier," Johnson dramatized his plight. Once again involved with the artist's feeling of lonely isolation, set apart as he is from the normal joys and preoccupations of the active life, Johnson invests his poem with a Rossettian sense of fatal powers. Although his use of the eyes as crystal spheres in which his doom is writ large is a kind of metaphysical conceit in keeping with the seventeenth-century setting of the poem, the powers revealed therein suggest the occult and remind one of the medieval world of Rossetti's "Rosemary," in which enigmatic, evil forces battle with the good. "What powers/ Prepare the secret of the fatal hours?" he asks. And as the clouds break and clear "from the crystal ball" and the moment of death draws near, the mystic stoically turns to face with manly fortitude the ministers who come to possess his soul.

O rich and sounding voices of the air!
Interpreters and prophets of despair:
Priests of a fearful sacrament! I come,
*   To make with you mine home.*

Expressing his inner struggle in terms of Christian warfare, Johnson in his poem "The Dark Angel," embodies the decadent's attempt to control his passions and suppress his bent toward the poisonous, forbidden pleasures of the flesh. Having described the "dark Paraclete's" power to "burn/ With flames of evil ecstasy/ . . . all the things of beauty" and to poison "the fair design/ Of nature," Johnson rather unconvincingly turns on the "Tempter" with the Christian's faith that, if steadfast, he will save his soul from "the second Death" and turn evil intent into good. Secure in these thoughts, the poet commands:

Do what thou wilt, thou shalt not so,
Dark Angel! triumph over me:
Lonely, unto the Lone I go;
Divine, to the Divinity.

In addition to some good poems by Yeats and several of the best poems
of Dowson and Johnson, the two Rhymers' Club volumes included interesting examples of Victor Plarr's early work, such as "In a Norman Church,"
and one of Arthur Symons' early triumphs, "Javanese Dancers: A Silhouette." Although most of the one hundred and thirty poems (fifty-seven in
the first volume and seventy-three in the second) are admittedly bad to
mediocre, the two books are distinguished collections of their kind. After
all, how many anthologies have the distinction of containing for the first
time in book form such minor classics as "The Lake Isle of Innisfree,"
"Non sum qualis eram bonae sub regno Cynarae" and "By the Statue of
King Charles at Charing Cross"? Perhaps even more important is the fact
that the two books provided an outlet for the creative energies of both
Dowson and Johnson at a time when they were producing their best work.

When in 1873 Alfred, Lord Tennyson voiced his scorn for "Art with poisonous honey stolen from the flowers of France," he was at the height of his influence, and the undisputed poetic voice of Victorian England. Yet that he would deign in lines penned "To the Queen" to take notice of Swinburne's celebration of Gautier's *Mademoiselle de Maupin* as "the golden book of spirit and sense,/ The holy writ of beauty," [1] suggests that he was aware of a tendency in English poetry to ignore the example of the Laureate and look elsewhere for inspiration. In the very year Tennyson's Epilogue appeared, Walter Pater in his *Studies in the History of the Renaissance* offered an alternative to the moral earnestness of the great Victorians — what Yeats was later to describe as a "life lived as 'a pure gem-like flame' " [2] — and in so doing set forth in English a concept of life and art closely akin to the French notion of *"l'art pour l'art,"* which had been announced by Gautier as early as 1835.[3] And although "all," according to Yeats, were to accept Pater "for master," [4] those who found his ideas congenial also found the artistic expression of similar concepts in contemporary French poetry of great interest.

A year before Pater's essays on the Renaissance appeared, Andrew Lang had published an attractive little volume entitled *Ballads and Lyrics of Old France,* which contained translations of a number of early and contemporary French poets including Villon (an artist of especial interest to Rossetti and Swinburne), Du Bellay, Ronsard, Victor Hugo, and Gerard

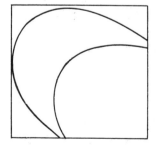

6 THE BODLEY HEAD POETS:
POISONOUS HONEY AND ENGLISH BLOSSOMS

de Nerval. Turning away with obvious relief from the didacticism and what was already thought of as the heavy rhetoric of Victorian poetry to the French Parnassians' preoccupation with form, Lang, in this his first book, and others of his generation created what Yeats was later to refer to as the Gosse, Lang, and Dobson school.[5] Following the advice of Théodore Banville, who in his *Petit Traité de poésie française* (1872) stressed Gautier's dictum that *"la forme . . . est tout,"* the English Parnassians thought of a poem as being, like an exquisitely carved jewel or cameo, sharply defined and sculptured in its effect. A desire for precision of image and frequently recurring rhymes, which had led to Banville's plea for a return to *"les poëmes traditionnels à forme fixe,"* also manifested itself in the books of verse of the English Parnassians as a profusion of rondeaus, villanelles, chant royals, triolets and virelais.[6]

So stimulated were the members of this minor English school of poets by the art and doctrine of the *Parnassiens* that Banville's treatise was interpreted to the English through Austin Dobson's poem, *"Ars Victrix"* and by Edmund Gosse's essay "A Plea for Certain Exotic Forms of Verse."[7] Consequently Parnassianism, with its emphasis on form and its penchant for trivial subjects, found its way into the poetry of a number of other poets during the seventies and eighties.

Although the Parnassian movement in England had largely faded out by the nineties, a few practitioners of the mode appear among the lists of Bodley Head authors. Arthur O'Shaughnessy, who had exhibited his interest in French literature with a translation of the *Lays of Marie de France* as early as 1872, published an important volume, *Songs of a Worker,* in 1881, which, in the section entitled "Thoughts in Marble," contained interesting examples of Parnassian poetry.[8] O'Shaughnessy died in that year, and his work was later edited by Louise Chandler Moulton and brought out by the Bodley Head in a volume entitled *Arthur O'Shaughnessy, His Life and His Work with Selections from His Poems* (1894). Despite its white cloth casing stamped with a typical *art nouveau* design of flowers on curving stems done in gold, the volume is a disappointment primarily because Mrs. Moulton, evidently hostile to the Parnassian mode, failed to include a single one of O'Shaughnessy's Parnassian poems although she did make room for a few excerpts from the *Lays.*

O'Shaughnessy's fellow clerk at the British Museum, Theo Marzials, also published in the early seventies a volume of verse, *The Gallery of Pigeons and Other Poems,* which especially in its dedicatory sonnet strongly reflected the influence of France. Another of those books of poetry which sold only a few copies when it first appeared, *The Gallery of Pigeons* was taken over by the Bodley Head in the early nineties, at which time the edition was apparently sold out.

The best examples of Parnassian poetry among the Bodley Head publications are to be found in Cosmo Monkhouse's *Corn and Poppies,* Walter Crane's *Renascence,* and Ernest Radford's *Chambers Twain.* Monkhouse, who was a friend of Henley's, was primarily an art critic, and his volume of poems, which appeared in 1890, shows the influence of various contemporary schools of poetry. Henley's *London Voluntaries* and the aesthetic desideratum of the day that poetry and art should aspire toward the condition of music doubtless were responsible for Monkhouse's poem entitled "Love, a Sonata," which is divided into five movements: "Love's Sweetness," *Adagio*; "Love's Courage," *Allegro*; "Love's Mirth," *Scherzo*; "Love's Holiness," *Andante*; and "Love's Laughter," *Rondo.* Further evidence that Monkhouse was also attuned to the influences coming to England's shores from France is found in his two attempts at translation — "The Rebel," from Baudelaire and *"Avant Qu'Amour"* from Ronsard. Among his Parnassian poems are the "Virelai Ancien" and two rondeaus, "Violet" and "To Punch."

Among the poems which Walter Crane composed and embellished with his own art work in *Renascence, A Book of Verse,* were seven rondeaus, two rondels, and a "Triolet," which is expressive of one of Crane's major themes:

> *In the light, in the shade,*
> *This is Time and Life's measure;*
> *With a heart unafraid,*
> *In the light, in the shade,*
> *Hope is born and not made,*
> *And the heart finds its treasure*
> *In the light, in the shade —*
>   *This is Time and Life's measure.*

Since Gautier and his *Parnassiens* sought to reproduce in verse "effects more directly obtained by painting and sculpture" [9] and often gave titles to their poems which suggested an artfully sculptured *objet d'art* — for instance, that of Gautier's famous volume, *Emaux et Camées* and Banville's *Améthystes* — it is not difficult to see why such fixed forms as the triolet appealed to artists like Crane. Not only were the fixed forms employed by the *Parnassiens* more congenial to the mind and sensibilities of an artist than less concrete forms of poetry, but they were also easily handled by poetasters such as Ernest Radford, who doubtless found pleasurable exercise in implementing the demands of the forms with commonplace sentiments such as that expressed in the triolet "A Broken Ring":

Lo, thy poor ring is broken!
These kisses bind for aye.
Let but this word be spoken,
Now thy poor ring is broken,
"True Love outlasts his token,
Yet cannot choose but stay."
Lo, thy poor ring is broken!
These kisses bind for aye.

In his attractive but very slender volume of verse, *Chambers Twain,* Radford included a number of deftly turned poems, including an envoy, as well as a translation from Gautier, entitled "Elegy."

In addition to these minor examples of the French influence on the poetry of the Bodley Head, two of Mathews and Lane's most important books are signal examples of the impact of French poetry on the literary milieu of the early nineties — Arthur Symons' *Silhouettes* and John Gray's *Silverpoints.* In *The Critic's Alchemy* Ruth Z. Temple has shown that Symons was the most important link between French and English poets during the *fin de siècle,* and his influence in this respect on Yeats is well known.[10] Like Le Gallienne and so many others, Symons was a provincial. Born in Wales of Cornish parents, he rebelled against the narrow morality of his clergyman father and the aesthetically negative milieu of Wesleyan parsonages and found in London and the literary and artistic life of the capital a more comely and meaningful existence. In the late summer of 1889, he made his first trip to Paris, in the company of Havelock Ellis. Having written poetry primarily under the influence of Browning, Rossetti, Swinburne, Meredith and Henley, the young Symons now came under the spell of the great French poets — Baudelaire and, in particular, Verlaine.[11]

The several accounts he was later to give of his first meeting with Verlaine in Paris on April 29, 1890, record the impact of the French aesthetic milieu in general and of Verlaine in particular on Symons. In the company of Charles Morice, a disciple of the master's, Symons "with delight and almost terror" approached the café François Premier, where the great man was wont to hold court amidst the glare of gas lights, surrounded by the noise and ribaldry of Montparnasse. Following Morice through the doors of the café, Symons went forward through the crowd to a table where he beheld Verlaine "smiling benevolently . . . surrounded by a crowd of young men." Although the poet's companions were arresting enough, Symons had eyes for one man alone, for no one "But Verlaine!" [12]

The effect of this second visit to Paris was decisive for his career as a poet. "As you are aware, I am spending some months in Paris," he wrote his friend Edmund Gosse in May. "Though I have been in Paris before, I have never before been able to study the life and the literature from a central standpoint. That is what I am able to do now." [13] According to his biographer, Roger Lhombreaud, "from the time of this visit to Paris," Symons discovered the manner and the genre which he was to cultivate "throughout the whole of his life." [14] It was during the ecstasy of these spring days in the French capital that Symons began to compose the poems in his new mode which were to be collected as *Silhouettes* and published by the Bodley Head in October 1892. The two issues, one of 250 small-paper copies and another of twenty-five large-paper copies, appeared with a distinctive title page lettered and drawn by H. P. Horne and covered in a gray paper with black lettering on the spine which might seem to belie the unusual nature of the contents. Yet, as we shall see, the book is unified by a gray mood of despair which objectifies itself in the poems.

Not unlike Pater's Leonardo, who found a decadent milieu a stimulus to his genius — "To Leonardo least of all men could there be anything poisonous in the exotic flowers of sentiment which grew there" [15] — Symons responded with an intense excitement and a keen sense of a first awakening to the "life of brilliant sins and exquisite amusements" which he found in the city of his soul, Paris. Born with that "certain kind of temperament, the power of being deeply moved by the presence of beautiful objects," [16] Symons was susceptible to the beauty that was Paris. His perceptive and sensitive mind drank deep of the aesthetic life lived along the Boulevard and in the cafés of St. Michel. Soon he was also to know the quiet sombre beauty of the French watering places. Under the stimulus of Verlaine, Rémy de Gourmont, Mallarmé, and a host of others, Symons came into his own. The artistic embodiment of these experiences is *Silhouettes,* which opens with a series of impressionistic pieces, "At Dieppe."

Composed during a brief stay at the famous seaside resort in mid-June 1890,[17] these sketches reveal the poet's gift for impressionistic expression and his predilection for the delicate, gray tones of nature, the subdued, half-light effects gained at dawn, twilight, or misty evening. Like those poets and artists most typical of the period, Symons saw life as through a veil. Sight of things reached him precisely as Pater's Leonardo perceived existence, "in no ordinary night or day, but as in faint light of eclipse, or in some brief interval of falling rain at daybreak, or through deep water." [18] It is not the brilliant primary colors of a flaming sun sinking far out over the sea that moves Symons' soul but the mauve-colored light of the opening poem, "After Sunset." "The heaped grey clouds" of the first stanza, suffused with "The grape's faint purple blush" fade into the pale light of evening as

> *Of delicate ivory,*
> *The sickle-moon and one gold star*
> *Look down upon the sea.*

"Night, a grey sky, a ghostly sea./ The soft beginning of the rain," is the setting of "On the Beach," a brief lyric in which the modern's sense of the oppressive weight of human experience is conveyed through the muffled sound of a rising tide, the stealthy descent of night, and the vague sight of black sails fading into the horizon. Although it is afternoon as the poet in "Under the Cliffs" lies quietly watching "the white sun walk across the sea/ . . . With feet that tread as whitely as the moon," the day is "pallid."

These sombre monochromes, which express the decadent's apprehension of experience and convey a mood of despair, give way in the final poem of the group, "Requies," to a monotone. Just as one color, gray, dominated the previous impressions, so one sound — "This slow sea-monotone" — creates the doubtful state of mind which is resolved in the poem's last lines by sleep:

> *O is it life or death,*
> *O is it hope or memory,*
> *That quiets all things with this breath*
> *Of the eternal sea?*

The sense of despair which clothes his world in the spectra of grays and blacks and reduces existence to a monotone — the note of Arnold's "Dover Beach" — also accounts largely for Symons' distinctive perception of man as a shadow, a silhouette. In his poem "The Quest," Symons chases "a shadow through the night,/ A shadow unavailingly." Only momentarily

> *Against the wall of sea outlines,*
> *Outlined against the windows lit,*

does he succeed in capturing the silhouette of the woman who leads him "through the night/ To the grey margin of the sea." [19] The possibility that man may be chasing shadows, that one may know only the shadow of reality, haunts Symons and underlies his characteristic way of seeing, which is again exemplified in "Pastel," the poem which opens the section of *Silhouettes* entitled "Masks and Faces." Composed in Paris on May 20, 1890, "Pastel" is a Verlaine-like[20] evocation of a fleeting, shadowy beauty emerging "through the dark." And if the lady's "lyric face" is but a momentary flush of color, "a rose," in the midst of darkness, the woman's "Monna Lisa" face in the poem, "In an Omnibus," is a vision of bizarre beauty against the commonplace background of a dreary Parisian day. And although her smile "is like a treachery" — "So smiles the siren where the sea/ Sings to the unforgetting shell" — the setting of "weary miles of walls/ That ache monotonously white" suggests to her observer the withering thought that behind all her seductive beauty may be nothing more than the inane mind and dreary personality of a very ordinary being:

> *Is there, in Tantalus's cup*
> *The shadow of water, nought beside?*

This world of shadows and silhouettes, which suggests that perhaps there is no reality to grasp, creates in Symons a strong sense of futility and depression occasionally given ultimate expression in a brief but touching lyric such as "Maquillage." Reminiscent of Baudelaire's evocations of artifice, the first stanza is a superb rendering of the harlot's face — as exotically beautiful and artificial as that of a priceless oriental figurine:

> *The charm of rouge on fragile cheeks,*
> *Pearl-powder, and, about the eyes,*
> *The dark and lustrous eastern dyes;*
> *A voice of violets that speaks*
> *Of perfumed hours of day, and doubtful night*
> *Of alcoves curtained close against the light.*

But the pale and subtly colored complexion, so "like the flower of dawn," those

> *. . . fleeting colours are as those*
> *That, from an April sky withdrawn,*

Fade in a fragrant mist of tears away
When weeping noon leads on the altered day.

The mask of artifice can beguile, can hide; yet it can also foretell the end and suggest the ruin, the doom that lies ahead.

This love of artifice, a predilection for what he later called "the *decor* which is the town equivalent of the great natural *decor* of fields and hills," [21] led Symons first to London then to Paris in search of new sensations, a quest for the kind of beauty which alone could satisfy one upon whom, in the words of Pater, "all 'the ends of the world are come'." [22] For a poet whose perception and sensibilities are the complex product of all the experiences and sensations man in a thousand years has come to know, neither the ideal of Grecian beauty with its serene, untroubled aura nor the natural beauty of pastoral and the country maiden was enough. How could a modern with all his sense of human evil, his awareness of the complexities and unfathomed depths of the human mind respond wholeheartedly to a beauty devoid of those touches — a sinister smile, perhaps — which are so suggestive of man's latter-day nature?

Occasionally, as the poem "Pattie" suggests, the ideal of a fresh, innocent country beauty was appealing to Symons. "Cool comely country Pattie" is fresh as the daisies she dwells among and attracts the poet, who turns a jaundiced eye upon the "courtly city dames,/ Pale languid-scented hot-house growth," but Symons' characteristic embodiment of beauty is his "Emmy," a lineal descendant of Rossetti's "Jenny" — a Pattie with a difference.

Written in Berlin in July 1891 and in Paris, May 11, 1892, the "Emmy" poems[23] are set in one of the prime locales of the early nineties, the music hall. Like Toulouse-Lautrec, Symons was fascinated by the whirling sights, the silhouettes dark against the light of the gas jets, the smoke, the talk, and the music of the café-dance hall and found in such haunts men like puppets abandoning themselves to a kind of madness and oblivion born of disillusionment and despair. But perhaps of even more interest to him was the kind of beauty found there, a tainted beauty all the more fascinating and significant for its signs of evil and artifice. Apparently still so simple, unpretentious, and pure as her name suggests, Emmy, for all her "exquisite youth and her virginal air" is already well on her way to becoming like "the women, haggard, painted and old" in whose midst she now stands.

There, in the midst of the villainous dancing-hall
Leaning across the table, over the beer,

While the music maddened the whirling skirts of the ball,
As the midnight hour drew near —

The poet recalls Emmy as she was then, a "fresh bud in a garland withered and stale." The pathos, the wistfulness with which she is recalled is increased by the signs — the "shameless" tales she told "out of Boccaccio's book," "the witching smile" — which tell of the evil nature within. Although her observer, like the prudish young man who moralizes over Rossetti's "Jenny," is outraged when he thinks on the man "who wronged you first, and began/ First the dance of death that you dance so well," Emmy is ultimately of interest precisely because she is a symbol of beauty which is credible to the mind and compelling to the sensibility of the men of the nineties.

Symons' "Emmy" poems are a bit too Victorian, but his "Morbidezza" is very much in the French impressionist vein. Though like Emmy in her "virginal" air, the "white girl" of the poem is, unlike Emmy, a wholly unnatural, exotic creature, a triumph of artifice in her deathlike "swoon/ Of whiteness" (an elaborate circumlocution which, if not death, suggests disease and debility). Reminiscent of Whistler's white girls, Symons' portrait shows a morbid fascination for the color white, which the aesthetes thought of as the subtlest of colors.[24] Impressionistically sketched for us in rhythms and rhymes which are more French than English, "Morbidezza" portrays another version of Symons' idea of beauty. There is about the white girl an unhealthy deathlike pallor — her "flesh is lilies/ Grown 'neath a frozen moon" — a strange stillness and an "alluring scent of lilies" which suggest "the fascination of corruption" which, in the words Pater used to describe the Medusa, "penetrates in every touch [her] exquisitely finished beauty." [25] A far better symbol than Emmy of the Medusan "type of beauty," which "is so exotic that it fascinates a larger number than it delights," [26] Symons' white girl is his ultimate embodiment of the morbid beauty so strangely attractive to his contemporaries.

Symons, whom Yeats was later to dub "a scholar in music-halls," [27] saw during his first visit to Paris a show which was to find its way into one of his best poems, "Javanese Dancers," a "silhouette" in its depiction of a group of shadowy, spectral dancers now motionless and still, now moving, swaying, "interthreading slow and rhythmically" across a stage. Although like "Morbidezza" an evocation of strange beauty, "Javanese Dancers" is an embodiment of the aesthetic ideal of perfect harmony of form and content, the desideratum expressed by Pater's dictum that *"all art constantly aspires toward the condition of music."* [28] Devoid of discursive meaning, the poem is in its form an integral part of the impression being created. Onomatopoetic

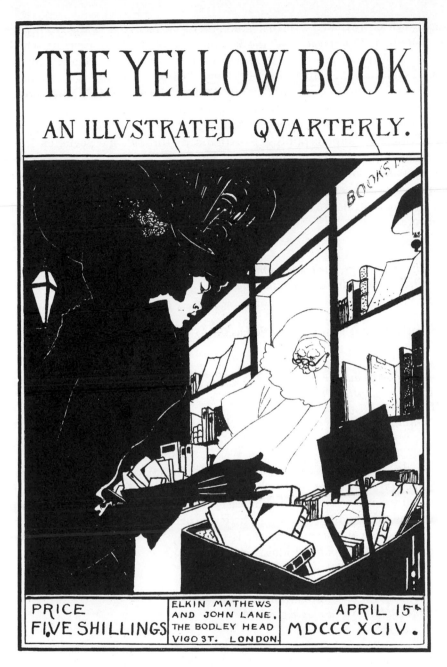

Design by Beardsley for the Prospectus of the *Yellow Book*.

words such as "twitched," "clang," and "shrill" suggest the strange, disquieting sounds of the music, and the rhythmic, repetitious movement which creates the hypnotic mood of the poem is enhanced by the frequent repetition of sounds — the alliteration of "clang," "cling," "continuous," "comes," "cat," and the assonance with "four," "forth," "fro," "row," and "slow." Symons' skillful use of sounds such as the long e in the final syllable of "stealthy" and in "three," and the long o in "fro" and "grove" which are threaded almost imperceptibly yet rhythmically through the poem, enriches the sense of mystery and motion.

A symbolist poem, "Javanese Dancers" is Symons' most potent evocation of an evil beauty comparable to something perhaps only Beardsley could create. The central dancer who comes stealthily on stage to the accompaniment of

Twitched strings, the clang of metal, beaten drums,
Dull, shrill, continuous, disquieting;

is essentially what Frank Kermode has described as the Romantic Image.[29]

Smiling between her painted lids a smile,
Motionless, unintelligible, she twines
Her fingers into mazy lines,
Twining her scarves across them all the while.

Enigmatic, fascinating, dangerous, her undulating form, her "fixed eyes" and "spectral hands that thrill" are symbolic of that forbidden beauty which found all too many idolaters in the early nineties. Nowhere is that worship of art and its essential character better evoked than in the poem's last stanza, in which the strange dancer is joined by her "little amber-coloured dancers" who, "like painted idols," are

. . . seen to stir
By the idolaters in a magic grove.[30]

The strange, at times evil, beauty which Symons worships in "Javanese Dancers" was found in the great cities of the world, places which had hitherto been in the nineteenth century most unpoetical. For example, Wordsworth had been able to see London as beautiful only when under the effect of dawn its "Ships, towers, domes, theatres, and temples" lay "Open into the fields and to the sky," [31] when the characteristic sounds and sights, its normal activities were halted. And as G. Robert Stange, in his recent essay on "The Victorian City and the Frightened Poets," has pointed out,[32] the mid-Victorian evocation of the city was very different from that of the nineties. For instance, Symons' "Emmy" poems and "Pattie" follow Rossetti's "Jenny" in representing through their central figure the typical Victorian antithesis between city and country. In "Emmy" we are never for a moment allowed to forget that she was once a pure and innocent little country maid whose laughter still rings "as bright,/ Fresh and sweet as the voice of a mountain brook."

Symons is typical of his time in that his most characteristic poems are not only about the city but about the beauty of the city. In his brief but important prefaces to the second editions of *Silhouettes* and *London Nights,* Symons defied those who would limit the artist to certain stereotyped kinds of beauty found only in the traditional locales— the countryside, in particular. In his search for new and more significant forms of beauty, like his French contemporaries, Symons claimed the right, in the words of A. J. A. Symons,

to a fresh freedom of subject-matter, the right to be restricted only by their ability to extract art from these new freedoms. They prized, and cultivated in themselves, the utmost sensitiveness of reaction both to the external world and to internal emotion; and so perceived, or thought they perceived, beauty in the common objects of the modern world, in things and thoughts commonly called wrong or ugly.[33]

A connoisseur of city sights and sounds, Symons, voicing his preference for the décor of the town in the *Silhouettes* preface, also expressed his pity for those who could not see any "beauty in the effects of artificial light, in all the variable, most human, and yet most factitious town landscapes." [34] Not only did Symons respond to the various beauties of the city but he also recognized it as a proving ground for the modern artist. In his essay on "Modernity in Verse," he wrote: "I think that might be the test of poetry which professes to be modern, its capacity for dealing with London, with what one sees or might see there, indoors and out." [35]

William Morris and his followers had sought to escape what he called derisively the "six counties overhung with smoke," but Symons and his fellows set out to find whether or not a county such as Middlesex overhung with smoke might possess some special, unperceived beauty. Addressing himself to what he described as "perhaps, the most difficult, as it is certainly the most interesting, of all artistic achievements," the task of representing in poetry "really oneself and one's surroundings, the world as it is to-day," [36] Symons sought to follow Baudelaire, the first of modern poets, and Verlaine, "the typical modern poet," [37] in creating poetry out of the most characteristic of modern phenomena, the city.

Although there is much of Whistler and his "when the evening clothes the riverside with poetry" in *Silhouettes*,[38] there is much, too, of Baudelaire's "Spleen de Paris" and Verlaine's impressionistic studies of the city. The section entitled "Nocturnes" and the poem of that name is definitely Whistlerian in its evocation of beauty along

> *. . . the Embankment with its lights,*
> *The pavement glittering with fallen rain,*
> *The magic and mystery that is night's,*

but in its wistful reminiscence of a moment of "human love without the pain" it is pure Verlaine.

It is what Edward Baugh has characterized as "a blending of Pater, his acknowledged master, of the early Verlaine, and of Impressionist painting," [39] that typifies the city poems of *Silhouettes*. This is especially true of the first of two "London Nights" poems, "Going to Hammersmith," in which a train is seen winding its way

> *. . . through the night of the town,*
> *Through a blackness broken in twain*
> *By the sudden finger of streets;*
> *Lights, red, yellow, and brown,*
> *From curtain and window-pane,*
> *The flashing eyes of the streets.*
>
> *Night, and the rush of the train,*
> *A cloud of smoke through the town,*
> *Scaring the life of the streets;*
> *And the leap of the heart again,*
> *Out into the night, and down*
> *The dazzling vista of streets!*

That Symons had what he later spoke of as "the vision and the point of view" to apprehend "the romance of what lies beneath our eyes, in the humanity of streets," [40] is abundantly clear in *Silhouettes*. In the section, "Masks and Faces," such poems as "In Bohemia," "In the Haymarket," "The Blind Beggar," and "The Absinthe Drinker" witness to Symons' ability to capture impressionistically the moods and experiences of those who lived apart from the main stream of Victorian life.

Although *Silhouettes* was reviewed in such diverse periodicals as Lord Alfred Douglas' *Spirit Lamp*[41] and the *London Quarterly Review,* the book's French orientation and its real value were seldom noticed. For the most part, Symons' reviewers were hostile and extremely obtuse like the anonymous reviewer for the [London] *Figaro* whose "first remark" apprised his readers of the fact that Mr. Symons was "none of your Nature's poets who deal in bosky dells and sport with Amaryllis in the shade. He is the laureate of the demirep, and carols of 'the charm of rouge on fragile cheeks' — a charm which it takes an exponent of the new poetry to discover." [42] Perceiving "now and then . . . a *soupçon* of Swinburne — Swinburne and water — tempered by an echo of Tom Moore" in the poems of *Silhouettes*, the reviewer soon tired of collecting "all Mr. Symons' bizarre phrases" and went on to a consideration of a rival volume also issued from the Bodley Head, Le Gallienne's *English Poems*.[43]

Another reviewer, Percy Pinkerton, was not only favorable in his response to the book but was able to recognize the impressionistic nature of the work. Referring to the poems of the "At Dieppe" section as "charming little scenes that Mr. Symons paints for us with great sensitiveness of touch," Pinkerton observed that "in their richness of suggestion and felicity of presentment they remind one of the work of Mr. Whistler. Perhaps," he suggested, "this is how, if he chose verse as the medium for his expression, he might appeal to our mental eye." [44]

Although he was not favorably disposed to the kind of poetry Symons wrote, the critic for the *London Quarterly Review* was the most perceptive and accurate in his comments. Referring to *Silhouettes* as "a collection of impressionist sketches, most of them very short, and each an attempt to give permanence to some flying glimpse of the visible world, some passing mood of the mind, some moment that stands out luminously distinct among the many lost in the grey distance of past years," the reviewer suggested that Symons as artist was something of a "strange mixture — half battered Bohemian, half unhappy child — " which accounted for the poet's "exquisite sensitiveness to every aspect of outer life," his "violin-like delicacy and subtlety of expression," and his "power of throwing the 'wizard twilight' of a strange and mystic significance about the objects that the ordinary man passes with the dull habitual glance of one who sees them without seeing, every day of his life." [45]

Aware of the fact that Verlaine's *Aquarelles* had "affected the development of Mr. Symons's poetic gift," the reviewer rather disappointingly ventured to think that the influence was unfortunate. "The charm of Verlaine," he observed,

is too special and individual to be the heritage even of the most devoted disciple, and it is that charm alone which gives value to work intrinsically so slight as this. There is power enough in the scattered sketches of *Silhouettes* to do justice to a large and solid conception on a basis of "fundamental brain-work." It seems a pity to have it frittered away in doing imperfectly a kind of thing that is only tolerable when it is exquisite.[46]

Accusing Symons of being one of those who put craft above content, the critic concluded with the popular opinion of the day that "the man, be he painter or poet, who views his subject merely as a means of illustrating his own dexterity of handling, is an idolater in the sacred fane of art." [47]

Even more than Symons' *Silhouettes*, John Gray's *Silverpoints* expressed the French poetic idiom in English. Not since John Payne's *Songs of Life and Death*, published in 1877, had England produced a book of verse so wholly French in its orientation. Like Symons and most of the central figures of the Bodley Head group, John Henry Gray was of a rather humble middle-class background. Gray's father was a journeyman carpenter employed in the London dockyards and his mother's father is said to have been a gipsy.[48] Born at Woolwich, London, March 10, 1866, the eldest of nine children, Gray left school at thirteen and worked in Woolwich arsenal before moving on to a position in the General Post Office and, later, to the post of librarian in the Foreign Office. A very precocious child, the young Gray seemingly taught himself to play the violin, to draw, and to paint, and to read and speak French expertly.

Not until his early twenties, however, was a more tangible link with things French afforded Gray, when in the summer of 1888 or 1889, he joined a friend, Marmaduke Langdale, and his family at their home in the little Breton village of St. Quay-Portrieux.[49] Shortly thereafter, Gray met, at Arthur Symons' rooms in Fountain Court, The Temple, the young man who was to become his most important link with France, "his friend of friends," as Brocard Sewell has expressed it, Mark André Raffalovich, a fashionable and aristocratic wealthy young Russian Jew, who had been educated in Paris and went to England to settle in 1884, at the age of 18.[50] John Gray became a frequent guest at the home of Raffalovich's mother in Paris, where he met Mallarmé and others of the symbolist poets whose work he was soon to translate. On occasion he contributed to several French periodicals including *L'Hermitage* and *La Revue Blanche*.[51]

In the early nineties, Gray became one of the most talked about young men of fashion in London, one who according to Dowson was "incurably given over to social things." [52] By 1892, his *annus mirabilis*, he numbered among his friends Oscar Wilde, Aubrey Beardsley, Lionel Johnson, Yeats, and — through Wilde, no doubt — Pierre Louÿs, the French poet, who had first called on Gray at his residence in Plowden Buildings, The Temple, in June.[53]

During this glorious year when Gray was at the height of his career as a poet and dandy, the greatest notoriety he was to know came in the form of a gossipy front-page article in the *Star* (February 6) entitled "Mainly about People." [54] Probably written by Le Gallienne, who was becoming more openly hostile to the English Francophiles, the article identified Gray as the original of Wilde's Dorian. Offended, the young poet threatened to sue the *Star* for libel, and the newspaper printed a retraction. Although *The Picture of Dorian Gray* had been published in *Lippincott's Monthly Magazine* in July 1890, presumably some time before Wilde knew Gray, Gray later became known in the fashionable circles of the day as "Dorian." Lionel Johnson, writing to Campbell Dodgson on February 5, 1891, conveyed the news that Wilde was proceeding to publish "Dorian Gray as a book, with additions, which improve it. . . . I have made great frends with the original of Dorian: one John Gray, a youth in the Temple, aged thirty, with the face of fifteen." [55]

During the same month, Gray had delivered what Wilde soon after was to write of as "the brilliant fantastic lecture on 'The Modern Actor' " at a meeting of The Playgoers' Club.[56] What Patricio Gannon has referred to as Gray's "first real claim to public notice," [57] the lecture was again given by the poet on Friday evening, March 4, in connection with the performance of his translation of Théodore Banville's "Le Baiser" by the Independent Theatre at the Royalty — an affair attended by such literary lions as Henry James, J. M. Barrie, George Moore, and, of course, Oscar Wilde who was there with "a suite of young gentlemen, all wearing the vivid dyed carnation which has superseded the lily and sunflower." [58]

Meanwhile under the impact of his experiences in France and his growing knowledge of the *Symbolistes*, Gray wrote his best poetry, and in 1892 he set about to make into a book a work which Wilde was prepared to underwrite.[59] Since Wilde himself was a Bodley Head author and Mathews and

Lane's firm was the only one which a young poet of fashion would deign to approach, Gray called to see Lane in Vigo Street and to leave "the roll of my poems" on May 27.[60] Disappointed not to find the publisher in, Gray doubtless returned soon after. By June 18, Lane had already perused the manuscript and apparently had accepted the book for publication.[61]

Although Lane has been celebrated through the years as a fearless man who dared to print material that — barring Leonard Smithers — no other publisher would touch, he seems to have immediately objected to one, then later to two, of Gray's poems on the grounds that they were indecent. Seemingly unperturbed and most agreeable, Gray replied to Lane on June 18, 1892: "By all means omit the 'Song of the Stars' from Silverpoints." [62] When the book finally appeared in March 1893, both the "Song of the Stars" and "Sound" were omitted because they were considered obscene.[63]

Gray's brilliant choice of the art term "silverpoints" for the volume's title suggests at once a close relationsip in his mind between his poems and this particularly subtle and shadowy form of art. A stylus which leaves on the surface of paper prepared with certain oxides a faint but indelible mark, the silverpoint was used by such masters as Botticelli and Dürer and in the later nineteenth century by Alphonse Le Gros and Burne-Jones to create the most delicate of drawings, whose silver-gray effect was especially delightful.[64] The connection between poetry and the visual arts explicit in Gray's title is exemplified most clearly in his poetic recreation of John Everett Millais's famous painting of Ophelia, "On a Picture." Also reminiscent of Rimbaud's "Ophélie," [65] Gray's contemplation of the beautiful suicide subtly suggests his own Hamlet-like preoccupation during what ostensibly was his most ecstatic year, 1892.[66]

One of a whole flurry of poems on pictures doubtless influenced by the practice of Blake and Rossetti, and the example of Pater's recreation of Leonardo's Mona Lisa,[67] "On a Picture" embodies Gray's deep desire to loose himself from the world and drift off silently, painlessly into an eternal state of "noble sloth." Millais's "Ophelia" evoked in Gray that sense of fulfillment and peace which only the static realm of art can afford. Keats's "in love with easeful Death," would have been a fitting epigraph to this poem, which evokes a placid beauty undisturbed "Until some furtive glimmer gleam across/ Voluptuous mouth . . . / And gild the broidery of her petticoat."

Another highly wrought, subtle bit of artifice which demonstrates the triumph of art over nature is the elegant and highly mannered, "Les Demoiselles de Sauve." [68] Employing the first and final stanzas as a frame to contain his "picture," Gray portrays three exotic women who pass as in some elegant, ceremonial dance through an orchard decked out in all the subtle colors of a Provençal spring. Heightening the decorous tone by his use of the historical present, Gray watches as *les Demoiselles*

> *Bend under crutched-up branches, forked and low;*
> *Trailing their samet palls o'er dew-drenched grass.*

As if each one is the embodiment of a quality of high art — its haughtiness, its exoticism, its religiosity, its sensuousness — the ladies command the attention of nature, which in deference to their superior beauty imitates them:

> *Pale blossoms, looking on proud Jacqueline,*
> *Blush to the colour of her finger tips,*
> *And rosy knuckles, laced with yellow lace.*
>
> *High-crested Berthe discerns, with slant, clinched eyes,*
> *Amid the leaves pink faces of the skies;*
> *She locks her plaintive hands Sainte-Margot-wise.*
>
> *Ysabeau follows last, with languorous pace;*
> *Presses, voluptuous, to her bursting lips,*
> *With backward stoop, a bunch of eglantine.*

So potent is their beauty in the eye of the beholder that as they pass through the last stanza, nature becomes a palace in which these "Courtly ladies . . ./ Bow low, as in lords' halls" while the "springtime grass/ Tangles a snare to catch the tapering toe."

Gray's love of artifice, which is conveyed through numerous touches such as the long, flowing lines of *art nouveau* which materialize as long hair, flames, and veils or as the "silver vine" in "Complaint," is most potently objectified in "The Barber." A monologue reminiscent of such sallies into the realm of madness as Browning's "Porphyria's Lover" and Swinburne's sadistic "The Leper," Gray's poem employs as its central figure the barber, who throughout history — especially in decadent ages — has dealt in the most extreme form of artifice, that of improving on nature through the use of cosmetics, wigs, masks, and strange dyes. A forerunner of Beardsley's barber, Carrousel, Gray's artificer is a symbol of the decadent artist whose love of *maquillage*[69] leads to madness. Dreaming that he was a barber beneath whose hands went "oh! manes extravagant" and "many a mask/ Of many a pleasant girl," the poet in his strangely beautiful yet terrible world of sleep runs the gamut of decadent moods, devices, and motifs.

Like a master of all the plastic arts, he dreams of transforming with ecstatic joy his pleasant clientele —

> *I moulded with my hands*
> *The mobile breasts, the valley; and the waist*
> *I touched; and pigments reverently placed*
> *Upon their thighs in sapient spots and stains,*
> *Beryls and crysolites and diaphanes,*
> *And gems whose hot harsh names are never said.*
> *I was a masseur; and my fingers bled*
> *With wonder as I touched their awful limbs.*

Shifting abruptly to the present tense in what becomes increasingly a hallucinatory situation beyond the control of the dreamer, the poet-barber beholds the last of his "pale mistresses," his ultimate *objet d'art*, come to life in a nightmare of surrealism:

> *So, at the sound, the blood of me stood cold.*
> *Thy chaste hair ripened into sullen gold.*
> *The throat, the shoulders, swelled and were uncouth.*
> *The breasts rose up and offered each a mouth.*
> *And on the belly pallid blushes crept,*
> *That maddened me, until I laughed and wept.*

Like "The Barber," a poem in the *symboliste* mode, Gray's "Mishka" yields up multiple meanings as the poet once again creates a hallucinatory state in which images blend into one another. For instance, Mishka, the bear, is a mingling of the human and the animal in the sense that he is also a "poet," has fists, and appears "white like a hunter's son." In stanzas two and three, the "honey-child," that is, the bee, is a monster and Mishka "hears" her eyes "saying" his name. A kind of parable like "The Barber," "Mishka" is an objectification of the artist's compelling desire or taste for beauty which leads him away from reality into the sterile world of fatal beauty. As Mishka, the "poet among the beasts," lies dreaming in his wintry cave, outside the world is dark and ugly, the roots are rotting, and the "rivers weep." Suddenly Mishka sees a monstrous eye — that of the honey-bee, the bearer of sweetness, Arnold's beauty — which turns him to stone. He has, so to speak, looked upon the face of the Medusa, that terrible beauty the glimpse of which destroys the beholder. Fascinated, Mishka follows the monstrous bee "into her lair/ Dragged in the net of her yellow hair" — a sequence of events which also suggests that the bee is its Swiftian opposite, the spider. Suddenly the monster is "the honey-child" whose hips "sing" and whose thighs each bear a "mound" of honey. Like Keats's knight-at-arms, Mishka finds himself in an exotic realm, the counterpart of the poet's dream of a paradisal place. Although the ominous note first struck by the advent of the monster is prolonged by the scream of "a far bird-note" and by "the triple coil" of the honey-child's hair which is "wound" "round his throat," Mishka has succumbed to the blandishments of a paradise as his enchantress strokes "his limbs with a humming sound."

Despite the fact that in reality

. . . he knows no more of the ancient south
When the honey-child's lips are on his mouth,
When all her kisses are joined in one,
And his body is bathed in grass and sun,

he, paradoxically, knows "all things." For as a poet, Mishka has by an act of the imagination been able to create for himself a realm of beauty — "the ancient south" — which is also the realm of ultimate truth.

Unlike Keats's "La Belle Dame sans Merci," in which the ominous motifs foreshadow the awakening of the knight into a world of death-in-life, the grotesque and terrible images seem in "Mishka" as if they were there primarily for effect. For Mishka does not awaken. Rather he is maintained in his state of sensuous, erotic ecstasy, and Gray's striking use of two quiet "correspondences" at the close, leaves the reader with the intangible essence of a highly satisfying experience:

The shadows lie mauven beneath the trees,
And purple stains, where the finches pass,
Leap in the stalks of the deep, rank grass.
Flutter of wing, and the buzz of bees,
Deepen the silence, and sweeten ease.

The honey-child is an olive tree,
The voice of birds and the voice of flowers,

> Each of them all and all the hours,
> The honey-child is a wingèd bee,
> Her touch is a perfume, a melody.[70]

Another poem in *Silverpoints* which suggests the difference between early and late Romantic poetry is the verse simply entitled "Poem," whose setting is a carefully trimmed formal garden with paved asphalt walks and flowers — "Geranium, houseleek, laid in oblong beds." This bit of "nature meth- odiz'd" located in the heart of the city is the antithesis of the natural locale of wild flowers and open fields so beloved by the early Romantics. And al- though there are daisies there, they are daisies with a difference: their lat- ter-day observer notices, for instance, that their "leprous stain/ Is fresh" and that "Each night the daisies burst again/ Though every day the gar- dener crops their heads." "A wistful child, in foul unwholesome shreds" ineffectually attempting to construct a daisy chain is also there to complete an un-Romantic trinity — "Sun, leprous flowers, foul child." The presiding deity of the formal garden, oddly enough, is Robert Burns in the form of a metal statue which serves as perch for "garrulous sparrows" who irreverently command, "Sing! Sing! . . . and flutter with their wings." Concluding his quiet, droll survey of the garden with delightful yet instructive irony, the observer muses:

> He does not sing, he only wonders why
> He is sitting there. The sparrows sing. And I
> Yield to the strait allure of simple things.

Although a general sense of languor pervades "Poem" as well as most of the other compositions — "indolent acrostics," Gray calls them in his epi- graph — the oppressive ennui of the volume here and there is counter- pointed with several poems about action and rebirth as if the desire to break away from the dreamlike, languorous state of "noble sloth" and achieve a more vital, activist life exists in Gray. For example, in "Wings in the Dark" a fishing boat which "the idle day/ Sees idly riding in the idle ranks," by night comes to life, and

> Like a young horse, she drags the heavy trawl,
> Tireless; or speeds her rapturous course unbound,

And passing fishers through the darkness call
Deep greeting, in the jargon of the sea.

As the clouds above shift in the night sky, "Low on the mud the darkling fishes grope,/ Cautious to stir, staring with jewel eyes" until . . .

Suddenly all is light and life and flight,
Upon the sandy bottom, agate strewn.
The fishers mumble, waiting till the night
Urge on the clouds, and cover up the moon.

This sense of pent-up vitality smothered by the dark is also present in such poems as "Song of the Seedling" and the curious "The Vines," which suggest emergent life constrained by winter waiting impatiently

. . . listening death away,
Till the day burst winter's bands.

As Gray's epigraph suggests, these "indolent acrostics" are, indeed, composed with much care and ingenuity. Gray's obvious relish for experimentation allowed him to employ just one fixed form, the sonnet, and in one of the three sonnets, "Song of the Seedling," he radically varied the line lengths. Gray's clever manipulation of the rhyme schemes of "Les Demoiselles de Sauve" and "The Vines" also suggests a mind in love with artifice. The rhymes of the last seven lines of "Les Demoiselles" leading away from the eighth are a mirror image of the rhymes of the first seven lines except for the switching of the last two rhymes, which surprises the reader and, as a result, enhances the meaning of the final line. Similarly the rhyme scheme of "The Vines" is the same going from the last line to the first as from the first line to the last. Such an ingenious rhyme scheme is not for ingenuity's sake alone — although, doubtless, that is part of the pleasure — for the complex intertwining of end rhymes and the judicious use of internal rhyme, especially the long e sounds in stanza three, do suggest the intricate coiling and interlacing process of the plants.

To enhance his meaning, Gray also makes skillful and effective use of internal rhymes in other of his poems. In the final stanza of "Wings in the Dark" when the sense of a sudden burst of swift activity is desired, the poet combines the sounds of "life" and "light" in the final word of the line "flight" to convey a sense of rapid movement.

Gray's attentiveness to French poetry and French literary customs of the day is most apparent in his translations — or what he preferred to call "imitations" — of Baudelaire, Verlaine, and others. But it can also be seen in his practice in *Silverpoints* of dedicating each of his poems to an individual — "Heart's Desmesne" to Verlaine, "Mishka" to Henri Teixeira de Mattos, "Summer Past" to Wilde, "On a Picture" to Pierre Louÿs — and his use of epigraphs from the French symbolists. Gray chose the epigraph to the volume " . . . *en composant des acrostiches indolents*" from Verlaine's "Langueur";[71] and he links two companion poems, the "Did we not, Darling, you and I" and the "Lean back, and press the pillow deep" by two epigraphs from Jules Laforgue's "IX" from *Derniers Vers,* an ironic poem about love.

It is in his twelve "imitations" that one is best able to judge Gray's sensitivity to and affinity for French symbolist poetry. Although he takes great liberties at times with the originals by altering words and shifting the emphasis so as to create effective English poems to his own taste, on the whole he captures the French remarkably well.[72] For instance, Gray develops *"Le Chevalier Malheur"* in a slightly different way from Verlaine by not telling us that the knight is kind until we see that he has renewed the speaker's heart. Verlaine begins the poem, *"Bon chevalier masqué,"* but Gray opens with "Grim visor'd cavalier." Gray describes the lance, which Verlaine does not characterize, as "unpitying." By omitting a line in which Verlaine has the knight say *"Tandis qu'il attestait sa loi d'une voix dure,"* he retains the original impression of his mysterious silence. Verlaine's closing line, *"Au moins, prudence! Car c'est bon pour une fois"* was spoken to him by a policeman the day he was released from prison. Gray alters the tone and impact when he says in less familiar and more explicit words, "Once only can the miracle avail. — Be wise!"

Although Gray loses some of the richness of imagery and meaning in his rendering of Mallarmé's *"Les Fleurs,"* considering how difficult Mallarmé is to translate, Gray's *"Fleurs"* is good. Gray omits the first stanza, in which Mallarmé uses compressed imagery to describe a former relationship between the stars, representing the absolute, and the earth. Gray, by his addition of "starless" to the last line of the poem, "For weary poets blanched with starless life," may allude to this symbolism of stars to indicate man's separation from the absolute. Gray's line, "Blushing the brightness of a trampled dawn," imitating *"Que rougit la pudeur des aurores foulées"* shows how successfully Gray can recreate Mallarmé's words. He loses, however, the impression of light in *"le myrte à l'adorable éclair"* and *"un sang farouche et radieux"* and omits the sobbing of the lilies. In the last stanza he alters the image: *"Calices balançant la future fiole,/ De grandes fleurs avec la balsamique Mort"* to "Challices nodding the not distant strife;/ Great honey'd blossoms, a balsamic tomb." Mallarmé's figure of death pouring from the flowers is superior to Gray's tombs.

Of Gray's several excellent translations of Baudelaire, *"A Une Madone"* is the freest. Although Gray retains the sadism in this poem, he makes the man and the woman less fierce than they are in Baudelaire. He omits the only reference to the man's physical desire, four lines beginning: *"Ta Robe, ce sera mon Désir, frémissant. . . ."* He also leaves out the content of the line describing the hatred which the serpent jealousy breeds in him: *"Ce monstre tout gonflé de haine et de crachats."* By changing *"En Vapeurs montera mon Esprit orageux"* to "So shall my soul in plaintive fumes arise," he continues to soften the picture of the speaker. Gray's lover is a "Torturer filled with pain" as Baudelaire's is a *"Bourreau plein de remords";* but Gray's is "sick with fear" at the same time as Baudelaire's is *"comme un jongleur insensible."* The niche in which Mary is to stand is *"d'azur et d'or tout émaillée"* in Baudelaire but "with mercy stained, and streaked with gold" in Gray. Baudelaire says, in an image of shoes, that the speaker's *"Respect"* will be *"humiliés"* by Mary's feet. Gray omits the idea of humiliation. Gray's Mary will "smile supreme" when she crushes the serpent, but Baudelaire's *"railles."* Where Baudelaire describes Mary as a *"sommet blanc et neigeux,"* Gray speaks of her "pitying eyes."

Gray's care in retaining the basic shape and movement of the French poems in his imitations, his painstaking efforts, for instance, to arrange the phrases within his stanzas in much the same order the French writers used, and his attempts to recreate the patterns of sound in the French poems as far as possible by substituting equivalent patterns in English, suggest a very serious and purposeful desire to convey an accurate impression of French symbolist poetry to the English reader. Under Gray's sensitive touch, the imitations, harmonizing with his original poems in themes and in style, form a fitting close to *Silverpoints*.

The other noteworthy Bodley Head books which contained "poisonous honey stolen from the flowers of France," were Oscar Wilde's *Poems* and *The Sphinx*. A reissue of a volume published in 1881 by David Bogue, Wilde's *Poems,* with its fresh cover and title page designed by Charles Ricketts, "was transformed into a charming edition de luxe." [73] The poems were the same, however, since the sheets of the unsold fifth printing were merely taken over and bound. The work of a very young man — largely a

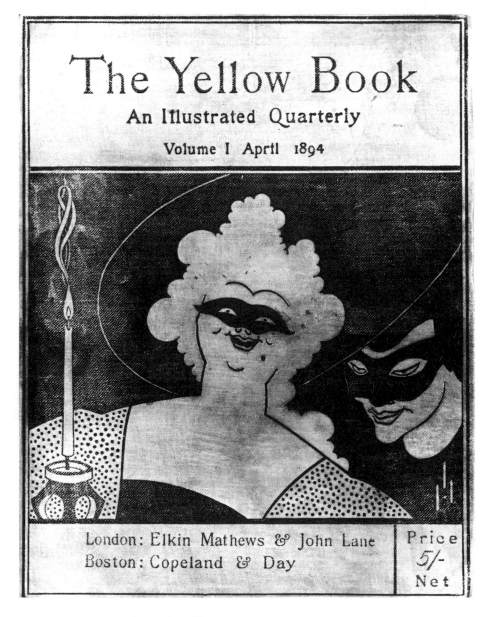

Front covers by Beardsley of the first two volumes of the *Yellow Book*.

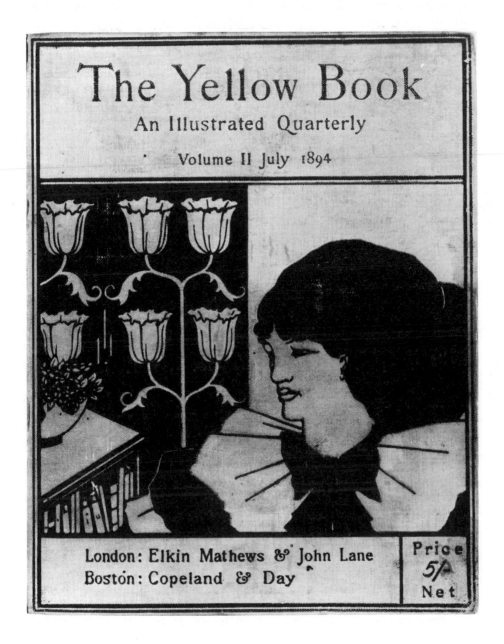

The Yellow Book

An Illustrated Quarterly

Volume II   July 1894

London: Elkin Mathews & John Lane
Boston: Copeland & Day

Price 5/- Net

product of his Oxford years — *Poems*, nevertheless, reflects Wilde's readings in contemporary French literature. Even before his several visits to Paris between 1881 and 1883, he had imbibed much from the Art for Art's Sake movement in France. Although Wilde's masters in English were Pater, Rossetti, and Swinburne, his poetry and criticism reflect his study of Gautier and Baudelaire — his critique, *Salon de 1846,* in particular.

Filled with much that is not French,[74] *Poems* does, however, contain two lyrics, *"Impression du Matin"* and *"Impression: Le Réveillon,"* which reflect the influence of French impressionist painting — especially its preoccupation with effects of light. Although the impress of Whistler is obvious in *"Impression du Matin"* in the opening line "The Thames nocturne of blue and gold," and in the titles "Symphony in Yellow" and "Harmony in the Gold Room," echoes of Gautier's *"Symphonie en Blanc Majeur"* are heard in Wilde's "Symphony" and there are reminiscences of Verlaine's *"Le Piano que baise une Main Frêle"* from *Romances sans Paroles* in "Harmony in the Gold Room."

Written in part during his stay at Oxford but completed in Paris in 1893, Wilde's *The Sphinx* was published by the Bodley Head on June 11, 1894 — the last publication before his arrest the following year. One of the few examples of a long poem in the nineties, *The Sphinx* is a far more elaborate poem than most of Wilde's work. According to B. Ifor Evans, *The Sphinx* is based on an incident from Huysmans's *À Rebours,* and reflects "most fully the influence of Baudelaire upon his work." [75] Certainly the characteristics of the Wildean Sphinx can be traced to Baudelaire's *Le Chat,* a poem in which he describes the physical charms of his "Green-Eyed Venus," Marie Daubrun.[76] The movement of *The Sphinx* from fascination and reverence to revulsion, too, has something of the Baudelairian spleen about it as does Wilde's condemnation of the Sphinx, which recalls the lines from *Le Chat*:

> Et, des pieds jusques à la tête
> Un air subtil, un dangereux parfum,
>   Nagent autour de son corps brun.[77]

Although Gray, Symons, Dowson, and Wilde, the Bodley Head poets who came under the direct influence of their French contemporaries, were unable to create poetry at all comparable to that which they sought to imitate, they did have a genuine appreciation for the French poetic idioms of the later nineteenth century. Writing to Symons in 1890, Wilde looked "forward to an evening together" when the two could "talk about French art, the one art now in Europe that is worth discussing — Verlaine's especially." [78] The high opinion of French art which these men maintained was hardly shared by the French public much less the English. And although we must be eternally grateful to Mathews and Lane for giving highly suspect and often maligned poets like Symons and Gray a voice, it is doubtful that the firm could actually have survived if their "nest of singing birds" had been made up solely of those whom the English public considered as one with the French *poètes maudits*.

The best sellers among the Bodley Head poets were those who, by and large, continued into the nineties the Romantic and Victorian modes — William Watson, Lord De Tabley, Ernest Rhys, Katharine Tynan, Laurence Binyon, Richard Garnett, T. Gordon Hake, A. C. Benson, Francis Bourdillon, and a host of others. These were the staple of the firm during the early nineties; and when during the *Yellow Book* crisis brought on by Wilde's arrest, Lane was faced with either dismissing Beardsley or losing William Watson and Alice Meynell, he fired Beardsley.

Although the reviews of Bodley Head poetry, whether it was French-oriented or traditional, were not always favorable, they suggest rather clearly the attitude of the general public toward the two groups of poets. For example, when both *Silhouettes* and Le Gallienne's *English Poems* appeared in October 1892, the two books were often reviewed together — far more often to the detriment of *Silhouettes*. Likewise, *Silverpoints* and William Watson's second edition of *The Prince's Quest* were issued from the Bodley Head in March 1893. After lauding Watson's work for its traditional beauties, the critic for the *Graphic* went on to speak of John Gray as a poet who "shows in his 'Silverpoints' . . . that if he would abandon the affectations of contemporary French verse, he might write excellent English poetry." [79] This attitude was often encountered. It was, for example, the attitude expressed by the Bodley Head's busiest and most prolific reviewer, Richard Le Gallienne, whose opinions were frequently read in the *Star,* the *Daily Chronicle,* the *Academy,* the *Illustrated London News,* and other periodicals of the day. Often to be counted on when a Bodley Head book needed a bit of logrolling, Le Gallienne's attitude toward the English Francophiles grew increasingly more hostile, an attitude suggested in his opinion of Theodore Wratislaw's volume of poems, *Love's Memorial.* In a letter to John Lane, Le Gallienne referred to the author as "a pessimistic Baudelairish singer," one who "is a[s] fond of rotting carcas[s]es as Baudelaire." Going on to describe the poem "Spring," Le Gallienne was repelled by the fact that though Wratislaw "opens with a pretty nature-description, birds, blossoms etc.," it only leads "up to the contrast of a dead man hanging from the branches of a blossomed apple-tree — & naturally a very Lord of Flies. Him the poet with grim humour addresses as 'fly-gatherer'!" [80]

Le Gallienne's traditionalist view of poetry and his deep seated antagonism to the *décadents* — both French and English — is also expressed in his review of Churton Collins' *Illustrations of Tennyson,* which, appearing in January 1892, was, in effect, Le Gallienne's opening salvo in a concerted effort of that year to destroy the *décadents.* Addressing himself to the question "What is decadence in literature?" Le Gallienne denied that it was either merely a question of style or primarily one of theme. It is, rather,

in the character of the treatment that we must seek it. In all great vital literature the theme, great or small, is considered in all its relations near and far, and above all in relation to the sum-total of things, to the Infinite, as we phrase it; in decadent literature the relations, the due proportions, are ignored. To notice only the picturesque effect of a beggar's rags, like Gautier; the colour-scheme of a tippler's nose, like M. Huysmans; to consider one's mother merely prismatically, like Mr. Whistler — these are examples of the decadent attitude. At bottom, decadence is merely limited thinking, often insane thinking.[81]

In an essay entitled "The Decadent Movement in Literature," Arthur Symons disagreed at length with Le Gallienne's point of view. This essay, which expressed its author's growing understanding and admiration for the literature of France, affords us another means of comparing Le Gallienne and Symons — both provincials who went down to London in the late eighties with a taste for literature yet responded so differently to the literary and artistic currents they found there.

Le Gallienne's response to the aesthetic milieu of the capital is recorded in the slightly disguised account of his first visit to London related in his autobiographical novel, *Young Lives.*[82] Though published in 1898, when most of the important personalities — Dowson, Beardsley, Johnson, Wilde, Davidson — either had died or, like Le Gallienne, slipped past their prime, the description of his first evening at the rooms of "the young publisher" (a thin disguise for John Lane) is an accurate reflection of Le Gallienne's and Lane's reaction to the "tragic generation," and a prejudiced and unfair account of the young writers observed.

Reminiscent of W. H. Mallock's satirical and jaundiced account of the Victorian intellectual elite in *The New Republic,* Le Gallienne's evening, related in Chapter XXXIV, "The Wits," begins with his arrival at "the pub-

lisher's little room about nine o'clock." Revealing his attitude immediately
in his description of the "half-a-dozen rather shy young men" whom he
found there "spasmodically" picking up "strange drawings or odd-looking
books, lying about on the publisher's tables," struggling "maidenly with
cigars," and sipping "a little whisky-and-soda," saying little, Mesurier is
first attracted to "a pale-faced lad" whom he takes to be "about fifteen." [83]
Startled by "his unexpectedly breaking out into a volley of learning, delivered in a voice impressively deliberate and sententious," Mesurier exclaims to the publisher, "What a remarkable boy that is!" The innocent
Mesurier's education begins with the first of a series of cynical if not contemptuous comments about his guests by the publisher. Referring clearly
enough to Lionel Johnson, he replies to Mesurier's outburst: "Yes; but he's
not quite a boy — though he's young enough. A curious little creature, mor-
bidly learned. A friend of mine says that he would like to catch him and
keep him in a bottle, and label it 'the learned homunculus'." [84]

After a conversation with "a being with a face that half suggested a faun,
and half suggested a flower," doubtless Yeats, Henry is further enlightened
by the worldly-wise young publisher, who sets about explaining "some of
these phenomena" to his rather "bewildered" friend:

This is a young Irish poet who, in the intervals of his raising the devil,
writes very beautiful lyrics that he may well have learned from the fairies.
It is his method to seem mad on magic and such things. You will meet with
many strange methods here to-night. Don't be alarmed if someone comes
and talks to you about strange sins. You have come to London in the
"strange sins" period.[85]

Immediately accosted by "a pallid young man, with a preternatural length
and narrowness of face" who talked "to him about the sins of the Borgias,"
Henry then is approached by "a supercilious young man, with pink cheeks,
and a voice which his admirers compared to Shelley's" who asked the young
Liverpudlian

what he thought of Mallarmé's latest sonnet; but finding Henry confessedly
at sea, turned the conversation to the Empire's ballet, of which, unfortunately, Henry knew as little. The conversation then languished, and the
Shelley-voiced young man turned elsewhere for sympathy, with a shrug at
your country bumpkins who know nothing later than Rossetti.[86]

In this parody of Symons, Le Gallienne again reveals his attitude toward a writer whose aesthetic point of view and whose genuine admiration for the French symbolists he doubtless never shared.

Le Gallienne's response to the early nineties is summed up most revealingly in the closing paragraphs of the chapter — an analysis of the situation, which strikingly illustrates its author's antipathy to all the distinctive characteristics of thought and attitude which set the central figures of the nineties apart from the Philistines.

And so it went on till past midnight, when Henry at last escaped, to talk it over with the stars. The evening had naturally puzzled him, as a man will always be puzzled who has developed under the influence of the main tendencies of his generation, and who finds himself suddenly in a backwater of fanciful reaction. Henry in his simple way was a thinker and a radical, and he had nourished himself on the great main-road masters of English literature. He had followed the lead of modern philosophers and scientists, and had arrived at a mystical agnosticism — the first step of which was, to banish the dogmas of the Church as old wives' tales. He considered that he had inherited the hard-won gains of the rationalists. But he came to London and found young men, feebly playing with the fire of that Romanism which he regarded as at once the most childish and the most dangerous of all intellectual obsessions. In an age of great biologists and electricians, he came upon children prettily talking about fairies and the philosopher's stone. In one of the greatest ages of English poetry, he came to London to find young English poets falling on their knees to the metrical mathematicians of France. In the great age of democracy, a fool had come and asked him if he were not a supporter of the House of Stuart, a Jacobite of charades. But only once had he heard the name of Milton — it was the learned boy of fifteen who had quoted him — a lifelong debt of gratitude; and never once had he heard the voice of simple human feeling, nor heard one speak of beauty, simply, passionately, with his heart upon his sleeve. Much cleverness, much learning, much charm, there had been, but he had missed the generous human impulse. No one seemed to be doing anything because he must. These were pleasant eddies, dainty with lilies and curiously starred water grasses, but the great warm stream of English literature was not flowing here.[87]

It is this insular, rather ignorant point of view — "In one of the greatest ages of English poetry, he came to London to find young English poets falling on their knees to the metrical mathematicians of France" — which materializes in *English Poems*. This volume, as he wrote his mother early in

1892, was deliberately designed "as a sort of protest against the deference to French criticism, etc., lately — ." Le Gallienne also told her: "Lane and several other people think it a good idea." [88]

A gathering up of all the poetry he had written since *Volumes in Folio*, *English Poems* reveals Le Gallienne's efforts since coming to London to take advantage of whatever poetic modes of the day seemed promising. Thus the book includes the poet's verses done somewhat in the manner of the decadents — "Hesperides" and "Neaera's Hair" (which G. B. Shaw in a review labeled immoral) [89] — as well as those such as "Sunset in the City" and "The City in Moonlight" which are vaguely reminiscent of the impressionists, whose subject often was the city at night.

Nevertheless *English Poems* is what Le Gallienne intended it to be — a gathering of poems on traditional English themes in traditional English verse forms with an introductory poem "To the Reader" and several other set pieces such as "Beauty Accurst" which voice clearly and directly his opposition to the latter-day "music of France." "Art was a palace once, things great and fair,/ And strong and holy, found a temple there," he reminds his readers. "Now 'tis a lazar-house of leprous men./ O shall we hear an English song again!"

Deriving his title from the highly successful volume of the day, *English Lyrics* by the future poet laureate, Alfred Austin, and his whole argument from the "Preface" written by William Watson, Le Gallienne's *English Poems* suggests how very unoriginal and opportunistic he really was. The fact that *English Lyrics,* first published in July 1890, had by April 1891 reached a third printing while the first printing of Symons' *Days and Nights* of 1889 was still largely unsold was not lost on Le Gallienne. Nor was the fact that William Watson, whose traditionalist position had been clear and unmistakable all along, was outselling all the younger poets by 1892.[90] While the decadents and the Francophile poets might have the adventage of sensationalism and the dubious acclaim of a very small elite, Alfred Austin and William Watson had the much greater advantage of a popularity based on the average English poetry reader's desire for good solid typical English fare. Besides, there can be no doubt that it was here that Le Gallienne's — and Lane's — true tastes really lay. Though he may have enjoyed playing himself up as a rebel against his Victorian father and the bourgeois materialist atmosphere of his native Liverpool while affecting the pose of the aesthetic young man who worshipped Pater and Rossetti, Le Gallienne was at heart a good old-fashioned Victorian sentimentalist who liked to gush over young love and write lyrics about birds and flowers and compose odes to autumn.

Consequently, Le Gallienne found Alfred Austin's "English" poems and especially Watson's defense of them of great interest. At a time when the modernists were making a strong bid in their attempt to oust Victorian rhetoric, themes and sentiment and choose new models and attend to a new subject matter, Watson's confident tone and prophetic voice had a profound effect on Le Gallienne, especially when his friend and rival poet moved with much fervor toward the climactic moment of his Preface: "Unless immemorial principles of right taste and judgment are to be annulled," Watson declared,

life, substance, reason, and reality, with a just balance of sense and sound, are what future generations will look for in our singers. And surely if poetry is not to sink altogether under the lethargy of an emasculate euphuism, and finally to die surfeited with unwholesome sweetmeats, crushed under a load of redundant ornament, and smothered in artificial rose-leaves, the strenuous and virile temper which animates this volume must come to be more and more the temper of English song.

Such a prediction clothed in such resounding rhetoric must not have been lost on one who was so very attentive to signs of how the popular literary current was running. Nor was Watson's assertion that "readers are growing weary, too, of the vaunted exotic graces — and uglinesses — which have been imported with so much pomp and circumstance into English verse," ignored by Le Gallienne, who doubtless applauded when Watson concluded:

We do not require these foreign reinforcements: the countrymen of Shakespeare have no need to borrow either their ethics or their aesthetics from the countrymen of Baudelaire; and if we be wise we shall turn more and more to whatsoever singer scents his pages, not with livid and noxious Fleurs du Mal, but with the blossoms which English children gather in their aprons, and with the candid breath of our hardy and hearty English sky.[91]

Watson's resounding dismissal of "livid and noxious Fleurs du Mal" from English poetry informs much of what Le Gallienne says in his "To the Reader" of English Poems. Watson's influence is clear in the tone Le Gallienne takes with the decadents, who have made the fair temple of English art "a lazar-house of leprous men" and in his assumption that the disturbing new voice in English poetry is derived from France:

Thou nightingale that for six hundred years
Sang to the world — O art thou husht at last!
For, not of thee this new voice in our ears,
Music of France that once was of the spheres;
And not of thee these strange green flowers that spring
From daisy roots and seem to bear a sting.

Coming before the English reader, "Not as a singer, only as a child," Le Gallienne promises in *English Poems* to oppose to the artifice and satiety of decadent verse the simple glories of nature and childhood. Above all, like Watson, he is indignant about the fact that while

An English May still brings an English thorn,
Still English daisies up and down the grass,
Still English love for English lad and lass —
Yet youngsters blush to sing an English song!

Since much of the book is given over to the theme of love, Le Gallienne began the volume with a long poem, which he entitled "Paolo and Francesca." Composed of Spenserian stanzas obviously modeled after Keats's "The Eve of St. Agnes," "Paolo and Francesca" is an example of what can come of nourishing oneself "on the great main-road masters of English literature." Devoid of all but the crudest and most debased echoes of the Keatsian poetic idiom, the first stanza is hardly better or worse than the remainder of the poem:

It happened in that great Italian land
   Where every bosom beateth with a star —
At Rimini, anigh that crumbling strand
   The Adriatic filcheth near and far —
   In that same past where Dante's dream-days are,
That one Francesca gave her youthful gold
   Unto an aged carle to bolt and bar;
Though all the love which great young hearts can hold,
How could she give that love unto a miser old?

"An Epitaph on a Goldfish" illustrates what he could do with something less demanding:

> *Five inches deep Sir Goldfish lies,*
> *Here last September was he laid,*
> *Poppies these that were his eyes,*
> *Of fish-bones were these bluebells made.*
> *His fins of gold that to and fro*
> *Waved and waved so long ago,*
> *Still as petals wave and wave*
> *To and fro above his grave.*
> *Hearken too! for so his knell*
> *Tolls all day each tiny bell.*

As Lionel Johnson once wrote, when Le Gallienne's "subject is in itself trivial he can be charming: when it is high he does not rise to it." [92]

Not always content simply to let his poetry illustrate his point of view, Le Gallienne in "The Decadent to His Soul" and "Beauty Accurst" openly resorted to didacticism, expressing his disgust for the decadent who worships a sinister and soul-debasing beauty. In his rather silly portrait of a "Decadent" who dreams "of new sin:/ An incest 'twixt the body and the soul," Le Gallienne, as Beckson has said, "satirizes the characteristic verse of the Decadents and their quest for new and strange sensations." [93] Having seduced his soul and having waited for "the purple thing that shall be born," the decadent exults, like Huysmans's Des Esseintes, over the strange flower which he now beholds —

> *Seven petals and each petal seven dyes,*
> *The stem is gilded and the root in blood:*
> *That came of thee.*
> *Yea, all my flowers were single save for thee,*
> *I pluck seven fruits from off a single tree,*
> *I pluck seven flowers from off a single stem,*
> *I light my palace with the seven stars,*
> *And eat strange dishes to Gregorian chants:*
> *All thanks to thee.*

Weeping "for both, — / The man was once an apple-cheek [sic] dear lad,/ The soul was once an angel up in heaven," the poet destroys any effect he might have derived from the satire by concluding with an exhortation designed to edify his readers:

O let the body be a healthy beast,
And keep the soul a singing soaring bird;
But lure thou not the soul from out the sky
To pipe unto the body in the sty.

Deriving a perverse pleasure from the worship she commands, Le Gallienne's "Beauty Accurst" delights in her newly won power over the minds of all — the "poet writing honey of his dear" as well as "the sleepy kine" who move round her "in desire/ And press their oozy lips" upon her hair. Intoxicated with such obeisance, she only waits

. . . the hour when God shall rise
Up from the star where he so long hath sat,
And bow before the wonder of my eyes
And set me there — I am so fair as that.

Just how successful Le Gallienne's poetic venture was is indicated by the public's eagerness to buy the book. In late July 1892, some two months before it was actually published on September 27, the edition evidently had already been subscribed for. On July 24, Le Gallienne had written in reply to a letter from Lane: "Your news of E. P. is in itself like a month at the sea-side. Why, reckoning the general[?] copies, the edn. is actually sold out." Printed at Constables, *English Poems,* according to the Day Books of the firm, appeared in a first printing of 800 ordinary copies, 150 large-paper copies and 25 (actually 30 printed) on Japanese paper. A second printing of 550 copies was called for in October and a third of 500 copies by mid-December — a total of 2,030 copies in all.

Although Le Gallienne's *English Poems* is neither the best nor the worst of the Bodley Head books of its kind, it does serve to heighten the contrast between what I have labeled the modernists and the traditionalists within the firm. That the Bodley Head could, by successfully purveying both poetic modes, create a minor revival of interest in poetry[94] at a time when poets good and bad were finding it very difficult to find either a publisher or an audience, is, indeed, an achievement of some worth to literature.

For us, the fact that books of so diverse a character were in the early nineties issued under the aegis of a single publishing firm suggests again the significance of the Bodley Head, the first seven years of which saw the death of both Arnold and Tennyson, the pre-eminent literary voices of Victorianism. So long as those two literary giants lived, traditional poetic matter and modes claimed the allegiance of a large but steadily dwindling audience. Young poets who like Watson sought to sustain the Victorian poetic voice on into the last decade of the century seemed at first to triumph. Yet by the death of Arnold in April 1888, a desire for a new subject matter and new poetic techniques was already evident. Although when Tennyson died in October 1892, none of the young English experimenters in the verse techniques of impressionism and symbolism were in serious contention for the Laureate's robes, the fact that there was a long-drawn-out struggle for the post Tennyson left vacant suggests the uncertain situation which prevailed in poetry at the time of which I write. The strenuous efforts which Richard Holt Hutton of the *Spectator* and other leading literary czars of the hour made toward gaining the Laureateship for a young traditionalist poet like Watson are indicative of a concerted effort in the early nineties to discredit and disarm young writers such as Symons, Gray, and Yeats, poets who were endeavoring to free English poetry from Victorian rhetoric and to search out a new path to the twentieth century.

What the Laureateship battle — fought as it was over a period of three years (November 1892 to December 31, 1895) — in a somewhat clouded way suggested is more clearly evident within the early Bodley Head itself. While reflecting the public demand for the verse of young traditionalists, the Bodley Head's book lists indicate the nature and extent of experimentation in English verse which in time was to lead to the new poetic voices of Ezra Pound and T. S. Eliot. The poetry of Watson published by the early Bodley Head suggests how feeble and exhausted were the poetic efforts of even the best of the young traditionalists, while the firm's examples of impressionism and symbolism in Symons' *Silhouettes* and Gray's *Silverpoints* represent the early gropings toward a new poetic tradition in England.

Dramatic Works

Although the early Bodley Head is most often acclaimed for its endeavors in the field of poetry, the firm, during its seven years of existence, certainly had its share of triumphs in several other areas of belles-lettres — in particular, the drama. The early nineties saw something of a revolution occur in the theater. By 1890, the old melodrama, which had been the staple of the Victorian stage, was on the wane, and a period of experimentation with new modes and new ideas came into existence. Though the Bodley Head's publication list of dramatic works is not large, only five volumes containing ten plays, it included significant examples of the work of three playwrights whose plays were produced by J. T. Grein's Independent Theatre in its first years of existence: Oscar Wilde's *Lady Windermere's Fan* and *Salome,* John Todhunter's *A Sicilian Idyll,* and Michael Field's *A Question of Memory* and *Stephania.*

Perhaps the most unsettling element in British drama during the years of the early Bodley Head were the Ibsenites — G. B. Shaw, William Archer, and Henry Arthur Jones — who through criticism and lectures called for a "renaissance of the drama." Although Ibsen had been in England since Edmund Gosse had begun to write about him in the seventies,[1] the storm over Ibsen which began to blow up when William Archer and Charles Charrington produced *A Doll's House* at the Novelty Theatre on June 7, 1889, burst forth in all its fury when in 1891 the Lord Chamberlain refused

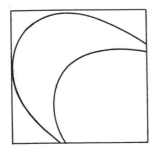

7 THE BODLEY HEAD AUTHORS:
A GATHERING OF PLAYWRIGHTS, ESSAYISTS, AND FICTIONISTS

to license a production of *Ghosts* by the newly established Independent Theatre. So extraordinary were these events in the theatrical world that, according to Holbrook Jackson, they aroused an interest "such as had not been known in artistic circles since the first performance of Wagner's operas, and the appearance of the Impressionistic painters." [2]

Founded in 1891 by Jack Thomas Grein, a drama critic, playwright, and manager, who had come to England from Holland, the Independent Theatre was established along the lines of Antoine's Théâtre Libre. Although his aim was to bring continental drama to the English stage, he also wanted to produce plays by talented young English authors who were in their various ways attempting to create a fresh and vital theater in London. Far from producing only Ibsen and his brand of realism, Grein exhibited an amazing sort of open-mindedness when he brought to the stage of the Independent such productions as John Todhunter's *The Black Cat*, Michael Field's *A Question of Memory*, and Wilde's *A Woman of No Importance*, as well as Shaw's *Widowers' Houses*. A program advertising the third season, for instance, brought together plays by dramatists as diverse in their aims as Zola, Strindberg, Shaw, Ibsen, Michael Field, and Todhunter.[3]

Although the search for a new drama led the playwrights and critics abroad to France, Russia, and Scandinavia, English dramatists also turned their attention to the drama of the nation's past, in particular to the drama of the Elizabethans and Jacobeans and to the poetic dramas of Shelley and Browning. *Fin de siècle* dramatists and audiences found the pastoral comedy of the Elizabethans, with its evocations of an age of innocence and rural joy, a pleasant means of escape from an urban world oppressive with its materialism and its hypocrisy, while the decadents in particular found the "lurid and chaotic world," as William Watson described it, of John Ford and John Webster as interesting as that of Ibsen.[4] Although the Jacobeans had been of great interest to earlier writers — Lamb and Hazlitt, for example — the attention given them by Swinburne and others in the late nineteenth century resulted in the Mermaid series, edited by Havelock Ellis and Arthur Symons.

Perhaps the similarity of theme and treatment between the works of the Jacobeans and Shelley's *The Cenci* had something to do with its being performed for the first time at the Grand Theatre in Islington on May 7, 1886, and the great enthusiasm which attended it. A production of the newly formed Shelley Society, *The Cenci* was a triumph for the actress Alma Murray, who in the long and arduous role of Beatrice won for herself "at one stroke an unassailable and world-wide reputation." [5] Having been acclaimed in such roles as Juliet in *Romeo and Juliet* and Portia in *The Merchant of*

Venice, Miss Murray seems to have made her greatest impact on her audiences as Beatrice in Shelley's play and as the heroines in the Browning Society's productions of "In a Balcony," "A Blot in the 'Scutcheon" and "Colombe's Birthday." So popular was Miss Murray in the early nineties that she was the subject of numerous pamphlets including *Miss Alma Murray as Beatrice Cenci, Miss Alma Murray's Constance in "In a Balcony,"* and the Bodley Head's contribution of 1891 bound in red paper wrappers, *Alma Murray, Portrait as Beatrice Cenci with Critical Notice Containing Four Letters from Robert Browning.*[6]

The controversy which the new trends in the theater stirred up can be gathered from the venom with which the revival of the Jacobeans was countered and from the torrent of invective, satire, and parody with which the conservative critics of the day met the efforts of the Ibsenites. For instance, Watson's *Excursions in Criticism,* which the Bodley Head published in 1893, contained two essays previously published, "Ibsen's Prose Dramas" and "Some Literary Idolatries," in which Watson vigorously opposed morbid, pessimistic representations of life. His main criticism of the dramas of Ibsen and of the Jacobean playwrights was that, unlike true tragedies, they failed — despite all their blood, thunder, and mental anguish — to "inspirit and rejoice the reader." Although Watson recognized Ibsen to be a writer of great power and genius, he felt the playwright failed as a dramatist because he confined his vision to only one side of life. Unlike Sophocles and Shakespeare who "deal with life," Ibsen, Watson believed, dealt "only with death-in-life. They treat of society; he treats only of the rottenness of society. Their subject is human nature — his, human disease." [7]

Allan Monkhouse, in his Bodley Head volume, *Books and Plays,* defended Ibsen and the effect of Ibsenism on the English theater in his essay entitled, "Ibsen's Social Plays," but the majority of critics of the day would not have concurred in his opinions of Ibsen or in his assertion in another essay, "The Politics of Dramatic Art," that "what is required" to save the theater "is to rouse the interest and intelligence of the people, who are bored by poetical plays of old types." [8]

Evidence that the playgoer of the early nineties still preferred to go to the theater to be entertained and amused rather than to be preached at and indoctrinated can be gathered from a poem, " 'The Playgoer' (New Style),'' which appeared in the *Anti-Jacobin* on Saturday, January 31, 1891.

> *There was a time I blush to say*
> *When, if I ventured on the play,*
> *I merely wanted to be gay.*

Now, however, the playgoer found that he must sit through naturalistic dramas which prove that burglars are "the Psychical Epitome/ Of Labour struggling to be Free" and that a murderer is but "a 'monad blown/ By grim Heredity's cyclone.' " Once, he recalled,

The wife who ran away, alack!
Was for the moment on the track
Of ruin, but at length came back,

She wasn't quintessential rant
Of hypnotism, Hegel, Kant,
Herr Ibsen, and the wormwood plant.

But now Shakespeare has been "quite misplaced," he found and

That not to Nature now must hold
The stage its mirror as of old,
With broad reflections manifold;
But, science-hit, be doomed, alas!
With finnikin reforms to glass
The prig-philosophaster class.

Consequently, he complained,

I "go" not now to plays, but cram
To pass them like a school exam.
I strive to be a solemn sham, —
And shan't be happy till I am.[9]

More to the taste of the *Anti-Jacobin* was a Bodley Head play by Dr. John Todhunter, *A Sicilian Idyll*, the title of which suggests how far from Ibsen it was. As a result, the reviewer found it free from what he described as "affectation of manner," and went on to conclude: "Restrained, simple, graceful, 'A Sicilian Idyll' deserves all these epithets in an age of gush, obscurity, and ugliness." [10] The result of a suggestion by Yeats, Todhunter's play is an example of a dramatic work in the early nineties which, while exhibiting tendencies opposed to naturalistic theater, was nevertheless a significant departure from the old farce and melodrama.

Yeats was just as opposed to Victorian tradition in the theater as were the Ibsenites and just as anxious as they to replace it with something new; but his early ideas about the renovation of the theater lay with a renewal of the poetic drama, a drama which in its language and its themes would be remote from actual life. Revolted by what he called the theater of commerce, which was typified by a journalistic clarity and an attempt to imitate the style and rhythm of common everyday speech, Yeats believed that "if modern drama is to be anything else than a muddy torrent of shallow realism," it must lift

us into a world of knowledge and beauty and serenity. As the Mohammedan leaves his shoes outside the mosque, so we leave our selfhood behind before we enter the impersonal temple of art. We come from it with renewed insight, and with our ideals and our belief in happiness and goodness stronger than before. Melodrama can make us weep more; farce can make us laugh more; but when the curtain has fallen, they leave nothing behind. They bring us nothing, because they demand nothing from us. They are excitements, not influences. The poetic drama, on the other hand, demands so much love of beauty and austere emotion that it finds uncertain footing on the stage at best.[11]

Of the opinion that if what he called "higher drama" was to come "once more into existence" it must first find its audience among "the refined and cultivated and well-read," [12] Yeats found in the early plays of Todhunter a reasonable approximation of his ideal. Todhunter had written several plays before *A Sicilian Idyll*: the classical tragedies *Alcestis* and *Helena of Troas*, which he had modeled on Swinburne's *Locrine*. Although entirely too oratorical for Yeats, the *Helena,* performed in Dublin at Hengler's Circus, which had been remodeled as a Greek theater, had, nevertheless, moved him: "Its sonorous verse, united to the rhythmical motions of the white-robed chorus, and the solemnity of burning incense," produced what he felt to have been "a semi-religious effect new to the modern stage." [13] In his continuing effort to define what was "new and creative" in the *Helena,* Yeats pointed to Todhunter's "attempt to apply the old conditions to the modern stage, to redeem the drama by mingling music and poetry, to add a new convention to the stage." [14]

Yeats saw in Todhunter, the Bedford Park coterie of which both were a part, and its little theater in the red brick Clubhouse, the perfect ingredients for the creation of "higher drama." Consequently he urged Todhunter, an elderly man many years his senior, to continue his experiments in this direction by writing a kind of drama so remote from the modern social setting of the naturalistic drama that, "nobody would expect . . . the succession of nervous tremors which the plays of commerce, like the novels of commerce, have substituted for the purification that comes with pity and terror to the imagination and intellect." [15]

Todhunter took his young friend's advice and wrote *A Sicilian Idyll,* which was an attempt to fulfill Yeats's early dramatic ideal. What Yeats described as "a little verse play of shepherds and shepherdesses, founded on a story in Theocritus," [16] the *Idyll* is in a sense a revival of a tradition in the English drama which began with Sir Philip Sidney's entertainment *The Lady of May* and continued with the masques and pastoral comedies of Ben Jonson and John Fletcher. Provided with choruses and incidental music composed by B. Luard-Selby, the *Idyll* is masquelike in several respects, including its use of the dance, especially the wild vintage or cymbal dance performed by Thestylis with what one reviewer called "that wild enthusiastic vehemence, coupled with perfect grace" [17] which so affected the London audiences.

In part a contribution to the neopaganism of the nineties, *A Sicilian Idyll* is the product of a sophisticated, predominantly urban elite trying to recapture the instincts of a genuine primitivism through a self-conscious imitation of its external manifestations. Yet for Todhunter, who was steeped in the poetry of William Blake, it was also an attempt to embody the Blakean idea that all art should labor to restore the Golden Age. Expressing in its Prologue an oblique criticism of the Iron Age of the present, the play in its setting, its style and language, and its theme, is an expression of its author's belief that art must raise us above the mortal world of time and change and elevate us if but for a moment into a realm of the ideal toward which one must aspire. An implied rejection of Philistia and its emphasis on the here and now, *A Sicilian Idyll* in its contrived and artificial style is also a rejection of the tendency of the theater of the nineties to use everyday speech, a language of the streets, which of necessity is subject to constant change. Archaisms abound in the *Idyll* because of their artificiality and immunity from modification.

Although "a sad yet kindly smile" from "the pale shade of old Theocritus" is "all our age/ Dare hope," the speaker of the Prologue invokes "his impassioned nightingale," which lingers still, as Muse and pleads —

> *O, let none sneer*
> *If, singing still, she strive to charm your ear*
> *With vowelled verse, to set before your eyes*

Title page and first page of text designed by C. S. Ricketts for *The Sphinx*.

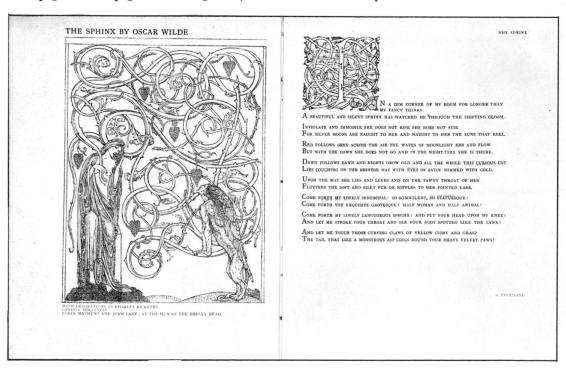

An Idyll, picturing 'neath sunnier skies
The shepherd folk of some dim age of gold.

Hegelian in his aesthetics,[18] Todhunter divided the *Idyll* into two scenes: the first centering around a challenge to the heroine's beliefs, which initiates the conflict and dilemma of the play; and the second leading to her reconciliation and marriage with Alcander. Amaryllis, the Amazonian heroine, is a beautiful, chaste but cold virgin, whose idealistic nature causes her to scorn life as it is. Having observed "The tedious tragedies of woman's life," she refuses to share the view of her friend, Thestylis, who lives and acts according to the idea that "we clothe in dreams/ The naked limbs of life that we may live/ Unscathed of the dread vision." Like Tennyson's Princess, Amaryllis is one who has "ever roamed the mind's high mountain-peaks" and as a "Lone shepherdess of thought's wide wandering flocks" has refused to have anything to do with ordinary men.

In a confrontation with the hero, Alcander, who, unlike Amaryllis, wants a real mate not a paragon of unearthly virtues, the heroine is forcibly kissed by the hero — an act which affects Amaryllis like a love potion — "I have drunk the wine of Circe," she exclaims to herself. After Amaryllis has "grown a woman" in the arms of Alcander, love once again triumphs and is welcomed as the reigning deity by the happy shepherds.

Thestylis. *Hail, conquering Eros, thou shalt be the lord*
              Of all our flocks and herds!
Amaryllis.   *And hearts and homes.*

Produced as Yeats had hoped at the little theater in Bedford Park, *A Sicilian Idyll* on its opening night, May 5, 1890, was an enormous success. With costumes and scenery designed by Lys Baldry, the production drew audiences which filled the theater "for twice the number of performances intended, for," as Yeats later explained, "artists, men of letters and students had come from all over London." [19] Yeats was delighted with the performance of Florence Farr, a leading actress of the day, as Amaryllis, and Heron Allen, an amateur, as Alcander. In his *Autobiography* he recalled that while these two "were upon the stage no one else could hold an eye or an ear. Their speech was music, the poetry acquired a nobility, a passionate austerity that made it akin for certain moments to the great poetry of the world." [20]

In its review of the play, the *Academy* seemed to have been of like mind with Yeats. It found pleasure in the fact "that a play of this kind can exercise so much attraction in days when art — and especially, perhaps, the dramatic art — tends so much to become a form of nervous excitement." And it also praised Todhunter's ability to subordinate thought, character, and plot "to grace — everything comes to us through a medium which subtly alters the stern or exuberant outlines of reality to delicate forms of rhythmic beauty." [21]

Shortly after the Bedford Park success, Todhunter moved swiftly to have the play published, and since Elkin Mathews and his sisters were his neighbors in the suburb,[22] he turned to the Bodley Head for a publisher. A prospectus of two pages was got out in July, and the Copyright Registry Book lists the date of publication as November 24, 1890. Very handsomely done at the Chiswick Press in both a small-paper and large-paper issue, *A Sicilian Idyll,* with its frontispiece and tail piece by Walter Crane, its handmade paper and its letterpress in an old-style font, is one of the Bodley Head's most attractive books.

Like Todhunter, John Davidson, too, turned to the pastoral tradition in creating several of his early plays and his first real literary success, a little volume of poems entitled *Fleet Street Eclogues,* which the Bodley Head published in 1893. A great admirer of Spenser's *Shepherd's Calendar* since his days as a lonely, oppressed schoolteacher in his native Scotland, Davidson turned his idea for a Teacher's Calendar into a Journalist's Calendar when he came to London in 1890 and began to know firsthand the horrors of the Fleet Street hack writer's situation.

A dramatization of an inner conflict between his will and his aesthetic temperament, *Fleet Street Eclogues,* like his plays, maintains a peculiar balance between fantasy and realism. As J. Benjamin Townsend has observed:

By contrasting the views of his journalist-shepherds and by opposing the urban dungeons in which they work to the rural scenes which they nostalgically recall, the poet sustains a nice balance and a peculiarly modern irony. Satire, sentiment, melody, color, wit, description of nature, and discursive opinion all woven into an intricate counterpoint of sound and sense.[23]

Highly recommended to Lane for publication by his reader, Le Gallienne, the book appeared in April 1893, in an edition of 300 copies issued in dark blue buckram lettered in gold. So popular were the *Eclogues* that a second printing appeared in July. It was probably on the basis of this success that Lane decided to issue Davidson's plays, which had between 1886 and 1889 fallen from the press almost stillborn. Of the five plays which were in 1894 to be brought together in the handsome Bodley Head edition entitled simply *Plays*, three — *An Unhistorical Pastoral, A Romantic Farce,* and *Scaramouch in Naxos* — had been published privately in one volume by the author at Greenock, Scotland, in 1889, before he had come to London. A second issue had then been published in the following year by T. Fisher Unwin. An advertisement included in the second issue read: "Under the title of 'plays' this volume was printed and published for private circulation. In issuing this edition the author takes the opportunity of correcting his title-page, and giving his work the title of the play he likes best." Davidson evidently objected to the change of title from *Plays* to *Scaramouch in Naxos: A Pantomime and Other Plays*, however, so when after much effort, Davidson and Lane were able to get the remainder of the sheets transferred to the Bodley Head in 1893, the third issue appeared with both the original title page and a new title page with the Mathews and Lane imprint, both entitled, *Plays*.[24]

In the spring and early summer of 1893, Davidson and Lane also sought to obtain the remainders of two other plays, *Bruce,* published by Wilson and McCormick at Glasgow in 1886, and *Smith,* brought out by Wilson and Brother of Glasgow in 1888. Again the author and publisher ran into much trouble. Since the demise of the firm of Wilson and McCormick, *Bruce* had come into the hands of a vendor who, on being approached by Davidson to sell him all the remaining copies, demanded a much higher price than expected. On May 2, 1893, Davidson wrote Lane to tell him how the matter with regard to *Bruce* then stood.

The vendor sent me an account of £5.5.8, which with 3/6 of carriage makes £5.9.2. I regarded this as a preposterous price and wrote offering him £2 which I think ample. I had thought of its not costing more than £1, and my intention was to destroy all the copies of "Bruce," as it contains one very wretched passage at least, and several lines I wish knocked out. When I said £3 to you yesterday, I calculated on the vendor reducing his terms by £2 in reply to my offer; I haven't his answer yet. I only want my expenses covered. "Bruce" cost me £12 to start with, and I've seen none of it, and I'm not disposed to be out of pocket by it any more. I couldn't very well go into these details yesterday with a customer in the shop. I shall let you have the copies, if you want them, at the lowest they cost me, which will I think be less than you could have bought them for.[25]

The problem with *Smith* was even more difficult to solve. In the fall of 1893, when it became known that the Bodley Head intended to issue a collected edition of five of Davidson's plays, including *Smith,* the firm received a threatening letter from Frederick Wilson, a partner in the then bankrupt Wilson and Brother publishing firm. Contending that *Smith* was to be a publication of his new firm, Frederick W. Wilson & Co., Wilson claimed title to the stock.

Frustrated and much outraged, Davidson wrote to Wilson offering ninepence per copy for the remainders of *Smith,* only to be ignored. Again he wrote, this time proposing to pay sixpence for every bound copy and threepence for any in sheets. Again no word. After writing and withdrawing all offers, Davidson received word that Wilson wanted a shilling and sixpence per copy. It was at this point that Davidson agreed to allow Lane to act for him in the matter and wrote out a four-page document entitled "After-Piece to *Smith*" for Lane's use, giving his version of the whole transaction with Wilson.[26] Lane was doubtless successful in his negotiations to secure what remained of the 300 copies of *Smith,* for it was included in the edition of *Plays* which appeared early in February 1894.

Although the Bodley Head had gone ahead and reissued both *Bruce* and the original *Plays* in 1893, Davidson's desire all along seems to have been to destroy all the remainders and bring out a revised version of the five plays in a collected edition. In his letter to Lane of May 2, 1893, Davidson in a postscript to his account of the negotiations concerning *Bruce* had written: "The advantage to me of course is considerable in getting a number of 'Bruces' destroyed. I look forward to the publication of all my plays revised in one volume — which will indeed be the first publication of them: none of them can properly be said to have been published." [27] In another letter to Lane of about the same date Davidson actually made a proposal to that effect: "Instead of trying to sell in the meantime these copies of first editions, [let us] issue a collected edition (300) of all my plays in the autumn, advertising a few copies remaining of first editions at end of volume." [28]

As it turned out, this was the way the Bodley Head handled the matter, and on November 2, 1893, Lane sent to Davidson the final agreement:

We undertake to publish your plays — including "an unhistorical pastoral," "a romantic farce," "Scaramouch in Naxos," "Bruce," and "Smith" — in an edition not to exceed 500 copies at 7/6 net the cost of paper printing binding advertising and distributing being at our sole charge. We agree to allow you a royalty of 1/- per copy on all copies sold, payable quarterly reckoning from one month after the first quarter-day subsequent to publication, and to supply you with six gratuitous copies and as many additional copies as you may require at the ordinary trade price. We shall at our own cost provide a frontispiece to the volume.[29]

Plays, which appeared in a handsome purple or puce-colored cloth casing with Beardsley's Pierrot figure stamped in gold at the right-hand bottom of the cover, also included the now famous frontispiece also by Beardsley, which the artist referred to as "a really wonderful picture for *Scaramouch in Naxos* [the last play in the volume]."[30] Composed of caricatures of Mabel Beardsley, Henry Harland (literary editor of the *Yellow Book*), Oscar Wilde, Sir Augustus Harris (manager of Covent Garden, Drury Lane, and Her Majesty's Theatre), Le Gallienne as Pierrot, and the dancer Adeline Genée, the frontispiece is also notable for the details of the landscape which, according to Brian Reade, "are remarkable for their date, being almost abstractions."[31]

Although three of the plays, *An Unhistorical Pastoral, A Romantic Farce,* and *Scaramouch,* share with Todhunter's *A Sicilian Idyll* the external trappings of Elizabethan pastoral comedy, they are very different in their inclusion of what Townsend has called a "contemporary message."[32] Like Todhunter, Davidson harbored a fierce hatred for the bourgeois world, yet unlike him, he insisted on facing it and denouncing it. Unwilling to escape into a realm of the beautiful, Davidson, in his comedies and the chronicle play *Bruce* and in the "tragic farce" *Smith* constantly was at war with Philistia and the blight of materialism. "Business — the world's work — " one of his characters in *Smith* proclaims, "is the sale of lies."[33] Davidson's Scaramouch, an unscrupulous impresario modeled on the American showman P. T. Barnum, has been described as "the epitome of Philistine opportunism as it might affect interstellar commerce."[34] Somehow in facing the world yet rejecting it and refusing to live on its terms, Davidson gained a sense of release, joy, and freedom. His King Bruce of Scotland gives voice to this view when he says, "I stand here free, though bound and doomed to die."[35]

In *Smith,* a Spasmodic drama in blank verse, Davidson, representing his two selves in the Byronic hero, Smith, and the poet-friend, Hallowes, ran into something of the decadent impasse. Hallowes in the end seeks refuge "from any breath of modern weariness"[36] in the mountains of the north, where in romantic despair he commits suicide. Smith and his beloved Magdalen likewise seek refuge from their pursuers in the mountains, where they leap together to their deaths.

Strikingly different in their bizarre mixture of dramatic elements from the past and the playwright's evolving philosophy of life, the plays were both attempts to discover the dramatic form of the future, a quest to which Davidson addressed himself outright in his Prologue to *Scaramouch in Naxos,* the play in which he came closest to success:

Which of the various dramatic forms of the time may one conceive as likeliest to shoot up in the fabulous manner of the beanstalk, bearing on its branches things of earth and heaven undreamt of in philosophy? The sensational dramas? Perhaps from them some new development of tragic art; but Pantomime seems to be of best hope. It contains in crude forms, humour, poetry and romance. It is the childhood of a new poetical comedy.[37]

Two close friends of John Todhunter and Elkin Mathews, Katherine Bradley and her niece Edith Cooper, wrote under the pen name of Michael Field, and published three books with the Bodley Head imprint — a volume of poems, *Sight and Song,* and two plays, *Stephania* and *A Question of Memory* — and continued after the breakup to publish with Mathews. Having published a volume of poems, *Bellerophon,* in 1881 and a play, *Callirrhoë,* in 1883, the two women largely retired from the world in 1888 to devote their lives solely to their art. Nevertheless their acquaintance with the literati and artists of the period grew until the ladies knew many of the important people of the day — Charles Ricketts (who designed several of their most beautiful books), Charles Shannon and Will Rothenstein, Oscar Wilde, George Meredith (whom they worshiped), and Bernard Berenson among them. Consequently, the name of Michael Field appears in almost every memoir and reminiscence of the nineties. The ladies were much admired for their devotion to their art and their assiduous cultivation of a life beyond the touch of the meanness and rapacity of modern life.

Symbols of gentleness of spirit and beauty of mind, the two women and their work gained the praise of many who in an age of uncertain values and vulgar pursuits looked to them for art which transcended the ugliness of reality. In his recollection of them, Will Rothenstein wrote:

I see them in my mind's eye, Michael stout, emphatic, splendid and adventurous in talk, rich in wit; Field wan and wistful, gentler in manner than Michael, but equally eminent in the quick give and take of ideas. But how to pass on to others their shining comments on people, on books and pictures, and on human experience — an impossible task! Both were endowed with an ecstatic sense of beauty — of the loveliness of the visible world, and in addition a sensitiveness to the subtleties of art and poetry which inspired them with a perception of the touching poetry which clings to all material things. . . . With so much beauty to occupy them, they had no time for, and no patience with, the meaner objects which too many men and women pursue. For their poet's integrity must be kept bright and spotless, as everything about them, furniture, silver, china, was to be kept.[38]

It was this life in art and the expression of that life in their work which made Michael Field as typical of the nineties as the decadents who lived the life of Bohemia and wrote of the lost days of wine and roses.

A passion for the Elizabethans is probably the single most glaring defect in Michael Field's dramatic work. As William Archer was quick to discern in his review of *A Question of Memory*, the authors, under the spell of Elizabethan drama,

conceived that the essence of drama lay, not in the nicely adjusted interplay of action and character, but in the copious effusion of highly figurative rhetoric. That style was the most dramatic which could boast the greatest number of metaphors to the square inch; and the diction and versification of 1590 or thereabouts were reverently accepted as the heaven-ordained stilts on which all lofty drama must move for evermore. Of the appropriateness of speech to character the poets took little thought. All their personages without distinction spoke the same archaic dialect, tense with imagery, and writhed, as it were, in the effort to find the most impossible expression for the most improbable feelings. Imaginative, philosophical, lyrical faculty abounded in their work — everything, in short, except dramatic impulse or inspiration. This worship of a dead convention has produced an infinite mass of still-born literature, and the dramas of "Michael Field" are among its most melancholy results.[39]

That Wilde and doubtless others of the nineties approved of this strange archaic language and settings remote from actual life can be gathered from his letter to the authors shortly before *A Question of Memory* was produced by the Independent Theatre on Friday, October 27, 1893. "Choose graceful personalities," he advised his friends. "Young actors and actresses who have charming voices — that is enough. . . . I look forward to listening to your lovely play recited on a rush-strewn platform, before a tapestry, by gracious things in antique robes, and, if you can manage it, in gilded masks." [40]

Although the ladies wrote over the years a number of volumes of verse, they longed to "earn the better title of a playwright." [41] And despite the fact that they labored hard to write a great play, their only real taste of success came when in 1893 J. T. Grein accepted their prose tragedy *A Question of Memory* for presentation at the Independent Theatre. In their journal, *Works and Days*, Michael (Miss Bradley) and Field (Miss Cooper) devoted what later became a whole chapter to an account of the trials and tribulations and the joys of the rehearsals. It is still not clear why Grein chose to do the play. William Archer's first thought was that he "was playing into his opponents' hands by converting the Independent Theatre into a *theatre ou l'on s'ennuie*," [42] but the performance attracted all the personages in the realm of art, and Oscar Wilde took a box.

The hero of *A Question of Memory* is a young Hungarian patriot living during the uprisings of 1848. After Ferencz Rényi is captured by the Austrians, the drama mounts to a tense and moving third act, in which the hero, who refuses to reveal the secret of his comrades' positions, watches as first his mother and then his sister are executed. When his betrothed, Kati, is brought forward, however, Rényi can stand no more and agrees to betray his comrades. But at the climactic moment he loses his memory, and on seeing Kati murdered, he goes violently insane. Generally applauded, the third act was, according to Wilde, "admirable — a really fine piece of work — with that touch of terror our stage lacks so much. I think the theatre should belong to the Furies. Caliban and Silenus," he went on to remark, "one educated and the other sober, seem now to dominate, in their fallen condition, our wretched English drama." [43]

Stephania, the earlier of the two plays published by the Bodley Head, is a "trialogue" spoken in blank verse by Otho III, the Holy Roman emperor; Gerbert, his tutor; and Stephania, a courtesan and widow of the murdered Roman consul, Crescentius. Set in Rome in the year 1002 A. D., it portrays the struggle and eventual triumph of Stephania over the Emperor, whose love for her destroys him. Issued in an edition of 250 copies, the volume is another handsome example of the Bodley Head book. Cased in gray paper boards, its distinction lies in its fine, decorated title page, colophon, and cover design by Selwyn Image.

Despite Oscar Wilde's admiration for Michael Field's plays, there is very little in his dramatic work which suggests theirs. His comment about *A Question of Memory* that "the theatre should belong to the Furies" does however remind one of *Salome*, for Wilde endowed his heroine and her mother, Herodias, with not a little of the wild and terrible qualities of those ancient mythical beings who seem present again, at least, in the wings of the Angel of Death heard fluttering ominously about the halls of Herod. Indeed, in its review of *Salome* the *Times* characterized the play as "an arrangement in blood and ferocity, morbid, *bizarre*, repulsive, and very offensive in its adaptation of scriptural phraseology to situations the reverse of sacred." [44]

In almost every respect a bombshell, *Salomé* stirred up controversy from the outset, when in late June 1892 Sarah Bernhardt's planned performance in the title role was banned by the Lord Chamberlain on the grounds that the play contained biblical characters. A naked and unrestrained embodiment of that sense of evil which Pater recognized in his portrait of the Mona Lisa and which was most fully expressed in the poetry of Charles Baudelaire, *Salome,* more than any other Bodley Head book caused a sensation and set the Philistines at open war with the artists of the nineties.

Written in the autumn of 1891 and submitted to Wilde's friend the French poet Pierre Louÿs for his corrections in December, *Salomé* first appeared in print in its original, French version on February 22, 1893. Printed in France and published jointly by the Librairie de l'Art Indépendant in Paris and Mathews and Lane in London, the play was only later translated into English and published by the Bodley Head in 1894.

The French version was printed *"sur les Presses de Paul Schmidt"* and bound in Paris in what Wilde described as "Tyrian purple" wrappers, lettered, and with a cover design in "fading" or "tired" silver.[45] Otherwise unadorned, *Salomé* appeared in England only through a very tardy and ill-agreed-upon arrangement between Wilde and John Lane. From what one can gather, Lane, on hearing about the proposed French edition, urged Wilde to increase the number of ordinary copies of *Salomé* from 250 to 600 and add the imprint of Mathews and Lane to that of the Librairie on the title page so that the Bodley Head could have the privilege of issuing the play in England. For some reason, however, Lane, despite numerous promptings on Wilde's part and repeated promises on his, failed to write out and sign a formal agreement.

In early February 1893, Wilde wrote Lane to say that he expected *Salomé* to "be ready in a fortnight — at any rate before the end of the month. I am printing 50 on large paper, of which you can have 25 if you like; they will be 10/– each, sale price. Of course you will have them at a proper reduction. But," he urged, "kindly let me have as you promised, a formal note about the whole thing, so as to have no misunderstanding about the agreement. Pray do this at once." [46] Nevertheless, it was not until the very eve of the day of publication that Lane sent a telegram to Wilde expressing his intent to take the copies allotted him. "Dear Mr Lane," Wilde wrote in reply,

Your letter has not yet arrived, but I have received your telegram, which I will now regard as a formal record of our agreement. You see now, I feel sure, how right I was in continually pressing you for a written agreement, and I cannot understand why you would not do so. I spoke to you on the subject at your own place; you promised to forward the agreement next day; this was in November last; I spoke to you twice about it at the Hogarth Club, you made the same promise. I wrote to you endless letters — a task most wearisome to me — on this plain business matter. I received promises, excuses, apologies, but no agreement. This has been going on for three months, and the fact of your name being on the title-page was an act of pure courtesy and compliment on my part; you asked me to allow it as a favour to you; just as my increasing the numbers printed from 250 to 600 was done to oblige you. I make no profit from the transaction, nor do I derive any benefit. As you are interested in literature and curious works of art I was ready to oblige you. The least return you might have made would have been to have spared me the annoyance of writing endless business letters. I can only tell you that when I did not hear from you in Paris last week I very nearly struck your name off the title-page of the book, and diminished the edition. As you had advertised it, however, I felt this would have been somewhat harsh and unkind to you.

I will now look on the incident as over, and accept the regrets expressed in your telegram. I hope that we may publish some other book of mine, but it must clearly be understood that the business matters are to be attended to by your firm properly and promptly: my sphere is that of art, and of art merely.

With regard to the edition on Dutch paper, I am only putting twenty-five on the market. Of these I have reserved ten for you.[47]

It was as a postscript to this letter that Wilde, obviously much chagrined by Lane's behavior, rebuked the publisher for advertising *Salomé* as "the play the Lord Chamberlain refused to license."

Please do not do this again. The interest and value of *Salomé* is not that it was suppressed by a foolish official, but that it was written by an artist. It is the tragic beauty of the work that makes it valuable and of interest, not a gross act of ignorance and impertinence on the part of the censor.[48]

The ill temper detected here is to some extent due to his recollection of the painful fact that when the rehearsals for the production of *Salomé* at the Palace Theatre in London were in full swing in June 1892, they were cut short by the refusal to license the play. A wholly unjust and bigoted move, the refusal to allow *Salomé* to be performed on the London stage was actually the decision of Edward F. Smyth Pigott, whom Wilde referred to "as a commonplace official . . . who panders to the vulgarity and hypocrisy of the English people, by licensing every low farce and vulgar melodrama." [49] Yet what may have hurt Wilde perhaps more than the censorship itself was the fact that with the exception of William Archer and G. B. Shaw every major drama critic and even such leading actors as Henry Irving supported the licenser and spoke strongly in favor of continuing stage censorship.[50]

So outraged was the author over this unexpected reversal of his plans for *Salomé* that he was quoted by several newspapers as having said that he would take his departure for France at once, a statement which gave rise to Watson's poem, "Lines to Our New Censor" which appeared in the *Spectator* for July 9, 1892:

> *And wilt thou, Oscar, from us flee,*
>   *And must we, henceforth, wholly sever?*
> *Shall thy laborious* jeux-d'esprit
>   *Sadden our lives no more forever?*

Watson once again seems to have expressed the sentiments of the English public accurately.[51] At the same time, Archer wrote a letter to the *Pall Mall Gazette* in which he not only strongly denounced the censorship of the stage but criticized Wilde's decision to turn tail and run "away from a petty tyranny which lives upon the disunion and apathy of English dramatic authors." Seeing in *Salomé* a work unique to the English stage, Archer urged that the play was necessary "to aid in the emancipation of art from the stupid meddling of irresponsible officialism." [52] When in February 1893, Wilde sent a copy of *Salomé* to Archer, he recalled with appreciation the drama critic's support.[53]

Although Wilde was doubtless stunned by the adverse reaction to his play, he did in time proceed to publish it, first in France, then a year later in England. It is the English version of *Salome* with its illustrations and cover designs by Aubrey Beardsley which is the more famous. Wilde, who rejected Beardsley's translation of *Salomé* in favor of another by Lord Alfred Douglas, nevertheless chose Beardsley to decorate the book presumably over Charles Ricketts, who had since 1891 been Wilde's choice. Perhaps the fact that John Lane had been so taken with Beardsley's gratuitous illustration of *Salomé*, the *J'ai Baisé Ta Bouche Iokanaan*, which appeared in the

Studio in April 1893, was the deciding factor in the choice of an illustrator. However that may be, a token of the playwright's esteem for the young artist is Wilde's inscription in his presentation copy to Beardsley of the 1893 edition of *Salomé*: "March '93. For Aubrey: for the only artist who, besides myself, knows what the dance of the seven veils is, and can see that invisible dance. Oscar." [54]

In the end both Wilde and Lane were something less than happy with Beardsley's illustrations. There were those obvious and hardly flattering caricatures of Wilde as "The Woman in the Moon" in the frontispiece and as Herod in "The Eyes of Herod," among others. Although Brian Reade agrees that this "doubtless annoyed" Wilde, he goes on to suggest that the caricatures need not be taken as proof of any real enmity toward the author on the artist's part. "Beardsley had a habit of caricaturing his friends and acquaintances without real malice. And the notion that he satirized the play and despised Wilde at the date of these drawings cannot be confirmed." [55] Nevertheless, the illustrations for *Salome* caused a rift between the two men which grew into an open break under the impetus of Wilde's trial and what Reade refers to as "the jealous influence" of André Raffalovich. Something of the artist's attitude toward Wilde can be gathered from a letter Beardsley wrote to Robert Ross either during the execution of or shortly after the *Salome* designs were done: "Have you heard from either him [Lord Alfred Douglas] or Oscar?" he asked. "Both of them are really very dreadful people." [56]

Beardsley was undeniably excited about his work for *Salome*. In a note to Ross in which the artist asked him to come and have lunch, he added: "If you happen to be near Elkin Mathews *today* they have a drawing (Salomé) to show you./ Aubrey!!!" [57] Soon after, however, as Beardsley's illustrations came in for Lane's careful inspection, real trouble began. "I suppose you've heard all about the *Salomé* Row," Beardsley wrote Ross in a letter of late autumn 1893,

I can tell you I had a warm time of it between Lane and Oscar and Co. For one week the number of telegraph and messenger boys who came to the door was simply scandalous. I really don't quite know how the matter really stands now. Anyhow Bozie's name is not to turn up on the Title. The Book will be out soon after Xmas. I have withdrawn 3 of the illustrations and supplied their places with 3 new ones (simply beautiful and quite irrelevant).[58]

The original title page, which can be seen as plate no. 274 in Reade's

Front and back covers of *The Sphinx* with Ricketts' designs.

241

Aubrey Beardsley, containing the name of Lord Alfred Douglas as translator was one of several of the original drawings that had to be changed in order not to offend the public. As Beardsley noted in another letter to Ross, "I think the title page I drew for *Salomé* was after all '*impossible*'. You see booksellers couldn't stick it up in their windows. I have done another with rose pattern and Salomé and a little grotesque Eros, to my mind a great improvement on the first." [59]

The English version of *Salome* was all in type at Constables in Edinburgh by November 13, 1893, and on February 9, 1894, the book was published in London by the Bodley Head and in Boston by Copeland and Day. An ordinary issue of 750 copies cased in rough blue canvas boards with lettering on the spine and Beardsley's cover designs in gilt was issued as well as a large-paper issue of 125 on Japanese paper cased in green silk. Shortly after, on February 15, the *Studio* reviewed the new edition of *Salome* and found "the irrepressible personality of the artist dominating everything — whether the compositions do or do not illustrate the text." [60] In this first full discussion of the question which immediately arose — do Beardsley's illustrations harmonize with Wilde's text? — the *Studio* brushed aside what it called the expedient of resorting to conventional criticism and justified the illustrations on the grounds that they were so "audacious and extravagant, with a grim purpose and power of achieving the unexpected — " that "one takes it for itself, as a piquant maddening potion, not so much a tonic as a stimulant to fancy." [61]

Although some of the illustrations have often been criticized as irrelevant to the text, there has recently been a shift in opinion on the part of both literary and art critics. In his recent book on Wilde, Epifanio San Juan, Jr., has pointed out that "there is much in Wilde's imagery of setting and speech that matches Aubrey Beardsley's notorious drawings for the play, his cloistral tableau of nudes and imps, his tortuous lines, his macabre ornamentation." [62] Similarly, Brian Reade asserts that Beardsley's artistic "conceptions immortalize in fact those strains in the play which the author shared unconsciously with its illustrator. Wilde disliked them possibly because they did just this, and also because they conveyed what Beardsley could seldom repress, an ironical comment on the text." [63] Beardsley's art then is a perfect complement to the text, for it is expressive of that same sense of strange beauty which Wilde's Salome and John embody.

Perhaps the best description of Beardsley as the creator of the *Salome* illustrations is to be found in Pater's account of Leonardo, the decadent *par excellence* of the Renaissance, who "wasted many days in curious tricks of design, seeming to lose himself in the spinning of intricate devices of line and colour." [64] What Pater wrote of Leonardo's art has special relevance to both the art and the text of *Salome*: "In such studies," he observed, "some interfusion of the extremes of beauty and terror shaped itself. . . ." [65] In the *Salome* of Wilde and Beardsley that sense of evil beauty which is the central motif of the decadence is most baldly and unrestrainedly objectified in English art. Consequently, it is what the *Studio* in 1894 claimed it to be — "the very essence of the decadent *fin de siècle*"; it was "the typical volume of the period." [66]

Although Wilde spoke of Pater's *Renaissance* as "my golden book; I never travel anywhere without it"; and proclaimed it "the very flower of decadence: the last trumpet should have sounded the moment it was written," [67] what he said could, with even more truth and far more timeliness, have been said about *Salome*. For the play was the beginning of the end not only for Wilde but for decadence as well. In the outraged cries of the British press, even in the way that the leading actors and drama critics almost to a man stood firm behind the Lord Chamberlain's decision, Wilde should have recognized the terrible hatred toward him and the kind of art he represented welling up like the lava of an explosive volcano ready to burst forth in sudden and fatal fury. The *Salome* which Wilde created, Beardsley decorated, and the Bodley Head published was the ultimate expression in English of the literary and aesthetic movement which ended with the arrest of Wilde the following year.

Wilde's first dramatic success had been *Lady Windermere's Fan*, which was produced in the year of Elizabeth Robins' production of *Hedda Gabler* — 1892. Perhaps it was because of so much Ibsenism in the air that Wilde's play, too, was built around a "problem" and emphasized such topics as marital relationships and even, to some extent, heredity. A play in which the virtuous Victorian wife is pitted against her own mother in the form of the New Woman of the nineties, *Lady Windermere's Fan* is another of Wilde's writings in which, as Richard Ellmann has said, "Wilde spreads the guilt from the artist to all men." [68] Lady Windermere, so self-righteous and certain of her goodness at the beginning of the action, comes in the end to know that she and Mrs. Erlynne are of the same mold. To her husband's naive and sentimental assertion — "Into your world evil has never entered" — she replies: "Don't say that Arthur. There is the same world for all of us, and good and evil, sin and innocence, go through it hand in hand. To shut one's eyes to half of life that one may live securely is as though one blinded oneself that one might walk with more safety in a land of pit and prejudice." According to Wilde if all men are hiding behind masks and, whether they know it or not, living insincere lives which amount to a lie, then, in Ellmann's words, "the artist cannot be blamed for not being white." [69]

In the confessions of Lady Windermere and Mrs. Erlynne one observes a ritual which is common to many of Wilde's works. The need to recognize the other, the evil, self is compulsive. Just as Salome in the famous dance "strips the veils from her body, and all semblance of restraint from her mind, so that the play ends in naked cruelty and lust," [70] so, in less violent but equally revealing ways, end *Lady Windermere's Fan* as well as *The Importance of Being Earnest* and *The Ideal Husband*.

Produced for the first time at St. James's Theatre on February 20, 1892, *Lady Windermere's Fan* was offered to Macmillan[71] before it appeared in book form in November 1893, under the auspices of the Bodley Head. The first of several of Wilde's plays to appear in a uniform format designed and furnished with title page and cover decorations by Ricketts' close friend and associate at the Vale Press, Charles Shannon, it was under negotiation early in 1893 as Wilde wanted to publish the play during the spring season. However, in a letter to Ricketts, probably written in June, in which Wilde expressed his pleasure with Shannon's "setting of *Lady Windermere*" — "it looks delightful and is exquisitely placed" — he ventured the opinion that it was "too late in the season" to publish the work.[72]

Although an agreement was not made final until August 3, 1893, a draft agreement had been drawn up by May,[73] which largely reflected Wilde's sentiments as Shannon had conveyed them to Lane in a letter written from The Vale, Chelsea, sometime earlier. "Oscar called tonight," Shannon explained, and

decided very wisely I think that the plays Lady Windermere's Fan etc, should be published at 7/6 net with a limited Edition de luxe at 1 guinea instead of the uniform price of 10/6. These you can announce simply in this way.

In a binding & title page specially designed by Charles Shannon.

.   .   .   .

Oscar says Lady Windermere which is to be the first of the series is to come out at once during the season[.] Oscar is averse to the idea of their being all bound in the same cover. Let me know when you have the material of Lady Windermere in hand & I will take it to the Ballantyne [Press, the printers] the next day.

The order of plays is
1 Lady Windermere's Fan
2 The Duchess of Padua
3 The Woman of No Importance
    You had better write to him concerning the proper order.[74]

As we now know, the suggested price for the large-paper issue (or "limited Edition de luxe," as Shannon termed it) of one guinea was reduced to fifteen shillings. Moreover, neither *Mr. W. H.* nor *The Duchess of Padua* was ever to appear under the Bodley Head imprint although the third play in the projected series, *A Woman of No Importance*, was published in an edition uniform (except for the cover design) with *Lady Windermere's Fan* by John Lane in October after the breakup. *Lady Windermere* appeared on November 9 in a small-paper issue of 500 copies and in a large-paper issue on handmade paper of 50 copies.

Essays — Familiar and Critical

Neither the playwrights nor the poets and prose essayists who gathered about the Bodley Head were in any real sense "Bohemians" simply because in the Parisian sense of the word there was no Bohemia in London. Although there was Soho and the few "literary" taverns in central London like the Crown and the Cock in Shaftesbury Street, the British capital provided nothing comparable, say, to the Latin Quarter of Paris as Baudelaire knew it in the early 1840s, a place largely inhabited by students and destitute artists, eating, drinking, and loving in a free and unruly manner. On coming up to London from the provinces, most of the Bodley Head authors took refuge in very respectable bachelor establishments such as Lane found in the home of Dr. Pritchard at 37 Southwick Street, Hyde Park, and Lionel Johnson found in the home of H. P. Horne and the Century Guild group in Fitzroy Street, both of which were remote from the wholly unsupervised situation Baudelaire knew at Pension Bailly in 1839. As Ernest Rhys later pointed out in an interview, on coming to London from Durham, he found the writers and artists scattered about the great city and not too disposed to indulge in one another's society. Although before his arrival "he had fancied the literary folk, in particular, as living all together in some such paradise of suburbanity as Miss Thackeray's old Kensington or Carlyle's Chelsea," he found that "nothing, of course, could have been further from the fact." [75]

Doubtless, there was something of the Bohemian about the London life of Francis Thompson, Arthur Symons, and Dowson in his later years; yet the more typical young Bodley Head author was Le Gallienne, who though a bit of a dandy and something of a rebel, had hardly gotten a regular job as reviewer for the *Star* before he married his hometown sweetheart and settled down in suburban London in a little middle-class villa, "Mulberry Cottage," to the life of a career writer. Similarly, in the early nineties even the British artists who had gone to Paris — Ricketts and Shannon, Will Rothenstein, Du Maurier — had returned home and settled down to a life of domesticity and serious work. And despite all the to-do Symons, Lane, Rothenstein, York Powell, and others made over Verlaine's visit to England in 1893, the poet, now an old man, did not care to tarry long in a London so unlike his beloved Paris, and his admirers were a bit relieved to see the unpredictable and shabby Frenchman with his uncouth habits and bizarre manners go.

The closest the Bodley Head came to the Parisian Bohemia was in the poetry of Symons' *Silhouettes*, in such poems as "The Absinthe Drinker," "In Bohemia," and "Emmy." Yet the Bodley Head valued among its authors another kind of Bohemian who was, in many respects, very different from his Parisian cousin. Although he shared an antipathy toward the regimented, thoroughly respectable life of the middle-class family man who went bored and no doubt a bit desperate to his work in the City fifty-one weeks of every year, he was himself a victim of this soul-destroying, exceedingly humdrum existence. Most of the time this Bohemian who had learned to repress his primitive, anarchic instincts led what outwardly appeared to be an exemplary life worthy of the approbation of Queen Victoria herself. He married, raised healthy, well-scrubbed, well-mannered children. One of them, Kenneth Grahame, rose to be Secretary of the Bank of England.

Yet the urge to throw it all up and take refuge in a secret world of lost childhood or run away to a remote, rural world still ruled by Pan and the irrational, natural instincts became overwhelming. At such moments, they took excursions in the country on week ends or during their holidays and wrote stories which evoked and recreated the wonderful world of an idyllic childhood. Arnold's Scholar-Gipsy was the prototype and guiding spirt of these Bohemians who, like him, sought the quiet joy of "some lone alehouse in the Berkshire moors" or haunted the remote reaches of "the stripling Thames at Bab-lock-hithe." Whenever Fortune briefly smiled it was they who threw off the cloak of conformity and sought for a day or a week to gain respite from "this strange disease of modern life,/ With its sick hurry, its divided aims,/ Its heads o'ertax'd, its palsied hearts."

It is this Bohemianism which is central to several of the Bodley Head's most famous books of informal essays: Kenneth Grahame's *Pagan Papers*, John Addington Symonds' *In the Key of Blue*, and John Davidson's *A Random Itinerary*. In each the "Romance of the Road" is rife, the desire "to get away from it all" is imperative, and, what is even more important, an implied rejection of both modern society and religion — its customs, creeds and values — is unmistakable.

Kenneth Grahame was a young clerk in the Bank of England when on January 19, 1893, he wrote to Mathews and Lane inquiring whether or not they would "care to publish a quite small selection of articles that I have had in the *National Observer* and *St. James's Gazette* during the past few years?" Aware of the Bodley Head's interest in distinctively different literary pieces, he added that his essays were, he thought, "just sufficiently individual and original to stand it." He bolstered his modest claim with the name of his chief mentor, William Ernest Henley, who, he pointed out, had once suggested "that a 'blend' of these short articles with verse would perhaps make a 'feature' that might take." Offering to leave the things with the publishers to look over, Grahame concluded with a statement which was surely pleasing to the enterprising young partners: "Your attractive 'format' — which you maintain so well — has mainly prompted my suggestion." [76]

The essays which Grahame had written were reminiscent of Alexander Smith's popular volume of 1863, *Dreamthorpe, A Book of Essays Written in the Country*, in particular the twelfth and last, "On Vagabonds," an obvious anticipation of Grahame's sort of Bohemianism. In style and theme, Grahame's essays were also reminiscent of Robert Louis Stevenson's recent collection entitled *Virginibus Puerisque*. Yet these pieces were very personal expressions of the young author's inner mental life — his imaginative, emotional self. Despite the fact that through his early years, Grahame had shown a marked inclination toward literary and academic pursuits, he had been forced to forgo Oxford and enter his uncle's business in Westminster until a clerkship became available for him in the Bank of England. The blow, although a severe one, was not disabling. As Peter Green, one of his biographers, has stated, the "pull towards discipline, duty, obligation, and conformity" within the young Grahame "was at least as strong as the anarchic individualism which complemented it." [77] Indeed, rather than driving him to a mental collapse, the tension set up within him by these two powerful drives generated the creative energy which produced his essays and stories.

Finding in Henley with his hatred of Puritanism and Victorian humbug an ideal editor, Grahame began to contribute to the *Scots Observer* in 1890. His essay "Of Smoking" appeared in October, and before "The Rural Pan" appeared on April 25, 1891, five other contributions had preceded it.

Pagan Papers includes six stories, later incorporated into *The Golden Age*, and eighteen essays largely concerned with the pleasures of idleness, walking tours, and nature worship. "The Romance of the Road," the first essay in the volume, describes the pleasures of a walk along one of those paths which like the Ridgeway of the North Berkshire Downs leads one almost as if by the hand "out and away from the habitable world." Grahame loved the feel of an old country road along which one could sense the presence of the past — the Roman legions wearily treading toward their camp or the Wessex levies hurrying "along to clash with the heathen and break them on the down where the ash-trees grew." Although there is much in this piece about that "certain supernal . . . deific, state of mind," that "particular golden glow of the faculties" that only a country vagabond can know "after severe and prolonged exertion in the open air," it is in "A Bohemian in Exile" that Grahame best describes the kind of man he longed to be. Having bought a pony and a barrow, Fothergill gives in to his desire to be free from all that his life as a Bloomsbury clerk stands for, and bidding his friends adieu he takes to "the old road-life" which "still lingered on in places, it seemed, once one got well away from the railway." Having discovered that "there were two Englands existing together, the one fringing the great iron highways wherever they might go — the England under the eyes of most of us," and "the other, unguessed at by many," Fothergill, with his clay pipe in his mouth and his pony, "heading west at a leisurely pace" set out to rediscover "the England of heath and common and windy sheep down, of by-lanes and village-greens — the England of Parson Adams and Lavengro."

But if as Peter Green has said, "the obvious central theme in these essays is what may be loosely described as Bohemianism," [78] Grahame's most revealing and permanently valuable ideas are expressed in "The Rural Pan," "The Lost Centaur," and "Orion," essays in which the paganism implied by the book's title is best elucidated. His sense of a life in nature, his longing for an animistic universe in which one could participate instinctively, and his hostility towards industrialism and the deadening effect it had upon the land as well as on the human mind so permeate these essays that the ending of Wordsworth's "The World Is Too Much with Us" might serve as a fitting epigraph.

The pre-Freudian and pre-Lawrentian theme of "The Lost Centaur," that "man has fatally neglected the instinctive, animal side of his nature through spiritual pride, puritan repression, and material greed," [79] is symbolized in Cheiron, the wise Centaur who nurtured and trained the young Achilles. Cheiron represents an ideal union of mind and body, a harmony of soul and sense which has been lost and can never be fully recovered. A similar note is sounded in "Orion," an essay in which Grahame contrasts the celestial hunter (his symbol of the primitive in man) with the children of the plough, the civilized but sadly regimented scions of past vigor. In a paragraph whose implications must have shocked his readers in the nineties, Grahame wrote:

Many a century has passed since the plough first sped a conqueror east and west, clearing forest and draining fen; policing the valleys with barbed-wires and Sunday schools, with the chains that are forged of peace, the irking fetters of plenty: driving also the whole lot of us, these to sweat at its tail, those to plod with the patient team, but all to march in a great chain-gang, the convicts of peace and order and law: while the happy nomad, with his woodlands, his wild cattle, his pleasing nuptialities, has long since disappeared, dropping only in his flight some store of flint-heads, a legacy of confusion. Truly, we Children of the Plough, but for you tremendous Monitor in the sky, were in right case to forget that the Hunter is still a quantity to reckon withal. Where, then, does he hide; deep in the breasts of each and all of us! And for this drop of primal quicksilver in the blood what poppy or mandragora shall purge it hence away?

Yet despite such apparent insights into the nature of the modern condition, Grahame was neither a Freud nor a Lawrence. For, as Green contends, "the political, sexual, and psychological implications of his thesis terrified him." [80]

A respectable and conforming "mid-Victorian" to the end,[81] Grahame, unlike a number of his contemporaries, fell into no perversions. Yet for John Addington Symonds the story was somewhat different. Manifesting itself in part in strong and irresistible homosexual tendencies, Symonds' other self was not so easily repressed and sublimated as were the "pagan" tendencies in Grahame. Although Symonds married and produced a family of four daughters, he was never able to endure the regimen of a man of business. The son of a wealthy west country physician, Symonds was schooled at Harrow and Oxford. Although after his marriage he attempted to settle himself down to the study of law, he spent most of his mornings writing essays on the Elizabethan dramatists and his afternoons visiting friends and viewing art galleries with his wife. When ill health threatened, Symonds deserted the legal profession altogether and devoted himself to the life of a writer. As a result, his catholicity of taste and his enormous learning were to be embodied in works of poetry, history, philosophy, aesthetics, science, and biography.

Suffering from chronic tuberculosis and seldom free from the strain of mental and emotional problems, Symonds traveled widely, especially in the south of France, Italy, and Switzerland. In January 1868 he suffered a serious mental breakdown while at Cannes, a nervous crisis Phyllis Grosskurth attributes "to the strain of suppressing his sexual cravings." [82] Now aware that peace would elude him so long as he continued to resist his own nature, Symonds returned to England, where through his close friend Graham

Dakyns he met an unusually intelligent, agreeable, and mature young man of seventeen, Norman Moor.[83] A homosexual relationship between the two developed which marked a turning point in Symonds' life. Later, having established himself and his family at "Am Hof," a great rambling frame house at Davos Platz in Switzerland, Symonds, often alone, made excursions into Italy, staying for extended periods in Venice, where the physical beauty of the gondoliers kindled his admiration. One afternoon in May 1881, his friend Horatio Brown pointed out to Symonds a striking young gondolier whose "hoarse voice, a mass of dark hair, and dazzling teeth under a short blonde moustache" [84] began to haunt him. Compelled to seek out the young man, Symonds in a turmoil of emotion composed a series of sonnets, "The Sea Calls," the first of a number of poems inspired by the twenty-four-year-old Angelo Furato, who became his closest companion for the remainder of his life.

Another *facchino*, Augusto, who also served Symonds, is the subject of his sketches in the title essay of *In the Key of Blue* and shared the travels recorded in the essay "Among the Euganean Hills." Published shortly before Symonds' death, *In the Key of Blue* is a collection of essays which are only vaguely related — a fault he attempted to explain away in his Preface by suggesting that his aim in the volume had been "to make the selection representative of the different kinds of work in which I have been principally engaged — Greek and Renaissance Literature, Description of Places, Translation, Criticism, Original Verse." [85] Although it has been said that the "whole collection" is modeled on the French Symbolist system[86] of choosing each word "not for its own beauty or excellence; but as a painter chooses his scheme of colour, or the musician his key," [87] such a description hardly applies to any but the title essay, a disappointing effort despite Symonds' conscious desire to extend Pater's dictum that all art aspires to the condition of music, to the informal essay. Starting with a disquisition on the inadequacy of language to express the various hues and tints of colors, and addressing himself to the challenge it presents the writer in English, Symonds set himself the problem of composing in prose and poetry "symphonies and harmonies of blue." Taking as his subject the male population of Venice, which largely attired itself "in blouses, sashes, and trousers of" blue, Symonds referred to the endless variety of tints as "modulations from the main chord" of blue and observed that "under strong sunlight, against the greenish water of the canals, the colour effects of such chromatic deviations are piquant and agreeable."

Having established his impressionistic point of view, Symonds concentrated the major portion of "In the Key of Blue" on a series of studies of Augusto posed in blue dress "in a variety of lights with a variety of hues in

Prospectus and order form for F. W. Bourdillon's *A Lost God*.

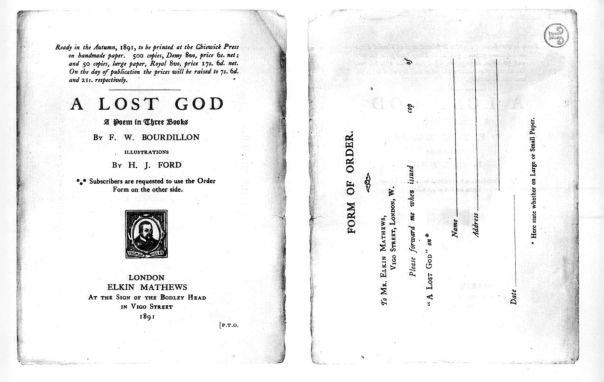

Ready in the Autumn, 1891, to be printed at the Chiswick Press on handmade paper. 500 copies, Demy 8vo, price 6s. net; and 50 copies, large paper, Royal 8vo, price 17s. 6d. net. On the day of publication the prices will be raised to 7s. 6d. and 21s. respectively.

A LOST GOD

A Poem in Three Books

By F. W. BOURDILLON

ILLUSTRATIONS

By H. J. FORD

₊ Subscribers are requested to use the Order
Form on the other side.

LONDON
ELKIN MATHEWS
AT THE SIGN OF THE BODLEY HEAD
IN VIGO STREET
1891

[P.T.O.

FORM OF ORDER.

To MR. ELKIN MATHEWS,
VIGO STREET, LONDON, W.

Please forward me when issued
"A LOST GOD" *on* *
_____ *cop* _____ *of*

Name _____

Address _____

Date _____

* Here state whether on Large or Small Paper.

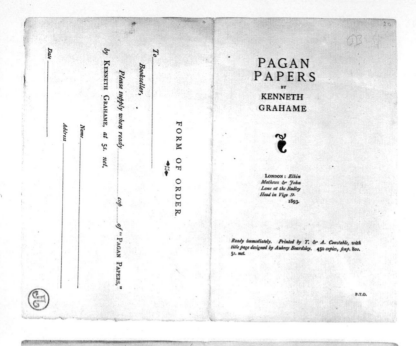

Prospectus and order form for Kenneth Grahame's *Pagan Papers*.

combination." A distinctly Whistlerian effect was gained in his first sketch, which pictures the gondolier sitting under the flaring gas-lamp "gazing dreamily and tired across the Grand Canal. Scattered lights broke the surface of the water, and gondolas, like glow-worms, now and then moved silently upon that oily calm. Augusto was intensely blue, giving the single blot of colour on a ground of gloom. This," Symonds observed, "suggested the first of my studies":

A symphony of black and blue —
Venice asleep, vast night, and you.
The skies were blurred with vapours dank:
The long canal stretched inky-blank,
With lights on heaving water shed
From lamps that trembled overhead.
Pitch-dark! You were the one thing blue;
Four tints of pure celestial hue:
The larkspur blouse by tones degraded
Through silken sash of sapphire faded,
The faintly floating violet tie,
The hose of lapis-lazuli.
How blue you were amid that black,
Lighting the wave, the ebon wrack!
The ivory pallor of your face
Gleamed from those glowing azures back
Against the golden gaslight; grapes
Of dusky curls your brows embrace,
And round you all the vast night gapes.

"Willing to pleasure" his nineteen-year-old *facchino*, who "had never left Venice for a day," Symonds proposed that the two "should spend a couple of days in the Euganean Hills," and they set forth from the city in search of the peace and beauty along the roads and byways of what then was a little-frequented upland. "Among the Euganean Hills" is a pleasant and often charming account of Symonds' journeys, in which his purpose was "to invade the Oreads of the Euganeans in their native haunts, and to pluck the heart out of their poetic mystery." Consisting of extracts from his diary which relate his "aimless but highly enjoyable ramblings about their gentle declivities and wooded valleys," the essay shows Symonds at his "Bohemian" or, if one prefers, "pagan" best. As attentive to the ancient history and mythological associations of the region through which he traveled as was Grahame, Symonds was particularly fascinated by the ancient neighboring towns of Battaglia and Abano, celebrated for their baths and springs of hot sulphurous water, which, Symonds pointed out, were, according to legend, opened by Hercules, who ploughed there with his oxen.

The ancients seem to have symbolized the volcanic nature of this country in several myths. It is difficult not to connect the legend of Phaethon, who fell from heaven into the Po, burned up the waters of Eridanus, and converted the tears of the river-nymphs to amber, with some dim memory of primitive convulsions.

The hot days of May during which Symonds was wont to wander through the Euganeans were a perfect complement to that mood of vagabondage which overtook him each spring. The landscape, the villages, the names on the land which were so richly evocative of the past were likewise congenial companions to his wanderlust. Although Symonds, who liked good food and wine, was not so frugal and utterly simple in his tastes as Grahame's Fothergill, few Bohemians would have denied him the bliss of that evening spent at a village inn where his supper of " 'Risi-bisi,' a Venetian mess of rice and young peas stewed in gravy; veal cutlets, with asparagus; lettuce-salad, home-made sausage, and cheese from the pastures" drunk down with a good white wine "was served in a corner of the kitchen: one of those large brick-floored rooms, with wooden rafters, and a pent-house chimney-piece half open to the air." Wandering "out into the moonlight, pacing country lanes alive with fire-flies and glow-worms," Symonds returned to "the divine night of sleep in lowly bed-chambers with open windows, through which entered the songs of nightingales, the plash of falling waters, and the sough of heavy-foliaged trees."

John Davidson's excursions from civilization to nature were not so far or so purely idyllic as those of Grahame and Symonds, but they served the same purpose. Davidson, more unfortunate and more bedeviled than either of his contemporaries, could afford only a walk now and then in the less-traveled environs of London itself. Described by Townsend as "a series of impressionistic, discursive travel sketches in prose," [88] *A Random Itinerary* is typically Davidson in its use of dialogue which, in the epilogue, turns into an altercation between the Itinerant and the Disputant, and in "Among the Chilterns," takes the form of a conversation between the Itinerant and a farmer, who discuss the properties of soot as manure and "that damned Home Rule Bill," among other things.

As his prefatory note suggests, Davidson's prose idyls grew out of a number of rambles about Epping Forest, Wood Green, Highgate, and other of the London environs during "the remarkable spring and summer of 1893." Although the sketches were written to be sold to newspapers, Davidson offered them to Mathews and Lane instead in July in hopes of securing an early publication date.

I am sending you with this [a receipt for royalties accruing from *Fleet Street Eclogues*] the m.s. of "A Random Itinerary." The nature of the book would require its early publication, and I have to ask for an early decision. Should it suit you, I beg to offer you an edition of 600 @ 5/ net for £20, payable as cash, or a bill, on the 31st of August next — unless you would propose a larger edition.[89]

The publishers must have dispatched the manuscript to Le Gallienne immediately, for his reader's report on the work notes that the manuscript was returned, presumably to the publishers, on August 3.[90] Although Le Gallienne recommended that *A Random Itinerary* be published, he offered a number of rather severe criticisms of the work, criticisms which Davidson answered in a letter to the publishers dated August 5, 1893. Thanking Mathews and Lane for a sight of the report and stating his pleasure at the good opinions expressed therein, Davidson went on to say, "But I disagree with the strictures. The itinerant has made as much out of his ideas as he intended to; *i.e.*, as he possibly could." Proceeding at some length to justify his method in the *Itinerary,* Davidson asserted that "all the highest literature consists of jottings, *e.g.*, the opening of the first chapter of Genesis; Lycidas, and the best dialogues in Shakespeare." [91]

Davidson did not stop there; he set about to write an epilogue based on the reader's report and his reply. As a result the Disputant in "By Way of Epilogue" is really Le Gallienne and the Itinerant is Davidson himself. Le Gallienne doubtless recognized as much when he saw the published book and addressed himself at length to the epilogue in his review of *A Random Itinerary* and thus, in a sense, had the last word. Turning his attention almost at once to what he described as "a bold epilogue, written as Mr. Stevenson once wrote a preface, 'by way of criticism'," Le Gallienne in his review described the situation as one in which the imaginary disputant who is represented as having "read the proofs of the foregoing 'Itinerary,' . . . takes upon himself to make certain mildly adverse criticisms upon it." Having done so he is countered by the Itinerant who "with true Scotch hardihood, and a pipe sturdily gripped within his pugnaciously smiling mouth, takes [hold of the disputant] much as a terrier takes a rat. Naturally the disputant, a poor wraith of tobacco-smoke, has little chance with the man who not only created him, but was also reporting the dialogue." [92]

Much to Davidson's chagrin *A Random Itinerary* was not rushed off immediately to the printer (perhaps because of Le Gallienne's reservations about the book). For one thing, Lane, probably on Le Gallienne's suggestion, urged that Davidson intersperse some poetry among the prose, a request Davidson was able to comply with, "having got an idea for a magnificent new ballad which I can inset naturally in the dialogue between the Itinerant and the Disputant." [93] The agreement, which largely incorporated Davidson's original proposal — 600 copies at 5/– and a royalty of £20 — was not signed until November 2. [94] Although the book was published during the last week of November 1893, it is dated both on the title page and spine 1894, in compliance with a request the author made in a letter written in October to Frederic Chapman, a Bodley Head assistant.

It occurs to me that as we are past the middle of October "The Random Itinerary" cannot now be out till November. Would it not be wise then to date it 1894? It is very unfortunate that the book is so long delayed, dealing as it does, with 1893: the excuse in my prefatory note will soon be a lame one. Can it by no means be got out at once? [95]

Davidson's worries lest *A Random Itinerary* lose all its relevance were ill founded, for his excursions through the Chilterns and into Buckinghamshire are still pleasant enough reading for those who love to escape the city and the press of daily chores and cares and indulge for a while their Bohemian longings.

Although many of the books of Bodley Head essays were not so enjoyable or interesting to the present-day reader as, say, *Pagan Papers* or some of the pieces from *In the Key of Blue,* they were in their various ways reflective of serious concerns of their times, especially Le Gallienne's *The Religion of a Literary Man* and Watson's *Excursions in Criticism.* Le Gallienne's controversial essay illuminates the religious state of mind of the nineties, which was still attempting to recover from the shock of Darwin's *Origin of Species.* The result of a controversy over a poem, *The Wandering Jew: A Christmas Carol,* published by Robert Buchanan (the "Thomas Maitland" of "The Fleshly School of Poetry" fame), *The Religion of a Literary Man* was Le Gallienne's most successful effort to parlay a review of a very minor poem into a major upheaval in the British press of which he was the

Beardsley's parody of C. S. Ricketts' cover designs for the Bodley Head (upper left). E. T. Reed's parody of Beardsley's cover designs and illustrations for the Keynotes series. It accompanied a *Punch* essay, "She-Notes" by Borgia Smudgiton (lower left). Linley Sambourne's drawing of Beardsley pulling the Yellow Book authors. It accompanied a *Punch* essay by "Max Mereboom" (right).

chief benefactor. It all began when Le Gallienne, taking exception to Buchanan's vision of Christ as an outcast in the nineteenth century, wrote an anonymous review which was published in the *Daily Chronicle* for January 11, 1893. On the following day, Buchanan, in a letter to the newspaper, replied to the reviewer, and Le Gallienne, this time over his own signature, replied to the reply and posed the question — "Is Christianity played out or not?" — which became the central issue of the whole controversy. As a result of this initial exchange of views between Le Gallienne and Buchanan, thousands of letters poured in to the *Daily Chronicle,* which even after several weeks was unable to extricate itself from the battle which raged in its Letters to the Editor column.[96]

As his biographers have said, "it would be grossly unfair to suggest that he [Le Gallienne] had contrived the quarrel with Buchanan for purposes of self-advertisement, [and] it would be equally untrue to deny that he was quick to cash in on the new and widespread fame which it had so conveniently brought him." [97] He kept his hand in the affair with a poem, "The Second Crucifixion," which appeared in the *Speaker* on February 4; and by March 11, it was reported in the *St. James's Gazette* that "Mr. Le Gallienne is not going to rest content with his controversy with Mr. Buchanan about Christianity in the *Daily Chronicle*. He is writing a small volume of essays to give his gospel of 'Essential Christianity.' " [98] There is evidence that Le Gallienne found it difficult to get his book going; on April 1 he wrote Lane that although other work was keeping him back from his "Religion book," he "simply *must* tackle" it "forthwith whatever else goes to the wall." [99]

The Bodley Head's anxious desire to publish the new work can be surmised from the publishers' tendering an agreement to Le Gallienne on May 6 and from their willingness to forward the author the sum of "£10 on account of the first edition of 'The Religion of a Literary Man'" and their decision to print 3,000 copies of a small-paper issue in addition to a large-paper issue.[100] Nevertheless, Le Gallienne was again plagued not only by ill health but also by a general inability to grind out each week as much as he had hoped. Consequently, the book was not done on August 28, 1893, when in the throes of an asthma attack he wrote Lane in a desperate mood: "if I am not better in the morning I shall discard the treatment for the time being I think, for I must get my 'Religion' done even if there is nothing for it but writing post, with relays of brandy." Yesterday, he reported, "I was able to cogitate somewhat fruitfully so if I can only get a vigorous day or so I think I shall finish my book no worse, at any rate, than I have begun." [101]

Having gained some respite from his illness with the onset of cooler weather, Le Gallienne completed his manuscript at last. On October 18, in an address to a small coterie — the Cemented Bricks — one of the brother-hoods to which he belonged, he gave what was reported to have been

a considerable foretaste of his new book, the lines of which may be suffi-ciently indicated by this passage towards the close of his address: "The Christian is the perfect lover, and those whom it helps to associate their lives with moving names may assume the honourable style of Christian without fear, though they cannot sign the Thirty-nine Articles." [102]

Although the table of contents is filled with such awesome and ponderous topics as "The Relative Spirit," "What Is Sin?," "What Is Pain?," "Free-Will," "The Hereafter," "Essential Christianity," "Dogma and Symbolism," "The Religious Senses," in addition to "Preliminaries" and a "Postscript" (which alone deals with such subjects as "The Evangel of the Demi-monde and the Music-hall," "The Dream of the Decadent," "The Anthropologist's 'explanation' of Religion" and "Religion the most ancient of the Sciences"), the body of the book is, as Whittington-Egan and Smerdon have suggested, "really little more than an essay tricked out to a book of 119 pages by the typographical ingenuity of the publisher who, by a system of wide marginal rulings and liberal spacing, contrived to limit the number of words per page to about 250." [103]

The tempest of interest created by the topic "Is Christianity Dead?" sug-gests that in 1893 it was a serious concern to many and that the position of the Church had become very precarious. A very commonplace and, by then, platitudinous statement of what had been, since F. D. Maurice and Charles Kingsley, essentially the Latitudinarian or Broad-Church position, *The Re-ligion of a Literary Man* was nevertheless a fairly honest statement of Le Gallienne's attitude toward religion, a position spelled out in *Young Lives* as "a mystical agnosticism — the first step of which was to banish the dog-mas of the Church as old wives' tales." [104]

Published during the last days of November 1893, the book was a huge success, calling forth a second printing of 2,000 copies in December. Al-though the reviews were generally favorable, the attitude of the intelligent-sia was indicated by Barry Pain's spoof *The Religion of a Cabdriver* and by a devastating critique in Henley's *National Observer*. Referred to by Max Beerbohm as "a superbly poignant article," [105] the review declared:

Here at last is a book that should have a vogue. For it is a book that meets the spiritual needs of the age. The tea-tables of the suburbs have been crying out for a Moses to lead them into the Promised Land where prigs are. And here is Mr Le Gallienne to bring them over Jordan under the twin banners of Literature and Religion. His book is just the article to supply the want. As a conjunction of pretentiousness and cheapness, affectation and simplicity, shallowness and foppery, it is all that the Heart of Woman could desire.[106]

Le Gallienne's excursion into the realm of religion was an offshoot or by-product of his major professional preoccupation, that of critic. As the statement of principles prefaced to his collected critical essays, *Retrospective Reviews,* makes clear, Le Gallienne was very much under the spell of Pater's critical point of view as embodied in *Appreciations.* For instance, his first principle was that "Criticism is the Art of Praise," and his sixth, merely a restatement of the point: "Praise is more important than judgment. It is only at agricultural societies that men dare sit in judgment upon the rose."

There were a number of critics who did not share Le Gallienne's concept of criticism, but his pet peeve was William Watson, who since his father's sudden death in 1887 had had to devote himself to the reviewer's art in order to earn a livelihood. In one of those early reviews, "Fiction — Plethoric and Anaemic," Watson attacked Le Gallienne's current idol, George Meredith, with a devastating denunciation of the novelist's style, which he characterized as "stiff without dignity and lax without ease; a style that attempts rapidity, to achieve fuss; a style aggressively marked and mannered, an intractable style that takes the initiative, leads the way, dominates the situation, when it should be . . . simply an obedient instrument, a blade to be carved with, not to be flashed in our eyes." [107] Le Gallienne, who at the time was writing his *George Meredith,* was outraged by Watson's diatribe and wrote his chapter "The Critics" as a direct rebuttal to Watson, whom Le Gallienne represented as the *National Review*'s Goliath.[108]

Watson, who was indeed a critical Goliath compared to Le Gallienne's David, was convinced that the critics of the day were not adequate to the task of saving literature from disaster. In his reviews of Pater's *Appreciations* and of George Saintsbury's *Essays in English Literature,* therefore, Watson set about to curb the modern tendency to weaken the critic's authority and to reassert the right of the critic to chastise the writer who failed to measure up to the high standards set by tradition. Tracing the history of criticism in the nineteenth century, Watson, in his essay on "Critics and Their Craft," found that during the early years there "was a general unanimity of opinion that a critic was primarily and above all else a judge. He himself never had any misgivings about that. He wore, with an air of judicial infallibility, the literary ermine; he grew grey in precedents; and he got into a habit of regarding authors generally as the accused in the dock." [109] Thinking primarily of such critics as Francis Jeffrey, John Wilson, and Thomas Babington Macaulay, Watson recognized the fact that they sometimes had judged wrongly and had articulated principles later reversed by posterity; nevertheless, these Solons of the literary world at least held firmly to the belief that their "business was to interpret and administer the literary law, and that this law, though not susceptible of regular codification — being, indeed, unembodied in formal statutes — was yet in spirit clearly deducible from tradition and generally approved usage." [110]

Modern critics, Watson found, preferred to appreciate rather than to judge. Their aim was to find something of value in every work and to expatiate upon these virtues either in vague, overly subtle language, or in an easy, familiar, at times vulgar, style which was in itself a sign of the very disease that the criticism should have been attempting to remedy. Pater, for instance, whose "critical posture is invariably one of extreme modesty," [111] irritated Watson because he humbly approached his authors with "admiration and sympathy" and occupied himself with seeking out and reverently transmitting to his readers "the essence" of their utterances. Although he did not go so far as to condemn Pater openly, Watson's dissatisfaction with his "creed of universal appreciation" is clear. Censure is implicit in Watson's statement that Pater's ambition is "simply to understand and report." Although he declared Pater to be "the subtlest artist in contemporary English prose," the admission carried no approval. Moreover, Pater was not only at fault in his critical approach but also in his use of the language. The "honeyed effeminacy" of Pater's style, his "mere daintiness," [112] was anything but reassuring to Watson, whose desire for virile, dignified prose led him to look with equal disfavor upon the easy, familiar style of Saintsbury. [113]

Since the critics had "ceased to assume the role of public censor" and had failed to take seriously their role as "guardians of law and order in literature," [114] Watson made a determined effort to reverse this trend by invoking the spirit of the earlier critic-judges. Certain that his critical principles were sound, Watson in his reviews never allowed anything to deter him from delivering "the maximum sentence" when "eminent offenses against good taste and good sense" were committed. Although he made it clear that it took a good deal of self-control "to go through the performance of such an unpleasant judicial duty," [115] one can readily see that he often delivered his "judicial" opinions with an unusual amount of gusto.

In addition to Watson's *Excursions*, the Bodley Head during its early years published other essays in criticism including James Ashcroft Noble's *The Sonnet in England and Other Essays*, G. A. Greene's study of the *Italian Lyrists of To-Day*, and Gleeson White's anonymously published *Letters to Living Artists*. But the firm's most noteworthy critical works were the important full-length critical studies — Le Gallienne's *George Meredith*, Lionel Johnson's *The Art of Thomas Hardy*, J. T. Nettleship's *Robert Browning, Essays and Thoughts*, and Henry Van Dyke's *The Poetry of Tennyson*, all of which have been lasting contributions to the study of these major literary figures.

Short Stories and Novels

Although the Bodley Head's contribution to the realm of fiction was not extensive or particularly distinguished, the firm did publish several books typical of the period. Perhaps the most significant event in this respect was the commencement of the Keynotes series, which within scarcely half a year's time after it was begun gave to the world not only George Egerton's title volume, published in December 1893, but also Florence Farr's *The Dancing Faun* and Lena Milman's translation of Dostoevski's *Poor Folk*. Also during the last few months of its existence, the firm published G. S. Street's amusing parody of the aesthetic novel, *The Autobiography of a Boy*.

Although the Bodley Head had published Le Gallienne and Robinson K. Leather's little book of Stevensonian stories entitled *The Student and the Body-Snatcher and Other Trifles* in 1890, it was not until George Egerton's *Keynotes* appeared that the firm issued a significant book of short fiction. The work of an Australian-born woman of considerable talent, Mary Chavelita Dunne, *Keynotes* is notable for its studies of the relationship between the sexes and the "new woman" and her pallid Victorian counterpart. With the knowledge of five languages at her command, George Egerton read widely in the literature of Continental writers at a time when few Englishmen knew much about literary trends beyond the Channel. Not only did she translate the work of Knut Hamsun and Björnstjerne Björnson into English, but she immersed herself in the work of the French realists, especially the short fiction of Guy de Maupassant. Consequently, given her subject and her mode of treatment, George Egerton's stories were something of a mild surprise when they appeared.[116]

Keynotes was first issued in pink paper wrappers with the designs by Beardsley in dark blue. It was an immediate success. Although Lane was interested in bringing out a series of fictional works very cheaply bound, he quickly decided to case the second issue in a light green cloth with Beardsley's designs in dark green. The artist's designs and the attractive format for *Keynotes* clearly had much to do with its popularity, and Lane went ahead with the series on the condition that Beardsley would continue to design the succeeding volumes in the mode of *Keynotes*. Thus began a distinguished set of books which in its typographical layout, its use of the lower case in the titles, and Beardsley's designs for the keys, covers, and title pages, "raised it," in the words of Brian Reade, "to the highest point in the category of well-produced cheap books of the 'Nineties." [117]

The second in the series, *The Dancing Faun,* a novel by the famous actress Florence Farr, bore on its front cover and title page the well-known Beardsley caricature of Whistler as faun. The novel did not continue the realist-naturalist mode of Egerton's *Keynotes.* Instead it looked to Oscar Wilde and the aesthetic fiction of the period for its cue. The novel is dominated by Mr. Travers, who is in every respect the young, slightly depraved aesthete who speaks in epigrams — "Yes, Lady Geraldine, the only beauty in modern life is its falsehood. Its reality is ridiculous." Travers is declared "a very, very bad man" by the dowager grand dames of London society. One who has the aura of a "charming languor" about him, Travers also arouses "violent" friendships in young men. At times reading like a Wilde play or the dialogue in "The Decay of Lying," *The Dancing Faun* is a notable example of the aesthetic novel of the day, which often was difficult to distinguish from its novelistic parodies such as Robert Hichens' *The Green Carnation.*

Although not quite so good as Hichens' work or Davidson's *Earl Lavender, The Autobiography of a Boy* was clearly an attack upon the aesthetes of the day by one of Henley's cronies, G. S. Street, who was often seen with the leader of the counter-decadents at Solferino's Restaurant in Rupert Street. As Le Gallienne noticed in his reader's report on the book, "the title is a misnomer. . . . The 'boy' is actually a 'superior' aesthetic young man of the Oscar Wilde type . . . extremely well done . . . makes one laugh . . . worth doing as a sort of companion to *Pagan Papers.*" [118]

At pains to parody the decadent characteristic of a lust for strange and exotic experiences, Street portrays Tubby, the hero, as a kind of Des Esseintes or Dorian Gray. Affecting a sated indifference to life, Tubby delights in the idea that no proper young lady will speak to him. Rather than marry and settle down, he prefers to spend all his time in courting new sensations. When his father gives him the choice of marriage or exile to Canada, he chooses the latter. "Yes," he tells himself, "my nature will expand in this wild land. Of course I have avoided, so far as I could, learning anything about it, that my impressions might be absolutely free." Although Tubby's father had intended that his son go into a bank on his arrival, the hero decides otherwise. "But I shall make straight for the forests, or the mountains, or whatever they are, and try to forget. I believe people shoot one another there," he muses. "I have never killed a man, and it may be an experience — the lust for slaughter."

Not only in poetry but in other genres of literature as well, the Bodley Head suggested the aesthetic temper of the early nineties. Its avoidance of the long, didactic poem, its emphasis on the brief lyric and the more personal embodiment of an author's feelings, all are reflected in the firm's avoidance of long works of fiction and in its emphasis on an often poetic, highly personal — even idiosyncratic — drama. The drama and the essays which the Bodley Head published were not only of a lyrical, belletristic nature but also rather experimental, reflecting the period immediately following the age of the great Victorians. The plays and to a lesser extent the essays tended to be "individualistic" and as a result remind us once more that the period saw an assertion of various kinds of individualism in defiance of an age of conformity.

Certainly the lack of fiction among the publications of the early Bodley Head and the emphasis on belles-lettres, in the strictest sense of that term, suggest the distaste on the part of the aesthetic temperament for fiction which, perhaps, in the form of the three-decker novel was too often associated with the large commercial publishing houses of the day, and which in its emphasis on the realistic events of bourgeois life was doubtless uncongenial. Until George Egerton's *Keynotes* appeared, the Bodley Head produced little that had the faintest taint of realism or naturalism about it. Consciously or not, the Bodley Head was of the same mind as Oscar Wilde when in "The Decay of Lying" he declared:

But from the standpoint of art, what can be said in favour of the author of *L'Assommoir, Nana* and *Pot-Bouille?* Nothing. Mr. Ruskin once described the characters in George Eliot's novels as being like the sweepings of a Pentonville omnibus, but M. Zola's characters are much worse. They have their dreary vices, and their drearier virtues. The record of their lives is absolutely without interest. Who cares what happens to them? In literature we require distinction, charm, beauty and imaginative power.[119]

The fact that in the last months before the breakup four works of fiction were published is indicative of the growing rift between Mathews and Lane. Mathews' great successes had been and were to continue to be in poetry, while Lane was already turning his attention to fiction, which was to be a staple item of the Bodley Head of the future. There is little to indicate that Mathews had much to do with the Keynotes series which was, like the *Yellow Book,* largely Lane's brain child. Since each partner seems to have been going his own separate way during the early months of 1894, it was only a matter of time until the two would make the break a formal one.

As the summer of 1894 approached, the fortunes of the Bodley Head were clearly in the ascendant. The *Yellow Book* had been launched with great acclaim and much notoriety in April, and George Egerton's *Keynotes* was in its fourth printing. Both the periodical and the series of new fiction were the result of John Lane's efforts alone. Neither Beardsley's bizarre and decadent art in the *Yellow Book,* nor the avant-garde views of George Egerton, nor the naturalistic bent of Dostoevski's *Poor Folk* were the kind of art which Elkin Mathews preferred. His tastes ran more to Dr. Todhunter's evocation of the Theocritan past, *A Sicilian Idyll,* or to the poetry of the young William Butler Yeats, which he was shortly to publish, and the art of Yeats's brother, Jack — all of whom were his neighbors in the respectably arty realm of Bedford Park, an upper middle-class London suburb. While Lane met with his young and occasionally risqué authors at 37 Southwick Street or with his cronies at the Hogarth Club, Mathews returned each evening to the pleasant environs of old Chiswick. Lane enjoyed the fast tempo, the business atmosphere and the slightly off-color world of central London; Mathews relished the slower pace, the purer air, and idyllic setting of Bedford Park.

The earliest of the planned garden suburbs, Bedford Park had been from its beginnings in 1875 connected in the minds of Londoners with William Morris, the Pre-Raphaelites, and the aesthetic movement in general. Yeats remembered the suburb "when the crooked ostentatiously picturesque

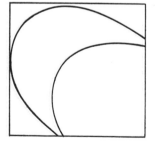 8 THE BREAKUP

streets with great trees casting great shadows had been a new enthusiasm: the pre-Raphaelite movement at last affecting life." [1] When in the early eighties the young Oscar Wilde was lecturing the nations on the subject of beauty and Gilbert and Sullivan's *Patience* was the rage, "The Ballad of Bedford Park" advertised the village as a place "Where men may lead a chaste/ correct aesthetical existence." [2]

The work largely of Norman Shaw, Bedford Park in its appearance and setting doubtless appealed to the aesthetic sensibilities of those who, eschewing both Philistia and Bohemia, sought refuge in the carefully laid-out suburb "with its curved streets, its carefully preserved old trees, and its novel variety of detached, semi-detached, and terrace houses." [3] Shaw's liking for red brick and Dutch gables and his use of decorative tiles was indicative of the influence of Dutch art and architecture in England during the seventies and eighties. The white window casements, the little oriels and cosy porches, the small gardens, the unusual church with its two-storied belfry suggestive of the fine seventeenth-century lanterns found in Holland, the red brick clubhouse with its little theater[4] — all must have held a special appeal for a cultivated, intelligent middle-class man like Elkin Mathews who enjoyed beauty in its serener, unadulterated forms.

As in our present-day suburbias, the families of Bedford Park busied themselves with a variety of social activities such as the garden party Ernest Rhys attended in the summer of 1890 given by "Willie Yeats and his sisters" [5] or the Waltonian "At Home" which Elkin Mathews and the "Misses Mathews" gave on the occasion of Izaak Walton's tercentenary, for which Jack Yeats drew up a charming card of invitation.[6] Of an even more literary turn were the meetings of the Rhymers' Club which took place on occasion at the home of Dr. Todhunter.[7] The theater, too, where Todhunter's plays often opened, with Florence Emery and other notables in the leading roles, was a center of much pleasant activity — the same "little theatre" which, according to Yeats himself, "began to stir my imagination." [8]

Although "The Ballad of Bedford Park," suggests that the village was

> *builded*
> *for all who are aesthete*
> *Whose precious souls it fill did*
> *with utter joy complete,*[9]

it is doubtful that either Elkin Mathews or his neighbors were quite the Wildeans the author implied. It is also doubtful that many even were accustomed to taking their "aesthetic cheer" by reading "Rossetti here/ by a Japanese-y lamp." [10] Yet the poem does suggest the milieu of the early nineties in which Elkin Mathews and a number of his friends were especially at home, the kind of sedate aestheticism which, while devoting itself to art and literature and objects of beauty, was a far cry from the sinister and perverse art of the decadence Lane was willing to encourage so long as there was no danger of his getting burned.

During its first five years the Bodley Head had, in the midst of London, taken on the serene, cultivated, mildly aesthetic aura of a Bedford Park, but John Lane's coming into the firm early in 1892 considerably altered all that. Mathews' quiet, decorous conduct of the business gave way to the lively, enterprising activities of a far different sort of person. J. Lewis May, in recalling the Bodley Head as it was in 1894, remembered Lane as a man

forever bustling in and out — always somewhere to go, something to see. Sometimes he would rush in with two or three people in his wake — artists, poets, journalists, printers, binders, or Heaven knows whom. Then what a buzz, what a hum of excited conversation! Mathews, secretly regretting Cathedral Yard, Exeter, where such disconcerting irruptions never disturbed the calm of his repose, would hover about on the outskirts of the group, like an ineffective football player vainly endeavouring to push his way into the "scrum." [11]

It was not long after Lane entered the business full time that Elkin Mathews seems to have been relegated to what Lane considered a secondary function of the firm, that of antiquarian bookseller, while Lane, himself, moved swiftly to take over and expand the publishing. Soon much that was going on within the narrow compass of the Vigo Street premises was only vaguely known to Mathews and at times highly distasteful or disquieting. As time went on, in order to handle things his own way and keep Mathews in the dark, Lane met with his authors and transacted business more and more outside the firm's office, often, according to Percy Muir, at the Hogarth Club, of which Mathews was not a member.[12]

That Lane early moved to establish himself as the effectual head of the firm is evidenced by the fact that even before he came into active partnership, he had established Le Gallienne as a power in the business. Then in 1892 Lane made two key appointments: Le Gallienne became the official reader for the firm, and a bookman named Frederic Chapman (who was later to be Lane's office manager) was hired as chief assistant. Chapman, who in April 1895 was to face the *Yellow Book* crisis alone, was, according

Oscar Wilde and Lord Alfred Douglas.

Ricketts and Shannon, 1897, by William Rothenstein.

Ernest Dowson.

to J. Lewis May, discovered by Lane "in a Leicester bookshop," where he managed a circulating library.[13] May, who attributed much of the success of the Bodley Head to Chapman's quiet, behind-the-scenes efforts, described his duties as that of "reader, editor, correspondent, and general counsellor." In nothing less than an encomium, May spoke of him in *The Path Through the Wood* as a "grave and studious" man who

had read enormously, and possessed a prodigious knowledge of English literature, not only of the main current, but of those lesser tributary streams which are not usually explored save by the specialists in particular periods or subjects. . . . Fastidious, though without pedantry, he had a delicate appreciation of style and a most sensitive literary conscience. But what probably endeared him to John Lane more than anything else was that he too was a collector, an antiquary, a lover of old and quaint and beautiful things — china, pewter, prints, furniture and, most of all, books.[14]

Chapman, who assumed his duties with the Bodley Head on Monday, February 13, 1892,[15] was one of five or six employees, all of whom appear to have been "Lane's men." There was J. Lewis May, whose parents discerning in their son some "nascent literary talent" sent him up to London to be guided by their old friend, John Lane, and to act as stock boy to the Bodley Head.[16] "There," wrote May, "I advanced my literary education by addressing the firm's envelopes. I served my articles to the Muses, I made acquaintance with the poets by stacking their works as they came in from the binders!" Keeping his eyes and ears open, May "saw and heard many people whose names are inscribed in the roll of fame." [17] In addition to May, there were the stock boy Edward Shelley, whom Oscar Wilde probably came to know through his visits to the Bodley Head, and Roland Clarke the cashier,[18] and a Mr. Iredale,[19] of whom next to nothing is known.

When the announcement about the dissolution of the partnership came, persons not closely associated with the firm were surprised, but those acquainted with the partners were not. For the Bodley Head was, as Le Gallienne had suggested, a Janus, whose two faces looked in opposite directions. It is very doubtful that Lane even from the first thought of the partnership with Mathews as a permanent arrangement. Indeed, a good case could be made for Lane's having used his partner to get ahead only to drop him once he found himself able to carry on alone. Lane, aggressive, seething with ideas, willing to take a chance and even skirt the law if necessary, was the opposite of Mathews, whom Lane doubtless looked upon as the "conservative and unenterprising" little man that J. Lewis May later made him out to be.[20] Consequently, the dissolution of the partnership was the result of a clash of personalities and a desire on Lane's part to move forward unencumbered to ever greater heights with none to share in or detract from his success.[21]

The initial decision to dissolve the partnership cannot be precisely dated, but its cause — continued incompatibility between Mathews and Lane — is certain. A growing number of what Mathews rightly or wrongly interpreted as provocations and affronts led him in time to the breaking point. As Mathews once wrote, "the climax came when [in the spring of 1894] the Editors of the *Yellow Book* gave a dinner to the contributors and Lane alone represented the firm." Hearing about the dinner only by accident — "Lane never volunteered any information about it until I taxed him" — Mathews interpreted the incident as another of a long series of infidelities on Lane's part, the latest affront, which Mathews felt must be the last.[22]

Mathews was hurt by this flagrant breach of the decorum inherent in partnerships and angered by Lane's duplicity. In a draft letter to Dr. Brushfield, he explained,

I learned afterwards that many *asked* where *I* was — and that when Lane was asked to speak for the publishers — he with the boldest effrontery said that he deeply regretted the unavoidable absence of his partner — and that he was not present to join in the general enthusiasm and so on.

As a matter of fact I could have attended the dinner with the greatest ease in the world, I had *absolute* leisure that evening, and there was not the slightest colour for him to make such a statement. He had evidently represented to the Editors that he alone was the partner interested in the working of the *Yellow Book,* and they did not take the trouble to act otherwise.

I heard that when Lane expressed his regret at my "unavoidable absence," one prominent author shouted out "that [is] a lie." [23]

Thus the *Yellow Book,* which was fateful in the careers of so many, was the immediate cause of the breakup of the early Bodley Head.

Although in his brief account of the beginnings of the Bodley Head, Lane suggested that the dissolution of the partnership had been wholly amicable, the evidence available suggests that this was something less than the truth. In fact, once the decision to part company was made, acts occurred which led to further unpleasant altercations between the partners, incidents which made it impossible for them to have parted so amicably as Lane suggested: "By mutual arrangement, for our separation was of a perfectly cordial character," he wrote, "the sign of *The Bodley Head* was transferred to my new offices opposite." [24] In no way does this placid statement convey to the reader the anger, concern, and misgivings which surrounded Lane's taking the revered sign from 6B Vigo Street and raising it above his premises in Albany.[25]

Mathews in the moment of crisis, trying to be fair and considerate, decided, since he was retaining the old premises, to offer Lane the sign. As he himself once explained it, in order "to cut the gordian knot" and secure his independence from an increasingly distasteful and untenable partnership, he told Lane he could have the Bodley Head sign, never "dreaming that he had up his sleeve permission from the Albany authorities to change one of the windows looking out upon Vigo Street into a doorway." [26] What a shock it must have been to the mild and gentlemanly Mathews when Lane not only accepted the offer but crossed the very narrow street, rehung the sign over his newly-cut door and christened his establishment "The Bodley Head, the Albany."

Doubtless Mathews was appalled and too late realized his serious tactical blunder. That his friends were outraged by the event is borne out by a series of letters Ernest Radford addressed to Mathews at the time of the breakup. On August 5, 1894, he wrote:

> Lane called here yesterday. If what he has told Mrs Radford is true[,]
> the advantage is on his side in the arrangement you have made. If he
> chooses to run an independent business in Vigo Street next door to you[,]
> you cannot prevent him but that you should allow him to remove the
> sign of "The Bodley Head" from your place to his is to me incredible. I
> must hear it directly from you before I believe it for a moment. I think
> you cannot have considered how much you will lose by allowing Lane to
> do any such thing.[27]

Another letter dated the following day makes clear that Radford was quite aware that by giving up the sign Mathews was losing a good deal more.

> In speaking so strongly about your abandoning to Lane the Sign of the
> Bodley Head, I was thinking in great part of you, and partly of what people
> would call the "good-will" of a business. The place is yours to do what
> you like with. You may decapitate Bodley or not as you think best. But
> please, in no case, allow Lane to retain any property in him, or to have any
> voice in the matter.[28]

Despite Radford's pleas and Mathews' second thoughts, the offer had been made and accepted. The Bodley Head had been lost. Within days, Lane was advertising his telegraphic code as "Bodleian" and Mathews was listing his as "Elegantia." The depth of Mathews' grief is indicated by the words he wrote some months later: "Since the *Bodley Head* is fast becoming identified with fiction of a very modern character — made up emotion and no morals [—] probably I shall in time get reconciled to its [The Bodley Head's] loss." [29]

Further serious friction between the partners arose when, in order to decide the question of which authors and artists would continue with Mathews and which would follow Lane, Lane made a private, confidential canvass of the writers involved. What Mathews wished to be purely a matter of asking was turned by Lane into a high-powered campaign to win over as many authors to his side as possible. Because, according to Mathews, Lane was "doing his best to get everything over for himself," [30] Mathews also made considerable efforts to thwart Lane's designs.

In a letter of August 24, 1894, Elkin Mathews wrote to Will Rothenstein to apprise him of the fact that he would "receive a circular in due course — directly the Accountant and Valuer have done their work. Our authors," he explained, "will be asked with which of the partners they would like their books to go." Telling Rothenstein that he would be glad to see him for a talk on his return to London, Mathews went on to say that some of the authors had already made their preference known. "Horatio Brown for instance writes to say he wishes Addington Symonds' 'In the Key of Blue' to come to me." Then referring to the fact that Lane had long made it his chief occupation to seek out authors and work with them alone, Mathews added:

Of course as Lane took upon himself to run after the authors *presumably* for the firm, but as it now appears from his own avowal, *really* for himself, many of them therefore feel they ought to offer them to Lane, and those who have no such compunctions Lane tries to *worry* over to his side[.] Lionel Johnson for instance is a case in point.[31]

Looking to the future, Mathews listed W. B. Yeats, Lionel Johnson, Percy Addleshaw, Frederick Wedmore, Herbert Horne, "and of course yourself & York Powell" as persons he could count on. "I don't aim at having a big list [of books and authors] to start with, so Lane is welcome to the Lion's share. I suppose there is no doubt the Editors of the Y. B. will offer it to Lane — I expect too, that the new book just announced as coming from Geo. Egerton 'Discords' will go to Lane." [32]

Faced with making a choice, the authors, in general, chose to stay with the partner through whom they had come into the firm — Le Gallienne with Lane, and Todhunter with Mathews, for instance. The avant-garde, the more bizarre items from the Bodley Head catalogue without exception continued under Lane's banner. For example, Lane kept the *Yellow Book* while Mathews kept the *Hobby Horse*; and of the two series of books begun before the dissolution, Keynotes and Diversi Colores, Lane continued to publish the former, Mathews the latter.

Some authors, including Lionel Johnson and Oscar Wilde, proposed to divide their work among the partners. Johnson, who probably preferred Elkin Mathews, nevertheless offered Lane *The Art of Thomas Hardy* and any future prose works while he promised Mathews his forthcoming volume of poems and any further volumes of verse.[33] Wilde, who disliked Lane and to show his contempt had named the manservant in *The Importance of Being Earnest* for him,[34] at first agreed with Lane's proposal that he take over the plays and relegate to Mathews the unpublished "Mr. W. H.," which was still hanging fire. "I am very pleased you like the plays," he wrote Lane early in September, "and hope they will be a success in your hands. We could bring out *The Duchess of Padua* in February." [35] This arrangement was apparently not acceptable to Mathews, for Lane soon after informed Wilde that his partner declined to publish "Mr. W. H." "at any price" because he did not approve of it.[36] Since the Bodley Head was under contract to publish the book, however, Wilde was determined that one or the other of the partners would bring out this work as his letters to Mathews and Lane of September 1894 fully bear out. Yet at the time of Wilde's debacle in the spring of 1895, neither Mathews nor Lane had proceeded with the publication of "Mr. W. H." [37]

Nevertheless, it seems that Mathews and Lane agreed that all of Wilde's works would "be handed over to Mr Lane" and Wilde was so informed.[38] This move proved unacceptable to Wilde, who took exception to the publishers' deciding the question. "I think," he wrote Mathews and Lane,

that it should be left to me to decide with which partner I will place my work. I have received the firm's circular on the subject, and am considering the point. There is after all no reason why I should not be treated with the same courtesy that is extended to obscure and humble beginners in the difficult art of Literature. Personally I am at present in favour of entrusting my plays to Mr Mathews, whose literary enthusiasm about them has much gratified me, and to leave to Mr Lane the incomparable privilege of publishing *The Sphinx, Salome,* and my beautiful story on Shakespeare's sonnets.[39]

Mathews and Lane's decision, nevertheless, prevailed. Not desirous of causing the partners any inconvenience in their publishing arrangements, Wilde in a further letter, pointing out that his proposal had been dictated only "by a desire to be fair and courteous to both," acquiesced in the decision that Lane "should have all my books" [40] and thereby settled the matter.

A special problem arose concerning the books of the Rhymers' Club. By September 1894, two volumes of verse by the members had been published by the Bodley Head and a third proposed. Since only *The Second Book of the Rhymers' Club* was still in print, only the Rhymers who had contributed to that volume were consulted.[41] Since Mathews attended meetings of the Club as early as January 1891 and as late as May 1895,[42] and since G. A. Greene, Ernest Radford, W. B. Yeats, and John Todhunter were his close friends, the Rhymers' Club members not only voted to leave *The Second Book* with Mathews but, according to Ian Fletcher,

to a man almost, elected to stay with Mathews: Radford (and his wife, Dollie); Greene, the Rhymers' Secretary who was to publish two further volumes of verse with Mathews; Plarr and Yeats who were to publish one volume each; while Arthur Symons' translation of Baudelaire's *Prose Poems* was to appear in the first of the [Vigo Street] Cabinet Series.[43]

Mathews, who wrote Herbert P. Horne that he "would grieve to lose the 'Rhymers Book'," made a concerted effort to keep the Rhymers in his camp even though he did not feel that there was "much doubt" about his getting "a majority of votes." On September 20, 1894, for instance, Mathews asked Horne if he minded using his "influence with Dowson, Plarr, or any of the other Rhymers you know." [44]

As secretary, Greene was the one asked by Mathews and Lane to poll the contributors. Acting accordingly, on September 17, 1894, he wrote to Ernest Radford:

Writers in 2nd Rh. Bk. have to decide whether Mathews or Lane is to be publisher. Will you kindly send me your vote at earliest convenience? If discussion at a meeting preferred, please let me know at once.[45]

That Mathews had strong support among the Rhymers is suggested by Radford's reply to Greene, which was immediate and vehement. "My dear Greene," he wrote,

> If others feel as strongly as I on the relative claims to respect of our publishers — there will be a row amongst members when we meet at the Cheshire Cheese.
> Please therefore register my vote for Mathews.
> I shall certainly withdraw from the Club if a third Book is offered to Lane.[46]

Although a third book of the Rhymers' Club never materialized, it most certainly would have been published by Mathews, for it was he who had the privilege of listing *The Second Book* among his publications in his advertisements of November 1894.

The Daniel Press books, some of which had been handled by the Bodley Head since 1890, were another potential problem. Lane apparently chose not to contest the disposition of these books, however, for in September Mathews simply informed Dr. Daniel of a *fait accompli:* "Dear Dr. Daniel," he wrote,

> You are no doubt aware that in a few days Mr. Lane and I dissolve partnership. I shall continue to carry on at the old premises in Vigo Street, the old book business together with the publishing on the lines we have hereto followed — Mr. Lane confines himself strictly to publishing.
> Consequently I have taken over all the books from your private press, and I hope you will kindly give me notice and the privilege of taking a certain number of copies as in the past of your private issues.[47]

The first indication of the results of the canvass appears to have been leaked to the press by Lane himself; and judging from the reaction of Elkin Mathews and Ernest Radford, the press releases were biased in favor of Lane and suggested that he had indeed come away with the lion's share of books and authors. On September 15, 1894, the *Publishers' Circular* carried the following announcement:

> On the termination of the partnership between Mr. Elkin Mathews and Mr. John Lane at the end of this month, Mr. Mathews will retain the

old premises, whilst Mr. Lane will open new offices opposite. The sign "The Bodley Head" and the telegraphic address "Bodleian" will in future be identified with Mr. Lane's business. As the result of a circular letter addressed to the authors, Mr. Mathews will continue to publish the books in the catalogue of the firm by Mr. Frederick Wedmore, the Rev. P. H. Wicksteed, Michael Field, Miss E. R. Chapman, Dr. Todhunter, the late Mr. J. A. Symonds, Mrs. De Gruchy, Mr. F. W. Bourdillon, and Mr. L. Binyon; Mr. Lane being in future the publisher of those by Mr. Grant Allen, Mr. John Davidson, Lord De Tabley, George Egerton, Mr. Norman Gale, Dr. Garnett, Mr. Edmund Gosse, Mr. Kenneth Grahame, Mr. G. A. Greene, Dr. Gordon Hake, Mr. W. P. James, Mr. Le Gallienne, Mrs. Meynell, Mr. Allan Monkhouse, Mr. J. T. Nettleship, Mr. J. A. Noble, Mr. Ernest Rhys, Mr. G. S. Street, Mr. Francis Thompson, and Mr. William Watson, as well as of "The Yellow Book" and the "Keynotes" series.[48]

Mathews evidently was completely taken by surprise when he read the announcement. Considerably chagrined, he wrote a letter of clarification which appeared a week later in the *Circular*:

Sir, — I observe you have published an announcement of my dissolution of partnership with Mr. John Lane, accompanied by an incomplete report of the result of a private and confidential canvass among our authors as to which of us should continue to publish the book or books "at present *bearing the imprint of the old firm*."

This circular was marked "private," and it was understood that the respective authors should be in no way committed to any subsequent definite course; and although the expression in your report "will continue to publish the books *in the catalogue* of the firm['] is strictly accurate (if the words "in the catalogue" are emphasised) it is misleading, as the new books of some of the authors claimed by Mr. Lane are arranged — or are likely — to be published by me.

In the list of authors sent to you whose books in the catalogue of the firm I continue to publish, the names of Mrs. Radford, Dr. Henry Van Dyke, Mr. Herbert P. Horne (I shall also in future be the publisher of the "Hobby Horse" and the "Diversi Colores" series) and others are I observe, omitted, for, as it was not contemplated to make the matter a public announcement, the authors whom we knew would publish with me were not troubled with this strictly private circular.[49]

Radford's vehement reaction to a similar announcement in the *Daily Chronicle* is to be found in a letter he wrote Mathews. "I was consumed with rage," he began, "at the scarcely concealed malice of the paragraph in last Saturday's Chronicle, and am very glad indeed to read your answer today." [50] Attempting to counter the announcement's insinuation that the journal Lane was to keep — the *Yellow Book* — and the Keynotes series were far more valuable and worthy of attention than those retained by Mathews, Radford went on to affirm: "The Hobby Horse is worth 10000 Yellow Books. Horne's *Diversi Colores* is compact of delights and a beautiful book to have published." Continuing with remarks and assurances which suggest the deep division which developed between the partners and their authors at this time, Radford wrote: "I wish that by raising my voice in public I could advance your cause at this critical time. As it is I have done all I can to make you feel that a close inner circle of friends is worth living and working for." [51]

Referring again to the inaccuracies of Lane's announcements, Radford pointed out to his friend the fact that he seemed not to have noticed that "two of the writers they give you are dead — namely J. Addington Symonds & Mrs De Gruchy." In closing, Radford, expressing his belief that Yeats would "take his stand at your side," went on to deliver himself of an opinion which largely suits with the facts of the case:

The fact that you are always too modest gives the enemy an advantage — at the same time it endears you to friends. Please give my love to your sisters. If they are kind enough to like me I hope it is at least partly because I am yours/ so sincerely/ Ernest Radford.[52]

Whether or not Elkin Mathews' fear that his partner was attempting to destroy him and discredit him as a publisher is true or not, the fact is that the two men concluded their partnership each with a sizeable list of publications and an adequate group of loyal authors. The formal announcement of the dissolution of partnership, dated September 1894, and signed Elkin Mathews and John Lane, is accompanied by an attachment of two pages, which lists side by side the apportionment of "the books hitherto published or announced as in preparation by the Firm." [53] Although forty-nine titles of books are listed under Lane's name while only thirty-two appear under that of Mathews, a glance at the lists suggests that each publisher, by and large, retained for himself the books and journals he most favored.

The chroniclers of the Bodley Head era — J. Lewis May, Le Gallienne, and others — have indicated that Lane took with him practically all the authors and carried on the publishing tradition of the firm,[54] but the evidence is obviously to the contrary. Le Gallienne's statement that Elkin Mathews "had none of Lane's initiative and had been content to remain a bookseller" [55] was contradicted shortly after it was published, by Mathews' widow, Edith Elkin Mathews, when in a letter to the *Times Literary Supplement* she pointed out that after the dissolution of the partnership her husband "was able to attract such men as Lionel Johnson, J. M. Synge, John Todhunter, John Masefield, Lord Dunsany, James Joyce, Gordon Bottomley." [56] To this list, of course, she could have added Yeats, Ezra Pound, Bliss Carman, and Richard Hovey among others.

That Mathews had no intention of abandoning the publishing business is clear from such lists of books as appeared in the *Publishers' Circular* for September 29, 1894, and the *St. James's Gazette* for November 2, in which no fewer than twenty-five titles, including Yeats's *The Wind among the Reeds,* were announced either as "just published," "ready," or "in preparation." It was Mathews, not Lane, who through the kind of books he published and the kind of business he maintained best carried on the tradition of the early Bodley Head in publishing.

Certainly it was Mathews who continued to nurture poetic talent through those lean years which stretched on beyond the nineties into the new century. Just as he and Lane had published the work of the Rhymers, Symons, Gray, and other struggling unknowns in the early nineties, so a decade later, Mathews was publishing not only Symons but Masefield, Binyon, Plarr, Gibson, Monro, Flecker, and Pound. As Ian Fletcher has said, "It is a roll of honour." [57]

However much their paths in publishing were destined to diverge in later years, Mathews and Lane despite — or perhaps because of — their very different talents, personalities, and points of view brought together in that climactic but brief span of years a unique blend of literary and artistic talent which expressed the quintessential spirit of the remarkable period that was the early nineties.

APPENDICES

NOTES

ILLUSTRATION CREDITS

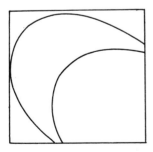

The following check list includes all books and periodicals which were published between March 1889 and October 1894 with the imprint of Elkin Mathews (or C. Elkin Mathews, in the case of Richard Le Gallienne's *Volumes in Folio*) or Elkin Mathews and John Lane, to which more often than not was added "at the Sign of the Bodley Head" or simply "at the Bodley Head."

The check list does not include what I refer to as the pre-Bodley Head books, which were published by Elkin Mathews before the appearance of Le Gallienne's *Volumes in Folio* (March 1889), the first book to appear with the imprint "at the Sign of the Bodley Head." The books which appeared with the imprint C. Elkin Mathews or Elkin Mathews before *Volumes in Folio* are, I feel, uncharacteristic of what was soon to be recognized as "the Bodley Head book." While Elkin Mathews was in business at Exeter, only one book appeared with his name attached to it: Maria Susannah Gibbons' *We Donkeys on the Devon Coast* (July 23, 1887). On moving to London in October 1887, Mathews issued three other pre-Bodley Head publications: J. S. Attwood's *Index* to Dr. George Oliver's *Lives of the Bishops of Exeter* (October 1887), William Crossing's *The Ancient Crosses of Dartmoor* (November 14, 1887), and Attwood's *Index* to Dr. Oliver's *Monasticon Dioecesis Exoniensis* (January 1889).

It must be remembered that a number of books and periodicals which appeared in Bodley Head lists of books and advertisements were merely issued from, that is, sold by, Elkin Mathews and John Lane at the shop in Vigo Street. For instance, the Daniel Press books at no time appeared with the Bodley Head imprint and, therefore, are not included in this list. All such books and periodicals are listed in Appendix F: Transfers.

The following entries include: (1) name of author; (2) title of book or periodical; (3) name of editor, translator, etc., if any; (4) date of publication; (5) number of copies printed, including ordinary (ord.) and special (spec.) issues as well as small-paper (SP) and large-paper (LP) issues; (6) name of printer. Since only a very few of the Bodley Head books were entered in *The Book of Registry of Copyrights and Assignments* kept at the Hall of the Stationers Company (now in the Public Records Office, London), it is often very difficult to affix a precise date of publication to each book. In a few cases bibliographers have been able to determine an exact date of publication for certain of the Bodley Head books, and occasionally letters and other documents in the Bodley Head files and elsewhere have enabled me to date the publication of a book with exactitude. Most helpful — and I suppose most reliable — have been the Inventory Sheets which list all Bodley Head publications still in print at the time of the breakup together with the date of publication of each. Yet for many of the Bodley Head volumes I have had to rely on the entries in the *Publishers' Circular* and the *English Catalogue of Books* and other approximate dates given in the firm's advertisements. Since much of the information concerning later printings and editions is based on secondary sources, the term edition (abbreviated "ed.") as used in those sources is retained here even though in many cases it is likely that printings rather than editions are involved.

1. Richard Le Gallienne. *Volumes in Folio.* 1889 [15–31 March]. SP, 250; LP, 50; spec., 3. Chiswick Press.

2. Emily H[enrietta] Hickey. *Verse-Tales, Lyrics, and Translations.* 1889 [spring]. SP, 300; LP, 50. John Robb.

3. John Keats. *Three Essays,* ed. H. Buxton Forman. 1889 [January 1890]. 50 copies. Chiswick Press.

4. Henry Van Dyke. *The Poetry of Tennyson.* 1890 [January]; 2nd ed., 1892; 3rd ed., 1893. 1st ed. consisted of 250 copies bought from Scribners' Sons, New York; 2nd ed., SP, 350; LP, 50. R. & R. Clark (2nd and 3rd eds. only).

5. J[ohn] T[rivett] Nettleship. *Robert Browning, Essays and Thoughts.* 1890 [February]; 2nd ed., 1890 [1–15 December]; 3rd ed., by July 1894. 1st ed., SP, 1,000; LP, 75; 2nd ed., 500. J. Miller & Son.

6. Antaeus[William Joseph Ibbett]. *The Backslider and Other Poems.* 1890 [March]. 100 copies printed (only 50 folded and stitched). Chiswick Press.

7. Ernest Radford. *Chambers Twain.* 1890 [15–30 April]. SP, 250; LP, 50. Chiswick Press.

8. [William] Cosmo Monkhouse. *Corn and Poppies.* 1890 [15–30 April]. SP, 350; LP, 50. R. & R. Clark.

9. Philip Schaff. *Literature and Poetry.* 1890 [16–30 June]. 100 copies. William A. Fell (Philadelphia).

10. *The Pioneer, A Journal of Literature, Social Progress, Economics and Ethics,* ed. G[eorge] Dyke Smith. Quarterly from July 1890.

11. Philip H[enry] Wicksteed. *Dante: Six Sermons.* 2nd ed., 1890 [16–30 August]; 3rd ed., 1892 [July]. Total copies printed, 1,000. H. C. A. Thieme, Nimeguen, Holland (3rd ed. only).

12. *Alma Murray, Portrait as Beatrice Cenci with Critical Notice Containing Four Letters from Robert Browning.* 1891 [1–15 November 1890]. Ord. issue, ?; Whatman paper issue, 30. Richard Clay & Sons.

13. Richard Le Gallienne. *George Meredith, Some Characteristics, with a Bibliography by John Lane.* 1890 [21 November]; 2nd ed., 1891 [wk. of 28 March]; 3rd ed., 1893 [wk. of 30 September]. 1st ed., SP, 750; LP, 75. John Robb.

14. John Todhunter. *A Sicilian Idyll.* 1890 [24 November]. SP, 250; LP, 50. Chiswick Press.

15. Roden Noel. *Poor People's Christmas.* 1890 [1–15 December]. Total printed, 250 (includes the handmade paper issue of an undetermined quantity). Hazell, Watson & Viney (Aylesbury Press).

16. *The Reading Guild Handbook.* n.d. [7 February 1891].

17. Robinson Kay Leather and Richard Le Gallienne. *The Student and the Body-Snatcher and Other Trifles.* 1891 [wk. of 28 March]. SP, ?; LP, 50. John Robb.

18. Charles Thomas Jacobi. *On the Making and Issuing of Books.* 1891 [wk. of 18 April]. SP, 435; LP, 50; spec., 15. Chiswick Press.

19. Richard Henry Stoddard. *The Lion's Cub with Other Verse*. 1891 [wk. of 18 April]. 100 copies. Trow's Printing & Bookbinding (New York).

20. Dollie Radford. *A Light Load*. 1891 [wk. of 2 May] George E. Over, Rugby Press.

21. Walter Crane. *Renascence, A Book of Verse*. 1891 [30 May]. SP, 350 for England, 150 for USA; LP, 65 for England, 35 for USA; spec., 25 plus 4 for England, 15 for USA. Chiswick Press.

22. *Igdrasil*, ed. William Marwick. Vol. III from June 1891–March 1892.

23. *World Literature*, ed. William Marwick. Vol. I (nos. 1–6) from 15 September 1891–1 March 1892.

24. Eugene Benson. *From the Asolan Hills*. 1891 [September–October]. 300 copies. Chiswick Press.

25. [Gleeson White]. *Letters to Living Artists*. 1891 [October]. SP, 500; LP, 25. J. Miller & Son.

26. Francis Bourdillon. *A Lost God*. 1891 [November]. SP, 500; LP, 50. Chiswick Press.

27. Philip Bourke Marston. *A Last Harvest*, ed. with Preface and biographical sketch by Louise Chandler Moulton. 1891 [late]. SP, 500; LP, 50. J. Miller & Son.

28. William Wilsey Martin. *Quatrains, Life's Mystery and Other Poems*. 1891 [late]. Bedford Press.

29. *The Book of the Rhymers' Club*. 1892 [February]. SP, 450 (350 for sale); LP, 50. J. Miller & Son.

30. Michael Field [Katherine Harris Bradley and Edith Emma Cooper]. *Sight and Song*. 1892 [24 May]. 400 copies. T. and A. Constable.

31. William Strang. *The Earth Fiend*. 1892 [May]. SP, 175 on Japanese paper; LP, 55 (45 for sale) Folio copies on old handmade paper.

32. William Watson. *The Prince's Quest*. 2nd issue, 1892 [May?]; 2nd ed., 1893 [7 April]. 2nd issue, 265 copies; 2nd ed., 1,000. T. and A. Constable.

33. Effie Johnson. *In the Fire and Other Fancies*. 1892. 500 copies. Wertheimer, Lee & Co.

34. Ian Hamilton. *The Ballad of Hádji and Other Poems*. 1892. 500 copies. Chiswick Press.

35. Michael Field [Katherine Harris Bradley and Edith Emma Cooper]. *Stephania, A Trialogue*. 1892. 250 copies. Folkard & Son.

36. John Leicester Warren, Lord De Tabley. *A Guide to the Study of Book-Plates*. 2nd issue, 1892.

37. Oscar Wilde. *Poems*. 2nd issue, 1892 [26 May]. 220 copies.

38. Richard Le Gallienne. *English poems*. 1892 [27 September]; 2nd ed., 1893; 3rd ed., 1894. 1st ed., SP, 800 for England and USA; LP, 150 for England and USA; spec., 30; 2nd ed., 550 copies; 3rd ed., 500 copies. T. and A. Constable.

39. Arthur Symons. *Silhouettes*. 1892 [wk. of 8 October]. SP, 250; LP, 25. R. Folkard & Son.

40. William Crossing. *The Old Stone Crosses of the Dartmoor Borders*. 1892 [4 November].

41. Alice Meynell. *The Rhythm of Life and Other Essays*. 1893 [3 December 1892]; 2nd ed., 1893 [April]. 1st ed., SP, 550; LP, 50; 2nd ed., SP, 500. T. and A. Constable.

42. Alice Meynell. *Poems*. 1893 [3 December 1892]; 2nd ed., 1893 [April]. 1st ed., SP, 550; LP, 50; 2nd ed., SP, 500. T. and A. Constable.

43. Frederick Wedmore. *Renunciations*. 1893 [January]. SP, 375; LP, 50. R. Folkard & Son.

44. Oscar Wilde. *Salomé, drame en un acte*. 1893 [22 February]. Ord., 600 (500 for sale); spec., 50. Paul Schmidt, Paris.

45. J[ames] Ashcroft Noble. *The Sonnet in England and Other Essays*. 1893 [24 February]. SP, 712; LP, 53. J. Miller & Son.

46. John Gray. *Silverpoints*. 1893 [wk. of 4 March]. Ord., 250; spec. ed. in vellum, 25. R. Folkard & Son

47. William Watson. *The Eloping Angels*. 1893 [23 March]; 2nd ed., 1893 [May]. 1st ed., SP, 2,025; LP, 290; spec., 102; 2nd ed., SP, 624. T. and A. Constable.

48. William Watson. *Excursions in Criticism*. 1893 [29 March]; 2nd ed., 1893 [April]. Total printed, SP, 2,000; LP, 110. J. Miller & Son.

49. John Leicester Warren, Lord De Tabley. *Poems, Dramatic and Lyrical*. 1893 [29 March]; 2nd ed., 1893 [May–June]. 1st ed., ord. issue, 750; Japanese paper issue, 102; 2nd ed., ord. issue, 500. T. and A. Constable.

50. John Davidson. *Fleet Street Eclogues*. 1893 [late April]; 2nd ed., 1893 [July]. 1st ed., 300; total copies (both eds.) printed, 702. J. Miller & Son.

51. William Bell Scott. *A Poet's Harvest Home*. 1893 [wk. of 6 May]. SP, 300; LP, 50.

52. *The Hobby Horse* [new series of the *Century Guild Hobby Horse*], ed. Herbert P. Horne. Nos. 1–2 (1893); no. 3 (1894).

53. Augusta De Gruchy. *Under the Hawthorn and Other Verse*. 1893 [31 May]. Ord., 300; spec., 30. George E. Over, Rugby Press.

54. Alfred Hayes [*From Midland Meadows*], Richard Le Gallienne [*Nightingales*], Norman Gale [*A Verdant County*]. *A Fellowship in Song*. 1893 [June]. SP, 310; LP, 50. George E. Over, Rugby Press.

55. John Addington Symonds. *In the Key of Blue and Other Prose Essays*. 1893 [wk. of 7 January]; 2nd ed., 1893 [29 July]. Trial issue bound in blue, ?; regular SP issue bound in white, ?; LP, 50; total number of copies printed, both eds., 1,927. Ballantyne, Hanson.

56. William Hazlitt, *Liber Amoris or the New Pygmalion,* ed. with Introduction by Richard Le Gallienne. 1893 [early June]. George E. Over, Rugby Press.

57. Longus. *Daphnis and Chloe,* trans. from the Greek by George Thornley; woodcuts drawn by Charles Ricketts from designs by Charles H. Shannon. 1893 [wk. of 10 June]. 200 copies. Ballantyne.

58. Arthur Henry Hallam. *The Poems of Arthur Henry Hallam, together with His Essay on the Lyrical Poems of Alfred Tennyson*. 1893 [22 June]. SP, 860; LP, 77 (50 for sale). T. and A. Constable.

59. William Rothenstein. *Oxford Characters,* with Text by Frederick York Powell and Others. Parts I–V, from June 1893–June 1894. SP, 200 sets per part; LP, Parts I and II: 50 sets each; Parts III–V: 25 sets each.

60. John Davidson. *Plays [Scaramouch in Naxos: A Pantomime and Other Plays].* 3rd issue, 1893 [summer].

61. John Davidson. *Bruce, A Drama in Five Acts.* 2nd issue, 1893 [summer].

62. Herbert Beerbohm Tree. *The Imaginative Faculty.* 1893 [wk. of 15 July]. 1,050 copies. T. and A. Constable.

63. Frederick Wedmore. *Pastorals of France; Renunciations.* 1st ed., 1893 [2 October]. 950 copies. J. Miller & Son.

64. G[eorge] A[rthur] Greene. *Italian Lyrists of To-day.* 1893 [2 October]. 1,000 copies. T. and A. Constable.

65. Arthur Christopher Benson. *Poems.* 1893 [14 October]. 550 copies. T. and A. Constable.

66. Michael Field [Katherine Harris Bradley and Edith Emma Cooper]. *A Question of Memory, A Play.* 1893 [early November]. 120 copies.

67. Norman Gale. *Orchard Songs.* 1893 [8 November]. SP, 2,080; spec., 175. T. and A. Constable.

68. Francis Thompson. *Poems.* 1893 [8 November]; 2nd and 3rd eds., ?; 4th ed., 1894. 1st ed., SP, 500; LP, 12; total copies printed, all eds.: 2,173. R. Folkard & Son.

69. Oscar Wilde. *Lady Windermere's Fan.* 1893 [9 November]. SP, 550; LP, 50. T. and A. Constable.

70. Richard Le Gallienne. *The Religion of a Literary Man.* 1893 [14 November]; 2nd ed., 1893 [December]; 5th thousand by June 1894. 1st ed., ord. issue, 3,000; spec. rubricated issue, 260; 2nd ed., 2,000; total copies printed, all eds.: SP, 5,283; LP, 253. T. and A. Constable.

71. John Davidson. *A Random Itinerary.* 1894 [24 November 1893]. 755 copies. J. Miller & Son.

72. Richard Garnett. *Poems.* 1893 [30 November]. 550 copies (350 for England). T. and A. Constable.

73. Kenneth Grahame. *Pagan Papers.* 1894 [30 November 1893]. 615 copies (450 for England). T. and A. Constable.

74. George Egerton. *Keynotes.* 1893 [2 December]; 2nd issue, 1893 [December]; 2nd ed., 1894 [March]; 3rd ed., ?; 4th ed. by May 1894; 5th ed., late summer 1894. Although the first issue (pink wrappers) was of only 500 copies, the first printing was of 1,100 copies. The second edition was of 2,000, and the third of 3,000; total printed, all eds. by midsummer 1894: 6,071 copies. T. and A. Constable.

75. Richard Le Gallienne. *Limited Editions, A Prose Fancy: Together with Confessio Amantis, A Sonnet.* 1893 [Christmas]; 2nd issue, 1894 [January]. 1st issue, 700 copies; 2nd issue, 300; spec. issue on Japanese paper, 50. T. and A. Constable.

76. Stephen Coleridge. *The Sanctity of Confession.* 2nd ed., [January 1894?]. 250 copies. Clowes & Son.

77. Frances Wynne. *Whisper! A Volume of Verse* with "Frances Wynne: A

Memory" by K[atharine Tynan] H[inkson]. 2nd issue, 1893 [wk. of 3 February 1894]. 308 sheets purchased.

78. Grant Allen. *The Lower Slopes*. 1894 [12 February]. 812 copies (600 for England, 150 for USA). T. and A. Constable.

79. Laurence Binyon. *Lyric Poems*. 1894 [12 February]. 356 copies. R. Folkard & Son.

80. John Davidson. *Plays*. 1894 [12 February]. 760 copies (500 for England; also a few copies of special trial issue in white buckram). Ballentyne, Hanson.

81. Oscar Wilde. *Salome, A Tragedy in One Act*. 1894 [24 February]. Ord., 755 (500 for England); spec., 125 (100 for England). T. and A. Constable.

82. Katharine Tynan Hinkson. *Cuckoo Songs*. 1894 [24 February]. 717 copies (500 for England). J. Miller & Son.

83. Thomas Gordon Hake. *The Poems of Thomas Gordon Hake*, selected with a Prefatory Note by Alice Meynell. 1894 [2 March]. 660 copies (500 for England). T. and A. Constable.

84. W[illiam] P. James. *Romantic Professions and Other Papers*. 1894 [2 March]. 663 copies (450 for England). T. and A. Constable.

85. Thomas Lovell Beddoes. *The Letters of Thomas Lovell Beddoes*, ed. with Notes by Edmund Gosse. 1894 [8 March]. SP, 848 (600 for England); LP, 61 (25 for England). Ballantyne, Hanson.

86. *The Yellow Book*, ed. Henry Harland (letterpress) and Aubrey Beardsley (Art). Vol. I, 1894 [15 April. Copyright Registry Book, Vol. 38, gives 2 April as date of first publication]. Vol. II, 1894 [July]. Vol. I, 7,000 copies; Vol. II, 5,000. Ballantyne Press.

87. Elizabeth Rachel Chapman. *A Little Child's Wreath*. 1894 [1 June]; 2nd ed., 1894 [July?]. 1st ed., 350 for England, 200 for USA; total copies printed, both eds., 617. R. Folkard & Son.

88. Christopher Marlowe and George Chapman. *Hero and Leander*, with Decorations by Charles Ricketts and Charles H. Shannon. 1894 [1 June]. 220 copies (200 for sale). Ballantyne Press.

89. Ernest Rhys. *A London Rose*. 1894 [8 June]. 560 copies (350 for England, 150 for USA). T. and A. Constable.

90. G[eorge] S[lythe] Street. *The Autobiography of a Boy, Passages Selected by His Friend*. 1894 [8 June]. 2nd ed., 1894 [July]. 650 copies (450 for England, 150 for USA); total copies printed, both eds.: 1,174.

91. Oscar Wilde. *The Sphinx*, with Decorations by Charles Ricketts. 1894 [8 June]. SP, 303; LP, 25. Ballantyne Press.

92. Florence Farr. *The Dancing Faun*. 1894 [wk. of 9 June]. 1,100 copies, of which the 1st issue was bound in light blue cloth with designs in dark blue and key on spine in gold; 2nd issue was bound in light green cloth with designs and key on spine in dark blue. T. and A. Constable.

93. Richard Le Gallienne. *Prose Fancies*. 1894 [15 June]; 2nd ed., 1894 [July]. 1st ed., SP, 1,112; LP, 117; 2nd ed., 1,015; T. and A. Constable.

94. Charles Conrad Abbott. *Travels in a Tree-Top*. 1894 [20 June]. 200 copies.

95. *The Second Book of the Rhymers' Club.* 1894 [20 June]. SP, 718 (450 for England, 150 for USA); LP, 76 (50 for England, 20 for USA). J. Miller & Son.

96. Allan Monkhouse. *Books and Plays.* 1894 [26 June]. 464 copies. J. Miller & Son.

97. F[eodor] Dostoevski. *Poor Folk,* translated from the Russian by Lena Milman, with a Preface by George Moore. 1894 [30 June]. 1,100 copies. T. and A. Constable.

98. A. Fraser Hill. *The Land and Wealth of New South Wales.* 1894 [24 August].

99. Lionel Johnson. *The Art of Thomas Hardy.* 1894 [wk. of 6 October]. SP, 1,500; LP, 150. T. and A. Constable.

100. *Arthur O'Shaughnessy, His Life and His Work, with Selections from His Poems,* with Preface and selections made by Louise Chandler Moulton. 1894 [transferred to John Lane from Stone and Kimball, October 1894]. De Vinne Press, New York.

APPENDIX B.   THE BODLEY HEAD ARTISTS
AND ILLUSTRATORS

The contributions of the major illustrators — Beardsley, Housman, Ricketts and Shannon, and Crane — to the design and overall image of the Bodley Head book have already been discussed (Chapter Two). It is my purpose here to address myself to the one Bodley Head book devoted solely to an artist's drawings, William Rothenstein's *Oxford Characters,* and to several other publications of artistic interest such as Ricketts and Shannon's *Hero and Leander* and *Daphnis and Chloe,* Walter Crane's *Renascence,* and William Strang's *The Earth Fiend.* A list of Bodley Head artists and illustrators and their work is also appended here.

Rothenstein's series of portraits of notable Oxford dons and undergraduates was the young artist's first published work and therefore an important consideration in any study of the evolution of his style. Rothenstein had come to London from his native Bradford in 1888, at the age of sixteen, to study with Alphonse Legros, who at the time was a professor at the Slade School. The following year, Rothenstein went to Paris, where he studied art under Benjamin Constant and Jules Lefèbre at Julien's Academy. Although he seems to have thoroughly enjoyed Paris, where he became the friend of many men of note — Rodin, Verlaine, and Toulouse-Lautrec, in particular — Rothenstein returned to London in 1893 and soon after, with a commission from Lane, set out for Oxford, where he was to reside on and off for the next year while working on his series of *Characters.*

Rothenstein seems to have come to Lane's attention through his Oxford friend, York Powell, whom Yeats described as "a famous Oxford Professor of History, a broad-built, broad-headed, brown-bearded man clothed in heavy blue cloth and looking, but for his glasses and the dim sight of a student, like some captain in the merchant service." (*Autobiography of William Butler Yeats* [New York: Macmillan, 1953], p. 72.) According to Rothenstein, Powell had shown Lane some of his caricatures, and although Rothenstein says nothing of it, Powell may even have suggested the idea of the series to Lane. Since Lane "was on the look-out for fresh talent," he sought out the young artist and commissioned him to do the series of drawings which was to become the *Oxford Characters.* (William Rothenstein, *Men and Memories,* I [London: Faber, 1939], 125.)

1893 seems to have been the year in which Lane's search for new talent led him to discover several of the most gifted young artists of the day. For he not only began the extraordinarily fruitful relationship with Beardsley in that year, but he also initiated his far less remarkable ventures in publishing with Rothenstein. Furthermore in September of that year Lane approached Max Beerbohm, whom he probably had met through Rothenstein, with a proposal that he "write the letterpress of a fantastic book of which Aubrey Beardsley is doing the illustrations." ([September 21, 1893], in *Letters to Reggie Turner,* ed. Rupert Hart-Davis [London: Rupert Hart-Davis, 1964], p. 66.)

Certainly, Beerbohm's belief that Lane's ventures — especially the *Yellow Book*

— would "make all our fortunes" seems to have been shared by Rothenstein as well as Beardsley. ([January 1, 1894], *Letters to Reggie Turner*, p. 88.) Yet it soon became apparent to these men that their relationship with Lane was destined to be unsatisfactory. Rothenstein's relationship with the publisher was to be a brief one. Almost from the outset he seems to have found Lane intolerable, and when in September 1893 Lane visited Paris and stayed with Rothenstein for a week, a serious altercation occurred, which Max Beerbohm reported shortly after in a letter to Reggie Turner:

It seems that John Lane is furious with Will Rothenstein, whose guest he has been for a few days in Paris. After conducting his publisher to the Louvre, taking him into every room and listening with great attention to his detailed opinions of all the pictures, he suddenly turned upon him with pent-up fury and insolence and told him never to mention Art again: inasmuch as he knew nothing whatever about it and probably cared less. John Lane is extremely bitter about him now in consequence and is probably going to get someone else to design a book-plate, instead of one for which he has already paid Will Rothenstein. Isn't it rather sad? (Postmarked September 22, 1893, *Letters to Reggie Turner*, pp. 69–70.)

A letter from Beardsley to Rothenstein suggests that as early as September 1893, he, too, had misgivings about the publisher, of whom he speaks with derision. "I am sure," Beardsley wrote, referring to Lane's recent visit to Paris, "you must have had a very funny time with Jean Lane (who by the way is behaving I think very treacherously both to you and to myself —)." (A.L.S., n.d., Houghton.)

Although Lane and Rothenstein seem to have gotten over their spat at Paris, the trouble which arose during the course of publishing the *Oxford Characters* series doubtless brought their relationship to the breaking point; several minor commissions for illustrations of books which Rothenstein was given were never carried out and, when the artist refused to contribute to the *Yellow Book* after Lane fired Beardsley, the contract between the two men ended. (Robert Speaight, *Sir William Rothenstein* [London: Eyre & Spottiswoode, 1962], p. 94.) It would seem that what had in 1893 promised to be a most fruitful relationship for both publisher and artists was not destined to flourish. Lane, whom Beerbohm referred to as "that poor fly in the amber of modernity" ([September 1893], *Letters to Reggie Turner*, p. 63) was to fail signally in his attempts to make the most of the great talents of three of his most gifted young artists, Rothenstein, Beerbohm, and Beardsley.

Nevertheless Rothenstein returned to London in September 1893 and hastened on to Oxford to carry on with his commission. His coming was attended by something of a minor storm in the quiet groves of academia. In his "Enoch Soames" (*Seven Men* [London: Heinemann, 1919], pp. 4–5), Beerbohm was later to write of Rothenstein:

In the Summer Term of '93 a bolt from the blue flashed down on Oxford. It drove deep, it hurtlingly embedded itself in the soil. Dons and undergraduates stood around, rather pale, discussing nothing but it. Whence came it, this meteorite? From Paris. Its name? Will Rothenstein. Its aim? To do a series of twenty-four portraits in lithograph. These were to be published from the Bodley Head, London. The matter was urgent. Already Warden of A, and the Master of B, and the Regius Professor of C, had meekly "sat." Dignified and doddering old men, who had never consented to sit to any one, could not withstand this dynamic little stranger. He did not sue: he invited; he did not invite: he commanded. He was twenty-one years old. He wore spectacles that flashed more than any other pair ever seen. He was a wit. He was brimful of ideas. He knew Whistler. He knew Edmond de Goncourt. He knew every one in Paris. He knew them all by heart. He was Paris in Oxford. It was whispered that, as soon as he had polished off his selection of dons, he was going to include a few undergraduates. It was a proud day for me when I — I — was included.

Whether the more staid dons shared the enthusiasm of the undergraduates for Rothenstein's venture is to be doubted, for it was with some trepidation that some of them acquiesced and sat for the young artist. When such worthies as Sir Henry Acland and Walter Pater turned with alarm and disapproval from Rothenstein's first representation of their highly prized physiognomies, there were serious repercussions.

The first part of the series had appeared in June 1893 and was composed of two portraits, one of them a drawing of Sir Henry Acland, K.C.B., F.R.S., M.D., a most distinguished and revered Oxonian. Rothenstein's caricature of Acland as a senile old man brought on one of the Bodley Head's most serious predicaments. So disturbed were the partners that Lane was dispatched to Oxford in December to try to calm things down, and Mathews wrote Rothenstein in much alarm declaring that in Oxford the initial publication of the *Characters* had been a failure "largely on account of the antipathy of Sir Henry Acland & his friends with portrait of Sir Henry in Part I" and further reporting that "the booksellers are mutinying against taking the 2nd and future parts." (A.L.S., dated December 1893, Houghton.)

Nevertheless, as Mathews also informed Rothenstein, Sir Henry was prepared to give the artist another sitting for a new portrait, and in time an entirely new likeness of the doctor was inserted in the much delayed second part, with a covering letter in ink on Bodley Head stationery begging subscribers to substitute it for the portrait issued in the first part. A far more serious and thoughtful looking gentleman, Rothenstein's second Acland was as much an idealization of the man as the first had been a caricature.

As if the embarrassment of Lane and Mathews over the Acland affair was not enough, the great to-do over the Pater drawing was also trying. At first reluctant to sit for Rothenstein, Pater in time agreed. By March 25, 1894, Rothenstein's portrait was ready to be inspected. Pater, who was leaving for an extended holiday in the north of England, informed Lane that his sisters would view the drawing and that he would abide by their decision. The sisters found the portrait so unlike their brother that Pater wrote Lane on April 5 to say that he was sorry but "the publication of it must be given up." (Quoted in *Letters of Walter Pater*, ed. Lawrence Evans [Oxford: Oxford University Press, Clarendon Press, 1969], Letters 262, 263, pp. 151–152.) Pater too was willing to sit again, and the result was the well-known drawing which suggests that he is anything but a monkish sort of aesthete.

If Rothenstein had at the outset contemplated a series of highly original and frank representations of his Oxford subjects, under the avalanche of criticism and great pressure from Lane he soon changed his attitude. "Poor Rothenstein," exclaimed Beerbohm in a letter to Reggie Turner, "his series 'va très lentement'." (Tuesday, [December 19, 1893], *Letters to Reggie Turner*, p. 85.) In March Beerbohm was again solicitous about his friend's welfare. "It is rather touching," he wrote.

You know how angry old Henry Acland was at the libellous portrait of him and how that Walter Pater refused to sit at all? Well, poor Rothenstein has turned idealist, in consequence — has done a second thing of old Henry, who no longer an old village-dotard, appears exactly like Gladstone, only far firmer, and Walter Pater, who as you know is a kind of hump-back *manqué,* figures as a young guardsman with curly mustachios — just what Kendal must have looked like twenty years ago. (A.L.S., [March 8, 1894], *Letters to Reggie Turner,* p. 90.)

Although the Bodley Head was under contract for twelve parts of two portraits each, only five parts were published before the breakup. All twelve parts (24 lithographs) were issued in one volume by Lane in 1896. The portraits were done as lithographs with the artist working with T. Way, Whistler's favorite printer. According to Sir John Rothenstein, Will's distinguished son, the *Oxford Characters*

reveal the same qualities which characterized his work in Paris. The dashing technique, the vigorous style, the strong sense of character are all there. But only in some of the portraits of the more ancient among the dons is there a trace of the restraint and austerity of the future. (*A Pot of Paint, The Artists of the 1890's* [New York: Covici, Friede, 1929], p. 197.)

Even though Rothenstein's series was the only work issued from the Bodley Head which can be strictly considered an art book, at least four other volumes can be loosely considered as art books in that they were initiated by artists primarily for the purpose of illustration. That artists would go so far as to choose a text or actually compose a poem in order to illustrate it suggests the high regard in which the art of illustration was held by the artists of the nineties. Certainly Ricketts and Shannon's illustrated editions of *Hero and Leander* and *Daphnis and Chloe* are among those artists' finest work; A. J. A. Symons' comment on Beardsley could with almost equal force have been applied to any of the best artists of the Bodley Head:

Beardsley was, more than any artist of modern times, the creature of the printed book . . . his drawings were created not so much to be beautiful in themselves (though they are that) but to be beautiful in reproduction; and apart from such trifles as Christmas cards and posters, his works were specifically intended for use as covers, title-pages, illustrations or embellishments to books. ("The Typography of the 1890's," *Fleuron,* VII [1930], 96.)

Like Walter Crane's *Renascence,* William Strang's *The Earth Fiend* exemplifies the beautiful book created by an artist-author of his own finely illustrated poetry. Strang, who had come to London from his native Dumbartonshire about 1879 to study at the Slade School, like Rothenstein, worked under Legros. Although some of his early things, such as his etched mezzotint of 1882, "Head of a Peasant," are strikingly Rembrandtesque in effect, it is the influence of Legros which is more noticeable in Strang's work. As Laurence Binyon once wrote, "Of all M. Legros's pupils, the one who is nearest akin to him, and who has imbibed most of his spirit, is William Strang." (*William Strang, Catalogue of His Etched Work* with an Introductory Essay by Laurence Binyon [Glasgow: James Maclehose & Sons, 1906].)

Strang's *Earth Fiend* is a poem reminiscent of Robert Burns in its use of Scots dialect and its rural setting. A native of the Burns country, Strang in both his poetry and art, as Binyon has said, "remains always a Lowland Scot." ("Introductory Essay," p. xv.) The poem tells the grim Scottish folk tale of a stout-hearted Scots peasant who comes upon and conquers an Earth Fiend, who does his bidding for a time but then turns upon him and destroys him.

A parable of man's thankless and often fatal struggle with the soil, *The Earth Fiend* is illustrated with eleven etchings, which do full justice to the harsh and ugly reality the subject matter evokes. In fact, it is a certain grotesque element in these etchings or what Binyon referred to as "something of the decadence," which characterizes Strang's peculiar sense of beauty, a quality which as Binyon said "has indeed been denied him by many altogether; these are convinced that he has a downright passion for ugliness." ("Introductory Essay," p. xii.)

Also most appropriate to the spirit of the poem is that aspect of Legros's temperament which was most congenial to Strang, "that side which was expressed in the French master's pictures of Death coming on the tramp or the wood cutter, surprising them by the wayside or in the midst of their labours" (Introduction to *William Strang, Supplement to the "Catalogue of His Etched Work 1882–1912"* [Glasgow: Maclehose, Jackson & Co., 1923], p. xii).

The Bodley Head's most highly priced book, *The Earth Fiend* appeared in 1892 in two handsome issues, 55 folio copies (45 for sale) on old handmade paper and 150 copies on Japanese paper; the etchings were printed and signed by F. Goulding and the letterpress was by T. and A. Constable. Both editions of *The Earth Fiend* were sold out before the date of publication. But the publishers soon after were able to repurchase a few copies, which they offered at the rate of seven guineas per folio copy and three guineas per small-paper copy.

Despite the fact that Eugene Benson did not illustrate his poem, *From Asolan Hills,* he should be mentioned here; for, like Crane and Strang, he was an artist and his poetry was written from the point of view of a painter. According to his close friend Walter Crane Benson "was another American artist of cultured tastes and much originality of conception, who had a literary side as well." (*An Artist's Reminiscences,* 2nd ed. [London: Methuen, 1907], p. 130.) Besides *From Asolan Hills,* Benson published an essay on Gabriele d'Annunzio in the *Yellow Book* (XI, 284–299).

Benson was born in 1837. When Crane met him, in the early 1870s Benson had already found his way to Rome and to Venice, where he took up residence in a fine old house on the Rio Marin, Palazzo Capello. Desirous of following Crane's procedure in publishing *Renascence* — that is, having the book printed at the Chiswick Press and then published and sold on commission by the Bodley Head — Benson asked his friend to approach Mathews and Lane on his behalf. On January 25, 1891, Crane mentioned in a postscript to a letter to Lane (Houghton): "a friend of mine who lives in Venice (Eugene Benson, the painter) sends me a poem of his own — 'From Asolan Hills' — which he would like to bring out through Elkin Mathews." A few weeks later, in a letter of March 3, 1891, Crane wrote of the matter to Mathews. Repeating what he had already written to Lane, Crane also volunteered his own opinion of Benson's poetic effort:

The poem seems to be a very interesting one, & has a certain distinct interest too
—apart from its intrinsic one—from its connection with *Browning* & *Asolo*
(where it was written). It deals with Venice from the Artist's point of view, touching
history & antiquity as well as life & nature. Mr. Benson's pictures are well known
in London & are often seen at the New as formerly at the Grosvenor. (E.M.)

In addition to Beardsley, Ricketts, Crane, and Strang, the Bodley Head employed the services of a number of other leading artists of the day, among the most notable of whom were H. J. Ford, the illustrator of Andrew Lang's famous books of fairy tales, and John Fulleylove, who was well known for his pictures of classic Greek landscapes and architecture. The Bodley Head used as frontispieces P. Wilson Steer's lithographed portrait of Richard Le Gallienne and Dante Gabriel Rossetti's watercolor of T. Gordon Hake.

The list of the Bodley Head illustrators and artists and their work given below indicates how extensive the art work was in the Bodley Head books.

Beardsley, Aubrey
 George Egerton, *Keynotes* (1893), binding designs, title page.
 Kenneth Grahame, *Pagan Papers* (1893), binding designs, title page.
 Oscar Wilde, *Salome* (1894), binding designs, title page, frontispiece and nine other full page illustrations.
 Florence Farr, *The Dancing Faun* (1894), binding designs, title page.
 Feodor Dostoevski, *Poor Folk* (1894), binding designs, title page.
 John Davidson, *Plays* (1894), binding design, frontispiece, title page.
Crane, Walter
 John Todhunter, *A Sicilian Idyll* (1890), frontispiece.

Ernest Radford, *Chambers Twain* (1890), title page.

Walter Crane, *Renascence* (1891), title page, head and tail pieces.

Effie Johnson, *In the Fire and Other Fancies* (1892), cover design, title page.

Augusta De Gruchy, *Under the Hawthorn* (1893), title page.

Davis, Louis

Dollie Radford, *A Light Load* (1891), title page.

Ford, Henry Justice

F. W. Bourdillon, *A Lost God* (1891), three full page illustrations.

Fulleylove, John

Frederick Wedmore, *Pastorals of France* (1893), title page.

Furse, Charles Wellington

G. S. Street, *The Autobiography of a Boy* (1894), title page.

Granby, the Marchioness of

Herbert Beerbohm Tree, *The Imaginative Faculty* (1893), portrait drawing of Tree for frontispiece.

Hogg, Warrington

William Watson, *The Eloping Angels* (1893), binding design, half title, title page.

Horne, H. P.

H. P. Horne, *Diversi Colores* (1891), binding design and title page.

Arthur Symons, *Silhouettes* (1892), lettering and design for title page, lettering for table of contents.

Housman, Laurence

Francis Thompson, *Poems* (1893), binding designs, frontispiece, title page.

John Davidson, *A Random Itinerary* (1894), binding design, frontispiece, title page.

Katharine Tynan Hinkson, *Cuckoo Songs* (1894), binding design, title page.

Image, Selwyn

Michael Field, *Stephania* (1892), binding design, frontispiece, colophon.

Laurence Binyon, *Lyric Poems* (1894), binding design and lettering, title page.

Elizabeth Chapman, *A Little Child's Wreath* (1894), binding design, title page.

Ernest Rhys, *A London Rose* (1894), binding design, title page.

Kay, J. Illingworth

Norman Gale, *Orchard Songs* (1893), binding design, half title, title page.

Richard Garnett, *Poems* (1893), half title, title page.

Grant Allen, *Lower Slopes* (1894), binding design, title page.

W. P. James, *Romantic Professions* (1894), half title, title page.

Meredith, W. Maxze

Richard Le Gallienne, *George Meredith* (1890), sketch of The Chalet at Boxhill.

Ricketts, Charles

Oscar Wilde, *Poems,* second issue (1892), binding design.

John Addington Symonds, *In the Key of Blue* (1893), binding design, title page design.

Lord De Tabley, *Poems, Dramatic and Lyrical* (1893), binding design, title page design, six full-page illustrations.

John Gray, *Silverpoints* (1893), binding design, title page design, initials.

Oscar Wilde, *The Sphinx* (1894), binding design, title page, initials, nine illustrations.

Ricketts, Charles, and *Charles Hazlewood Shannon*

Longus, *Daphnis and Chloe* (1893), woodcuts drawn on wood and engraved by Ricketts and Shannon.

Christopher Marlowe, *Hero and Leander* (1894), decorations designed and cut on wood; also decorated colophon.

Rossetti, Dante Gabriel

T. G. Hake, *The Poems of Thomas Gordon Hake* (1894), portrait of Hake for frontispiece.

Rothenstein, William

York Powell and others, *Oxford Characters* (1893–   ), twelve portraits.

[Projected work for Bodley Head which was never done:

Richard Le Gallienne, *Prose Fancies* (1894), portrait of Le Gallienne for frontispiece.

Norman Gale, *Orchard Songs* (1893), title page.]

Scott, William Bell

Lord De Tabley, *Poems, Dramatic and Lyrical* (1893), book plate.

Shannon, Charles Hazlewood (see also Ricketts and Shannon)

Oscar Wilde, *Lady Windermere's Fan* (1893), binding designs.

Steer, Philip Wilson

Richard Le Gallienne, *Prose Fancies* (1894), lithographed portrait of the author (English edition only).

Strang, William

Cosmo Monkhouse, *Corn and Poppies* (1890), etched frontispiece (large-paper edition only).

William Strang, *The Earth Fiend* (1892), designs and illustrations.

Ian Hamilton, *The Ballad of Hádji,* second issue (1892), etched frontispiece.

Lionel Johnson, *The Art of Thomas Hardy* (1894), etched portrait of Hardy.

White, Gleeson

T. G. Hake, *The Poems of Thomas Gordon Hake* (1894), lettering and designs on binding.

Young, Austin

James Ashcroft Noble, *The Sonnet in England* (1893), lettering and design on binding.

APPENDIX C. THE BODLEY HEAD PERIODICALS

The most famous of the Bodley Head periodicals, of course, is the *Yellow Book*, two issues of which appeared before the breakup (April and July 1894). Since it has received much attention over the years and at least one detailed study, Katherine Lyon Mix's *A Study in Yellow* (Lawrence, Kans.: University of Kansas Press, 1960), little need be said here.

The *Yellow Book* was conceived of by Aubrey Beardsley and Henry Harland, who with the enthusiastic cooperation of John Lane brought it into being. According to a letter which Beardsley wrote to Robert Ross (dated by Margery Ross as December 1893 in *Robert Ross, Friend of Friends,* ed. Margery Ross [London: Jonathan Cape, 1952]), the idea of a new quarterly had already led to decisive action. "I am sure," wrote Beardsley,

you will be vastly interested to hear that Harland and myself are about to start a new literary and artistic Quarterly. The title has already been registered at Stationers Hall and on the scroll of fame. It is *The Yellow Book.* In general get up, it will look like the ordinary French novel. Each number will contain about 10 contributions in the way of short stories and discursive essays from the pens say of Henry Harland, Henry James, Crackenthorpe, George Egerton, and Max Beerbohm. The drawings will be independent and supplied by Aubrey Beardsley, Walter Sickert, Wilson Steer, and Will Rothenstein and other past masters. The publication will be undertaken by John Lane, and the price will be 5/–.
(No. 1 appears on April 15th.)
We all want to have something charming from you for the first number. Say an essay or a short story. . . .
Our idea is that many brilliant story painters and picture writers cannot get their best stuff accepted in the conventional magazine, either because they are not topical or perhaps a little risque.

As Beardsley's letter suggests, the *Yellow Book* was the joint responsibility of two men — the artist himself and Henry Harland, one serving as art editor and the other as literary editor. Beardsley had met Harland in the waiting room of the celebrated Dr. Symes Thompson, who specialized in the treatment of tuberculosis, a disease from which both Beardsley and Harland suffered. Despite the fact that he pretended to have been born in St. Petersburg (like Whistler?), Harland had been born in New York and with his wife had come to London in 1889.

During the summer of 1893 Beardsley visited the Harlands, who were sojourning in France, and presumably the two men continued to see each other in London during the following autumn. According to Harland,

The *Yellow Book* was first thought of one fearful afternoon in one of the densest and soupiest and yellowest of all London's infernalest yellow fogs. Aubrey Beardsley and I sat together the whole afternoon before a beautiful glowing open coal fire and I assure you we could scarcely see our hands before our faces, with all the candles lighted, for the fog, you know. . . .

So we sat together the whole day and evening and were a gay and cheerful couple I assure you. We declared each to each that we thought it quite a pity and a shame that London publishers should feel themselves longer under obligation to refuse any more of our good manuscripts. Fancy having our brains stowed away for so long in their editorial sideboards that we lost our chance of even having our ideas served up cold.

"'Tis monstrous, Aubrey," said I.

"'Tis a public scandal," said he. And then and there we decided to have a magazine of our own. As the sole editorial staff we would feel free and welcome to publish any and all of ourselves that nobody else could be hired to print.

That was the first day of January . . . and the next day we had an appointment with Mr. John Lane. (Manuscript quoted in *A Study in Yellow*, p. 68.)

Once the idea matured a bit, it apparently took very little time for news of the proposed magazine to get about town, for shortly the names of Beardsley and Harland as well as the *Yellow Book* were on the lips of all the literati. On February 17, 1894, Ernest Rhys concluded a long, gossipy letter to Arthur Stedman with an account of the previous evening, at which time he had met at the Hogarth Club

the inconceivable Beardsley, still a mere boy of about twenty, who is Harland's co-editor in the new "Yellow Book" (for which by the way H. H. has just taken a story of mine). H. H. was very witty & excitable as usual at supper, — too excitable, I'm afraid, for health, but not the less amusing for that! It's wonderful that he pulled through his last illness. (C. U. L.)

In addition to all the excitement Beardsley, Harland, and Lane stirred up among Londoners of the smart set, the Bodley Head did much else to create interest in the imminent appearance of the *Yellow Book*. Among Beardsley's notable work are his designs for an advertisement for the magazine and the prospectus for the first volume (see Brian Reade, *Aubrey Beardsley* [New York: Viking, 1967], plates 341 and 343). The prospectus depicted a "new woman" standing in front of the Vigo Street shop picking and choosing her own reading matter from among tables of books while a disapproving Elkin Mathews as Pierrot looked on.

Although there had been much speculation as to what the *Yellow Book* was to be, little of substance could be depended upon until the appearance of the *Sketch*, V (April 11, 1894), 557–558, which contained an interview with Harland and Beardsley. To the question "What is to be the leading note of the *Yellow Book*?" the editors replied:

All magazines, if they are any good at all, must have clever stuff in them; that is a primary essential. We want, also, to be distinctive, to be popular in the best sense of the word. And we don't want to be precious or eccentric. We feel that the time has come for an absolutely new era in the way of magazine literature. . . . Distinction, modernness — these, probably, so nearly as they can be picked out, are the two leading features of our plan.

Having denied that most of the contributors to the first issue of the *Yellow Book* belonged to "the Vigo Street school," Beardsley and Harland went on to further enunciate the aims of the new magazine. In pointing out that the magazine would be receptive to long short stories, the editors went on to say that "in many ways our contributors will employ a freer hand than the limitations of the old-fashioned periodical can permit." The only limitation, it was suggested, would be craftsmanship. If a piece of literature or a work of art was well made, it would be acceptable. "What goes into the *Yellow Book*," the editors stressed, "will go in on the absolute rule of workmanship — value from the literary point of view. In fine, the notion is that the *Yellow Book* should contain what is literature, and only what is literature — literature in all its phases."

Another point which, according to Beardsley and Harland, set the new magazine apart from others was the fact that the text and the illustrations or art work were to be given equal emphasis. Art, they insisted, would not be in the *Yellow Book* the handmaid to literature. "We want to put literature and art on precisely the same level." Accordingly, "a picture will have to recommend itself purely as a work of art — that will be the one and final test. If you were to bring us a bad picture of the Crucifixion, we should not take it; but if you brought us a good picture of a pumpkin, it's highly probable we should take it."

Clearly Beardsley, Harland and Lane thought of the *Yellow Book* as beginning a new era in magazine publishing. Although much of what the *Yellow Book* purported to be had been anticipated by the *Century Guild Hobby Horse*, no magazine with such high and uncommercial aims had hitherto been planned for a wide audience. Certainly compared to practically all its contemporaries, the *Yellow Book*'s announced policies were distinct and new, for it was to deal entirely with literature and art. No news, politics, or sociological subjects were to be found in its pages, nor were any commercial book reviews to be included.

Typographically too the *Yellow Book* differed radically from most of its competitors. In keeping with the ideals of the Revival of Printing, the magazine was printed entirely in Caslon old-face type. Not only was the title page, like those Beardsley designed for *Keynotes* and *The Dancing Faun*, strikingly different from the weak, crowded, unaesthetic title pages of the usual Victorian journal, but the typography of each essay began in a new and attractive way. The heading was set a quarter of the way down the page in upper and lower case, not centered but to the left, with the author's name a line beneath on the right. Other distinctive features, as A. J. A. Symons in his essay on fine printing in the *Fleuron* (VII [1930], 101) pointed out, were a catchword on each page and the luxury of fly-titles preceding each plate.

The day of publication, April 15, 1894, was followed by the celebrated "Yellow Book Dinner," from which Elkin Mathews was excluded. A first printing of 5,000 copies was issued and exhausted in five days only to be followed by a second and third printing before the public's demand for copies was assuaged.

As had been planned, the *Yellow Book* enjoyed something of a *succès de scandale*. With a good deal of pride, Beardsley wrote Henry James, who was a friend of

Harland's: "Have you heard of the storm that raged around No. 1. More of the thunderbolts fell on my head. However, I enjoyed the excitement immensely." (A.L.S. April 30, Houghton.) While the aesthetes exulted and the Philistines raged, the reviewers had a field day; some, like the *Times* reviewer, cried out in wrath against the new magazine, others bestowed lavish praise:

From the Bodley Head, Vigo Street (very aptly called "the London Hippocrene") there comes one more triumph of aesthetic art. We refer to an exquisite new quarterly magazine, entitled "The Yellow Book," which must charm the eye and mind alike of every reader who can appreciate the perfection of modern book-making. Not only is "The Yellow Book" fascinatingly fantastic to the cultured eye, but it is also goldenly interesting and joy-dispensing to the cultured mind. Those who can revel in the consummation of artistic expression, and in the most restrained and most refined language of English modernity will find here a sumptuous feast. ([Katharine Tynan?], the *Weekly Irish Times* [Dublin], Saturday, April 28, 1894, XX, no. 954, 4.)

Much in the way of satire and parody appeared, among the best of which was an announcement concerning the imminent publication of "The Yellow Boot" to be sent forth from "The Blodey Head/ Prigo Street, W." which appeared in the *Granta,* VII, no. 133 (April 21, 1894), 270–271. Illustrated with a take-off on Beardsley's prospectus — a Mrs. Grundy with high buttoned boots smugly kicking Pierrot in the face — the parody offered this enlightening explanation of its title:

The Yellow Boot: *Yellow* as the complexion of the poet and as the gold which inspires him: *Boot,* because Art can dispense with all other clothing, and because our contributors, if they get nothing else, may at least hope to get the Boot — above all because there is nothing like leather.

Among the list of contributors were such worthies as Richard Le Guineahenne, Flaubert Crockonwheales, Melia Mascula Dowdie, Oswald Siesic, and E. Leary Bacchus.

Many of the Bodley Head authors were also displeased by the *Yellow Book.* Both Alice Meynell and Lord De Tabley refused to write for it; William Watson published a number of his poems in the magazine, but his attitude, as expressed many years later in a letter to R. Ellis Roberts, was definitely disapproving:

I have just been reading with great interest your review, in the Guardian, of "The Beardsley Period" — a book whose title perhaps seems less exquisitely facetious to those who did not know Beardsley than to me who did. I suppose we shall now be having "The Dowsonian Age" & perhaps "The Life and Times of John Lane."

I must say that whilst those Nineties were running I was quite unaware that the world was being suffused with the hue of jaundice, or that a quarterly magazine to which I had with difficulty been prevailed upon to contribute was so seriously disturbing the equilibrium of the universe. What I & some others mainly saw in the Yellow Book was the crude amateurishness of much of its contents, some of which seemed to us the last word in bad writing. (A.L.S. in my possession, dated from Hawkshead, Ambleside, February 25, 1925.)

Although the *Yellow Book* was the only periodical which the Bodley Head initiated, Mathews and Lane advertised and issued five other periodicals which had previously been published by other firms, including the two most beautifully printed and decorated journals of the nineties, the *Hobby Horse* and the *Dial*. Like the *Yellow Book,* these two magazines were products of the aesthetic movement in England and were devoted — like their forerunner, the short-lived Pre-Raphaelite journal, the *Germ* — solely to literature and the arts.

The organ of the Century Guild, an organization of artists and craftsmen formed in 1881 by the architect Arthur Mackmurdo with the aid of Herbert Horne and his mentor, Selwyn Image, the *Century Guild Hobby Horse* (as it was entitled until 1893) began with a trial issue published at Orpington in April 1884 and continued to be published from 1886 through 1894. Deriving its aims and ideas from the Pre-Raphaelites and the teachings of John Ruskin, the journal was dedicated to the revitalization of the decorative or minor architectural arts by recovering them from the province of the mere tradesman and thereby making them once again available to the artist-craftsman. Much opposed to the commercialism of the age, the proprietors of the *Hobby Horse* sought, like William Morris, to extend Ruskin's ideas into the realm of everyday life where even "the man whose work, though it be but the making of household stuffs, or of the common utensils of daily life, expresses the better part of himself, and of his hopes and thoughts." ("A Preface" to the *Century Guild Hobby Horse,* no. 13, for January 1889.)

The principle upon which the Guild operated and which gave to the periodical its name and device — "a vignette of two Hobby-horsemen up to the neck in roses," as Ernest Rhys, in *Wales England Wed* (London: Dent, 1940), p. 109, was later to describe it — was that of a free rein in artistic expression. As stated in "A Preface,"

it was the hope of this periodical to provide a quiet place in which men, who were at one in their fundamental ideas about Art, might give free expression to their individual thoughts and sentiments, might assert that individuality of conception and of treatment, which is so interesting, which is so important, which is not in the very least incompatible with a clear apprehension of what are the immutable principles which underlie all Art, everywhere and for ever. "De gustibus non est disputandum," that is, as we find it translated in "Tristram Shandy," there is no disputing about Hobby Horses. This is the precise title of our Periodical, and the significance of it will be evident in the light of what has just been said. Only, be it remembered, it is not in the matter of the fundamental, immutable principles of Art, but in the matter of their individual expression, that what we playfully call "men's hobbies" have their place.

Printed and published by the Chiswick Press between 1889 and 1892, the *Century Guild Hobby Horse* during its last two years was published by the Bodley Head through an arrangement made with the editor, H. P. Horne. A letter from Horne to Mathews dated January 5, 1893 (E.M.) indicates that the preparations for a new and even more aesthetically pleasing series to be entitled simply the *Hobby Horse* were well under way. Ill with the flu, the editor wrote Mathews that after a lengthy correspondence he found it necessary

to have a special mould made for The Hobby Horse paper. There is one great advantage in this. We can then have a special water mark, which will increase its value in the eyes of collectors. The mould will cost about 100 francs. I am designing the mark, or rather trying to: despite headaches & shivers. I will get back the agreement from my lawyer, as soon as I can.

The first of the numbers issued from the Bodley Head was carefully publicized. Among the descriptive materials published in anticipation of the new series was a prospectus which displayed on its cover the Hobby Horse device. Inside was a list of contributors, which included Laurence Binyon, Ford Madox Brown, Burne-Jones, Lionel Johnson, May Morris, William Morris, Hubert Parry, Christina Rossetti, John Ruskin, Simeon Solomon, Katharine Tynan, and Oscar Wilde. Opposite was the following announcement:

Messrs. Elkin Mathews and John Lane beg to announce, that they have concluded arrangements with the Proprietor of the "Hobby Horse," by which they are now prepared to receive subscriptions for the issue of a New Series of that Magazine, to be edited by Mr. Herbert P. Horne, under whose direction the publication originally appeared, from 1886 to 1891. The Magazine will continue to be published in quarterly numbers; and the price of subscription for the four numbers, commencing with the January number of each year, and including packing and postage, will be One Pound. Separate numbers will be issued only to subscribers. It has been necessary to raise the price of the Magazine, in order to publish what was formerly issued in a half-private manner, and without regard to loss; but, upon the other hand, the most scrupulous care will be expended upon the form and matter of the forthcoming series. A new title-page, and new ornaments, will be designed by the Editor; and all copper-plates and lithographs will be printed as India-proofs. The paper will be expressly hand-made for the Magazine, and will bear a special water-mark; and new type will be cast for the fresh Series. All communications to be addressed to Messrs. Elkin Mathews and John Lane, at The Bodley Head, Vigo Street, London, W.

Obviously inspired by the *Hobby Horse*, the *Dial*, edited by Charles Ricketts, was published at irregular intervals from 1889 to 1897 — five numbers in all. Featuring the "Vale type" designed by Ricketts and his experiments with offset reproductions of line drawings done on copper and printed on heavy paper, the

Dial also exhibited the art work of Reginald Savage and Charles H. Shannon as well as Lucien Pissarro's woodcuts with their weird humanesque landscapes. An early repository of the poetry of John Gray and T. Sturge Moore, the *Dial* in both its art work and letterpress is distinguished by a mystical and pseudo-medieval bent reflected in its cover, which displayed a medieval maiden seated in a study decorated with symbols of mystical knowledge: roses, sundial, alchemical devices and musical instruments.

On seeing the first number, Oscar Wilde was so delighted that he urged Ricketts and Shannon not to bring out a second number — "all perfect things should be unique." (*Oscar Wilde: Recollections by Jean Paul Raymond and Charles Ricketts* [London: Nonesuch Press, 1932], p. 28.) As it happened, the first series consisted of just this one number. Of the new series, which extended to four numbers, the Bodley Head advertised and distributed the first two, neither of which ever bore the firm's imprint. The 200 copies of each number sold for a guinea each.

In addition to the *Hobby Horse* and the *Dial*, the Bodley Head also issued for a time the publications of the Ruskin Reading Guild, *Igdrasil* and *World Literature*. Unlike the aesthetic journals, *Igdrasil* emphasized Ruskin's social gospel and, according to the "Editorial Note" to the first number for January 1890, took as its aim "a face-to-face and heart-to-heart inspection of Human Existence — of what has been done, what is doing, and what will be done by man — not, however, by any manner of means in the way of an encyclopaedic survey of literature, science, and art, but 'for the sake of humanity that these influence and illustrate.' " In the "Editorial Note," the editor, William Marwick, chose the old Norse representation of Life by the Tree Igdrasil as a symbol of the publication's aim.

Between January 1890 and March 1892 three volumes of *Igdrasil* were published before the journal became known as *World Literature,* the first six numbers of which (from September 15, 1891, to March 1, 1892) had been issued as supplements to *Igdrasil*. Elkin Mathews and another London publisher, E. W. Allen, published volume three of *Igdrasil* and the first six numbers (or volume one) of *World Literature*.

One other journal which was issued for a short time by Elkin Mathews and E. W. Allen, the *Pioneer,* a journal of literature, social progress, economics and ethics, was edited by George Dyke Smith. The official organ of the Pioneer Club, the journal, according to the prospectus for the July 1890 number, was, despite its social orientation, to be decked out in a manner befitting the best aesthetic periodicals of the day. "Henceforth The Pioneer," it read, "will be printed on hand-made paper, in the finest manner, and published quarterly. The conductors aim to give a 'pioneer' character to its form as well as to its contents by making it an example of modern artistic letter-press printing." The aim of the *Pioneer* was, as reported in the prospectus,

to deal in a helpful way with the many complex problems of individual and social life that are now pressing for solution. Its text is Human Life, and its treatment thereof is as fresh, undogmatic and unconventional, and as non-temporary and non-local as its conductors can make it. It is a journal of whatever is of service, in letters, ethics, economics and handicraft, to men and women who think for themselves and are interested in the amelioration of suffering and the progress of culture.

APPENDIX D. THE RECEPTION OF BODLEY HEAD BOOKS IN AMERICA

Although American publishers had been importing Bodley Head books since the American Book Company began to distribute Richard Le Gallienne's *George Meredith, Some Characteristics* in 1890, it was not until 1893 that a considerable interest in Bodley Head books was stimulated largely through the efforts of two new publishing firms, Copeland and Day of Boston and Stone and Kimball of Cambridge and Chicago, both founded by enterprising young men who purposed to cater in America to the same kind of small but sophisticated audience to which in England the Bodley Head had addressed itself. During the last years of the partnership between Mathews and Lane these two firms were to publicize and issue in the United States a number of the Bodley Head's most interesting books.

Of the two firms, it was Copeland and Day which was more oriented toward the English book trade, and, consequently, got the choice of Bodley Head books in America from 1893 until 1896, when Lane established a branch in the United States. (See Sidney Kramer, *A History of Stone and Kimball and Herbert S. Stone & Co.* [Chicago: University of Chicago Press, 1940], p. 20). Its first book list, in fact, was made up entirely of editions of English authors, several of them imported from the Bodley Head. That Copeland and Day was to a large extent modeled on the Bodley Head is suggested by the *Publishers' Weekly* notice of the new firm's existence. The issue for December 2, 1893 (p. 927) pointed out to its readers that the new firm was headed by "young men of literary taste and ability, who have gone into the business with the intention of publishing only fine limited editions of high-class works." Among the firm's books mentioned by the *Publishers' Weekly* were such Bodley Head imports as Francis Thompson's *Poems*, Oscar Wilde's *Salome*, Richard Garnett's *Poems* and the *Century Guild Hobby Horse*.

It was, in particular, the *Hobby Horse* and Rossetti's *The House of Life* in a small-paper issue of 500 copies and a large-paper issue of fifty copies "on thick hand-made Michalet paper" that reflected the decidedly aesthetic tastes of one of the firm's two founders, Fred Holland Day. Devoted to Rossetti and the Pre-Raphaelites, Day also found the *Century Guild Hobby Horse* to his taste because it often contained essays on Rossetti and his circle and reproductions of Pre-Raphaelite art. In a letter to Herbert Horne, the editor of the *Hobby Horse*, dated December 14, 1892 (Dugdale), Day introduced himself as one who had made "futile efforts" to obtain information concerning the fate of the *Hobby Horse*. Telling Horne that his essay on Rossetti in the seventh number of the journal had "quite charmed" him, the young man went on to say that he had for some years "been collecting everything relating to Rossetti that came within my knowledge."

In this same letter Day also lauded Horne's little volume of verse issued through the Bodley Head, *Diversi Colores*. "For beauty and grace and delicacy, there is nothing in the public's hands today, that has been produced during the century, that may truly be called its equal." Regretful that there was not an edition of

Horne's poems that could not be exhausted — "one from which the *true people* could know you, as only the *Elect* may now" — Day inquired: "Pray is not such an one in hand?"

Soon after the founding of Copeland and Day, the young partners sought the permission of Mathews and Lane to issue the *Hobby Horse* and other Bodley Head books in America. Doubtless it was the firm's interest in the *Hobby Horse* which later led Lane to offer the *Yellow Book* to Copeland and Day when Macmillan refused to act as the publisher in America for the famous journal.

Having issued seven separate Bodley Head titles in addition to the *Hobby Horse* and the *Yellow Book* by the summer of 1894, Messrs. Copeland and Day of Boston were mentioned in the *Star* (London, August 9, 1894) as

becoming for America much what Messrs. Mathews and Lane are for England. They publish books with an ideal beyond the mere commercial profit to be made out of them. They first of all aim at publishing books that have a true literary raison d'etre, and their next concern is to give them a beautiful setting that shall be worthy of them.

A similar credo was also adopted by Copeland and Day's friendly rival, Stone and Kimball, whose "first aim," as it was reported in the *Publishers' Weekly* for September 9, 1893,

after the worth and truth of a book is assured, is to give it a beautiful setting. . . . They are using the best papers in the market — Dutch, English and American — are decorating their books with designs by the best artists in this country and England and are printing and binding their books at the leading establishments in the country. . . . The ambition of this new firm is, in short, to attain to the ideal realized by Messrs. Elkin Mathews and John Lane, of London.

Less involved with Pre-Raphaelitism and English aestheticism than Day and Copeland, Herbert Stuart Stone and Hannibal Ingalls Kimball, while still undergraduates at Harvard, sought to create their own coterie of young, promising American authors similar to the Vigo Street "nest of singing birds." Nevertheless, the new publishing firm imported some of the Bodley Head's most notable books, Kenneth Grahame's *Pagan Papers* among them.

On May 15, 1894, Stone and Kimball along with Bliss Carman began publishing a little bimonthly literary journal, the *Chap-Book*, largely devoted to advertising the firm's book lists, which did much to publicize the Bodley Head in America. This was done, in part, through the advertisements not only of Stone and Kimball's imports from the Bodley Head but those of Copeland and Day as well. For instance, the first few numbers of the *Chap-Book* brought before the American public descriptive lists including Wilde's *Salome* and *The Sphinx*, and John Davidson's *Plays* and *A Random Itinerary* as well as full-page advertisements of *The Poems of Thomas Gordon Hake* and Ricketts and Shannon's *Hero and Leander*.

Through brief notices, excerpts, sketches of authors and reviews of Mathews and Lane's belles-lettres, the *Chap-Book* also did much to familiarize the American reader of the nineties with the Bodley Head and its literary and artistic milieu. For example, the *Chap-Book* for August 15, 1894, printed William Watson's epigram, "To a Lady Recovered from a Dangerous Sickness," because it was "too pretty to miss quoting"; and, in the review of the *Yellow Book* in the same number, Pierre La Rose (obviously a properly aesthetic pseudonym) affirmed that "after all, the quiet, pervading charm of *The Yellow Book* is its brazen inessentiality." Of the opinion that "in the long run, the ancient love of simple dignity and self-respect in literature and in art will probably prevail again," the reviewer counseled, "meanwhile, *The Yellow Book* is winning a well-deserved popularity. So let us sigh '*finis.*'"

Without doubt the hero of the early issues, Aubrey Beardsley, rated not only serious encomiums on his art, but an amusing poem as well, entitled "The Yellow Bookmaker," which appeared in the second number (June 1, 1894). With rollicking good humor, the editors of the *Chap-Book* dismissed Victorianism and advertised their wares at one and the same time.

> *There once was a certain A. B.*
> *And a Yellow Bookmaker was he,*
> *His dead black and white*
> *Was such a delight,*
> *All Vigo street came out to see.*

Having made some choice remarks in this limerick sort of fashion concerning Wilde's *Salome*, the poet continued:

> *And everyone whispered, "Dear me,*
> *How very extraordinary!"*
> *And poor Mrs. Grundy*
> *Was buried on Sunday,*
> *Oscarified such things could be.*

> *Now this is the tale of A. B.*
> *The grotesque black and white devotee,*
> *The decadent fakir,*
> *The Yellow Bookmaker,*
> *The funny-man over the sea.*

> *P. S. If you're anxious to see*
> *This most up to date Salomee,*
> *Send over the way*
> *To Copeland and Day,*
> *Cornhill, in the Hub, Dollars three —*
> *And seventy*
> > *five*
> > > *cents.*

Having heard by September 15, 1894, of the impending dissolution of the Bodley Head partnership, the spokesman for the *Chap-Book* considered the matter

of not a little interest and import to book lovers and book collectors and even, I conceive, to book readers as well. The firm has done so much that is attractive in manufacture, has shown, at times, such excellent taste, and has brought out so many new and novel things, that I cannot help feeling unhappy that the association has to end.

Another source of information about the Bodley Head in America was the New York *Critic*, referred to by the London *Academy* as "the first literary journal in America." Through its "London Letter" and its "Chicago Letter" (which the publishers added to its "Boston Letter" in March 1893), the journal conveyed news of Bodley Head celebrities such as that given by Arthur Waugh from London, on July 8, 1893. Reporting "that Mr. Oscar Wilde will shortly give the public, through the hands of that artistic firm, Messrs. Elkin Mathews & John Lane, the librettos of 'Lady Windermere's Fan' and 'A Woman of No Importance,' " Waugh considered it "a wise step, for the clever dialogue will doubtless read even better than it plays."

Through the Chicago critic, Lucy Monroe, American readers received news of the latest Stone and Kimball imports. For instance, in her "Chicago Letter" of November 11, 1893, she spoke of Kenneth Grahame as "a new name on this side of the water," but, she continued,

the fact that he is one of Henley's assistants on *The National Observer* prepossesses one in his favor. A volume of his essays will soon be published by Stone & Kimball of this city in conjunction with those rarely courageous London publishers, Elkin Mathews & John Lane. The Chicago firm is entering the same field as the English one, and there is a certain charming quaintness in the rich simplicity of the dress of the books it issues.

In addition to reviews of Bodley Head books by Louise Chandler Moulton in such periodicals as the *Chap-Book* and the *Boston Herald,* the important Chicago review, the *Dial*, was a further means of establishing in the minds of American readers the names of Bodley Head authors. In its pages appeared reviews of most of the Bodley Head books published in the United States by American publishers, including Walter Crane's *Renascence*, John Addington Symonds' *In the Key of Blue*, Grant Allen's *The Lower Slopes*, Richard Garnett's *Poems*, and William Watson's *The Eloping Angels*. And in 1893–1894, half-page and full-page advertisements of Copeland and Day's, and Stone and Kimball's book lists appeared in its pages. For instance, the Copeland and Day advertisement in the *Dial* for December 16, 1893 (XV, no. 180, 375), listed the *Hobby Horse* and Francis Thompson's *Poems*. And of Beardsley's illustrations for *Salome,* the advertisement spoke of the artist's "masterly handling of black and white in more than abundant masses" and declared that such designs "cannot fail to influence our illustrative art."

More conservative in its literary and artistic views than the *Chap-Book,* the *Dial,* edited by Francis F. Browne, was very receptive to Bodley Head authors like William Watson but much less pleased with the more avant-garde items from Vigo Street such as Beardsley's art and the *Yellow Book.* In the *Dial* for June 1, 1894 (XVI, no. 191, 335–336), there appeared a discussion of "The Initial Number of the 'Yellow Book'" in which the cover was looked upon with disfavor because, in the view of the journal, Mr. Beardsley's imagination "had been permitted to run riot." The generally hostile attitude of the *Dial* toward the new publication is apparent in the concluding remarks to the effect that

the sponsors of this new-born periodical have kept their promise in excluding "actuality" from its pages. There is nothing timely about any of the contents as far as subject-matter is concerned. But the sort of "actuality" that finds expression in mannerism is abundantly present, and we doubt if the beginning of the twentieth century will find this volume nearly as readable as we now find it late in the nineteenth.

APPENDIX E. BODLEY HEAD EXPORTS AND IMPORTS: ENGLAND, AMERICA, AUSTRALIA

Entries include: (1) author, (2) title and date of publication, (3) number of copies exported or imported. Entries are listed in order of publication.

EXPORTS TO:

Charles Scribner's Sons, New York

Le Gallienne, Richard. *Volumes in Folio* (1889)	50
Wedmore, Frederick. *Pastorals of France* (1893)	375

American Book Co., New York

Le Gallienne, Richard. *George Meredith* (1890)	325

Macmillan, New York

Crane, Walter. *Renascence* (1891)	200 (150 SP, 35 LP, 15 Jap. vellum)
Symonds, John A. *In the Key of Blue* (1893)	450(?)
Watson, William. *Excursions in Criticism* (1893)	300(?)
De Tabley, Lord. *Poems, Dramatic and Lyrical* (1893)	150(?)
The Poems of Arthur H. Hallam (1893)	200
Greene, George A. *Italian Lyrists of To-day* (1893)	250
The Letters of Thomas L. Beddoes (1894)	200
James, W. P. *Romantic Professions* (1894)	100

Cassell, New York

Le Gallienne, Richard. *English Poems* (1892)	150(?)

Roberts Bros., Boston

Marston, Philip Bourke. *A Last Harvest* (1891)	100
Egerton, George. *Keynotes* (1893)	?
Farr, Florence. *The Dancing Faun* (1894)	?
Dostoevski, Feodor. *Poor Folk* (1894)	?

G. P. Putnam's Sons, New York

Le Gallienne, Richard. *Religion of a Literary Man* (1893)	?
Gale, Norman. *Orchard Songs* (1893)	520(?)
Le Gallienne, Richard. *Prose Fancies* (1894)	?

Copeland and Day, Boston

Garnett, Richard. *Poems* (1893)	100
Thompson, Francis. *Poems* (1893)	?
Davidson, John. *A Random Itinerary* (1894)	100
Le Gallienne, Richard. *English Poems*, 3rd edition (1894)	?
Hero and Leander (Ricketts and Shannon), (1894)	25
The Hobby Horse (1893–1894)	?
Wilde, Oscar. *Salome* (1894)	200
—— *The Sphinx* (1894)	50
The Yellow Book (April 1894) vol. 1	?

————(July 1894)   vol. 2   600
   Hinkson, Katharine Tynan. *Cuckoo Songs* (1894)   150
Dodd, Mead, New York
   The Second Book of the Rhymers' Club (1894)   160
   Rhys, Ernest. *A London Rose* (1894)   160
   Johnson, Lionel. *The Art of Thomas Hardy* (1894)   ?
   Chapman, Elizabeth. *A Little Child's Wreath* (1894)   210
Stone and Kimball, Chicago and Cambridge
   Grahame, Kenneth. *Pagan Papers* (1894)   100
   Davidson, John. *Plays* (1894)   150
   Allen, Grant. *The Lower Slopes* (1894)   150
   The Poems of T. Gordon Hake (1894)   100
J. B. Lippincott, Philadelphia
   Monkhouse, Allan. *Books and Plays* (1894)   105
   Street, G. S. *The Autobiography of a Boy* (1894)   155
American Importer Unknown
   Nettleship, J. T. *Robert Browning* (1890)   364

IMPORTS FROM:
Charles Scribner's Sons, New York
   Van Dyke, Henry. *The Poetry of Tennyson* (1st ed.   400 (2nd ed.; 350 SP,
   1890; 2nd ed. 1892)   50 LP)
   Schaff, Philip. *Literature and Poetry* (1890)   100
   Stoddard, Richard Henry. *The Lion's Cub with Other*
   Verse (1891)   100
J. B. Lippincott, Philadelphia
   Abbott, Charles C. *Travels in a Tree Top* (1894)   200
Stone and Kimball, Chicago and Cambridge
   Moulton, Louise C., ed. *Arthur O'Shaughnessy, His Life*
   and His Work (1894)   ?
Central Press Agency Ltd., Sydney, Australia
   Hill, A. Fraser. *The Land and Wealth of New South Wales*
   (1894)   ?

APPENDIX F. TRANSFERS

I list here all books and journals originally issued by some publisher other than Elkin Mathews and John Lane at the Sign of the Bodley Head even though some were reissued with a cancel title page bearing the Bodley Head imprint. Generally speaking, when Mathews and Lane chose to reissue a volume previously published by another firm, they *preceded* the original title page (which was not removed) by one with their own imprint. Such, for instance, is the case with Ian Hamilton's *A Ballad of Hádji,* Lord De Tabley's *A Guide to the Study of Book-Plates,* Frances Wynne's *Whisper!,* William Watson's first edition of *The Prince's Quest and Other Poems,* and John Davidson's *Bruce* and *Plays,* 1893. Any volume which I have found bearing the Bodley Head imprint has also been included in the Check List.

Since I have found no evidence that Alfred Forman's translation of Wagner's *Tristan and Isolde* and Walter Fairfax's *Robert Browning and the Drama,* both published by Reeves and Turner, 1891, were ever published or sold by the Bodley Head, despite their appearance in Bodley Head lists, I have not included them here.

The financial difficulty experienced by Kegan Paul, Trench & Co. in 1892 (see p. 78 above) may have accounted for several transfers to the Bodley Head in that year including Beeching, *et al., Love in Idleness,* Hamilton's *A Ballad of Hádji,* Watson's *A Prince's Quest,* and Wynne's *Whisper!*

Entries below include: (1) author, (2) title, (3) original publisher and date; (4) Bodley Head method of issue and date.

Beeching, H. C., J. W. Mackail, and J. B. B. Nichols. *Love in Idleness,* Kegan Paul, Trench, 1883; 2nd issue, 1892.

Bourdillon, F. W. *Ailes D'Alouette,* Daniel Press, 1890; sold by, 1890.

Bridges, Robert. *The Feast of Bacchus,* Daniel Press, 1889; sold by, 1890.

———— *The Growth of Love,* Daniel Press, 1890; sold by, 1890.

Coleridge, Stephen. *The Sanctity of Confession,* Kegan Paul, Trench, 1890; 2nd issue, 1894.

Davidson, John. *Bruce, A Drama in Five Acts,* Wilson & McCormick, 1886; 2nd issue, 1893.

———— *The North Wall,* Wilson & McCormick, 1885; 2nd issue, 1893.

———— *Plays,* privately printed at Greenock, Scotland, 1889 (2nd issue by T. Fisher Unwin as *Scaramouch in Naxos: A Pantomime and Other Plays,* 1890); 3rd issue, 1893.

De Tabley, Lord. *A Guide to the Study of Book-Plates,* J. Pearson, 1880; 2nd issue, 1892.

The Dial. Edited by Ricketts and Shannon, C. H. Shannon, The Vale, 5 nos., 1889–1897; issued nos. 2 and 3 (nos. 1 and 2 of 2nd series), 1892–1893.

Gale, Norman. *A June Romance,* George E. Over at Rugby, 1892 (also by Simpkin, 1894); 3rd issue, 1894.

Hamilton, Ian. *The Ballad of Hádji and Other Poems*, Kegan Paul, Trench, 1887; 2nd issue, 1892.

The Hobby Horse. Edited by H. P. Horne as the *Century Guild Hobby Horse*, Kegan Paul, Trench and later by Chiswick Press, 7 vols., 1884–1894; issued nos. 1 (1893), 2 (1893), 3 (1894).

Horne, Herbert P. *Diversi Colores*, Chiswick Press, 1891; 2nd issue, 1891.

Igdrasil. Edited by William Marwick, George Allen, vols. I–II (1890–1891); vol. III (1891–1892).

Leather, Robinson K. *Verses*, T. Fisher Unwin, 1891; 2nd issue, 1891.

Le Gallienne, Richard, *The Book-Bills of Narcissus*, Frank Murray, 1891; 2nd edition, 1892–1893.

Marzials, Theo. *The Gallery of Pigeons and Other Poems*, Henry S. King, 1873; 2nd issue, 1893.

Pinkerton, Percy E. *Galeazzo; A Venetian Episode with Other Poems*, Sonnenschein, 1886; 2nd issue, 1893.

Watson, William. *The Prince's Quest and Other Poems*, Kegan Paul, Trench, 1880; 2nd issue, 1892 and 2nd edition, 1893.*

Wynne, Frances. *Whisper! A Volume of Verse*, Kegan Paul, Trench, 1890; 2nd issue, 1893 [Feb. 1894].

* *The Prince's Quest* was first issued by Kegan Paul, Trench in 1880. In 1892 Elkin Mathews and John Lane brought out a second issue in two forms: (1) the first issue of Kegan Paul, Trench with "1880–92" stamped in gold on lower spine where the Kegan Paul, Trench emblem had been previously; (2) the original sheets, including title and half-title, with a new title and half-title.

APPENDIX G. PRODUCTION COSTS AND FINAL INVENTORY

1. Production Costs, Chiswick Press

Check list number	Number of copies		Total composing, printing, and paper	
	Small paper	Large paper	Small paper	Large paper
1	250	50	£14. 6. 0	£ 6.13. 6
3	50	—	—	—
6	100[c]	—	—	—
7	250	50	20.16. 3	7. 2. 6
14	250	50	12. 1.10	3. 3. 5
18	435	50	—	—
21	500	100	44.17. 0	14.19. 0
24	300	—	23. 5. 6	—
26	500	50	20.16. 6	4. 5. 6

Binding Costs		Other costs[a]	Total
Small paper	Large paper		
—	—	£ 2. 9. 2	£ 24. 5. 2[b]
—	—	—	3. 3. 6
—	—	—	10. 0. 6
—	—	9. 5. 3	37. 4. 0
—	—	6. 6. 7	21.11.10
—	—	—	21.19. 9[d]
£16.13. 4	£ 5. 0. 0	19.14. 0	126. 2. 4[e]
7.10. 0	—	4.17. 0	35.12. 6
20. 7. 4	5. 0. 0	1. 2. 6	51.11.10

Source: Chiswick Press Records, B.M.

[a] Usually includes alterations, proofs, increasing margins for large-paper editions, etc.

[b] Includes sixteen shillings, sixpence for three special copies on Japanese vellum.

[c] Fifty copies only folded and stitched.

[d] Includes cost of fifteen special copies.

[e] Includes £24.19. 0 (£17. 5. 0 for composing, printing, paper and £7.14. 0 for binding) for forty-four special copies.

2. Production Costs, T. and A. Constable

Check list number	Number of copies		Sheets per copy	Total composing, printing, and paper		Other costs[a]	Total
	Small paper	Large paper		Small paper	Large paper		
30	400	—	4½	£16.10. 9	—	£ 6. 7. 0	£ 22.17. 9
31	175	55	—	—	—	—	7.14. 0
32	1000	—	10¼	28.19. 2	—	2. 2. 2	31. 1. 4
38	800	150	4½	23. 8. 0	£ 9.14. 0	11. 6. 0	51.18. 6[b]
38*	550	—	4¾	10. 9. 0	—	11. 6	11. 0. 6
38*	500	—	4½	9.17. 0	—	15. 0	10.12. 0
41	550	50	6¾	15. 3. 9	4.14. 6	1. 5. 6	21. 3. 9
41*	500	—	7¾	7. 0. 0	—	2.15. 6	9.15. 6
42	550	50	5½	12. 7. 6	3.17. 0	2.19. 0	19. 3. 6
42*	500	—	6	5. 5. 0	—	2. 2. 8	7. 7. 8
47	2000	250	—	13. 7. 0	7.12. 0[c]	1.11. 0	22.10. 0
47*	600	—	—	4. 2. 0	—	19. 3	5. 1. 3
49	750	100	7¼	57. 1.11[d]	—	7. 5. 6	64. 7. 5
49*	500	—	7¼	15. 0.11	—	7. 2. 0	22. 2.11
58	850	75	11½	23. 0. 0	10. 1. 3	4.19. 6	38. 0. 9
62	1050	—	3¼	9. 0. 5	—	4.19. 0	13.19. 5
64	1000	—	17	59.10. 0	—	8. 9. 0	67.19. 0
65	550	50	13	29. 5. 0	1. 6. 0	3. 2. 6	33.13. 6
67	2080	175	8	36. 0. 0	1.16. 0[e]	4.18. 0	42.14. 0
69	550	50	9¼	24. 1. 0	8.14. 3	9.18. 0	42.13. 3
70	3000	260	8¼	57.15. 0	39. 0. 0	34. 1. 9[f]	130.16. 9
70*	2000	—	10	35. 5. 0	—	4. 0	35. 9. 0
72	550	—	11¾	27.12. 3	—	4. 1. 0	31.13. 3
73	550	50	11	22.11. 0	11. 0	4.15. 6	27.17. 6
74	1100	—	12(16pp.)	30. 1. 7	—	6.19. 0	37. 0. 7
74*	2000	—	13(16pp.)	30.15. 2	—	8. 5. 0	39. 0. 2
74*	3000	—	6(32pp.)	45. 6.11	—	2. 0. 6	47. 7. 5
75	700	—	—	6.10. 0	—	—	6.10. 0
75*	300	—	—	—	—	—	3.15. 0[g]
78	800	—	5½	13. 3. 7	—	2.12. 0	15.15. 7
81	750	125	6	13.16. 0	7.10. 0	4. 8. 0	25.14. 0
83	650	—	10¼	16. 2.11	—	4.11. 0	20.13.11
84	650	—	15	31. 2. 6	—	5. 4. 0	36. 6. 6
89	560	—	7	15.11. 6	—	3.14. 0	19. 5. 6
90	650	—	8	15. 8. 0	—	3.13. 0	19. 1. 0
92	1100	—	10	25. 5. 0	—	4.11. 6	29.16. 6
93	1100	115	13½	34. 1. 9	16.17. 6	21.16. 0[h]	72.15. 3

2. Production Costs, T. and A. Constable—*continued*

Check list number	Number of copies		Sheets per copy	Total composing, printing, and paper		Other costs[a]	Total
	Small paper	Large paper		Small paper	Large paper		
93*	1000	—	14½	19. 4. 3	—	7. 2. 0[i]	26. 6. 3
97	1100	—	13¼	33. 9. 2	—	12. 1. 6	45.10. 8
99	1500	150	22	45.13. 0[j]	23. 2. 0	34.11. 8[k]	103. 6. 8

Source: T. and A. Constable's ledgers, day books, letters, etc.

* Indicates editions and printings subsequent to the first (in order of publication).

[a] Usually includes alterations, proofs, increasing margins for large-paper editions, and, often, composing, printing and paper for Bodley Head catalogues of books.

[b] Includes £7.10. 6 for thirty special copies.

[c] Includes cost of 100 special copies on Japanese vellum.

[d] Includes cost of large-paper copies as well.

[e] Excludes cost of paper.

[f] Includes £9.18. 0 for electrotyping 132 pp. of text.

[g] Includes cost of 50 copies on Japanese paper.

[h] Includes £10. 9. 0 for one set of electro shells for America.

[i] Cost of stereotyping 213 pp. @8d.

[j] Excludes cost of paper for small-paper copies.

[k] Includes £22. 7. 2 for 36½ reams of Double Crown paper for small-paper copies.

3. Transcript of Final Inventory Sheets of the Bodley Head, Listing the Stock of the Firm on Hand as of June 30, 1894(?)

Date published	Number subscribed	U.S. sales	Large paper			Ordinary			Title
			Quires[a]	Cloth[b]	Cost of binding	Quires[a]	Cloth[b]	Cost of binding	
2/12/94	234	150	—	—	—	—	242	—	*The Lower Slopes*
6/20/94	21	—	—	—	—	—	126	—	*Travels in a Tree Top*
2/12/94	107	—	—	—	—	—	103	—	*Lyric Poems*
6/1/94	146	210	—	—	—	—	52	—	*A Little Child's Wreath*
2/12/94	150	150	—	—	—	—	271	—	*Plays* (J. Davidson)
11/24/93	118	100	—	—	—	—	229	—	*A Random Itinerary*
5/31/93	140	—	—	—	—	—	64	—	*Under the Hawthorn*
3/29/93	412?	150?	—	—	—	—	104	11d.	*Poems, Dramatic and Lyrical*
5/24/92	165	—	—	—	—	—	94	—	*Sight and Song*
11/ 8/93	1422?	520?	—	15	—	—	215	—	*Orchard Songs*
11/30/93	143	100	—	—	—	—	93	—	*Poems* (R. Garnett)
3/ 8/94	176	200	—	23	—	—	336	—	*Beddoes' Letters*
11/30/93	142	100	—	—	—	—	68	—	*Pagan Papers*
2/?/90	—	260 +104	—	—	—	—	—	—	*Robert Browning*
2/24/93	205	—	—	13	—	—	207	—	*The Sonnet in England*
6/20/94	194	160	—	64	—	—	217	—	*The Second Book of the Rhymers' Club*

Number printed	Price	Molds or stereos	Cost per copy	[Domestic] sales		Trade price	Terms with author
				to Dec. 1893	Jan. to June 1894		
812	5/-	—	1/5 cloth	—	104	4/2	Royalty 1/- ea. Eng.; 6d. ea. U.S.
200	—	—	2/1¾ cloth	—	21	4/2	Bought sheets from Lippincott
356	5/-	—	1/2 cloth	—	86	4/2	Royalty of 10%
617 as 600	3/6	—	9½d. cloth	—	59	2/11	Royalty 6d. ea. Eng.; 3d. ea. U.S.
760 as 700	7/6	—	2/9½ cloth	—	115	6/3	Royalty 1/- ea. Eng.; 6d. ea. U.S.
755	5/-	—	2/2 cloth[c]	198	60	4/2	£20 paid Royalty for edition of 600
332	5/- 15/- large paper	—	1/8½ cloth	4	2	4/2	Royalty 10%
1352[d]	7/6	—	1/4 in sheets	48	23	6/3	Royalty 1/- small paper copies, 2/- large paper copies Eng.; 6d. U.S.
400	—	—	1/8¾ cloth	1	3	4/2	Royalty 10%
2270[e]	5/-	—	9¼d. cloth[f]	159	67	4/2	Half profits
550	5/-	—	1/9 cloth	46	44	4/2	Royalty 10%
848 small paper; 61 large paper	5/-	—	1/5½ cloth[g]	—	280?	4/2	Royalty 1/- ea. small paper; 2/- ea. large paper
615	5/-	—	1/5 cloth	73	155	4/2	Royalty 10%
1500[h]	7/6[i]	Ster.	—	—	—	—	Royalty 4d. ea.
712 small paper; 53 large paper	5/-	—	1/7 cloth; 5/10 large paper	3	32	4/2	£25 for an ed. of 650
718 small paper; 76 large paper	5/-	—	1/1½ cloth[j]	—	32	4/2	£5 paid to Rhymers' Club

Transcript of Final Inventory Sheets of the Bodley Head,
Listing the Stock of the Firm
on Hand as of June 30, 1894(?)

Date published	Number subscribed	U.S. sales	Large paper			Ordinary			Title
			Quires[a]	Cloth[b]	Cost of binding	Quires[a]	Cloth[b]	Cost of binding	
6/8/94	82	160	—	—	—	—	203	—	*A London Rose*
6/1/94	154	25	—	—	—	—	34	—	*Hero & Leander*
6/8/94	118	155	—	—	—	—	308	3¾d.	*Autobiography of a Boy*
11/8/93	250	—	—	—	—	—	97	—	*Poems* (F. Thompson)
2/24/94	110	150	—	—	—	—	280?	—	*Cuckoo Songs*
—	—	—	—	—	—	150	83	5d.	*Poetry of Tennyson*[1]
6/2/93	685?	450?	—	—	—	297	64	11d.	*In the Key of Blue*
3/23/93	1269	—	—	43	—	—	579	—	*The Eloping Angels*
3/29/93	1249?	300?	—	2	—	—	391	—	*Excursions in Criticism*
4/7/93	506	—	—	—	—	—	152	—	*The Prince's Quest*
10/2/93	—	375	—	—	—	150	76	4½d.	*Pastorals of France*
—	—	—	—	—	—	250	40	3¾d.	*A Study of Dante*
10/2/93	202	250	—	—	—	250	19	8d.	*Italian Lyrists*
3/2/94	100	100	—	—	—	258	32	6½d.	*Poetry of Hake*
6/22/93	—	200	—	1	—	—	65	—	*Hallam's Poetry*

Number printed	Price	Molds or stereos	Cost per copy	[Domestic] sales		Trade price	Terms with author
				to Dec. 1893	Jan. to June 1894		
576	5/–	—	1/1¾ cloth	—	48	4/2	Royalty 8d. ea. Eng.; 4d. ea. U.S.
200	35/–	—	20/10 vellum	—	42	29/2	Bought from Ricketts and Shannon at 20/10 ea.
1174	3/6	—	6d. in sheets	—	355	2/11	Royalty[k]
2173	5/–	—	1/0½ cloth	385	1322	4/2	Royalty 1/3 ea. Eng.; 6d. ea. U.S.
717	5/–	—	1/1¾ cloth	—	110?	4/2	Royalty 6d. on first 400, 1/– on next 100 Eng.; 3d. U.S.
—	5/6	—	2/– in sheets	9	30	4/7	Bought from Scribners
1927[m]	—	Molds	1/3½ in quires	9	36	7/1	Royalty 1/– ea.
2649 small paper; 290 large paper; 102 Japon Vellum[n]	3/6	Molds	6¾d, cloth; 1/1¾ large paper	14	18	2/11	Half profits
2000 small paper; 110 large paper[o]	5/–	Molds	1/1½ cloth; 3/8 large paper	24	17	4/2	Royalty 1/– ea. Eng.; 6d. ea. U.S.
1113	4/6	Molds	1/– cloth	35	23	3/9	Half profits
950	5/–	—	1/6½ cloth	43	76	4/2	Royalty 9d. ea. Eng.; 4½d. ea. U S.
1000[p]	2/–	—	4¼d. in sheets	72	145	1/8	Royalty 2d. ea.
1000	5/–	—	1/4¾ in sheets	74	52	4/2	Royalty 8d. ea. Eng.; 4d. ea. U.S.
660	5/–	—	1/3 in sheets	—	90	4/2	Royalty 6d. ea. £5/5– paid for editing
860 small paper; 77 large paper	5/–	—	1/7¼ cloth; 4/5 large paper	14	13	4/2	Royalty[q]

Transcript of Final Inventory Sheets of the Bodley Head,
Listing the Stock of the Firm
on Hand as of June 30, 1894(?)

Date published	Number subscribed	U.S. sales	Large paper			Ordinary			Title
			Quires[a]	Cloth[b]	Cost of binding	Quires[a]	Cloth[b]	Cost of binding	
3/2/94	193	100	—	—	—	—	183	—	*Romantic Professions*
6/15/94	945	—	—	28	—	500	236	—	*Prose Fancies*
9/27/92	694?	150?	—	—	—	—	129	$3\frac{3}{4}$d.	*English Poems*
1890	—	325	—	—	—	—	—	—	*G. Meredith*
11/13/93	1618	—	—	76	—	50	1609	—	*Religion of a Literary Man*
12/3/92	95	—	—	14	—	—	54	—	*Poems* (Meynell)
12/3/92	90	—	—	17	—	—	138	$7\frac{1}{2}$d.	*The Rhythm of Life*
4/15/94	—	—	—	—	—	—	633	—	*Yellow Book* vol. I
—	—	600	—	—	—	—	1030	—	*Yellow Book* vol. II
6/26/94	—	105	—	—	—	—	104	—	*Books and Plays*
6/8/94	—	50	—	—	—	128	6	4s. 2d.	*The Sphinx*
2/24/94	194	200	—	10[w]	—	—	150[w]	—	*Salome*
—	—	—	—	—	—	—	110	—	*Whisper*
—	—	—	—	—	—	1000	444	$3\frac{3}{4}$d.	*Keynotes*
—	—	—	—	—	—	300	104	$3\frac{3}{4}$d.	*Dancing Faun*

Number printed	Price	Molds or stereos	Cost per copy	[Domestic] sales		Trade price	Terms with author
				to Dec. 1893	Jan. to June 1894		
663	5/-	Molds	—	—	211?	4/2	Royalty 6d. ea. Eng.; 3d. ea. U.S.
2127 small paper; 117 large paper	5/-	Ster.	Cost[r]	—	125	4/2	Half profits
2030	5/-	—	9d. in sheets	57	358	4/2	Royalty 1/- ea.
—	5/6	—	1/-	16	85	4/7	Royalty 8d. ea.
5283 including 253 large paper	3/6	Electros	$5\frac{1}{2}$ in sheets; $3/5\frac{1}{2}$ large paper	974	628	2/11	Half profits
1050 small paper; 50 large paper	3/6	Molds	6d. in sheets; 2/- large paper	131	124	2/11	Royalty 15% on 1st ed. (on trade price) & other eds. 7d. ea.
1050 small paper; 50 large paper	3/6	Molds	7d. in sheets; $2/5\frac{1}{2}$ large paper	38	115	2/11	Same as above
7000	—	—	1/7 cloth	—	3609[s]	11/2	Royalty[t]
5000	—	—	2/7 cloth	—	—	4/2	Royalty[u]
464	5/-	—	—	—	33	4/2	Royalty 10%
303 small paper; 25 large paper	42/-	—	8/- ea.[v]	—	81	35/-	Royalty 10% on trade price
755 small paper; 125 large paper	15/-; 30/- large paper	—	$3/7\frac{1}{4}$ cloth; 4/3 silk	—	164	12/6	Royalty 1/- ea. small paper; 3/- ea. large paper
308 sheets purchased	2/6	—	—	54	43	2/-	Remainder from Kegan Paul
6071[x]	3/6	Ster.	$5\frac{1}{4}$d. in sheets	819	3188	2/11	Royalty 6d. ea. 1st 5000 then 8d. See contract with author
1100	3/6	—	8d. in sheets	—	40	2/11	Royalty 6d. ea.

Transcript of Final Inventory Sheets of the Bodley Head,
Listing the Stock of the Firm
on Hand as of June 30, 1894(?)

Date published	Number subscribed	U.S. sales	Large paper			Ordinary			Title
			Quires[a]	Cloth[b]	Cost of binding	Quires[a]	Cloth[b]	Cost of binding	
—	—	—	—	—	—	—	687	—	*Poor Folk*
—	—	—	—	—	—	—	137	—	*Fleet Street Eclogues*
—	—	—	—	—	—	—	—	—	*Hobby Horse* Parts I & II. Under contract as to III & IV
—	—	—	—	—	—	—	—	—	*Oxford Characters* I to V. Under contract for 12 parts

Number printed	Price	Molds or stereos	Cost per copy	[Domestic] sales		Trade price	Terms with author
				to Dec. 1893	Jan. to June 1894		
1100	3/6	—	1/10¾ cloth	—	27	2/11	Translator £25; editor £10; 10% of gross returns
702	5/-	—	1/0½ cloth	25	83	4/2	Royalty ?
—	—	—	Parts I & II cost £151.1.0. Receipts £136.3.3 from subscriptions paid on 4 parts.				
—	—	—	Parts I to V cost £125.4.4.				

Source: Inventory sheets in the possession of Mr. Percy Muir.

[a] Refers to number of copies still in sheets and as yet unbound.
[b] Refers to number of copies bound in cloth.
[c] Includes royalty.
[d] Includes total number printed in two printings.
[e] Includes 170 large paper copies.
[f] Large paper copies cost 3/7 each.
[g] Large paper copies cost 6/8 each.
[h] Includes 1000 copies of the first printing and 500 of the second.
[i] Reduced to 5/6 each on last 250 copies.
[j] Large paper copies cost 3/10 each.
[k] 6d. each on first edition; 8d. each on second edition, Eng.; 6d. on first 50, then 3d. on remaining 100, U.S.
[l] Entry probably refers to the third edition of 1893.
[m] Includes total number printed in two printings.
[n] Includes total number printed in two printings.
[o] Includes total number printed in two printings.
[p] Entry refers to the third edition, 1892.
[q] 6d. ea. to holder of copyright, £10.10.0 paid for editing.
[r] 1/1 cloth; 9¼d. sheets; 4/1¾ large paper.
[s] Stock does not include copies on sale.
[t] £200 paid to Editors and Contributors. Editors(?) to receive 20% of sales.
[u] £235 paid to Editors and Contributors (does not include copies out on sale). Agreement covers first two volumes only.
[v] Indicates cost of small-paper copies in sheets.
[w] Approximate figures.
[x] Includes total number printed in three printings

NOTES

1. The Beginnings of the Bodley Head

1. A.L.S., dated April 26, 1885, E.M. A heading cut from his fifth catalogue dated 1887 in the City Library, Exeter, indicates that Mathews issued at least five catalogues while at Exeter.

2. The quotation appears on the "fancy title page" Mathews drew up on the back of the letter to his sister, dated April 26, 1885.

3. According to Lane in his introduction to his reprint of *The Life of Sir Thomas Bodley Written by Himself*, privately printed for his friends, Christmas 1894, pp. v–vi, the name for the new premises in Vigo Street was the result of the following colloquy with Mathews: " 'It should have a sign,' I said, 'and I have thought *The Bodley Head* is what it should be.' 'The very same idea was in my own mind,' answered my partner, fresh from Exeter, Sir Thomas Bodley's birthplace; and consumed as he was at the time with that passion for old literature which would, Exeter even apart, have made the coincidence perfectly natural. So *The Bodley Head* it became." That the idea of a Bodley *Head* derived from the fact that the Vigo Street shop had previously been known as the "Rembrandt Head" is indicated in Lane's account on pp. iv–v.

In a draft letter to a Dr. Brushfield, dated February 7, 1895 (E.M.), Mathews corrected Brushfield's notion that his shop in Vigo Street had been known as the "Bodley Head" when he rented it. Then he went on to say that had he remained in Exeter "I should have called my place in the Close after Bodley — I did indeed draw up a catalogue before I left the city and named it the 'Bodley Catalogue,' and Lane knew of the scheme."

4. The facts are based primarily on my conversations with Mathews' daughter, Miss Nest Elkin Mathews, and on "Elkin Mathews — Poets' Publisher (1851–1921)" in an Exhibition Catalogue of the same title issued by the University of Reading, May 1967, by Patricia Hutchins.

5. "A Chat with Mr. Elkin Mathews," in *Publisher and Bookseller*, February 24, 1906, p. 417.

6. "About Mr. Elkin Mathews," *St. James's Budget*, "Literary Supplement," XXIX, no. 749 (November 2, 1894), 26.

7. *The Path Through the Wood* (New York: Dial Press, 1931), p. 142.

8. Quoted by Miss Hutchins in "Elkin Mathews — Poets' Publisher," n.p.

9. See also "A Chat with Mathews," p. 418.

10. The uncle, Charles Elkin, and his wife were the proprietors of a hotel called "Warrior House" at St. Leonards-on-Sea near Hastings in Sussex.

11. "A Chat with Mathews," p. 418.

12. This information appears on the printed letterhead which he used in the Exeter shop, E.M.

13. "About Mr. Elkin Mathews," p. 26.

14. Copyright Registry Book, vol. 32, January 14, 1887–February 23, 1888 (IND 5826), now in the Public Records Office, London.

15. A.L.S. from Mathews to his sister, dated April 26, 1885, E.M.

16. *Ibid.*

17. "A Chat with Mathews," p. 418.

18. *D.N.B., s.v.* John Lane. Another of Lane's friends who knew him from his early years, R. Pearse Chope, also records that "Lane was a keen collector, not only of books, but also of bookplates, glass, and other bric-a-brac." See "John Lane, a Personal Note," *Devonian Year Book*, 1926, p. 37. This essay also appears in *The Hartland Chronicle*, no. 352, March 1, 1927.

19. In an A.L.S. from Lane to Mathews, dated May 16, 1887, Lane wrote: "I have seen nothing in the shape of premises at all suitable as yet." (E.M.)

20. "John Lane, a Personal Note," *Devonian Year Book*, 1926, p. 37. Lane until 1894 shared the house at 37 Southwick Street with Dr. Pritchard, "a fellow bibliophile whose sympathy with the ambitions of the aspiring publisher took the practical form of an offer of a home in return for ten shillings a week and a half-share of the grocery bills." Richard Whittington-Egan and Geoffrey Smerdon, *The Quest of the Golden Boy* (Barre, Mass.: Barre Publishing, 1962), p. 133.

21. A.L.S. from Symons to J. Dykes Campbell, dated March 5, 1890, B.M.

22. A.L.S. from Lane to Mathews, dated May 16, 1887, E.M.

23. Perhaps in Lane's conservative nature, which he inherited from his father, one can find the basis of his love for old and rare books. According to Chope in "John Lane," p. 37, "Lane's father was one of the old school and observed the old folk customs." C. Lewis Hind in *Naphtali* (New York: Dodd, Mead, 1926), p. 100, says that although Lane was "very much a man of actuality, keenly alive to the shifting lights of the present, his heart was much in the past; he loved old things — pictures, prints, miniatures, silver, glass, anything that time had hallowed."

24. *D.N.B.* (1922–1930), p. 477; also see R. Pearse Chope, *The Book of Hartland* (Torquay, 1940), p. 146.

25. *Path Through the Wood*, pp. 139–140.

26. "A Chat with Mathews," p. 418.

27. J. Lewis May in the *D.N.B., s.v.* John Lane.

28. *Path Through the Wood*, p. 139.

29. A.L.S. from Lane to Mathews, dated May 16, 1887, E.M. Lane's business acumen is also illustrated in a letter to Mathews, dated November 9 [1887?], in which he reports that he knows two brothers who work "at Cox & Co's the army agents, they have promised to watch all cheques payable to well known *booksellers* & to supply us with the names & addresses of their clients, which will be a good thing I fancy." (A.L.S., E.M.)

30. A.L.S. dated August 4, 1887, and August 10, 1887, E.M.

31. The premises located at 6B Vigo Street were actually a part of a building situated at 1 Savile Row, Burlington Gardens, owned and then occupied by the Royal Geographic Society.

32. A.L.S., dated June 15, 1887, E.M. Lane in his introduction to *Sir Thomas*

Bodley, p. iv, says that it was in July 1887 that he visited, in the company of Mr. R. W. Wilson, "an exhibition in the Rembrandt Head Gallery in Vigo Street; and, casually asking the proprietor, Mr. Dunthorne, if he knew of any cosy little corner where a book-shop would be in fit setting, he at once rejoined that the premises in the same street, where he had originally hung up the sign of the Rembrandt Head, were vacant, and that he would be pleased to show them to me. I saw them, liked them, and at once made up my mind that here was the spot I had been looking for."

33. *Sir Thomas Bodley,* p. v.

34. A.L.S. from Mathews to W. Taylor, the agent for the Royal Geographic Society, E.M. The term "cabinet" derived from the fact that the Vigo Street premises had been known for the past seven years not only as Dunthorne's "Rembrandt Head" but also as "The Cabinet of Fine Arts." Mathews retained the use of the term and some years later issued a one shilling, paper-bound series of books known as "The Vigo Cabinet Series, an Occasional Miscellany of Prose and Verse." "Publishers' Premises," Part III, *Literary World* (August 9, 1901), p. 93. For further information see a draft in Elkin Mathews' hand of "From Vigo Street to Cork Street," an essay probably written to advertise his move in 1912 to Cork Street. (E.M.)

35. Draft letter dated February 7, 1895, E.M. In this draft letter to Dr. Brushfield, Mathews says that he "was on the lookout for London premises" in 1887 and that Lane, knowing this, "gave me no peace, until I discovered that through taking some of his books I had practically made him a partner — I only discovered this some years ago when I sought to get rid of him — for mark you, at that early stage I had not received from him one shilling in cash, — and then when I found there was no choice and that I had to submit to a partnership deed being drawn up, all the money he put into my concern was £50 which he borrowed from Mr. J. W. Darton the publisher.

36. E.M.

37. A.L.S., E.M. Also Chope in "John Lane," p. 38, recalls having helped Lane "in the long and tedious task of listing his books which formed his share of the stock when he entered into partnership with Elkin Matthews [*sic*]."

38. See esp. A.L.S. from Lane to Mathews dated July 21, 1887; September 2, 1887; September 14, 1887; and September 24, 1887, E.M.

39. Undated A.L.S. from Lane to Mathews, E.M.

40. Undated A.L.S., E.M.

41. A.L.S. from Lane to Mathews, undated (probably October 5, Wednesday, 1887), suggests that Mathews was finally to appear in town on Friday. (E.M.)

42. *Path Through the Wood,* pp. 171–172.

43. Vigo Lane applied to the whole Lane from Regent Street to Bond Street until 1831, when the western half became known as Burlington Gardens. The best accounts of the street are in "Publishers' Premises," p. 93, and in the draft history of Vigo Street written by Mathews. (E.M.)

44. *Path Through the Wood,* p. 141.

45. *Ibid.*

46. *Minding My Own Business* (London: Chatto & Windus, 1956), p. 4. An engraving of the shop appeared on the front covers of the Vigo Cabinet Series books.

47. Undated A.L.S. from Lane to Mathews, E.M.

48. *Wales England Wed* (London: J. M. Dent, 1940), p. 152.

49. *Minding My Own Business*, pp. 3–4.

50. My description here is of one of the large-paper copies.

51. *Academy*, no. 829 (24 March 1888), pp. 200–201. Noble's review may also have led Lane to Gleeson White's recent *Ballades*, where he would have found Le Gallienne's "Ballade of Old Sweethearts." Le Gallienne also reviewed Philip Bourke Marston's *Song-Tide*, edited with a memoir by William Sharp in the May 19, 1888, edition of *Academy*, pp. 337–338.

52. *Academy*, no. 831, p. 238.

53. *Academy*, no. 833, p. 273.

54. *Academy*, no. 832, pp. 255–256.

55. *Quest of the Golden Boy*, p. 101 n. 1.

56. Noble's review of *My Ladies' Sonnets*, pp. 200–201.

57. *Quest of the Golden Boy*, p. 101 n. 1 See Le Gallienne's barely disguised account in his autobiographical novel, *Young Lives* (Bristol: Arrowsmith, 1898), pp. 239–240: "The second was a letter forwarded, care of his [Henry Mesurier's, i.e. Le Gallienne's] printer, by one of the London reviews which had noticed his verses. It was from a rising young London publisher [i.e. Lane] who, it appeared from an envelope enclosed, had already tried to reach him direct at Tyre. 'Henry Mesurier, Esq., author of *The Book of Angelica*, Tyre,' the address had run: but the post-office of Tyre had returned it to the sender, with the words 'Not known' officially stamped upon it."

58. A.L.S. to Lane, May 20, 1888, Le G.

59. *Ibid.*

60. A.L.S., dated May 30, 1888, Hales.

61. Le G.

62. A.L.S. from Le Gallienne, E.M. On April 16, 1889, Le Gallienne, recovering from a "severe bilious attack" and preparing to remove himself to "new 'diggings' at Hampstead," sent his apologies to Mathews and his sisters for not having been able to visit them on the previous Sunday. (E.M.)

63. *Minding My Own Business*, p. 5.

64. *Quest of the Golden Boy*, p. 41.

65. Le Gallienne's diary and letters of this period often mention Ireland, who numbered among his friends Leigh Hunt, Carlyle, and Emerson (whose biography he wrote). His best known work was *The Book-Lover's Enchiridion,* a collection of passages in praise of books, published in 1882 under the pseudonym of "Philobiblos." *D.N.B., s.v.* Richard Le Gallienne.

66. Temple Scott, "Richard Le Gallienne, Reminiscences by an Old Friend," prefaced to Robert J. Lingel's *A Bibliographical Checklist of the Writings of Richard Le Gallienne* (Metuchen, N.J.: Americana Collector, 1926), pp. 7–8.

67. See L. D. Jacobs, *"The Quest of the Golden Boy*: R. Le Gallienne and Some Unpublished Evidence," *English Literature in Transition*, X, no. 4 (1967), 195.

68. According to Temple Scott, p. 8, Le Gallienne would often during his noon visits to bookshops "buy or exchange some book, adding to a collection which I later found to be of rare quality and gathered with fine and understanding discrimination."

69. I quote from the third edition, published in London and New York, 1895, pp. 4–5. The diary shows that Le Gallienne was writing *Book-Bills* in late 1889– 1890. According to the diary entry for June 26, 1890, the book was sent off to Murray, the publisher, on that date.

70. *Book-Bills*, p. 5.

71. See esp. A.L.S., October 5, 1889, Hales.

72. *Young Lives*, pp. 104–105.

73. *Ibid.*, p. 107.

74. *Ibid.*, p. 68.

75. *Quest of the Golden Boy*, p. 75; see esp. Jacobs, pp. 196–197.

76. *Young Lives*, p. 69.

77. *Ibid.*, pp. 71–72.

78. *Quest of the Golden Boy*, pp. 44–45.

79. *The Letters of Oscar Wilde* (New York: Harcourt, Brace & World, 1962), p. 209 n. 1.

80. *Ibid.*, p. 209.

81. A.L.S., dated July 1, 1888, Le G.

82. *Letters of Wilde*, p. 230 n. 3. The manuscript volume of poetry was probably *Volumes in Folio*.

83. *Quest of the Golden Boy*, pp. 108–109. Since no book with the title Le Gallienne mentions, "Oblivion's Poppy," was ever published, it is quite possible that Le Gallienne simply dreamed up the rather exotic title to please Wilde and hoped at a later date to write some essays to go with it. There is no evidence that anything other than the title ever existed. No doubt the *George Meredith* volume was the only book-length work Le Gallienne could handle at this time.

84. *Letters of Wilde*, p. 242.

85. *Ibid.*, p. 310.

86. Entry for February 23, 1890, Diary.

87. A.L.S. dated December 22, 1889, Le G. Many diary entries show that Le Gallienne was reading much Pater during the winter of 1889 and the early months of 1890. For instance, on November 29, 1889, he writes: "Reading Pater still with much joy." And again on March 9, 1890, he notes: "Reading *Marius* with much joy." Also see *Quest of the Golden Boy*, p. 121.

88. See Diary. For instance, the entry for November 17, 1889: "Reading *Far from the Madding Crowd* which held me very much, despite its intolerable affectations of style"; February 27, 1890: "Reading *Daniel Deronda* with much pleasure"; on March 26, 1890, the diary indicates that Le Gallienne was reading Coleridge's "Rime of the Ancient Mariner," some Charles Lamb, and Carlyle's *Heroes*; "also

Sir P. Sidney, out of Jim's old folio"; and on March 28, he is "at Clough again. I foresee he is to be the new enthusiasm." Through May and June he is reading Keats's letters.

89. Entry for June 20, 1890, Diary.

90. Reported by Le Gallienne in an A.L.S. to Samuel Hales double dated November 8 and 11, 1888, Hales. Wilson Barrett (1846–1904) was an actor-manager and author, who was highly successful in a number of melodramas including *The Silver King* and his own *The Sign of the Cross*.

91. In a letter to Hales, dated January 24, 1889, Le Gallienne wrote that his father had received the news that he had failed his accountancy examinations and planned to give up his job with the firm of Chalmers and Wade temporarily in order to join Barrett's entourage, with understanding and kindness. "Strange to say," Le Gallienne continued, "he had during the last few months been coming to the conclusion that, for various reasons, it wd be better to delay opening a business for a year or so." Farther on in the letter, Le Gallienne says that his father "is very anxious for me to make a determined effort to get thro' the exam — I have given him my word for that. . . ." See Le Gallienne's letter to his father concerning Barrett's offer, *Quest of the Golden Boy*, pp. 102–105.

92. *Publishers' Circular*, no. 1237 (April 1, 1889), p. 364.

93. *Letters of Wilde*, p. 230.

94. Description is of one of the large-paper copies.

95. *Ballades in Blue China* and *Proverbs in Porcelain* were titles of attractive little volumes of "Parnassian" verse previously published by Lang.

96. A.L.S., dated October 30, 1888, E.M.

97. A.L.S. to Mathews, E.M.

98. "Richard Le Gallienne," p. 10.

99. *Ibid.*, pp. 10–11.

100. Quoted in *Quest of the Golden Boy*, p. 109.

101. Add. MS. 50913, C.P.R.

102. No. 1235, p. 219.

103. A.L.S., dated April 17, 1889, E.M.

104. *Quest of the Golden Boy*, p. 109.

105. Quoted in an advertisement dated February 1890 at the back of J. T. Nettleship's *Robert Browning* (1890).

106. *Ibid.*

107. *Quest of the Golden Boy*, p. 110.

108. *Young Lives*, pp. 43–44.

109. See A.L.S. to Lane, May 23, 1889, Le G.

110. A.L.S., October 5, 1889, Hales.

111. Entry dated November 12, 1889, Diary.

112. A.L.S. dated December 22, 1889, Le G. Also quoted in *Quest of the Golden Boy*, p. 120.

113. *Quest of the Golden Boy*, pp. 127–128.

114. Entries for November 28, 1889, and March 31, 1890, Diary.

115. *Book-Bills*, pp. 107–108.

116. Although the book was announced in *Publishers' Circular* for December 1–15, 1890, Le Gallienne in a letter to Mathews dated March 3, 1891, wrote: "I propose publishing *The Body-Snatcher* along with the 2nd edition [of George] Meredith." Morever, Le Gallienne's request further on in the letter that Mathews advertise the book "only in two papers — say *Athenaeum* & *Academy* — as we [Le Gallienne and Leather] cannot afford to spend much in adv[ertisemen]t," suggest that Le Gallienne had the book printed and probably published at his and Leather's expense. A.L.S., University of Iowa Libraries.

117. A.L.S. from Le Gallienne, Le G.

118. A.L.S., dated July 27, 1890, Le G.

119. Quoted in *Quest of the Golden Boy*, p. 129.

120. No. 1303 (June 20, 1891), p. 661.

121. *Quest of the Golden Boy*, p. 134.

122. *Ibid*. Le Gallienne's first literary effort in behalf of Barrett had appeared in the *Star*. See *Quest of the Golden Boy*, p. 108.

123. *Quest of the Golden Boy*, p. 135. In a letter to Hales, June 13, 1891, Le Gallienne, referring to the trial columns, tells his friend not to "think that all those unsigned columns were mine. The second one after the disappearance of 'Tatler' was my first — & that only a trial one in competition with other people, who wrote the several foll[owin]g weeks."

124. A.L.S. from Le Gallienne, Le G.

125. *Quest of the Golden Boy*, p. 147.

126. Le G.

127. A.L.S. to Hales, Hales.

128. Harry Cozens-Hardy, *The Glorious Years* (London: Robert Hale, 1953), p. 123.

129. Quoted in *Glorious Years*, p. 124.

130. *Glorious Years*, p. 123.

131. Walter Crane, *An Artist's Reminiscences*, 2nd ed. (London: Methuen, 1907), p. 373 n. 1.

132. *Wales England Wed*, p. 152.

133. *Path Through the Wood*, pp. 160–161.

134. As chief reader Le Gallienne must have read hundreds of books in manuscript. When John Lane's library was sold in 1929, Le Gallienne's reports on about 160 books came to light. According to the catalogue, the length of the reports varied from a brief "commonplace and impossible" to a lengthy criticism of several pages. A brief sampling of his remarks includes such illuminating comments as that on Ernest Rhys's *A London Rose*: "Mr. Rhys's gift is slight but real!" Of Florence Farr's *Dancing Faun*, Le Gallienne wrote: "A very clever and original story." Lena Milman's translation of Dostoevski's *Poor Folk* struck him as "one of the most beautiful, touching stories I ever read." See Dulau entry 1054.

In addition to Le Gallienne, John Davidson also read a number of manuscripts, and Cosmo Monkhouse was the reader for Le Gallienne's *English Poems*. (See Dulau entry 347.)

135. A.L.S. to Lane, October 28, 1890, Le G.

136. A.L.S. dated June 26, 1889, Le G.

137. A.L.S., dated March 24, 1890, Le G.

138. Le G.

139. A.L.S., December 22, 1889, Le G.

140. A.L.S., B.M.

141. A.L.S., December 31, 1889, Le G.

142. May in *Path Through the Wood*, p. 142, is of the opinion that Mathews "had a conservative and unenterprising spirit." According to Muir in *Minding My Own Business*, p. 7, "Lane had in overflowing measure that buccaneer spirit, a modicum of which is indispensable to the success of any publisher. Mathews was timid and almost entirely unadventurous."

143. Quoted in item no. 366 in *Books of the 'Nineties*, Catalogue 42, issued by Elkin Mathews Ltd., London, n.d.

144. Reported in a letter to Lane dated July 27, 1890, Le G.

145. See Chapter Four, "Le Gallienne's *George Meredith*."

146. A.L.S., dated October 30, 1890, Le G.

147. A.L.S., dated October 26, 1889, Le G.

148. A.L.S., dated December 8, 1891, E.M.

149. A.L.S., Le G.

150. AL.S., Le G.

151. A.L.S. in my possession.

152. A.L.S., Le G.

153. A.L.S., dated December 22, 1889, Le G.

154. A.L.S., dated October 30, 1890, Le G.

155. A.L.S., dated October 22, 1890, Le G.

156. A.L.S., dated December 22, 1889, Le G.

157. A.L.S., Le G.

158. In his letter to Lane of January 3, 1892, Le Gallienne writes: "By this time, it [the Bodley Head] has two 'Heads' tho', hasn't it? — 'two-headed Janus'," which suggests that Lane became a full and active partner in the firm on the first day of the year although the announcement about the partnership did not appear in the *Publishers' Circular* until February 6.

159. LV, no. 1336, 156.

160. LV, no. 1340 (March 5, 1892), 271.

2. The Bodley Head Book

1. Richard Le Gallienne, *The Romantic '90s* (Garden City, N.Y.: Doubleday, Page, 1925), p. 168.

2. "Walter Biggar Blaikie," an essay by D'Arcy Wentworth Thompson reprinted from the *Edinburgh Academy Chronicle,* in *Walter Biggar Blaikie, 1847–1928* (Edinburgh: Constable, 1929), p. 5.

3. *Ibid.,* pp. 6–7.

4. *Ibid.*

5. *Blaikie,* p. 7.

6. *Brief Notes on the Origins of T. and A. Constable Ltd.* (Edinburgh: Constable, 1937), p. 9.

7. "Walter Blaikie: Personal Note" in *Blaikie,* p. 60.

8. *Ibid.,* pp. 61–62.

9. *Blaikie,* p. 9. According to *Brief Notes on T. and A. Constable,* p. 11, Morris "in the choice of his types and the design of his page, aimed at producing a beautiful book, of which the essential was the *appearance,* while the first consideration of the books issued from Thistle Street [site of Blaikie's office in Edinburgh] was *legibility,* bearing in mind the fitness for their purpose."

10. Another reason for Blaikie's success was the care with which he chose the paper for his books. During an age when cheap paper was extensively used in printing by the big commercial publishers, Blaikie's attention to handmade papers was unusual. His interest is attested to, for instance, by the efforts he made to get the Bruces at Currie to "make a light, 'feather-weight' paper without any 'loading' at all." Although the papermakers said it could not be done, Blaikie "persisted, and it was done, and *Barrack-Room Ballads* was the first book to be printed on the new material." *Blaikie,* p. 9.

11. "An Unacknowledged Movement in Fine Printing, The Typography of the Eighteen-Nineties," *Fleuron,* VII [1930], 115.

12. "How the Perfect Book Is Made," *Scottish Leader* (January 18, 1894), p. 3.

13. *Ibid.*

14. Born in London on November 20, 1853, Jacobi began work at the Chiswick Press as a printer's devil at the age of twelve and a half. The grandson of John Samuel Jacobi, a native of Coburg, Germany, who settled in England in 1823, Jacobi rose to be a leading authority on printing and in addition to *On the Making and Issuing of Books,* published a number of other monographs on the art of printing. See John Bassett, "Mr. Charles Thomas Jacobi," in the "Eminent Living Printers" series, *The Effective Advertiser* (September 1, 1890), pp. 43–47.

15. See "The Chiswick Press," *Modern Presses,* p. 192.

16. *Victorian Book Design and Colour Printing* (London: Faber and Faber, 1963), p. 106.

17. *Ibid.,* p. 162.

18. *On the Making and Issuing of Books* (London: Elkin Mathews, 1891), p. 12.

19. *Ibid.,* p. 21.

20. *Ibid.,* pp. 19–20.

21. Ricketts also did some illustrating for several commercial publications such as the *Magazine of Art, Black and White* and *Woman's World* (edited by Wilde). Although this work shows clearly the influence of Dante Gabriel Rossetti, Burne-

Jones, and William Blake on the early work of Ricketts, in the opinion of Richard Quinn, "Charles Ricketts and the Dial," Ph.D. Dissertation, University of Wisconsin, 1971, much of this early work is undistinguished.

22. Robert Steele, essay prefaced to *The Revival of Printing; A Bibliographical Catalogue of Works Issued by the Chief Modern English Presses* (London: Macmillan, 1912), p. xix.

23. *Letters of Oscar Wilde,* ed. Rupert Hart-Davis (New York: Harcourt, Brace & World, 1962), p. 276.

24. Stuart Mason, *Bibliography of Oscar Wilde* (London: T. W. Laurie, 1914), pp. 341–343.

25. Carl J. Weber, *The Rise and Fall of James Ripley Osgood* (Waterville, Me.: Colby College Press, 1959), pp. 253–255. Ricketts also designed for Osgood & McIlvaine *The Bard of the Dimbovitza* by Hélène Vacaresco and perhaps the English edition of Mary E. Wilkins' *A New England Nun.* See Weber, esp. chapters XIV, XV.

26. "Charles Ricketts and His Books," *Colby Library Quarterly,* III (November, 1951), 54.

27. John Rothenstein, *A Pot of Paint, The Artists of the 1890's* (New York: Covici, Friede, 1929), p. 182.

28. *Ibid.* See also Sturge Moore's account of these early years, *Self-Portrait Taken from the Letters & Journals of Charles Ricketts, R. A.,* collected and compiled by T. Sturge Moore and edited by Cecil Lewis (London: Peter Davies, 1939), pp. 14–18. Sturge Moore's account also serves as the Introduction to *Charles Ricketts, R. A.; Sixty-Five Illustrations* (London: Cassell, 1933).

29. A[nna] M. Stirling, *William de Morgan and His Wife* (New York: Henry Holt, 1922), p. 199.

30. *Ibid.* The Vale is depicted in de Morgan's last novel, *Old Man's Youth.*

31. See William Rothenstein, *Men and Memories* (New York: Coward-McCann, 1931), I, 312; Charles J. Holmes, *Self and Partners (Mostly Self)* (New York: Macmillan, 1936), p. 165.

32. John Rothenstein, *Pot of Paint,* p. 182.

33. *Letters of Wilde,* p. 250.

34. *Pot of Paint,* p. 183.

35. "A Neglected Virtuoso: Charles Ricketts and His Achievements," *Apollo* (February 1966), p. 141.

36. *A Defence of the Revival of Printing* (London: Hacon and Ricketts, 1899), p. 18.

37. *Ibid.,* p. 19.

38. *Ibid.*

39. *Ibid.,* pp. 24–25.

40. *Ibid.,* p. 25. In his Introduction to *Charles Ricketts,* n.p., Sturge Moore says that "*The Sphinx* was the first book which Ricketts made one thing from cover to cover."

41. In a letter to Mathews (September 1894), quoted in *Letters of Wilde,* p. 367,

Wilde writes of having handed the manuscript of "Mr. W. H." over to Ricketts so "that he might select the type and form and suitable setting for the book, and convey the manuscript to the printers."

42. "Fine Printing," p. 102.

43. Symons in "Fine Printing," p. 105, says that *Silverpoints* is "perhaps the finest 'trade' book to which he [Ricketts] set his hand."

44. *Ibid.*, p. 102.

45. Introduction to *A Bibliography of the Books Issued by Hacon and Ricketts* (London: Ballantyne Press, 1904), pp. vi–vii.

46. *Studio,* II (November 15, 1893), 57.

47. *Ibid.*, p. 58.

48. *The Unexpected Years* (London: Jonathan Cape, 1937), p. 115. Moreover, Wilde having seen Housman's illustrations for *The Green Gaffer* brought his name to the attention of Ricketts. *Ibid.* Although William Blake was a very important influence on Housman, whose first published work was a selection of Blake's writing, Ricketts' influence was also very strong. The shape and cover design Housman created for Christina Rossetti's *Goblin Market* is clearly modeled after Ricketts' *Silverpoints.*

49. "Fine Printing," p. 109.

50. McLean in *Victorian Book Design,* p. 12, says that Pickering used Caslon "for several title-pages in 1840; Herbert's *Temple* and *Lady Willoughby's Diary,* both of 1844, were among the first books wholly set in Caslon. . . . It remained in comparatively rare use until revived by Emery Walker and William Morris."

51. McLean in *Victorian Book Design,* p. 12, says that "to Pickering, perhaps the chief attraction of Caslon was that it looked (he thought) old-fashioned in the best sense."

52. *Modern Book Design* (Fair Lawn, N.J.: Essential Books, 1959), p. 4.

53. *Ibid.*, pp. 5–6.

54. Quoted in *Letters of Walter Pater,* ed. Lawrence Evans (Oxford: Oxford University Press, Clarendon Press, 1969), Letter 13, p. 8.

55. Simon Nowell-Smith, ed., *Letters to Macmillan* (London and New York: Macmillan, 1967), p. [142].

56. *Ibid.* Pater's personal interest in the appearance of his books was not lost on his disciples. When Arthur Symons came to publish his first book of verse, *Days and Nights,* he chose a paper and binding which he thought would "be similar to those used in Pater's books — a sort which was prepared under his personal supervision and which I think very charming." A.L.S. to Charles Churchill Osborne, dated December 12, 1888, P.U.L.

57. *Letters to Macmillan,* p. 143.

58. Charles L. Graves, *Life and Letters of Alexander Macmillan* (London: Macmillan, 1910), pp. 312–313.

59. *Letters to Macmillan,* p. 144 n. 1.

60. Oswald Doughty and John R. Wahl, eds., *Letters of Dante Gabriel Rossetti* (Oxford: Oxford University Press, Clarendon Press, 1965), II, 851–852.

61. Rossetti's first essay in bookbinding was the first edition of Christina Rossetti's *Goblin Market* (1862), the cover of which is done in "a severe design of straight lines with tiny circles blocked in gold on blue cloth." *Victorian Book Design,* p. 158. McLean goes on to say that "it is disconcerting to find this date on a design which might have been made in the 1890s or 1900s."

62. Paul Thompson, *The Work of William Morris* (London: Heinemann, 1967), p. 137.

63. J[oseph] and E[lizabeth] Pennell, *The Life of James McNeill Whistler,* rev. ed. (Philadelphia and London: Lippincott, 1911), p. 291. Speaking of *The Gentle Art,* the Pennells write that "Whistler was constantly at the Ballantyne Press. . . . He chose the type, he spaced the text, he placed the Butterflies, each of which he designed to convey a meaning."

64. "Fine Printing," p. 89.

65. *Ibid.*

66. John Russell Taylor, *The Art Nouveau Book in Britain* (Cambridge, Mass.: M.I.T. Press, 1966), pp. 51–52.

67. *Ibid.,* p. 52.

68. *Ibid.,* pp. 52–53.

69. *Victorian Book Design,* p. 166.

70. *Ibid.*

71. *Pot of Paint,* p. 183.

72. *Letters of Wilde,* p. 348.

73. *Arts and Crafts Essays* (London: Rivington, Percival, 1893), p. 121.

74. *Ibid.*

75. *Ibid.,* p. 127.

76. *Ibid.,* p. 129.

77. *Ibid.,* p. 130.

78. *Ibid.,* p. 132.

79. *Ibid.,* p. 133.

80. The second edition was imported from America by Elkin Mathews.

81. *Art Nouveau Book,* p. 74.

82. *Ibid.,* p. 54.

83. Quoted in Will Ransom, *Private Presses and Their Books* (New York: Bowker, 1929), p. 45.

84. *Sunday Sun* [London], II (October 2, 1892), 1.

85. *Victorian Book Design,* pp. 164–166. McLean, p. 164, says that "it was from amateurs, not professionals, that new ideas entered the design of books. One of the first was the Rev. C. H. O. Daniel." And in *The Daniel Press, Memorials of C. H. O. Daniel with a Bibliography of the Press, 1845–1919* (Oxford: Oxford University Press, 1921), p. 44, F. Madan says that Dr. Daniel has "strong claims to be regarded as the chief precursor of the Kelmscott Press and consequently of the Revival of Printing in English."

86. *Ibid.,* p. 166.

87. *Ibid.*

88. Other books which might be considered anticipations of the Bodley Head book were published by the Driver Press at Chelmsford, which published the poems of the bizarre and decadent writer John Barlas, who wrote under the name of Evelyn Douglas, and some of those published by David Nutt in the Strand.

89. *Art Nouveau Book,* p. 27.

90. "Perfect Book," p. 3.

91. *Minding My Own Business* (London: Chatto & Windus, 1956), p. 33.

92. Walter Pater, "Two Early French Stories," *The Renaissance* (London: Macmillan, 1910), pp. 8 and 15.

93. Pater, "Preface," *Renaissance,* p. x.

94. Pater's retelling of the Cupid and Psyche myth in his novel, *Marius the Epicurean,* not only led to new translations and interpretations such as Lang's, but his emphasis on the themes and sentiments of Provençal poetry and his decadent reading of the Amis and Amile, the Heloise and Abelard, and the story of Aucassin and Nicolette in "Two Early French Stories" created a vogue for such stories printed and published in a manner befitting the preciosity and sentiment of the subject. Ricketts and Shannon's *Daphnis and Chloe* and *Hero and Leander* are obvious examples. Also see *Of Aucassin and Nicolette, a Translation in Prose and Verse from the Old French, Together with Amabel and Amoris* done by Laurence Housman with drawings by Paul Woodroffe, engraved on wood by Clemence Housman (London, n.d.), and the Kelmscott *Of the Friendship of Amis and Amile* (1894).

95. From a *Daily Chronicle* review quoted in the Bodley Head list of October 1892.

96. A.L.S., dated July 24, 1888, Hales.

97. *Letters of Wilde,* p. 294.

98. *Ibid.,* p. 378.

99. "Fine Printing," p. 89.

100. Oscar Wilde, *The Picture of Dorian Gray* (Paris: Charles Carrington, 1908), p. 264. Again Pater is probably behind such sentiment. Although his *Renaissance* was Wilde's "golden book" and his *Marius* was George Moore's, it was Pater who established the fad in Chapter V of *Marius,* entitled "The Golden Book." The "'golden' book of that day [second century A.D.]" was a gift to Marius' friend Flavian, the young aesthete, whose name was written on the handsome yellow wrapper in purple ink. The book "was perfumed with oil of sandal-wood, and decorated with carved and gilt ivory bosses at the ends of the roller." Internally the book was "not less dainty and fine, full of the archaisms and curious felicities in which that generation delighted."

101. Ellen Moers, "Literary Economics in the 1890's: Golden Boys for Sale," *Victorian Studies,* VII (December 1963), 189.

102. "Fine Printing," p. 89.

103. *Ibid.,* p. 84.

104. *Ibid.*

105. This distinctive type, according to Alfred F. Johnson, *Type Designs: Their History and Development,* 2nd ed. (London: Grafton, 1959), p. 83, has "a heavy

face, with an oblique stroke to the eye of the e, and other characteristics which ally it with fifteenth-century types. The stress is definitely diagonal, so much so that the o has an angular appearance." See esp. Chapter 4, "Old-Face Types in the Victorian Age."

106. Louis Dudek, *Literature and the Press* (Toronto: Ryerson, 1960), p. 60.

107. *Victorian Book Design*, p. 9.

108. *Ibid.*

109. *Modern Book Design*, p. 6.

110. *Ibid.*, p. 5.

111. Also see the title page to William Watson's *The Prince's Quest*, 2nd ed. (London, 1893).

112. *Art Nouveau Book*, pp. 109–110.

113. *Ibid.*, p. 111.

114. A.L.S., Huntington.

115. *Ibid.*

116. A.L.S. from Housman, September 6, 1893, Huntington.

117. A.L.S. from Housman, September 9, 1893, Huntington.

118. Some idea of the painstaking efforts Housman made to get the title page printed in accordance with his exact wishes is suggested in a letter to Lane which he wrote probably some time in October 1893: "Since writing last night have found my original sketch of the 'Random Itinerary' title-page. Lay the tracing over the proof and make them correct till it comes right. Be sure that 'Elkin,' 'and' 'Vigo' [which is omitted from the title page actually printed] 'London' etc all *'toe the line'* with the title, to the left, and 'Davidson' the ornament and the date to the right.

"Why on earth cannot the miserable printer [J. Miller & Son of Edinburgh] set up his type by the copy which is set before him, instead of vexing the soul of an unhappy artist away for his holiday./ Yours very faithfully/ Laurence Housman.

"P.S. See also that they get the spaces *between* the different lines right. 'John Davidson' should be closer to the scroll [Housman's term for the ornament?] than to the title, as in sketch. Dont let the design come near[er] the inner edge of the page than I have given it." (A.L.S., Huntington.)

119. Walter Crane, *Of the Decorative Illustration of Books Old and New*, 3rd ed. (London: G. Bell, 1911), pp. 287–288.

120. *Ibid.*, p. 287.

121. *Art Nouveau Book*, pp. 69–70.

122. *Wales England Wed* (London: J. M. Dent, 1940), p. 152.

123. "Fine Printing," p. 112.

124. Taylor, in the *Art Nouveau Book*, p. 93, considers Ricketts and Beardsley the central figures.

125. Robert Ross in *Aubrey Beardsley* (London and New York: John Lane, 1909), p. 24, says that "towards the end of 1893 he [Beardsley] commenced working for Mr. John Lane." According to Brian Reade, *Aubrey Beardsley* (New York: Viking, 1967), p. 333 n. 261, it was Beardsley's "J'ai Baisé Ta Bouche Iokanaan,"

published in the first number of the *Studio,* which led Lane to commission him to do the *Salome* illustrations.

126. "Fine Printing," p. 99.

127. *Aubrey Beardsley,* p. 338 n. 297.

128. *Art Nouveau Book,* p. 52.

129. *Century Guild Hobby Horse,* III, no. 10 (April 1888), 58–59.

130. *Ibid.,* p. 63.

131. According to McLean in *Victorian Book Design,* p. 7, "the binder Archibald Leighton put on the market the first cloth specially manufactured for covering books, a stiffened dyed calico impervious to the glue required to stick it to the boards."

132. *Ibid.,* pp. 155, 158.

133. In "John Leighton, 1822–1912," *Connoisseur,* CLII (1963), 263.

134. *Ibid.,* p. 265.

135. Ireland's *Enchiridion* appeared in 1882 and went through five editions.

136. That persons were beginning to value books in their original boards is evidenced by the activities of T. J. Wise, the famous bibliographer and book collector, who in the 1880s was much interested in the original condition of books, especially those temporarily bound in boards and wrappers. See John Carter, *Taste and Technique in Book-Collecting* (New York: Bowker, 1948), p. 20.

137. The review, entitled "The Beauties of Bookbinding," first appeared in the *Pall Mall Gazette,* November 23, 1888. I quote from the essay in *Miscellanies,* (London: Methuen, 1908), pp. 102–105.

138. Unidentified newspaper clipping, E.M.

139. *Aubrey Beardsley,* p. 335 n. 273. Reade also notes that "the diagram roses with petals something like the scale-shapes he adapted from Whistler's peacock-feathers at 49 Prince's Gate were to become familiar in *art nouveau* decorations in all media." Wilde despised the coarse-grained blue-green binding of the ordinary issue. See his letter to Lane, *Letters of Wilde,* p. 348.

140. *Aubrey Beardsley,* p. 335 n. 272.

141. The binders' initials are engraved in gold on the cover. The bindings of *In the Key of Blue* and *Poems, Dramatic and Lyrical* also bear the initials of Leighton Son and Hodge.

142. The influence of Rossetti on these men was great, especially early in their careers. Ricketts' full-page illustration for Christina's sonnet, "An Echo from Willowwood," *Magazine of Art* (1890), p. 385, is directly influenced by Rossetti's Pre-Raphaelite style. Ursula Bridge in *W. B. Yeats and T. Sturge Moore: Their Correspondence, 1901–1937* (London: Routledge & Kegan Paul, 1953), p. 42, says that Ricketts was "entirely absorbed in Rossetti in 1890–91."

143. *Victorian Book Design,* p. 158.

144. *Art Nouveau Book,* see esp. pp. 29, 31.

145. McLean, *Victorian Book Design,* p. 158, gives a list of the binding designs done by Rossetti.

146. *Ibid.*

147. J. Lewis May, *John Lane and the Nineties* (London: John Lane, 1936), p. 116, refers to the cover design as "long tresses of willow." The brass used to impress Ricketts' design on the binding is preserved in the Constance Meade Collection, Oxford University Press, Oxford (now in the Bodleian).

148. In *A Defence of the Revival of Printing*, p. 21, Ricketts wrote that "the name 'saddle book' is of Persian origin, this format being placed in the pocket of a saddle on journeys that preclude other larger and more usual shapes: I give this for what it is worth, bearing in mind the oriental influences upon Venice, notably upon Venetian bindings."

149. "Fine Printing," p. 106.

150. Alfred L. Bush in "The Exhibition: A Retrospective View," *Wilde and the Nineties,* ed. Charles Ryskamp (Princeton, N.J.: Princeton University Library, 1966), p. 64, refers to the design as "gilt arabesque lily-of-the-valley."

151. *Letters of Rossetti*, II, 855.

152. A.L.S., September 20, 1893, Huntington. A later letter from Housman to Lane indicates that the brown ink — the "second colour" — mentioned in the previous letter did not work out. Housman must have wanted the design and lettering — or at least a portion of it — printed in this dark brown color. But since, as he told Lane, "neither colour had at all hit off my idea," he decided to "keep sides & back of Thompson cover all plain gold." A.L.S., October 11, 1893, Huntington.

153. A.L.S., October 4, 1893, Huntington.

3. Belles-Lettres to Sell

1. Percy Muir, *Minding My Own Business* (London: Chatto & Windus, 1956), p. 6.

2. A.L.S. to Mathews, E.M.

3. A.L.S., dated August 10, 1887, E.M.

4. Among Nutt's most popular and attractive little books were William Ernest Henley's first volume of poems, *A Book of Verse* (1888), and Norman Gale's *A Country Muse* (1892).

5. E.M.

6. W. Roberts, "The First Edition Mania," *Fortnightly Review,* LXI (March 1894), 352.

7. Richard Whittington-Egan and Geoffrey Smerdon, *The Quest of the Golden Boy* (Barre, Mass.: Barre Publishing, 1962), p. 71.

8. *Quest of the Golden Boy*, p. 113. John Carter in *Taste and Technique in Book-Collecting* (New York: Bowker, 1948), p. 17, says that first editions of Browning's last volume, *Asolando* (which appeared posthumously in December 1889), "were hoarded by booksellers for an expected rise."

9. *Quest of the Golden Boy*, p. 109.

10. Louise Chandler Moulton, writing about the possibility of placing Marston's

Collected Poems with an English publisher, told her American publisher, Mr. Niles, of Roberts Bros., "since I sent you the offer of Kegan Paul I have heard from *three* different sources that the firm can't be depended upon — & is supposed to be near bankruptcy." A.L.S., dated August 26, 1892, in my possession.

11. According to Rupert Hart-Davis, *Letters of Oscar Wilde* (New York: Harcourt, Brace & World, 1962), p. 302 n. 4, the unsold sheets of the fifth Bogue edition of *Poems* were "presumably" taken over by the firm of Osgood & McIlvaine "after Bogue's bankruptcy." In a letter to Mathews dated December 1891 in *Letters*, p. 302, Wilde indicated that he would ask Osgood & McIlvaine to hand over the remainder of *Poems* to the Bodley Head as soon as the payment to Ricketts was settled.

12. *Ibid.*, p. 302 n. 4.

13. No. 1413 (July 29, 1893), p. 103.

14. "First Edition Mania," p. 347.

15. *Ibid.*, p. 352.

16. *Ibid.*, p. 353. Gale's earliest things were printed by George E. Over at Rugby, where Gale as a young man was a local schoolmaster. The craze was not lasting. According to an entry in Selwyn Image's diary (Bodleian) dated March 29, 1908, Lane told Image "that the publication of books of poetry and belles lettres generally has never recovered from the blow given it by O. Wilde's disaster. Till then they sold like wild-fire."

17. "New and Forthcoming Works," a list of Elkin Mathews' books bound into the back of Todhunter's *A Sicilian Idyll* (1890).

18. *Ibid.*

19. "First Edition Mania," p. 347.

20. I am indebted to John Carter for the information in this paragraph.

21. "First Edition Mania," p. 347.

22. *Ibid.*, pp. 353–354.

23. List in the possession of Percy Muir.

24. "First Edition Mania," p. 354.

25. LVI, no. 8822, 4.

26. LVII, no. 8846, 4.

27. LVII, no. 8847 (July 31, 1893), 4. Le Gallienne's rejoinder to the press's criticism, "Limited Editions, a Prose Fancy," was bound up along with a sonnet, "Confessio Amantis," and issued as a Christmas gift for Lane, Mathews, and Le Gallienne in December 1893.

28. Marjorie Plant, *The English Book Trade*, 2nd ed. (London: Allen & Unwin, 1965), p. 402.

29. *Ibid.*

30. *Ibid.*

31. *Ibid.*

32. *The Romantic '90s* (Garden City, N.Y.: Doubleday, Page, 1925), p. 170.

33. *Wales England Wed* (London: J. M. Dent, 1940). In a letter to a friend, John Davidson spoke of Lane's feat of making poetry pay: "To discover & create

a buying public for minor and other poetry must always be a great feat; to have achieved it nowadays [in a commercial age], and in the manner in which it has been done at the Bodley Head, is to have established a record." A.L.S., n.d., National Library of Scotland.

34. Quoted in a Bodley Head advertisement.

35. *Ibid.*

36. "First Edition Mania," p. 347.

37. R. D. Brown, "The Bodley Head Press: Some Bibliographical Extrapolations," *Papers of the Bibliographical Society of America,* LXI (First Quarter, 1967), 41.

38. *Ibid.,* p. 42.

39. Ellic Howe, *The London Compositor* (London: Bibliographical Society, 1947). See Chapter XIII, "The Scale of 1891," esp. pp. 328–355.

40. T. and A. Constable. Day Book (#20), p. 371.

41. See Brown's resumé of these essential facts, "Bodley Head Press," p. 41.

42. *Ibid.* Brown's conclusions can only apply to such books as Radford's *Chambers Twain,* which was published on commission by the Bodley Head. Dr. Garnett's *Poems,* for example, actually cost more to print than a similar volume of prose. (See pp. 88–89 above.)

43. See Appendix G, Table 1, Production Costs, Chiswick Press.

44. Add. MS. 50914, pp. 122b–123, C.P.R.

45. Add. MS. 50913, p. 173b, C.P.R.

46. *Ibid.*

47. *Ibid.,* pp. 89 and 163.

48. Constable. Letter Book (#19) contains an entry for February 12, 1892, which indicates that Lane was expected in Edinburgh on the thirteenth.

49. *Ibid.,* entry for January 18, 1892, p. 580.

50. *Ibid.,* entries for January 14 and 18, 1892, pp. 556, 580.

51. Constable. Day Book (#19), p. 324.

52. Constable. Letter Book (#20), pp. 249–250.

53. *Ibid.,* p. 265.

54. Constable. Day Book (#20), p. 103.

55. Constable. Day Book (#19), p. 324. Letter Book (#20), p. 4.

56. Constable. Day Book (#20), p. 643.

57. Constable. Day Book (#20), p. 619.

58. *Ibid.*

59. Emery Walker, "Printing," in *Arts and Crafts Essays* (London: Rivington, Percival, 1893), p. 130.

60. Charles T. Jacobi, *On the Making and Issuing of Books* (London: Elkin Mathews, 1891), p. 18.

61. "How the Perfect Book Is Made," *Scottish Leader* (January 18, 1894), p. 3.

62. Walker, "Printing," p. 130.

63. *Ibid.*

64. *Making and Issuing Books,* p. 53.

65. According to Jacobi, *Making and Issuing Books,* p. 53, "a ream of writing

or hand-made paper usually consists of twenty quires of twenty-four sheets each, 480 in all; but machine-made paper is generally made up to 516 sheets (twenty-one and a half quires), termed 'printers' reams'."

66. Constable. Day Book (#20), p. 642.

67. Constable. Day Book (#21), p. 293.

68. Constable. Day Book (#20), p. 383.

69. Constable. Day Book (#20), p. 642.

70. Constable. Day Book (#20), p. 383.

71. In the possession of Percy Muir. See Appendix G, Table 3, Inventory Sheets.

72. Estimate dated February 13, 1892, from Leighton Son and Hodge, U.C.L.A.

73. E.M.

74. Add. MS. 50914, pp. 122b–123, C.P.R.

75. *Ibid.,* p. 118b.

76. See *Making and Issuing Books,* p. 40. Marjorie Plant, *Book Trade,* p. 409, says that "round about 1840 the author who could undertake his own advertising was being advised to publish by commission. He had only to send the books, ready printed, to a publisher and call every six months for the proceeds less a commission of 7½ per cent." Also see her section on "The Author's Remuneration," p. 410.

77. B.H.F.

78. B.H.F. Brackets in original.

79. U.T. There is a draft of this document at U.C.L.A.

80. B.H.F. Also excerpted in *Letters of Wilde,* p. 318 n. 4.

81. "Mr. W. H.," *A Woman of No Importance, The Duchess of Padua.*

82. B.H.F.

83. James G. Nelson, *Sir William Watson* (New York: Twayne, 1966), pp. 95–96.

84. B.H.F.

85. A.L.S. from Robinson Watson to Lane, January 11, 1893, B.H.F.

86. Agreement dated "(Monday) 16 [in different ink] Jany 1893," B.H.F.

87. B.H.F.

88. Jacobi, *Making and Issuing Books,* p. 47, lists five: British Museum; Bodleian, Oxford; Trinity College, Cambridge; Trinity College, Dublin; and Advocates' in Edinburgh.

89. B.H.F.

90. *Letters of Wilde,* p. 344 n. 3.

91. B.H.F.

92. Draft agreement (n.d.), B.H.F.

93. Agreement dated December 20, 1893, B.H.F.

94. Since this second Bodley Head edition of *Liber* was not published until November 1894, I do not include it among the early Bodley Head books.

95. B.H.F.

96. B.H.F.

97. B.H.F.

98. The New York branch was actually established in 1896.

99. In J. Lewis May, *John Lane and the Nineties* (London: John Lane, 1936), p. 158.

100. Houghton.

101. A.L.S., dated January 25, 1891, Houghton.

102. E.M.

103. A.L.S. from Crane to Mathews, dated April 25, 1891, E.M.

104. E.M.

105. *Ibid.*

106. Macmillan. Letter Book (#61).

107. E.M.

108. Macmillan. Letter Book (#66), copies of letters dated November 7, 1892, and December 19, 1892, respectively.

109. Macmillan. Letter Book (#66).

110. Macmillan. Letter Book (#66), copy dated November 11, 1892.

111. Macmillan. Letter Book (#68), copy dated April 12, 1893.

112. Macmillan. Letter Book (#68).

113. Macmillan. Letter Book (#69).

114. Macmillan. Letter Book (#71).

115. See her "Biographical Sketch of Philip Bourke Marston," prefaced to *The Collected Poems of Philip Bourke Marston* (London: Elkin Mathews, 1892).

116. A.L.S. in my possession.

117. *Making and Issuing Books*, p. 66.

118. Constable. Letter Book (#24), May 1, 1894, p. 303.

119. A photograph of Le Gallienne replaced a lithograph drawing of the author by J. Wilson Steer in the American edition.

120. Constable. Letter Book (#24), p. 862. The American edition appeared with the first page of the chapter entitled "The Devils on the Needle" and that of the chapter on "Irrelevant People" switched.

121. *Ibid.*

122. According to the Inventory Sheets, about 520 copies of Gale's *Orchard Songs* went to America. Although I have no record, *Keynotes* probably sold more copies than any other early Bodley Head book in the U.S.A.

123. See Copeland and Day advertisement in Stone and Kimball's *Chap-Book,* no. 4 (June 15, 1894), on back of front cover.

124. Copeland and Day advertisement in *Chap-Book,* no. 1 (May 15, 1894), p. 2.

125. See Appendix E: "Bodley Head Exports and Imports." The new avant-garde publishers in America, Copeland and Day, and Stone and Kimball, seem to have priced their imports higher than did the large established firms. For instance, G. P. Putnam's Sons priced Le Gallienne's *Prose Fancies* and *The Religion of a Literary Man* at $1.00 each.

126. Sidney Kramer, *A History of Stone & Kimball* (Chicago: University of Chicago Press, 1940), p. 208.

127. Data taken from Appendix G, Table 3, Inventory Sheets.

128. *Pall Mall Gazette,* LVI (April 8, 1893), 3.

129. Data taken from Appendix G, Table 3, Inventory Sheets. In a letter to George Egerton dated April 25, 1895 (P.U.L.), Le Gallienne wrote that he and Lane "were told that your 'Keynotes' had had the largest sale in America of any short stories except Kipling's."

130. *Ibid.*

131. B.M.

132. See Appendix G, Table 3, Inventory Sheets.

133. Ruari McLean, *Victorian Book Design and Colour Printing* (London: Faber and Faber, 1963), p. 10.

134. *Ibid.,* p. 16.

135. Constable. Day Book (#20), August 1893, p. 529.

136. Agreement dated September 1, 1893, B.H.F.

137. Constable. Day Book (#21), February 1894, p. 58.

4. The Birth of a Book

1. Richard Whittington-Egan and Geoffrey Smerdon, *The Quest of the Golden Boy* (Barre, Mass.: Barre Publishing, 1962), p. 105.

2. B.H.F.

3. A.L.S., dated May 30, 1889, Le G.

4. *Ibid.*

5. A.L.S., dated June 15, 1889, Le G.

6. *Ibid.* Le Gallienne reiterated this wish in his letter to Lane of June 26, 1889, and mentioned having "just finished a careful reading of the 1851 vol. [*Poems*]." Quoted in *Quest of the Golden Boy,* p. 113.

7. Preface to R. J. Lingel, *Bibliographical Checklist* (Metuchen, N.J., 1926), p. 10. Whittington-Egan and Smerdon suggest it was John Robb who gave Le Gallienne the novel. *Quest of the Golden Boy,* p. 108.

8. *Ibid.,* pp. 117–120.

9. Hales.

10. A.L.S., dated June 15, 1889, Le G.

11. A.L.S., dated October 26, 1889, Le G.

12. *Ibid.*

13. A.L.S., dated November 7, 1889, Le G. The terms of the agreement with Mathews allowed Le Gallienne to publish any two chapters in magazines before January 1, 1890.

14. *Ibid.*

15. Diary.

16. Diary, November 27, 1889.

17. A.L.S., dated December 22, 1889, Le G.

18. *Ibid.* The agreement listed the chapters as follows: (I) Introduction; (II)

Style, Storyteller, Word painter; (III) Meredith's Epigram and Humour; (IV) Meredith's Women; (V) Meredith's Comedy; (VI) Some Characters with their Originals; (VII) Poet; (VIII) Meredith's Ethics or Philosophy.

19. *Ibid.*

20. *Ibid.*

21. *Ibid.*

22. *National Review,* XIV (October 1889), 174. For a fuller discussion of Watson's article, see my *Sir William Watson* (New York: Twayne, 1966), pp. 66–67.

23. The essay was later accepted by *Time,* a London journal, and published in March 1890. See Diary, February 5, 1890.

24. A.L.S. to Lane, dated December 22, 1889, Le G.

25. *Ibid.*

26. *Ibid.*

27. *Ibid.*

28. A.L.S. to Lane, dated December 31, 1889, Le G.

29. Le G.

30. Diary, March 5, 1890.

31. Diary, February 4, 1890.

32. Diary, February 9, 1890.

33. Recounted in Diary entry for February 9, 1890. Also see an A.L.S. to Lane, February 7, 1890 (U.C.L.A.), in which Le Gallienne expressed pleasure on hearing of Whiteford's verdict, "for I value his opinion much." Then he continued, "you may rely that I will give any suggestions he has been good enough to make the most thoughtful consideration."

34. A.L.S. from Le Gallienne to Lane, dated February 18, 1890, Le G.

35. *Ibid.*

36. *Ibid.*

37. *Ibid.*

38. *Young Lives* (Bristol: Arrowsmith, 1898), pp. 231–232.

39. Robb also printed another Bodley Head book, Le Gallienne and Robinson K. Leather's *The Student and The Body-Snatcher,* in the autumn of 1890 while printing the *Meredith.*

40. Diary, March 5, 1890.

41. *Ibid.*

42. Lane had made arrangements with William Morton Fullerton to publish as an appendix to the *Meredith* his "Some Notes on George Meredith in America."

43. Le G.

44. A.L.S., dated March 24, 1890, U.C.L.A.

45. *Ibid.*

46. Herbert P. Horne, whose poems *Diversi Colores* were published by the Bodley Head, was a prominent man of letters and a central figure of the Century Guild along with Arthur Mackmurdo and Selwyn Image.

47. A.L.S., dated March 24, 1890, U.C.L.A.

48. A.L.S. to Lane, dated December 22, 1889, Le G.

49. A.L.S. to Lane, dated March 24, 1890, U.C.L.A.

50. Le G.

51. *Taste and Technique* (New York: Bowker, 1948), p. 14.

52. *Ibid.*

53. A.L.S. to Lane, dated February 18, 1890, Le G. Swinburne's letter to Lane was brief: "I never wrote anything about any of Mr. George Meredith's works except the letter of 28 years since to the 'Spectator' newspaper which you mention." A.L.S., dated February 15, 1890, Berg.

54. Berg. Reprinted in *The Collected Letters of George Meredith*, ed. C. L. Cline (Oxford: Oxford University Press, Clarendon Press, 1970), II, 956–957.

55. A.L.S. to Lane, dated March 24, [1890], Berg.

56. Diary.

57. Diary, September 26, 1890.

58. Diary, September 30, 1890.

59. Diary.

60. Diary, October 21, 1890.

61. A.L.S. to Mathews, dated September 26, 1890, U.C.L.A.

62. A.L.S. to Lane, dated October 6, 1890, U.C.L.A.

63. *Ibid.*

64. LIII, no. 1271 (September 1, 1890), 1090.

65. *Ibid.*, 1062.

66. A.L.S. to Lane, dated October 26, 1890, Le G.

67. Le G.

68. Reported in Le G., A.L.S. to Lane, dated October 28, 1890.

69. *Ibid.*

70. *Ibid.*

71. A.L.S. to Lane, dated October 30, 1890, Le G.

72. *Ibid.*

73. A.L.S. to Lane, Le G.

74. A.L.S. to Lane, dated October 29, 1890, Le G.

75. *Ibid.*

76. *Ibid.*

77. Le G.

78. A.L.S. to Lane, dated October 30, 1890, Le G.

79. Stationers' Registry Books, Public Record Office. *Quest of the Golden Boy*, p. 124.

80. A.L.S., dated October 22, 1890, Le G. Ye Sette of Odde Volumes was a literary club to which Lane belonged.

81. *Ibid.*

82. *Quest of the Golden Boy*, p. 124.

83. Le Gallienne's A.L.S. to Hales, dated November 24, 1890, Hales.

84. Advertisements in back of *George Meredith* (1890).

85. *Ibid.* (publ. November 27, 1890).

86. *Ibid.*

87. A.L.S., dated December 5, 1890, Le G.

88. Le G. In an A.L.S. to Lane, December 12, 1890, Le Gallienne wrote: "I am surprised Symons wrote the *P.M.G.* We must have mistaken him somewhat." If this is true, Symons wrote two reviews of the *Meredith.* One signed by him appeared in the *Academy,* January 24, 1891.

89. Advertisements in back of *George Meredith.*

90. *Ibid.*

91. A.L.S., dated December 8, 1890, Le G.

92. Advertisements in back of *George Meredith.*

93. A.L.S., dated December 12, 1890, Le G.

94. A.L.S. to Lane, dated December 4, 1890, Le G.

95. *The Letters of Oscar Wilde,* ed. Rupert Hart-Davis (New York:Harcourt, Brace & World, 1962), p. 277.

96. LIII, no. 1277 (December 1, 1890), 1555.

97. A.L.S., dated December 4, 1890, Le G.

98. A.L.S. to Lane, Le G.

99. Le G.

100. In *George Meredith: Some Characteristics* (London: Elkin Mathews, 1890), p. [v].

101. Le G.

102. Much the same information was conveyed to Lane: A.L.S., dated January 21, 1891, Le G.

103. A.L.S., dated January 27, 1891, Le G.

104. A.L.S. to Lane, dated October 28, 1890, Le G.

105. I quote from an anonymous biographical monograph entitled *Lord De Tabley* found in the British Museum, p. 13.

106. *Ibid.*

107. Lane urged him to allow the Bodley Head to reprint the *Guide* once the remainders were all sold, but De Tabley refused. See A.L.S. from De Tabley to Lane, dated May 20, 1893, Berg.

108. *Lord De Tabley,* p. 13.

109. Gordon Pitts, "The Poetry of John Byrne Leicester Warren, Lord De Tabley," Ph.D. Dissertation (University of Pennsylvania, 1956), p. 7.

110. *The Romantic '90s* (Garden City, N.Y.: Doubleday, Page, 1925), p. 174.

111. *Lord De Tabley,* p. 3.

112. The fullest study of De Tabley's classical plays, *Philoctetes* and *Orestes,* is Gardner B. Taplin, "The Life, Work, and Literary Reputation of John Byrne Leicester Warren, Lord De Tabley," Ph.D. Dissertation (Harvard University, 1941).

113. See Pitts, p. 36. De Tabley's poems appear in Alfred H. Miles, ed., *The Poets and the Poetry of the Century, William Morris to Robert Buchanan* (London: Hutchinson, 2nd ed. 1896), pp. 183–218.

114. "Lord De Tabley," *Athenaeum,* no. 3553 (November 30, 1895), p. 755.

115. *Lord De Tabley,* p. 16.

116. *Romantic '90s,* p. 177.

117. *Ibid.,* pp. 177–178.

118. *Ibid.,* p. 179.

119. "Lord De Tabley," p. 755.

120. Quoted in *Romantic '90s,* p. 178.

121. *Ibid.,* p. 179.

122. A.L.S., dated August 15, 1892, Bodleian.

123. A.L.S. from De Tabaley to Lane, dated September 10, 1892, Bodleian.

124. *Ibid.*

125. *Ibid.*

126. *Ibid.*

127. A.L.S., dated October 4, 1892, Bodleian.

128. *Ibid.*

129. *Ibid.*

130. A.L.S., dated October 6, 1892, Bodleian.

131. *Ibid.* In his letter to Lane of October 16 (Bodleian), De Tabley was still quite concerned about the relation of text to page. "I am quite ready to adopt with your concurrence, a page of this size [Grimm's *Household Tales* of 1882, illustrated by Walter Crane] for the reprint. My only doubt being whether I shall not have to print say 20% more copy to each page than I did in 'Rehearsals'."

132. A.L.S., dated October 7, 1892, Bodleian.

133. T. and A. Constable. Letter Book (#21), entry for October 21, 1892.

134. *Ibid.,* entry for November 7, 1892.

135. *Ibid.*

136. See A.L.S. from De Tabley to Lane dated October 16, 1892, Bodleian.

137. See Letter Book (#21), A.L.S. from Blaikie to Elkin Mathews and John Lane, dated November 7, 1892, Constable.

138. *Ibid.*

139. Constable. Letter Book (#21), p. 286.

140. A.L.S. to Lane, dated October 8, 1892, Bodleian. De Tabley's *Rehearsals* bore the subtitle, "A Book of Verses."

141. *Ibid.*

142. A.L.S. from De Tabley to Lane, dated October 24, 1892, Bodleian.

143. A.L.S. to Lane, dated October 31, 1892, Bodleian.

144. *Ibid.*

145. Bodleian.

146. Bodleian.

147. At least one advertisement mentioned a cover of "Petals" only.

148. A.L.S., dated November 3, 1892, Bodleian.

149. In a letter to Mathews, December 22, 1892, Bodleian, De Tabley suggests the stoppage was caused by the printers' running "out of some of their capital letters; and I suppose till they break up some old type, they will not get a fresh supply." Later in the letter De Tabley reported that Constables "wasted fully a

week, saying they wanted your authority to print some fifteen necessary pages. But I expect their type was run out rather than they seriously thought I should send them to print something unauthorized."

150. Quoted in *Lord De Tabley*, pp. 15–16.

151. A.L.S., dated December 31, 1892, Berg.

152. A.L.S., De Tabley to Lane, dated January 1, 1893, Berg.

153. A.L.S. from Mathews to De Tabley, dated June 7, 1893, B.H.F.

154. A.L.S., De Tabley to Lane, dated January 1, 1893, Berg.

155. *Ibid.*

156. *Ibid.*

157. Bodleian.

158. Berg.

159. Bodleian.

160. A.L.S., De Tabley to Mathews, dated January 3, 1893, E.M.

161. A.L.S., De Tabley to Lane, dated January 4, 1893, Berg.

162. *Ibid.*

163. Constable. Letter Book (#21).

164. De Tabley's letters (Berg) to the Bodley Head on January 7, 15, 23, 1893, all indicate that the plates were still tied up at Dawsons.

165. Constable. Letter Book (#21).

166. Constable. Day Book (#20), p. 309.

167. Constable. Letter Book (#21), entry for January 18, 1893, indicates that on December 17, 1892, Mathews and Lane ordered that 750 ordinary and 100 Japanese vellum copies of *Poems* be printed. Then on January 15, 1893, they ordered 800 ordinary and 110 Japanese vellum copies. On January 18, 1893, the Letter Book entry read, "have printed according to first order."

168. A.L.S., dated October 24, 1892, Bodleian.

169. A.L.S. from De Tabley to Lane, dated February 3, 1893, Berg.

170. A.L.S. from De Tabley to Lane, dated February 25, 1893, Berg.

171. See A.L.S. from De Tabley to Lane, dated March 29, 1893, Berg.

172. *Ibid.*

173. Quoted in *Lord De Tabley*, p. 16.

174. A.L.S., dated March 29, 1893, Berg.

175. A.L.S., dated April 14, 1893, Berg.

176. *Ibid.*

177. *Athenaeum,* no. 3417 (April 22, 1893), p. 498.

178. *Ibid.*

179. A.L.S., dated April 21, 1893, Berg.

180. *Saturday Review,* LXXV (May 13, 1893), 522.

181. A.L.S. from De Tabley to Lane, dated May 14, 1893, Berg.

182. *Spectator,* LXX (June 10, 1893), 776.

183. *Nineteenth Century,* XXXIII (May 1893), 899–904. Reprinted in Le Gallienne's *Retrospective Reviews* (London: John Lane; New York: Dodd, Mead, 1896), I, 263–271.

184. Day Book (# 20, p. 426), May 1893, Constable. The total cost for printing and paper was £22.2.11.

185. Copy of a letter on Bodley Head stationery from Elkin Mathews to De Tabley, dated June 7, 1893, B.H.F.

186. *Ibid.*

187. A.L.S. from De Tabley to Lane, Berg.

5. The Bodley Head Poets: The Books of the Rhymers' Club

1. Although LeGallienne made several attempts at writing decadent verse — see, for instance, "A Ballad of London" — his attitude toward the Decadents is expressed best in his poem, "To the Reader," in *English Poems,* in which he likens decadent art to "a lazar-house of leprous men."

2. From Wilde to Lane concerning the French edition of *Salomé, The Letters of Oscar Wilde,* ed. Rupert Hart-Davis (New York: Harcourt, Brace & World, 1962), p. 327.

3. Lane's reputation for being attentive to literature considered objectionable to others is attested to by a letter written to him by Laurence Housman: "The story [by his sister Clemence] is a modern problem in an old dress. The one or two publishers who have seen it seem scandalised at her solution of it. I don't think you will be, and therefore offer it you." A.L.S., dated January 9, 1894, Huntington.

4. Reported in Kathryn Mix, *A Study in Yellow* (Lawrence, Kans.: University of Kansas Press, 1960), p. 149.

5. In the early nineties, Lane seems to have been a leading member of this group which Walter Crane, in *An Artist's Reminiscences,* 2nd ed. (London: Methuen, 1907), p. 310, described as "a dining club, with a literary and artistic flavour, which used to meet about once a month. Like many societies, it began, as I remember Mr. Quaritch saying, in a very small way; but when I was a guest, the company was a large one, and the dinner long and elaborate. The *pièce de résistance,* however (outside the menu), was a paper by one of the members, followed by a discussion. The chairman or president for the year was called 'His Oddship,' and before calling on the paper reader, it was the odd custom for each 'brother' to introduce his guests — describing them and their achievements, hitting off their peculiarities over their heads, in a brief speech."

6. John M. Munro, in his "Introduction" to *English Poetry in Transition, 1880–1920* (New York: Pegasus, 1968), p. 24, points out that although the Decadents are usually associated with the Rhymers' Club and the Counter-Decadents with Henley, who gathered his group about him at Solferino's Restaurant, "they were far from mutually exclusive groups. W. B. Yeats, for example, appears to have felt no inconsistency in being associated with both camps simultaneously." Munro suggests that the unifying principle was the poets' "determination to discover new modes of poetic expression," p. 26.

7. *Savoy*, no. 1 (January 1896), p. [5].

8. *Studies in Two Literatures* (London: Smithers 1897), pp. [vi]–vii.

9. "The School of Giorgione," *The Renaissance* (London: Macmillan, 1910), p. 135.

10. Again Pater seems to have pointed the way. For instance, in his essay on Dante Gabriel Rossetti, first published in 1883, Pater was attentive to the qualities and characteristics of Rossetti's work which set him apart as a new poetic voice. "At a time when poetic originality in England might seem to have had its utmost play," he observed, "here was certainly one new poet more, with a structure and music of verse, a vocabulary, an accent, unmistakably novel, yet felt to be no mere tricks of manner adopted with a view to forcing attention. . . ." *Appreciations*, 3rd ed. (London and New York: Macmillan, 1901), p. 206.

11. "The Decadent Movement in Literature," *Harper's New Monthly Magazine*, LXXXVII (November 1893), 858–867.

12. *Ibid.*

13. "Modernity in Verse," *Studies in Two Literatures*, p. 190.

14. Both the curious interrelation of the arts and the mutual respect among artists of very different views and modes is suggested by the Beardsley posters which were seen about London in 1894 advertising Todhunter's *A Comedy of Sighs*. See "A Comedy of Sighs," *Sketch*, V (March 28, 1894), 444.

15. *The Autobiography of William Butler Yeats* (New York: Macmillan, 1953), p. 101.

16. *Ibid.*, p. 102.

17. *Prose Fancies* (London: Mathews and Lane; New York: Putnam's Sons, 1894), pp. 119–125.

18. A.L.S., December 8, 1891, E.M.

19. Le G.

20. A.L.S. from Le Gallienne to Lane, dated August 20, 1893, Le G.

21. A.L.S., March 20, 1893, E.M.

22. Quoted in Richard Whittington-Egan and Geoffrey Smerdon, *The Quest of the Golden Boy* (Barre, Mass.: Barre Publishing, 1962), p. 174.

23. "The Rhymers' Club," *Letters to the New Island*, ed. Horace Reynolds (Cambridge, Mass.: Harvard University Press, 1934), p. 143. Yeats, of course, ignores the fact that *The Book of the Rhymers' Club* included T. W. Rolleston's "A Ballade of the 'Cheshire Cheese' " and G. A. Greene's "The Song of the Songsmiths," both of which upheld the Parnassian ideals of craft and form.

24. See Chapter 6, pp. 185–187.

25. *New Island*, p. 144.

26. *Ibid.*, p. 145.

27. *Ibid.*, p. 146.

28. Desmond Flower and Henry Maas, for instance, suggest in *The Letters of Ernest Dowson* (London: Cassell, 1967), p. 181 n. 2, that a meeting of the club on Saturday, January 3, 1891, at H. P. Horne's (referred to by Dowson in a letter of Friday, January 2, 1891), "was probably the first meeting."

29. *The Path Through the Wood* (New York: Dial Press, 1931), p. 169.

30. "New Dates for the Rhymers' Club," *English Literature in Transition*, XIII, no. 1 (1970), pp. 37–38.

31. *Ibid.*, p. 38.

32. *Autobiography of Yeats*, p. 101. Also see Rhys's account in *Everyman Remembers* (New York: Cosmopolitan Books, 1931), pp. 220–229. Some scholars include Yeats's friend T. W. Rolleston among the founders. See Allan Wade, ed., *The Letters of William Butler Yeats* (London: Rupert Hart-Davis, 1954), p. 181 n. 1. Flower and Maas, *Letters of Dowson*, p. 181 n. 2, assert that the club began "as a gathering of Irishmen living in London" and was "reorganized on a broader basis." Edgar Jepson in his *Memories of a Victorian* (London: Gollancz, 1933), p. 237, says of the Rhymers: "They were all very Celtic, for it was the days of the Celtic Fringe." That the club was made up of a nucleus of Irishmen and grew out of their earlier gatherings is also suggested by the fact that Yeats, Rolleston and Todhunter had been involved with Æ's Dublin Lodge of the Theosophical Society founded in 1886 and had contributed to *Poems and Ballads of Young Ireland* (1888). Moreover, Rolleston, Greene, and A. C. Hillier were classmates at Trinity College, Dublin, in the 1870s, when Wilde was a student there.

33. A.L.S., C.U.L.

34. A.L.S. to Stedman, dated July 9, 1890, C.U.L.

35. *Ibid.*

36. *Ibid.* In *The Book of the Rhymers' Club* version, Rhys changed "rhymesters" to "Rhymers" and altered the first and second lines thus: "With wine and blood and reckless harlotry/ He sped the heroic flame of English verse."

37. *Ibid.*

38. *Ibid.*

39. Andrew Lang, in his review of *The Book of the Rhymers' Club*, *Daily News* (February 20, 1892), p. 5, in referring to these latter lines, quipped: "Perhaps these are questions for the zoologist."

40. Yeats once described Todhunter's Bedford Park home as "charming" with "a Morris carpet on the drawingroom floor," and "upon the walls early pictures by my father painted under the influence of Rossetti." "Preface," *New Islands*, pp. viii–ix.

41. *Naphtali* (New York: Dodd, Mead, 1926), pp. 96–97.

42. A.L.S. from Johnson to Campbell Dodgson, February 5, 1891, British Museum Add. MS. 46363. This is probably the gathering Victor Plarr describes in *Ernest Dowson* (London: Elkin Mathews, 1914), pp. 63–64, as "an evening of notabilities."

43. Although there was a secretary, G. A. Greene, arrangements, at least early on, seem to have been made haphazardly. For instance, in a letter to Victor Plarr in *Letters of Dowson*, p. 234, dated May 19, 1892, Dowson wrote: "it seems agreed that the Rhymers should meet au Cheshire, on Friday, but nobody has arranged to send out the notices. Will you, or Johnson do this, as we have not the list of addresses?"

44. A.L.S., postmarked January 19, 1891, in Dugdale Collection.

45. John Gray, the author of *Silverpoints,* whose aesthetic pose and friendship with Wilde led to his nickname "Dorian'" and to the erroneous belief that he was the original of Wilde's hero.

46. According to Flower and Maas, *Letters of Dowson,* p. 183 n. 6, the name was that of Dickens' Mr. Mantalini. Whistler had once said to Wilde: "Never let me see you . . . in the combined costume of Kossuth and Mr. Mantalini."

47. A.L.S. to Arthur Moore, [February 2, 1891], *Letters of Dowson,* pp. 182–183.

48. A.L.S., British Museum Add. MS. 46363.

49. A.L.S. quoted in Rhys's *Letters from Limbo* (London: Dent, 1936), p. 97.

50. A.L.S. from Yeats to John O'Leary, [?November 1891] *Letters of Yeats,* p. 181.

51. *Memories of a Victorian,* pp. 235–236.

52. *Autobiography of Yeats,* p. 191.

53. *Ibid.,* p. 180.

54. *Ibid.,* pp. 180–181.

55. *Letters of Dowson,* pp. 124–125.

56. A.L.S., [in week ending June 27, 1891], *Letters of Yeats,* p. 170.

57. *Letters of Dowson,* p. 202.

58. Ghose (1869–1924), a student at Christ Church, Oxford, in the late 1880s, along with Stephen Phillips, Arthur Cripps, and Laurence Binyon, published in 1890 a volume of verse, *Primavera.* In 1894 he returned to India, where he later became a professor at Presidency College, Calcutta.

59. *Letters of Dowson,* pp. 202–203.

60. *Ibid.,* p. 203.

61. *Ibid.*

62. Quoted in *Letters of Dowson,* p. 125.

63. Mathews and his sisters lived at no. 1 Blenheim Road and Yeats and his family at no. 3.

64. E.M.

65. Quoted in *Letters of Dowson,* p. 125. Among the stipulations Mathews imposed was that none of the poems included in the volume be published elsewhere till after March 1892. Yeats mentions the negotiations in a letter to O'Leary [?November 25, 1891], *Letters of Yeats,* p. 185.

66. *Ibid.,* p. 187.

67. Lionel Johnson in a letter to Campbell Dodgson, *c.* December 16–19, 1891, wrote: "Before Christmas will be published a small book called 'The Book of the Rhymers' Club,' by twelve minor poets." British Museum Add. MS. 46363.

68. Unidentified cutting entitled "The Rhymers' Club," E.M.

69. In a letter to Plarr, written about February 14, 1892, Dowson spoke of the book as "very good — better than I expected, on the whole, although the binding leaves much to be desired." *Letters of Dowson,* p. 225.

70. *Black and White*, III (1892), 72.

71. *Letters of Dowson*, p. 227.

72. A.L.S. written about February 23, 1892, *Letters of Dowson*, p. 274.

73. A.L.S. to Arthur Moore, *Letters of Dowson*, p. 227.

74. "Poetry's Chances," *Daily News* (February 22, 1892), p. 5. For other comments by reviewers see Karl E. Beckson, "The Rhymers' Club," Ph.D. Dissertation (Columbia University, 1959), p. 64.

75. A.L.S. to J. B. Yeats, July 21, [1906], *Letters of Yeats*, p. 474.

76. "Poetry's Chances," p. 5.

77. "The Book of the Rhymers' Club," *Church Reformer*, XI (March 1892), 65. The reviews which appeared in the *Daily Chronicle*, February 26, 1892, p. 3, and the *Star*, February 11, 1892, p. 2, may both have been written by Le Gallienne.

78. Unidentified cutting in E.M.

79. *Letters of Yeats*, p. 181 n. 1.

80. According to Flower and Maas, *Letters of Dowson*, p. 125, "Gale promised to send his quota [of verses], and as earnest of his serious interest sent in four lighthearted pastiche verses beginning: One more unfortunate/ Volume ungodly/ Rashly importunate/ Gone to the Bodley."

81. See Roberts' "The Rhymers' Club," *John O'London's Weekly*, XXIX (September 30, 1933), 901–903.

82. See Plarr's list of permanent guests in *Ernest Dowson*, p. 133.

83. *Letters of Dowson*, p. 286.

84. A.L.S., *c.* August 20, 1893, *Letters of Dowson*, p. 287.

85. "The Rhymers' Club," p. 67.

86. See, for instance, *Athenaeum*, no. 3487 (August 25, 1894), p. 252; *National Observer*, XII (July 21, 1894), 257.

87. *Letters of Yeats*, p. 232.

88. Edmund Gosse in "A Plea for Certain Exotic Forms of Verse," *Cornhill Magazine*, XXXVI (July 1877), p. 54, wrote: "The worship of Milton by Keats, of Milton through Keats, pushed to an extravagant excess, set the Spasmodic School in motion; blustering blank verse, studded with unconnected beauties of fanciful phrase, formed the instrument for these brilliant discords."

89. "The School of Giorgione," *Renaissance*, p. 137. Also recall Poe's "I hold that a long poem does not exist." ("The Poetic Principle").

90. *Autobiography of Yeats*, p. 95. Yeats wrote: "In London I saw nothing good."

91. "Preface," *New Island*, p. xii.

92. *Ibid.*

93. *Autobiography of Yeats*, p. 92.

94. *Ibid.*

95. *Ibid.*, p. 93.

96. *New Island*, esp. pp. 177–178.

97. *Ibid.*, p. 177.

98. "Father Gilligan," *Book of the Rhymers' Club*, p. 38.

99. "The Lake Isle of Innisfree" first appeared in *The Book of the Rhymers' Club*. Yeats in the *Autobiography,* p. 94, tells of the poem's genesis: "I had still the ambition, formed in Sligo in my teens, of living in imitation of Thoreau on Innisfree, in a little island in Lough Gill, and when walking through Fleet Street very homesick I heard a little tinkle of water and saw a fountain in a shop-window which balanced a little ball upon its jet, and began to remember lake water. From the sudden remembrance came my poem *Innisfree,* my first lyric with anything in its rhythm of my own music."

100. In a letter to Katharine Tynan, quoted in Richard Ellmann, *Yeats, The Man and the Masks* (New York: Macmillan, 1948), p. 77, Yeats wrote: "The real fact of the matter is that the other things at present for many reasons make me anxious and I bury my head in books as the ostrich does in the sand. . . . On the rare occasions when I go to see anyone I am not quite easy in my mind, for I keep thinking I ought to be at home trying to solve my problems."

101. Arthur Symons in "A Literary Causerie: On a Book of Verses," *Savoy,* no. 4 (August 1896), p. 92, wrote of Dowson: "Always, perhaps a little consciously, but at least always sincerely, in search of new sensations, my friend found what was for him the supreme sensation in a very passionate and tender adoration of the most escaping of all ideals, the ideal of youth."

102. *Ibid.,* pp. 92, 93.

103. See *Memories of a Victorian,* p. 246; also Mark Longaker, "Introduction," *Poems of Ernest Dowson* (Philadelphia: University of Pennsylvania Press, 1962), pp. 19–20.

104. Printed as sonnet IV in the sonnet sequence, "Of a Little Girl," in *The Poetical Works of Ernest Christopher Dowson,* ed. Desmond Flower (London: Cassell, 1934), pp. 124–131.

105. According to Longaker, Dowson met Adelaide "in her father's restaurant, 19 Sherwood Street, Soho, a cheap but entirely respectable eating place which he and his friends called 'Poland'." *Poems of Dowson,* p. 186.

106. *Memories of a Victorian,* p. 112.

107. *Poems of Dowson,* p. 204.

108. "Leonardo," *Renaissance,* p. 124.

109. "Literary Causerie," p. 92.

110. In a letter to Plarr, written some time in the fall of 1894, Dowson wrote: "What a terrible, lamentable thing growth is! It 'makes me mad' to think that in a year or two at the most, the most perfect exquisite relation I ever succeeded in making must naturally end." Quoted in *Poems of Dowson,* p. 204.

111. Cf. Brooks and Warren's loaded questions concerning "Cynara" in *Understanding Poetry,* 3rd ed. (New York: Holt, Rinehart & Winston, 1960), p. 256.

112. See the letter to Arthur Moore [February 7, 1891], in which Dowson enclosed the just finished "Cynara" and spoke of the poem as "an experiment." *Letters of Dowson,* p. 184.

113. *Ibid.*, p. 128.

114. *Ibid.*, pp. 127–128.

115. *Ibid.*, p. 128. Dowson was received into the Catholic church on September 25, 1891.

116. Granville Hicks, in *Figures of Transition* (New York: Macmillan, 1939), p. 258, writes that both the church and the Decadents distrusted contemporary society. "For especially in England, where its position was always difficult, the church stood apart from the progress of capitalism. Not only was it the one organization that could look back to a pre-capitalist past; not only did it set its values against the values of a competitive world; it was relatively unpolluted by the vulgarity that had overcome the representative churches of the British middle class."

117. See *Autobiography of Yeats*, p. 183.

118. *Ibid.*, pp. 186–187. Also see Le Gallienne's account of his first meeting with Johnson, *The Romantic '90s* (Garden City, N.Y.: Doubleday, Page, 1925), pp. 187–188.

119. *Autobiography of Yeats*, p. 183.

120. *Ibid.*, p. 182.

121. Cf. Andrew Marvell's poem on Charles I.

122. In "The King's Tragedy," Rosetti concludes his poem with the words of Catherine, the narrator: "And 'O James!' she said, — 'My James!'/ she said, — / 'Alas for the woful thing,/ That a poet true and a friend of man,/ In desperate days of bale and ban,/ Should needs be born a King!' "

123. Cf. also Tennyson's "Ulysses" and his idea in *In Memoriam* that life after death is an "Eternal process moving on,/ From state to state the spirit walks" (lxxxii).

124. *Autobiography of Yeats*, p. 135.

6. The Bodley Head Poets: Poisonous Honey and English Blossoms

1. See his "Sonnet, with a copy of *Mademoiselle de Maupin*."

2. "Introduction," *Oxford Book of Modern Verse: 1895–1935* (New York: Oxford, 1937), p. ix. Also see *The Autobiography of William Butler Yeats* (New York: Macmillan, 1953), pp. 181–182.

3. See the Preface to *Mademoiselle de Maupin*.

4. "Introduction," p. ix.

5. "The Rhymers' Club," *Letters to the New Island*, ed. Horace Reynolds (Cambridge, Mass.: Harvard University Press, 1934), p. 144.

6. For a more thorough discussion of the influence of the French *Parnassiens* on English literature, see James K. Robinson, "A Neglected Phase of the Aesthetic Movement: English Parnassianism," *PMLA*, LXVIII (1953), 733–754, and Enid Starkie, *From Gautier to Eliot* (London: Hutchinson, 1962), pp. 36–38.

7. *Cornhill Magazine*, XXXVI (July 1877), pp. 53–71.

8. In a section entitled "Translations from Contemporary French Poets," the volume also contains O'Shaughnessy's translations of Francois Coppée. Verlaine, Sully Prudhomme, and Catulle Mendès, among others.

9. "English Parnassianism," p. 739.

10. *The Critic's Alchemy* (New York: Twayne, 1953), Part III, "Arthur Symons," esp. pp. 122–125.

11. Enid Starkie in *Gautier to Eliot*, p. 107, also finds the influence of Baudelaire in Symons' first volume of poetry, *Days and Nights*. Of course, Symons had come "under the spell" of Villiers de l'Isle Adam in 1888 and at Wilde's request published an article on him — the first in England — in the *Woman's World* in 1889.

12. Quoted from *Mes Souvenirs* (Eure, France: Hours Press, n.d.), p. 6.

13. Quoted in Roger Lhombreaud, *Arthur Symons* (London: Unicorn Press, 1963), pp. 72–73.

14. *Ibid.*, p. 73.

15. *The Renaissance* (London: Macmillan, 1910), p. 109.

16. *Ibid.*, p. x.

17. Lhombreaud, p. 75. Also compare "Les Silhouettes," the first of Oscar Wilde's "Impressions."

18. *Renaissance*, p. 111.

19. "Quest" was the only poem Symons added to the second edition of *Silhouettes*.

20. In *Song of a Worker* O'Shaughnessy included his translation of Verlaine's "Pastel."

21. Preface to second edition of *Silhouettes*.

22. *Renaissance*, p. 124.

23. "Emmy" and "Emmy at the Eldorado."

24. See Robert L. Peters, "Whistler and the English Poets of the 1890's," *MLQ*, XVIII (1957), 254.

25. *Renaissance*, p. 106.

26. *Ibid.*, p. 99.

27. "The Rhymers' Club," *New Island*, p. 144.

28. *Renaissance*, p. 135.

29. See his *Romantic Image* (London: Routledge and Kegan Paul, 1957), esp. Chapter Three: "The Image."

30. I quote here from the stanza as it was later revised.

31. Sonnet "Composed upon Westminster Bridge, September 3, 1802."

32. *Victorian Studies*, XI (Summer 1968), 627–640.

33. "An Unacknowledged Movement in Fine Printing, The Typography of the Eighteen-Nineties," *Fleuron*, VII (1930), 85.

34. Preface, *Silhouettes* (2nd ed.). Compare with this passage, Symons' statement in "Modernity in Verse," *Studies in Two Literatures* (London: Smithers, 1897), p. 188, in which he praises Henley's "sense of the poetry of cities, that rarer than pastoral poetry, the romance of what lies beneath our eyes, in the humanity of streets, if we have but the vision and the point of view."

35. "Modernity in Verse," p. 188.

36. *Ibid.*, pp. 188–189. This view is very close to Pater's contention in "Winckelmann," *Renaissance*, that modern art must contain the experience of the modern world.

37. *Ibid.*, p. 189.

38. See Peters, "Whistler and the English Poets," pp. 253–255.

39. "Arthur Symons, Poet: A Centenary Tribute," *Review of English Literature,* VI (1965), p. 72.

40. "Modernity in Verse," p. 188.

41. No. 4 (December 6, 1892). Douglas became editor with this issue.

42. No. 1928 (January 26, 1893), p. 8.

43. *Ibid.*

44. Unidentified cutting, E.M.

45. [William Archer?], "Three Poets of the Younger Generation," *London Quarterly Review*, LXXXI [N.S. XXI] (October 1893), 44.

46. *Ibid.*, p. 46.

47. *Ibid.*

48. For biographical facts, I rely on Brocard Sewell's article "John Gray and André Sebastian Raffalovich," in *Two Friends, John Gray & André Raffalovich,* ed. Father Brocard Sewell (Aylesford: St. Albert's Press, 1963), pp. 7–8.

49. *Ibid.*, p. 9.

50. *Ibid.*, p. 10.

51. *Ibid.*, p. 14.

52. In a letter of 1892 written to Victor Plarr and quoted in "Gray and Raffalovich," *Two Friends*, p. 9.

53. *Ibid.*

54. See Patricio Gannon, "John Gray the Prince of Dreams," *Two Friends*, p. 108.

55. British Museum Add. MS. 46363. Also see Victor Plarr, *Ernest Dowson* (London: Elkin Mathews, 1914), p. 60. In 1961 a first edition of Wilde's novel was sold in New York which contained a letter from Gray to Wilde which bore the complimentary close and signature of "Yours ever, Dorian." As Brocard Sewell, "Gray and Raffalovich," *Two Friends*, p. 10, suggests, "had the existence of this letter been known to the *Star* . . . the case might have been decided differently."

56. Wilde to the Editor of the *Daily Telegraph*, February 19, [1892], *The Letters of Oscar Wilde* (New York: Harcourt, Brace & World, 1962), p. 311.

57. Gannon, "John Gray," p. 112.

58. *Ibid.*, pp. 113–114, quoted from the column, "Mainly about People," *Star.* On May 2, 1892, Gray wrote to Lane "with a view to some arrangement for the publication of a verse translation I have made of Théodore de Banville's 'Le Baiser'. I should be glad to hear what you think of the possibility." A.L.S., Berg.

59. See Chapter Three, p. 95.

60. See A.L.S. from Gray to Lane, May 27, 1892, Berg.

61. See A.L.S. from Gray to Lane, June 18, [1892], Berg.

62. *Ibid.* In this same letter Gray wrote, "The publication [of *Silverpoints*] will not take place until the middle or end of September, I suppose."

63. John Gawsworth in "Two Poets 'J. G.'" in *Two Friends*, p. 167, tells of seeing in Foyle's bookshop window "an elegant French marble-board-bound *manuscript*" of *Silverpoints,* "written out for the author's immortal friend, Pierre Louÿs, with two suppressed poems, 'Song of the Stars' and 'Sound'," which he went in and bought for £5. Later Gawsworth printed the text of the poems in his *Known Signatures.* A complete MS. of *Silverpoints* in Gray's hand, which includes the poems "suppressed from the volume on the grounds of indecency" with the proofs of the green cloth casing designed by Ricketts, is in the Princeton University Library. See *Wilde and the Nineties, An Essay and an Exhibition,* ed. Charles Ryskamp (Princeton, N.J.: Princeton University Library, 1966), p. 44.

64. See "Silver-points by Mr. Charles Sainton, at the Burlington Gallery," *Studio,* II (November 15, 1893), 72–73.

65. Often called Pre-Raphaelite in style, Rimbaud's "Ophélie" describes Ophelia in the water. But according to Daniel A. de Graaf, *Arthur Rimbaud* (Assen Pays-Bas: Van Gorcum, 1960), pp. 20–21, Rimbaud had not seen Millais's picture when he wrote his poem.

66. See a letter from Pierre Louÿs to Gray [November 27, 1892], in which Louÿs shows concern for Gray's despair and contemplated suicide. Quoted in Roger Lhombreaud, "*Arcades Ambo,* The Poetical Friendship of John Gray and Pierre Louÿs," *Two Friends,* pp. 126–127.

67. See, for instance, Michael Field's *Sight and Song,* a volume of poems on pictures, published by Mathews and Lane in 1892.

68. Sauve is a town in southern France.

69. Baudelaire's essay, "Eloge du Maquillage," influenced the work of both Gray and Symons.

70. "Mishka" should probably be read with Gray's strange story, "The Great Worm," *Dial,* I (1889), 14–18, in which again there is a mixture of the human and animal as well as a suggested relationship between the poet and the worm. The garden worm, like Mishka, has dreamed that he was transformed. Too, there occur in the story such phrases as "honeyed words ever left his gentle lips," "the white child," and "her breasts were like mounds."

71. According to A. E. Carter, *The Idea of Decadence in French Literature* (Toronto: University of Toronto Press, 1958), pp. 107–108, Verlaine's "'Langueur" contains the essence of decadence.

72. This discussion of the imitations is based almost entirely on a paper written by my student Mrs. Mary D. Davis, who is a far better judge of translations from the French than I.

73. A. J. A. Symons, *Fleuron,* VII (1930), 106, 109.

74. See Evans' review in *Poetry of the Later Nineteenth Century,* 2nd ed. (London: Methuen, 1966), pp. 392–400.

75. *Ibid.,* pp. 399–400.

76. Enid Starkie, *Baudelaire* (London: Faber and Faber, 1957), pp. 266–267.

Also cf. Baudelaire's "Les Chats," esp. the lines: "Ils prennent en songeant les nobles attitudes/ Des grands sphinx allongés au fond des solitudes."

77. Evans, p. 400.

78. October 22, 1890, *Letters of Wilde*, p. 276.

79. "Among the Brotherhood of Bards," *Graphic*, XLVII (April 8, 1893), 383. *Pall Mall Gazette*, LVI (May 4, 1893), 3, labeled Gray "Le Plus Decadent des Decadents" in its headline to the review.

80. A.L.S., July 1892, Le G. Wratislaw (1871–1933), was a lineal descendant of a count of Bohemia and a count of the Holy Roman Empire. He was a friend of the Bodley Head poets Arthur Symons and Norman Gale. His first collection of verse, *Love's Memorial*, is, according to Miss Starkie in *From Gautier to Eliot*, p. 109, "only a parody of Baudelaire, but his *Caprices*, published in 1895, is of a higher quality. It borrows its title from Verlaine, and he is the chief influence on poems such as *A Moment, Silhouettes*, and *On the Embankment*." Wratislaw submitted the manuscript of *Caprices* to Lane, but it was not accepted because of a severely critical reader's report, probably written by Le Gallienne. A volume of *Caprices* listed in the Dulau Catalogue of Lane's library contains a two-page letter from Wratislaw to Lane complaining about the report.

81. *Retrospective Reviews* (London: John Lane; New York: Dodd, Mead, 1896), I, 24–25.

82. The events of Mesurier's first visit to London are a composite of two separate visits to the city: the one Le Gallienne made shortly after his *My Ladies' Sonnets* was published in August 1887, when he sought out the editor of the *Academy* in hopes of getting literary work, and the visit made in early June 1888, when he met Lane and probably Mathews for the first time at an evening at Dr. Pritchard's at 37 Southwick Street. See Chapter 1, p. 15.

83. *Young Lives* (Bristol: Arrowsmith, 1898), p. 308.

84. *Ibid.*, p. 309.

85. *Ibid.*, pp. 309–311.

86. *Ibid.*, pp. 311–312.

87. *Ibid.*, pp. 314–316.

88. Quoted in Richard Whittington-Egan and G. Smerdon, *The Quest of the Golden Boy* (Barre, Mass.: Barre Publishing, 1962), p. 192. Further evidence of Lane's approbation of Le Gallienne's poetic efforts is found in a letter of July 27, 1892 (Le G.), in which Le Gallienne, referring to what Lane had said in a recent letter, wrote: "I am glad to know you care abt. my verses, as I had a sort of idea that your private opinion of them — well, did not quite come up to your public opinion."

89. Under the pseudonyn of Corno di Bassetto, Shaw wrote at length on *English Poems* in the *Star* a review which is quoted in full in *Quest of the Golden Boy*, pp. 199–201.

90. Le Gallienne had followed the career of his friend William Watson with a good deal of interest since the two had been budding young poets in the Liverpool of the 1880s who shared the encouragement of James Ashcroft Noble, a local

arbiter of literary taste, and Edward Dowden of Dublin University. Although maintaining a semblance of brotherly friendship, they were in fact rivals, always anxious to best the other. While their poetic tastes were similar, as critics they differed sharply — Le Gallienne warmly embracing Pater's appreciative approach in criticism, Watson stoutly preserving the stern approach of Dr. Johnson and Macaulay.

91. Alfred Austin, *English Lyrics*, 4th ed. (London and New York: Macmillan, 1896), p. xxiv. Watson, who received ten guineas for the Preface (see Macmillan Receipt Book, entry for July 8, 1890), evidently was far more outspoken and severe in his draft submitted to Macmillan, for on July 1, 1890, he wrote the publisher, Frederick Macmillan, that he was "much gratified by your kind expression of approval of my work, barring the obnoxious passages indicated." See Macmillan Letter Books.

92. See his letter to Katharine Tynan in Ezra Pound's *Literary Essays* (London: Faber & Faber, 1954), p. 365.

93. Karl Beckson, *Aesthetes and Decadents* (New York: Vintage, 1966), p. 135.

94. See, for instance, the chapter entitled "The Minor Poet" in Holbrook Jackson, *The Eighteen Nineties* (New York: Mitchell Kennerley, 1914). In a draft of an essay which he wrote at the time of his removal from Vigo Street to Cork Street (E.M.), Mathews spoke of "the remarkable poetical renascence of the early nineties," which he had helped to create.

7. The Bodley Head Authors: A Gathering of Playwrights, Essayists, and Fictionists

1. See his gathering of these essays, *Northern Studies* (London: W. Scott, 1890).

2. Chapter XV, "The Higher Drama," *The Eighteen Nineties* (New York: Mitchell Kennerley, 1914).

3. P.U.L.

4. "Some Literary Idolatries," *Excursions in Criticism* (London: Elkin Mathews and John Lane; New York: Macmillan, 1893), p. 2. John Addington Symonds, who began to contribute articles on the Elizabethan dramatists in the sixties, found them appealing because, as one of his biographers suggests, "in the conventional mode of the day they seemed vital creatures, men who were able to express themselves freely, unhampered by Victorian taboos." Phyllis Grosskurth, *The Woeful Victorian, A Biography of John Addington Symonds* (New York: Holt, Rinehart and Winston, 1965), pp. 101–102.

5. *Alma Murray, Portrait as Beatrice Cenci* (London: Elkin Mathews, 1891), p. 5.

6. The British Museum contains a number of these pamphlets, which evidently were published with the imprints of various publishers (see vol. no. 011795.h67.19). Most of them were handled by Reeves and Turner, publishers for Miss Murray and her husband, Alfred Forman (brother of Buxton Forman). A page of advertisements at the back of the Bodley Head pamphlet, *Alma Murray,*

Portrait as Beatrice Cenci, lists seven separate pamphlets obtainable from the Bodley Head.

7. "Ibsen's Prose Drama," *Excursions in Criticism,* pp. 129–130.

8. *Books and Plays* (London: Elkin Mathews and John Lane; Philadelphia, Lippincott, 1894), p. 195.

9. *Anti-Jacobin,* no. 1 (January 31, 1891), p. 17.

10. *Ibid.,* no. 10 (April 4, 1891), p. 240.

11. "A Sicilian Idyll," *Letters to the New Island,* ed. Horace Reynolds (Cambridge, Mass.: Harvard University Press, 1934), p. 113.

12. "The Children of Lir," *New Island,* p. 175.

13. "A Sicilian Idyll," *New Island,* pp. 113–114.

14. "Children of Lir," *New Island,* p. 175.

15. "The Theatre," *Essays and Introductions* (New York: Macmillan, 1961), p. 165. Compare Yeats's similar remark about *A Sicilian Idyll* in *The Autobiography of William Butler Yeats* (New York: Macmillan, 1953), p. 73: "Since I was seventeen I had constantly tested my own ambition with Keats's praise of him who 'left great verses to a little clan,' so it was but natural that I should persuade him for the moment that we had nothing to do with the great public, that it should be a point of honour to be content with our own little public, that he should write of shepherds and shepherdesses because people would expect them to talk poetry and move without melodrama."

16. "A Sicilian Idyll," *New Island,* p. 114.

17. "Dr Todhunter's Plays," *Anti-Jacobin* (June 20, 1891), p. 495.

18. See John Todhunter, "Theory of the Beautiful," *Essays* (London: Elkin Mathews, 1920), esp. pp. 38–39.

19. *Autobiography of Yeats,* p. 73. Also see the report in the *Theatre,* XV (June 1, 1890), 330–331. The *Idyll* was performed on Monday, Wednesday, Friday, May 5, 7, 9, and at a matinee on Saturday, May 17.

20. *Ibid.,* p. 74.

21. T. W. R[olleston]. *Academy,* XXXVII (May 17, 1890), 344–345.

22. In *Works and Days, From the Journals of Michael Field,* ed. T. and D. C. Sturge Moore (London: John Murray, 1933), p. 184, Michael Field talks of going to spend the evening with "Toddy" [Todhunter] at his Bedford Park house and mentions: "Elkin is there, with a procession of virgin sisters with eyes that shine like tin plates."

23. J. Benjamin Townsend, *John Davidson, Poet of Armageddon* (New Haven, Conn.: Yale University Press, 1961), p. 205.

24. *Ibid.,* p. 164.

25. Lane.

26. See the A.L.S. from Davidson to Lane probably written in the autumn of 1893 which refers to an earlier version of the "After-Piece," now in P.U.L. Both the letter and the version I refer to are in C.U.L.

27. Lane.

28. A.L.S. (P.U.L.)

29. B.H.F.

30. Quoted in *Robert Ross, Friend of Friends*, ed. Margery Ross (London: Jonathan Cape, 1951), p. 29.

31. *Aubrey Beardsley* (New York: Viking, 1967), pp. 340–341 n. 317.

32. *John Davidson*, p. 55.

33. John Davidson, *Plays* (London: Mathews and Lane; Chicago: Stone and Kimball, 1894), p. 226.

34. *John Davidson*, p. 90.

35. Davidson, *Plays*, p. 167.

36. *Ibid.*, p. 227.

37. *Ibid.*, pp. 251–252. One of the most acute criticisms of Davidson's plays can be found in William Archer's essay on the playwright in *Poets of the Younger Generation* (London: John Lane, 1904), pp. 119–161.

38. Introduction, *Works and Days*, pp. ix–x.

39. *The Theatrical 'World' for 1893* (London: Walter Scott, n.d.), pp. 252–253.

40. *The Letters of Oscar Wilde*, ed. Rupert Hart-Davis (New York: Harcourt, Brace & World, 1962), p. 345.

41. *Note to Callirrhoë* (1883).

42. *Theatrical 'World' 1893*, p. 25.

43. *Letters of Wilde*, p. 346.

44. Quoted in *Letters of Wilde*, p. 335 n. 4.

45. In a letter to Campbell Dodgson, Wilde wrote: "Bosie [Lord Alfred Douglas] is very gilt-haired and I have bound *Salome* in purple to suit him." *Letters of Wilde*, p. 333. Also see letters to William Archer on p. 332.

46. *Letters of Wilde*, p. 326.

47. *Ibid.*, pp. 327–328.

48. *Ibid.*, p. 328. See Bodley Head advertisements at back of John Addington Symonds' *In the Key of Blue* (1893). There is little to suggest that Wilde and Lane ever thought well of each other. In a telegram to More Adey, November 23, 1893, Wilde wrote: "The wicked Lane has been routed with slaughter." *Letters of Wilde*, p. 347. Shortly after Wilde's arrest had brought about a stoning of the Bodley Head premises in Vigo Street by outraged citizens, Lane, in a letter to George Egerton remarked: "You don't know the trouble that brute Wilde has caused me." A.L.S., May Day, 1895, P.U.L.

49. *Letters of Wilde*, p. 316.

50. *Ibid.*, p. 317 n. 1.

51. In another stanza of the poem, Watson wrote: "And as for us — to our disgrace,/ Your stricture's truth must be conceded:/ Would any but a stupid race/ Have made the fuss about you *we* did?" (Reprinted in *Lachrymae Musarum* [London and New York: Macmillan, 1892], pp. 48–49).

52. Quoted in *Letters of Wilde*, p. 317 n. 1.

53. *Ibid.*, p. 332.

54. Quoted in *Letters of Wilde*, p. 348 n. 3.

55. *Aubrey Beardsley*, p. 336 n. 283. Wilde's response to Beardsley's illustrations

is discussed by Frances Winwar, *Oscar Wilde and the Yellow Nineties* (New York: Harper, 1940), pp. 210–214.

56. Quoted in *Robert Ross, Friend of Friends,* ed. Margery Ross (London: Jonathan Cape, 1952), p. 29.

57. *Ibid.,* p. 25.

58. *Ibid.,* p. 28. Also quoted in *Letters of Wilde,* p. 344 n. 3.

59. *Friend of Friends,* pp. 29–30.

60. *Studio,* II (February 15, 1894), 184.

61. *Ibid.,* pp. 184–185.

62. *The Art of Oscar Wilde* (Princeton, N.J.: Princeton University Press, 1967), pp. 119–120.

63. *Aubrey Beardsley,* p. 336 n. 283.

64. *The Renaissance* (London: Macmillan, 1910), p. 104.

65. *Ibid.*

66. *Studio,* II (February 15, 1894), 185.

67. Quoted by Yeats in the *Autobiography,* p. 80.

68. "The Critic as Artist as Wilde," *Wilde and the Nineties,* ed. Charles Ryskamp, (Princeton, N.J.: Princeton University Library, 1966), p. 15.

69. *Ibid.*

70. Introduction, *Oscar Wilde, Selected Writings,* ed. Richard Ellmann (London: Oxford University Press, World's Classics ed., 1961), p. x.

71. Wilde offered it to the publishing firm in May 1892. See *Letters of Wilde,* p. 341 n. 5.

72. *Ibid.,* p. 341.

73. B.H.F.

74. B.H.F.

75. "Bohemia in London, An Interesting Chat with Mr. Ernest Rhys" from an unidentified cutting in a Boston newspaper, E.M.

76. Quoted in Peter Green, *Kenneth Grahame* (London: John Murray, 1959), pp. 131–132.

77. *Kenneth Grahame,* p. 53.

78. *Ibid.,* p. 120.

79. *Ibid.,* p. 121.

80. *Ibid.,* p. 123.

81. Grahame in a letter dated April 18, 1933, described himself this way. Quoted in *Kenneth Grahame,* p. 2.

82. *Woeful Victorian,* p. 125.

83. *Ibid.,* p. 128.

84. *Ibid.,* p. 241.

85. In a letter to Mathews dated September 20, 1892, Symonds wrote of the Preface: "The last paragraph is meant to give a certain unity to the collected essays." (Bodleian, MS. Eng. lett. d. 122, fols. 114–115.)

86. Enid Starkie, *From Gautier to Eliot* (London: Hutchinson, 1962), p. 38.

87. The statement is Lionel Johnson's as quoted in *Gautier to Eliot,* p. 38.

88. *John Davidson,* p. 152.

89. A.L.S. to Elkin Mathews and John Lane, dated July 28, 1893, Lane.

90. Undated reader's report by Le Gallienne, P.U.L.

91. Quoted in Dulau, no. 205. In a letter to Lane dated August 20, 1893, Le Gallienne said that he was returning Davidson's criticisms and admitted, "possibly I was a little severe on the 'itinerary.'" Then he went on to criticize Davidson's criticisms along the lines he was soon to follow in his review of the published book. Le G.

92. *Retrospective Reviews* (London: John Lane; New York: Dodd, Mead, 1896), II, 35.

93. A.L.S. to Mathews and Lane, n.d., Lane.

94. B.H.F.

95. A.L.S., October 19, 1893, Lane.

96. Richard Whittington-Egan and Geoffrey Smerdon, in *The Quest of the Golden Boy* (Barre, Mass.: Barre Publishing, 1962), pp. 206–223, give a very full account of the controversy.

97. *Ibid.,* p. 211.

98. Quoted in *Quest of the Golden Boy,* p. 211.

99. Le G.

100. B.H.F. On September 8, 1893, Le Gallienne wrote Mathews for help "in a money matter." He suggested "that as the publication of my 'Religion'" is so near at hand "perhaps you would not mind counting the cheque for £10 you hold of mine, as on a/c of the £75, & whether also you could kindly let me have another £10 to tide over momentary expenses. You know how ill & unable to work I have been just lately, & what little I have written I cannot get paid for — to wit 'The New Review' article on your patron saint [Izaak Walton]." E.M.

101. Bodleian, MS. Walpole d. 11.

102. *Publishers' Circular,* no. 1425 (October 21, 1893), p. 481.

103. *Quest of the Golden Boy,* p. 212.

104. *Young Lives* (Bristol: Arrowsmith, 1898), p. 314.

105. See A.L.S. [December 3, 1893], *Letters to Reggie Turner* (London: Rupert Hart-Davis, 1964), p. 82.

106. Quoted in full in *Quest of the Golden Boy,* pp. 218–220.

107. *National Review,* XIV (October 1889), 183.

108. "The Critics," *George Meredith* (London: Elkin Mathews, 1890), p. 149.

109. *Excursions in Criticism* (London: Elkin Mathews & John Lane; New York: Macmillan, 1893), p. 81.

110. *Ibid.,* p. 82.

111. Review of *Appreciations, Academy,* XXXVI (December 21, 1889), 399.

112. *Ibid.,* p. 400.

113. "Critics and Their Craft," *Excursions in Criticism,* p. 85.

114. *Ibid.,* p. 84.

115. "The Fall of Fiction," *Fortnightly Review,* n.s. XLIV (September 1, 1888), 336.

116. See Wendell V. Harris, "Egerton: Forgotten Realist," *Victorian Newsletter,* no. 33 (Spring 1968), pp. 31–35. *Keynotes* was first sent to the publisher William Heinemann, who returned the manuscript immediately with a note to the effect that the firm was not interested in mediocre short stories. *A Leaf from The Yellow Book,* ed. Terence De Vere White (London: Richards Press, 1958), pp. 27–28.

117. Brian Reade and Frank Dickinson, *Aubrey Beardsley* (Catalogue of the Victoria and Albert Exhibition, 1966), entry no. 343. See also W. V. Harris, "John Lane's Keynotes Series and the Fiction of the 1890's," *PMLA,* LXXXIII (1968), 1407–1413.

118. Excerpt quoted in Dulau, no. 1055.

119. *Oscar Wilde, Selected Writings,* p. 8.

8. The Breakup

1. *The Autobiography of William Butler Yeats* (New York: Macmillan, 1953), p. 69. The aesthetic character of the Bedford Parkites is portrayed in G. K. Chesterton's *The Man Who Was Thursday.*

2. Quoted in *Richard Norman Shaw, R.A.,* by Reginald Blomfield (London: Batsford, 1940), p. 34. Appeared originally on December 17, 1881, in *St. James's Gazette.*

3. Nikolaus Pevsner, *The Buildings of England: Volume Three, Middlesex* (Harmondsworth, Middlesex: Penguin Books, 1951), p. 25.

4. *Ibid.,* pp. 25–26; also see *Richard Norman Shaw,* p. 33.

5. *Wales England Wed* (London: Dent, 1940), p. 122.

6. In its "Jottings by the Way" column, the *Fishing Gazette* (August 12, 1893), p. 147, carried the following notice: "Mr. and the Misses Elkin Mathews kept 'St. Izaac's Day' on Wednesday last by giving an 'At Home,' at their residence in Bedford Park. It is needless to say that the function was a brilliant success." The event was also recorded in *Publishers' Circular,* no. 1415 (August 12, 1893), p. 164. The card of invitation drawn by Mathews' nextdoor neighbor, Jack Yeats, is preserved in the Elkin Mathews Collection.

7. See J. Lewis Hind, *Naphtali* (New York: Dodd, Mead, 1926), p. 96.

8. *Autobiography of Yeats,* p. 79.

9. *Richard Norman Shaw,* p. 36.

10. *Ibid.*

11. *The Path Through the Wood* (New York: Dial Press, 1931), p. 142.

12. *Minding My Own Business* (London: Chatto and Windus, 1956), p. 9. Muir writes that Lane also "would ask his business correspondents to mark as 'Private' letters addressed to him at Vigo Street."

13. *Path Through the Wood,* pp. 142–143.

14. *Ibid.,* p. 143.

15. A.L.S. from Chapman to Mathews and Lane dated January 31, 1892, E.M.

16. *Path Through the Wood,* p. 159.

17. *Ibid.*, pp. 159–160.

18. See J. Lewis May, *John Lane and the Nineties* (London: John Lane, 1936), p. 38.

19. See Wilde's letter to Iredale of March 1893, *The Letters of Oscar Wilde*, ed. Rupert Hart-Davis (New York: Harcourt, Brace & World, 1962), p. 336.

20. *Path Through the Wood*, p. 142.

21. Percy Muir, in *Minding My Own Business*, p. 9, says that Mathews' conservative, unadventurous attitude toward publishing "got no sympathy from Lane who, on the contrary, became increasingly contemptuous of his timidity, and dealt with it in his own peculiar way."

22. Rough draft of a letter to Dr. Brushfield dated February 7, 1895, E.M.

23. *Ibid.*

24. "Introduction," *The Life of Sir Thomas Bodley* (London: John Lane, 1894), p. vi.

25. Albany records do not give the exact date Lane moved into the famed building. According to the present secretary, Lt. Col. G. A. L. Chetwynd-Talbot, the chambers Lane took were G. 1., situated at the northern (Vigo Street) end of Albany. Lane was allowed to convert the bow window into an entrance. Nowadays Albany is referred to as such and not as "The" Albany. Col. Chetwynd-Talbot says that although "The" Albany was common in the nineteenth century, at the beginning of the twentieth "The" was dropped — probably because some thought that reference to "The" Albany sounded like a public-house.

26. Letter to Brushfield, E.M.

27. A.L.S. from Radford to Mathews, E.M.

28. A.L.S. from Radford to Mathews, E.M.

29. Letter to Brushfield, E.M.

30. A.L.S. from Mathews to H. P. Horne, September 20, 1894, Dugdale.

31. A.L.S. from Mathews to Rothenstein, Harvard.

32. *Ibid.*

33. *Minding My Own Business*, p. 10.

34. *Letters of Wilde*, p. 318 n. 3.

35. *Ibid.*, p. 365.

36. *Ibid.*, pp. 365–366.

37. See *Letters of Wilde*, esp. pp. 366–368.

38. *Ibid.*, p. 367.

39. *Ibid.*, pp. 367–368.

40. *Ibid.*, p. 368.

41. Mathews in his letter of September 20, 1894, to H. P. Horne (Dugdale) makes it clear that only *The Second Book* and its contributors were involved.

42. In a P. S. to his letter to Mathews, dated January 13, 1891 (E.M.), Ernest Radford wrote: "Will you oblige me by sending straight on to Cosmo Monkhouse the enclosed letter. It invites him to the 'Rhymers' who meet *here* on Thursday evening. I believe you do not rhyme but I shall be very glad if you will join us." Although it has been assumed that the Rhymers' Club ceased to be before 1895,

there is a postcard in the Elkin Mathews Collection from Greene to Mathews dated May 13, 1895, which reads as follows: "Rhymers' Dinner postponed. Cannot be managed. Longer notice must be given, in fairness to all. I understand you will be in town all June? I hope to fix date in a few days. Trust you can communicate with your guest, if any, in time to avoid inconvenience to him."

43. "A Note on the Reputation of Elkin Mathews," *Elkin Mathews — Poets' Publisher* (Reading, Berks.: Reading University Library, 1966), n.p.

44. A.L.S. from Mathews to Horne, September 20, 1894, Dugdale.

45. A.L.S. from Greene to Radford, E.M.

46. A.L.S. from Radford to Greene, September 19, [1894], E.M.

47. A.L.S. from Mathews to Daniel, September 25, 1894, Worcester College Library MS. 328 (Daniel Letters).

48. No. 1472, p. 266.

49. No. 1473 (September 22, 1894), p. 293. An announcement which reflects both Lane's announcement and Mathews' letter appeared in *Publishers' Weekly,* XLVI (October 6, 1894), 549–550.

50. A.L.S. dated September 18, [1894], E.M.

51. *Ibid.*

52. *Ibid.*

53. E.M. In order to distinguish the books which he took over after the dissolution of the partnership, Elkin Mathews placed a printed slip inside each book which read: "This book is now supplied by Elkin Mathews Vigo St. W." He also had the words on title pages: "and John Lane at the Sign of the Bodley Head" stricken out with ink. Lane, likewise, inserted in each book he issued a slip bearing a picture of Sir Thomas Bodley and the words: "This book is now published by John Lane at the Bodley Head in Vigo St. London W."

In a letter of August 7, 1894, T. and A. Constable notified Mathews and Lane that the following books were all in type: Francis Adams' *Child of the Age* and *Essays in Modernity,* José Echegaray's *The Great Galeoto,* and Wilde's *A Woman of No Importance.*

54. Percy Muir, *Minding My Own Business,* pp. 9–10, for instance, writes that at the breakup "nearly every one chose Lane; the only exception I can find was Lionel Johnson who asked that Lane might publish his prose, and Mathews his poetry."

55. *The Romantic '90s* (Garden City, N.Y.: Doubleday, Page, 1925), p. 167.

56. Thursday, June 24, 1926, p. 432.

57. "A Note on the Reputation of Elkin Mathews," n.p.

ILLUSTRATION CREDITS

Title pages by W. B. Blaikie for *Sight and Song* by Michael Field (London: The Bodley Head, 1892); Walter Crane for *Chambers Twain* by Ernest Radford (London: Elkin Mathews, 1890); Laurence Housman for *Cuckoo Songs* by Katharine Tynan Hinkson (London: Mathews and Lane; Boston: Copeland and Day, 1894); C. S. Ricketts for *Silverpoints* by John Gray (London: The Bodley Head, 1893); J. Illingworth Kay for *Orchard Songs* by Norman Gale (London: Mathews and Lane; New York: G. P. Putnam's Sons, 1893); Selwyn Image for *Lyric Poems* by Laurence Binyon (London: Mathews and Lane, 1894); H. P. Horne for *Silhouettes* by Arthur Symons (London: Mathews and Lane, 1892); border within a border title page for Richard Le Gallienne's *The Religion of a Literary Man* (London: Mathews and Lane; New York: E. P. Putnam's Sons, 1894).

Elkin Mathews, 1895, from a drawing by Arthur J. Gaskin, courtesy of Miss Nest Elkin Mathews and the Library, Reading University; John Lane from a caricature by Max Beerbohm, courtesy Sir Allen Lane and Mrs. Eva Reichmann. Statement of limitation and title page for Richard Le Gallienne's *Volumes in Folio* (London: C. Elkin Mathews, 1889). Some bindings for the early Bodley Head: Francis Thompson's *Poems,* Lord De Tabley's *Poems, Dramatic and Lyrical,* J. A. Symonds' *In the Key of Blue,* T. Gordon Hake's *Poems,* Allan Monkhouse's *Books and Plays.*

Title pages by Aubrey Beardsley for *Salome* by Oscar Wilde (London: Mathews and Lane; Boston: Copeland and Day, 1894); *The Dancing Faun* by Florence Farr (London: Mathews and Lane; Boston: Roberts Brothers, 1894); *Poor Folk* by F. Dostoevski (London: Mathews and Lane; Boston: Roberts Brothers, 1894); frontispiece and title page by Beardsley for *Plays* by John Davidson (London: Mathews and Lane; Chicago: Stone and Kimball, 1894). Design by Beardsley for the prospectus of the *Yellow Book;* front covers by Beardsley for the first two volumes of the *Yellow Book* (London: Mathews and Lane; Boston: Copeland and Day, April and July, 1894). Title page and first page of text designed by C. S. Ricketts for *The Sphinx* by Oscar Wilde (London: The Bodley Head, 1894); front and back covers of *The Sphinx* with C. S. Ricketts' designs. Prospectuses and order forms for F. W. Bourdillon's *A Lost God* and Kenneth Grahame's *Pagan Papers,* courtesy of the John Johnson Collection, the Bodleian Library, Oxford.

"The Book Trills of Pernicious," a parody by Aubrey Beardsley of C. S. Ricketts' cover designs for the Bodley Head. E. T. Reed's parody of Beardsley's cover designs and illustrations for the Keynotes series, *Punch* (March 10, 1894), p. 109; Linley Sambourne's drawing of Beardsley pulling the Yellow Book crowd, *Punch* (April 28, 1894), p. 194, courtesy *Punch,* London.

Oscar Wilde and Lord Alfred Douglas from a photograph in the William Andrews Clark Memorial Library, University of California, Los Angeles. C. S. Ricketts and C. H. Shannon, 1897, from a lithograph by William Rothenstein, courtesy of Sir John and Michael Rothenstein. Ernest Dowson from a photograph in the Lessing J. Rosenwald Collection in the Library of Congress.

INDEX

Abbott, Charles Conrad, 106, 289; *Travels in a Tree-Top,* 312, 318

Academy, 111, 211, 229, 309; Le Gallienne's poems in, 14; Bodley Head ads in, 81

Acland, Henry: Rothenstein's portrait of, 292–293

Addleshaw, Percy, 273

Aesthetic Movement: Le Gallienne's relation to, 20–21; 41

Albany (The Albany): Lane's premises in, 272, 307n25

Allen, Grant, 58, 65, 277, 288, 296, 309; *The Lower Slopes,* 90, 312, 316, 318

Allingham, William: *Irish Songs and Poems,* 172

Alma Murray as Beatrice Cenci, 54, 109, 223, 284. *See also* Murray, Alma

American Book Co.: Bodley Head exports to, 306, 311

Antaeus, *see* Ibbett, W. J.

Anti-Jacobin: poem on playgoers in, 223–224

Archer, William, 221, 238; review of *A Question of Memory,* 234, 235

Arnold, Matthew, 177–178, 179, 219, 220

Art nouveau, 51, 55, 67, 74, 341n139; title pages in style of, 65; elements of in poetry of John Gray, 201

Arts and Crafts Essays, 53; Cobden-Sanderson's essay in, 72

Arts and Crafts Society, 40

Athenaeum, 33, 130; Bodley Head ads in, 81; review of De Tabley's *Poems* in, 147–148

Attwood, J. S.: friendship with Mathews, 3; index to *Lives of the Bishops of Exeter,* 3, 13, 283; index to *Monasticon Dioecesis Exoniensis,* 13, 283

Austin, Alfred, 44; *English Lyrics,* 215

Ballantyne, Hanson, 286, 288

Ballantyne Press, 46, 98, 286, 288

Banville, Théodore: influence on Parnassians, 185; *Améthystes,* 186; "Le Baiser," John Gray's translation of, 199

Barlas, John (Evelyn Douglas), 339n88

Barrett, Wilson, 24, 26, 110; employs Le Gallienne, 22

Baudelaire, Charles, 236, 245; influence on Arthur Symons, 187, 196; John Gray's translations of, 207; influence on Wilde, 210; *Salon de 1846,* 210; *Fleurs du Mal* attacked by William Watson, 216

Beardsley, Aubrey, 12, 44, 60, 73, 151, 199, 201, 212, 266, 288, 290; Japanese influence on, 67; illustrations for *Le Morte Darthur,* 67; title pages designed by, 67–69, 70; dismissed by Lane, 211; designs for Davidson's *Plays* (1894), 232; rift with Wilde, 239; designs for Keynotes series, 262–263; Lane's relations with, 290, 291; A. J. A. Symons on, 293–294; Bodley Head art work, 295; William Watson's opinion of, 301; reception of in U.S.A., 308

    Salome: designs for, 58, 238–239, 242; binding design for, 73; payment for illustrations, 99; illustrations for, 309–310

    Yellow Book: genesis, 298–299; prospectus, 299; concept of, 299–300; art work for, 300

Beckson, Karl, 157, 169, 218

Beddoes, Thomas Lovell, 288; *The Letters of,* ed. Edmund Gosse, 103, 311, 318

Bedford Park, 159, 160, 225, 228, 229, 266–268, 369n1

Bedford Press, 285

Beeching, H. C., J. W. Mackail, J. B. B. Nichol: *Love in Idleness,* 79, 313

Beerbohm, Max, 259, 293, 298; on Lord De Tabley, 133; approached by Lane, 290; description of Rothenstein, 291–292

belles-lettres: demand for limited editions of, 77–82*ff.*

Benson, Arthur Christopher, 211, 287; *Poems,* 109, 316

Benson, Eugene, 285, 294–295; *From the Asolan Hills,* 92, 315; Crane's friendship with, 294–295

Bernhardt, Sarah: and *Salomé,* 236

Binyon, Laurence, 151, 211, 277, 279, 303; on the art of William Strang, 294; *Lyric Poems,* 66, 107, 288, 296, 318

Blaikie, Walter Biggar, 36, 46, 56, 60, 75, 87, 89, 145; joins T. and A. Constable, 37; as designer of books, 37–39; rivalry with William Morris, 38; concept of title page, 38–39; title pages designed by, 61–62; and format of *English Poems,* 88;

and format of De Tabley's *Poems*, 138–140; success of, 335n10

Blake, William, 48, 226

Bodley, Sir Thomas, 1, 7, 271

Bodley Head, the: founding of, 1–10, 271; named for Sir Thomas Bodley, 1; pre-Bodley Head publications of, 3; sign of, 12; Lane as silent partner in, 12, 30, 31, 34; early publications of, 13; Le Gallienne's early role in, 30, 31, 34; books of described, 37, 38 *passim;* range of publications, 54–55, 221; and demand for belles-lettres, 77–84; policies of, 78, 87, 92–93, 107, 150, 154; remainders issued by, 79; and demand for limited editions, 80*ff;* accusations against, 82; and large-paper editions, 82–83; printers for, 85–87; conduct of business, 87–88, 268; Inventory Sheets of, 91, 108, 318–325; typical contract of, 94–95; exports-imports of, 106, 306–312; financial status of, 106; success of, 106–109, 266; margin of profit, 109; aesthetic orientation of, 150–151; literary and artistic milieu of, 150–151, 308; as gathering place of poets, 150–151; divergent views of authors and artists, 151; as voice of early nineties, 151–152; philosophy of, 154–155; receptive to new poetic voices, 155–156; French influence on poetry of, 184–215 *passim;* best sellers of, 211; staple authors of, 211; anti-decadent poets of, 211–219; created poetic renascence in nineties, 219, 344n33, 364n94; variety and diversity of poetry issued from, 219; plays published by, 221–245; dramatic criticism published by, 222–223; typical authors of 245–246; essays published by, 245–262; criticism published by, 262; fiction published by, 262–265; representative nature of, 264, 279; growing interest in fiction of, 264–265; J. Lewis May's description of, 268; Mathews and tradition of, 279; artists and illustrators of, 290–297; artist-authors of, 294; influence on American publishers of, 306, 307–309; Daniel Press books sold by, 313; books transferred to, 313–314; final inventory of, 315–325; production costs of, 315–325; readers for, 333n134, 348n33
  premises: search for, 6–8; location of, 7, 10, 328n31; interior of, 12; quaint aura of, 151, 268
  royalties and other payments, 87, 321, 323, 325; to authors, 92–110; to artists, 99
  poets: Parnassians among, 185–186; and vogue of poems on pictures, 200; French influence on, 210–211; best sellers among, 211; public attitude toward, 211; anti-decadents among, 211–219; as forerunners of modern poets, 220; and Laureateship battle, 220; displeasure with *Yellow Book,* 301
  breakup of: reasons for, 264–265, 270–271; differences between Mathews and Lane, 266, 268, 270–271; controversy over disposition of sign, 272–273; apportionment of authors, 273–278; apportionment of the business, 274–275; announcement of, 276–277, 278; disposition of books, 278, 371n53; reaction to in U.S.A., 309; books in type at, 371n53; 108, 271–279

Bodley Head book, the: and the Revival of Printing, 53, 58–59; *art nouveau* milieu of, 55, 56; characteristics, 55, 56–58*ff.;* forerunners, 55–56; 79; and Kelmscott Press editions, 55, 58; vogue for, 56–57; type faces used in, 59; quality paper used in, 59-60, 89–90; title page, 60–70; binding designs and features, 70–76, 91–92; small editions, 80–81; advertising, 81, 107; production costs, 84–109 *passim;* printing, 86–88; binding costs, 91–92; binders, 91–92; publication in U.S.A., 101–106, 107, 306–308; prices in U.S.A., 105–106; prospectuses, 107; subscriptions, 107; sales, 107–108; selling price, 108–109; attractive format, 247; art of illustration in, 293–294; illustrators of listed, 295–297

Bodley Library Catalogue, 1

Bogue and Co., 79, 207

Bohemians: in London, 245–246; Ernest Rhys's essay on, 367n75

Book of the Rhymers' Club, The, 56, 72, 158, 159, 177, 285; purpose of, 156; publication of, 157, 166; genesis of, 162–163; plans for, 162–163; expense of, 163; selection of verse for, 163; format of, 166; reviews of, 166–167; verse characterized, 170–171; Parnassian verse in, 354n23

Bourdillon, Francis W., 211, 277; *A Lost God,* 56, 86, 92, 107, 285, 296; *Ailes D'Alouette,* 313

Bradley, Katherine, *see* Field, Michael

Bridges, Robert, 57, 82; Daniel Press books of, 56; *The Feast of Bacchus,* 313; *The Growth of Love,* 81, 82, 313

Browning, Robert, 21, 202, 284, 295; influence on Arthur Symons, 187; dramas of, 222; heroines portrayed by Alma Murray, 223, 284, 295

Buchanan, Robert: *The Wandering Jew: A Christmas Carol,* controversy with Le Gallienne over, 256

Burne-Jones, Edward, 56, 67, 200, 303

Carman, Bliss, 279, 307

Carter, John, 121

Caslon, William, 48

Cassell and Co.: Bodley Head exports to, 311

Celtic Movement, 151

Central Press Agency, Ltd.: Bodley Head imports from, 312

Century Guild: 120, 160, 245, 302; founders of, 66; members of, 151

Century Guild Hobby Horse, see Hobby Horse

Chap-Book, the, 307–309

Chapman, Elizabeth R., 277; *A Little Child's Wreath,* 67, 288, 296, 312, 318

Chapman, Frederic, 270, 256, 268

Chiswick Press, 24, 36, 45, 48, 51, 58, 86, 87, 229, 284, 285, 295, 303, 314; reputation, 39; records of, 91; production costs, 315

Clark, R. and R., 81, 105, 284; Bodley Head books printed by, 87

Clay, Richard and Sons, 284

Clowes and Son, 287

Cobden-Sanderson, T. J.: lecture on bindings of books, 72

Coleridge, Stephen: *Sanctity of Confession,* 287, 313

Commin, J. G., 2, 3, 13

Constable, T. and A., 36, 39, 48, 59, 85, 104–105, 138, 145, 148, 219, 242, 285, 286, 287, 288, 289, 294; W. B. Blaikie joins, 37; Bodley Head books printed by, 87–89; transactions with Bodley Head, 87–89; printing costs of Bodley Head books, 88–89; production costs, 316–317

Cooper, Edith, *see* Field, Michael

Copeland and Day, 82, 242, 309; published *Yellow Book* in U.S.A., 103; price of Bodley Head books published by, 105; influence of Bodley Head books on, 306–

307; Bodley Head books imported by, 306–312 *passim*

Corkhill, Fanny (Mrs. Percy): influence on Le Gallienne, 19

Crackanthorpe, Hubert, 298

Crane, Walter, 67, 151, 160, 161, 166; title pages designed by, 66; decorations for Todhunter's *A Sicilian Idyll,* 229; Bodley Head art work of, 295–296

    Renascence, 40, 48, 56, 58, 60, 285, 290, 294, 295, 296, 309; title page, 66; production costs, 86, 315; binding costs, 91–92; published on commission, 92; exported to U.S.A., 101–103, 311; Parnassian verse in, 186

Critic, the (New York): notices of Bodley Head books in, 309

Crossing, William, 3; *Ancient Crosses of Dartmoor, The,* 3, 13, 54; *The Old Stone Crosses of the Dartmoor Borders,* 285

Daily Chronicle, the, 211, 258, 277

Daniel, Rev. C. H. O., 48, 81, 276; founder of Daniel Press, 55–56; influence of, 338n85

Daniel Press, 276, 283; genesis of, 55–56; books sold by Bodley Head, 313

Davidson, John, 157, 158, 161, 162, 168, 212, 277; anti-decadent attitude of, 151; plays of, 230–233; attitude toward society, 232; dispute with Le Gallienne, 255–256; reader for Bodley Head, 334n134

    A Random Itinerary, 47, 246, 287, 296, 307; title page, 65, 340n118; binding, 76; payment for, 94; Le Gallienne's opinion of, 155; discussed, 254–255; offered to Bodley Head, 255; publication, 256; exported to U.S.A., 311; production costs, 318

    Plays (1894), 59, 70, 287, 288, 295, 307; title page, 69; genesis, 230–232; contract for, 231–232; Beardsley's designs for, 232; publication, 232; exported to U.S.A., 312; production costs, 318

    Fleet Street Eclogues, 56, 255, 286; genesis, 229; influence of Spencer on, 229; publication, 229–230; production costs, 324

    Bruce, 287, 313; remainders of, 230; reissued, 231

    Plays (1889): issues of, 230, 313

Smith: remainders of, 230, 231; Spasmodic elements in, 232

Davis, Louis: Bodley Head art work of, 296

Day, Fred Holland: interest in *Hobby Horse,* 306; aesthetic interests of, 306–307

Decadents, the, 151, 152, 153, 215, 234; poetry of, 58, 153, 187–211 *passim;* attitude of Bodley Head toward, 150; attitude of mind of, 173; attacked by William Watson, 216–217; interest in Jacobean drama, 222; and Salome, 242–243; satires on, 263; Le Gallienne's hostility to, 150, 212–219, 353n1; relations with counter-decadents, 353n6; attitude toward Roman Catholic church, 359n116

De Gruchy, Augusta, 277, 278, 296; *Under the Hawthorn,* 60, 66, 286, 318

De Tabley, John Leicester Warren, Lord, 211, 277; scholarly interests of, 132; literary career, 132–134; early writings, 133; poetry characterized, 133; temperamental nature, 135; hostility toward Ricketts, 138; refuses to write for *Yellow Book,* 301

    Poems, Dramatic and Lyrical, 45, 46, 47, 56, 57, 60, 76, 87, 110, 286, 296, 297; title page, 69–70, 144–145; binding, 74; binding costs, 91; sales, 107; history of publication, 132–149; genesis, 133–134; correspondence with Mathews and Lane, 136*ff.;* format, 138–140; controversy over title, 140–141; cover design, 141; royalties, 143, 148–149; production costs, 146, 316, 318; publication, 146–147; reviews, 147–148; success, 132, 147–148; second edition ordered, 148; exported to U.S.A., 311

    A Guide to the Study of Book-Plates: re-issued, 132; 285, 313

De Vinne Press, 289

Dial, the, 41, 44, 45, 47, 313; features, 303–304; art work in, 304; publication, 304; Wilde's praise of, 304

Dial, the (Chicago), 309; receptive to Bodley Head books, 310

Diversi Colores series, 274, 277

Dobson, Austin, 80; Parnassian poetry of, 185

Dodd, Mead and Co., 170; Bodley Head exports to, 312

Dostoevski, Feodor, 94, 262, 266, 289, 295; *Poor Folk:* title page, 67; George Moore's

Preface to, 100; exported to U.S.A., 311; production costs, 317, 324

Douglas, Lord Alfred, 239; and the *Spirit Lamp,* 197; translation of *Salome,* 242

Douglas, Evelyn, *see* Barlas, John

Dowson, Ernest, 157, 160, 161, 162, 167, 168, 170, 171, 210, 212, 245, 301; on meeting of Rhymers, 160; role in publication of *Book of the Rhymers' Club,* 162–163; contributions to *Second Book of the Rhymers' Club,* 169; and London society, 173; Paterian response to life, 173, 174; and cult of little girls, 173–174; Rhymer's Club verse of, 173–178, 183; Symons on, 174; and Adelaide, 174, 176, 177; enters Catholic church, 177; religious verse of, 177–178; verse compared with Matthew Arnold's, 177–178

    "Cynara," 169, 175–176, 183; essence of decadent poetry, 174

Driver Press (Chelmsford), 339n88

Dunne, Mary Chavelita, *see* Egerton, George

Egerton, George (Mary Chavelita Dunne), 262, 298

    Keynotes, 59, 87, 262, 263, 264, 266, 274, 277, 287, 295; title page, 67; binding, 91; contract for, 100–101; exported to U.S.A., 103, 311; printings of, 106; sale of, 107; "new woman" in, 262; Beardsley designs for, 262–263; publication of, 262–263; production costs, 316, 322; rejected by Heinemann, 369n116

Eighteen Nineties, the: attitude toward Victorian literature in, 151–152; aesthetic temper of, 151–154; revolution in theater of, 221; popular attitude toward drama of, 223–224; poetic drama of, 224–226; neo-paganism in, 226; art of illustration in, 293; William Watson's opinion of, 301–302; poetic renascence in, 364n94

    poetry of, 170–219; French influence on, 184–215 *passim;* traditional elements in, 211*ff.,* 220; experimentation in, 220; effect of Wilde's trial on, 343n16

    poets of: reaction to Victorian poetry, 151–153, 184–185, 220; influence of French poetry on, 153, 156, 184–215 *passim;* and the city, 195–197

Eliot, George, 111, 264

Eliot, T. S., 85, 220
Ellis, Edwin J., 157, 161, 163, 168
Ellis, Havelock, 187, 222
Ellmann, Richard, 243
Evans, B. Ifor, 210
Exeter: birthplace of Sir Thomas Bodley, 1; Mathews' bookshop in, 1–4

Fairfax, Walter: *Robert Browning and the Drama*, 313
Farr, Florence: in *Sicilian Idyll*, 228; Yeats's praise of, 228
    The Dancing Faun, 262, 263, 288, 295; title page, 67; contract for, 101; aesthetic hero of, 263; Beardsley's designs for, 263; exported to U.S.A., 311; production costs, 316, 322
Field, Michael (Katherine Bradley and Edith Cooper), 277; Bodley Head books of, 233; much admired, 233–234; Rothenstein's description of, 233–234; plays of, 233–235; *Works and Days*, 235
    Sight and Song, 35, 36, 56, 91, 108, 233, 285; title page, 61; format, 87–88; production costs, 88, 316, 318
    Stephania, 221, 233, 285, 296; title page, 66; publication, 235
    A Question of Memory, 221, 233, 287; production of at Independent Theatre, 222, 234; Wilde's opinion of, 234, 235; William Archer's review of, 234, 235; plot, 235
Figaro (London): review of *Silhouettes* in, 197
Fin de siècle: dramatists of, 222; *Salome* as typical of, 243
Flecker, J. E., 279
Fletcher, Ian, 275, 279
Flower, Desmond, 176
Folkard, R. and Son, 285, 286, 287, 288
Foltinowitz, Adelaide: and Ernest Dowson, 174
Ford, H[enry] J[ustice]: Bodley Head art work of, 295, 296
Forman, H. Buxton, 121, 284. *See also* Keats, John: *Three Essays by John Keats*
Fortnightly Review, the, 78, 81, 113, 115
Fullerton, William Morton: "Some Notes on George Meredith in America," 119–120
Fulleylove, John: Bodley Head art work of, 295, 296

Furse, Charles Wellington: Bodley Head art work of, 296

Gale, Norman, 80, 83, 168, 277; *A June Romance*, 313; "A Verdant County." *See* Hayes, Alfred, *et al.: A Fellowship in Song*
    Orchard Songs, 56, 87, 287, 296, 297; title page, 65; binding, 76; payment for, 92; subscriptions for, 107; exported to U.S.A., 311; production costs, 316, 318
Garnett, Richard, 211, 277, 287, 296
    Poems, 65, 306, 309; production costs, 89, 316, 318; exported to U.S.A., 311
Gautier, Théophile: Swinburne's admiration for, 184; and English Parnassians, 185; *Emaux et Camées*, 58, 186; influence on Wilde, 210
Genée, Adeline, 232
Germ, the, 47
Gibbons, Maria Susannah, 3; *We Donkeys on the Devon Coast*, 3, 283
Gladstone, William Ewart: admirer of De Tabley's poetry, 134; 293
Gosse, Edmund, 146, 188, 277, 288; editor of *The Letters of Thomas Lovell Beddoes*, 103, 288, 311, 318; review of De Tabley's *Poems*, 148; Parnassian doctrine of, 185
Grahame, Kenneth: Bohemian element in, 246–248; *The Golden Age*, 247; influence of Henley on, 247; inner life of, 247
    Pagan Papers, 59, 87, 256, 263, 277, 287, 295; title page, 69; contract for, 94–95; production costs, 88–89, 316, 318; Bohemianism in, 246–248; rejection of modern society in, 246–248; discussed, 246–249; genesis of, 247; exported to U.S.A., 307, 312
Granby, the Marchioness of: Bodley Head art work of, 296
Granta: parody of *Yellow Book* in, 301
Gray, John, 151, 160, 168, 210, 211, 220, 279; early life of, 198–199; visits Raffalovich in Paris, 198–199; friendship with Wilde, 199; knowledge of *Symbolistes*, 199; lecture on "The Modern Actor," 199; submits *Silverpoints* to Bodley Head, 199–200; and the "Dorian" controversy, 199, 356n45, 361n55; translation of Banville's "*Le Baiser*," 199, 361n58; love of artifice, 201; poetry in *Dial*, 304
    Silverpoints: modeled on Aldus, 45;

decadent verse of, 58; use of italics in, 59; title page, 69; suppressed poems, 74, 362n63; binding design, 74; contracts for, 95; French influence on, 187, 198–207 *passim;* discussed, 198–207; publication of, 200; significance of title, 200; artifice in, 200–201*ff.;* "Les Demoiselles de Sauve" analyzed, 200–201; "The Barber" analyzed, 201–202; sadistic element in, 201–202; "Mishka" analyzed, 202–204; "Poem" analyzed, 204; experimentation in, 205–206; translations from the French analyzed, 206–210; public attitude toward, 211; reviews of, 211; and modern poetic tradition, 220; manuscript of, 362n63

Green, Peter, 247, 248, 249

Greene, George A., 157, 161, 162, 163, 166, 168, 169, 170, 275, 276, 277
  Italian Lyrists of To-day: title page, 61: exported to U.S.A., 311; production costs, 316, 320

Grein, Jack T.: and the Independent Theatre, 221, 222, 235

Hacon, Llewellyn, 46. *See also* Hacon and Ricketts

Hacon and Ricketts, 45

Hake, T[homas] Gordon, 211, 277
  The Poems of Thomas Gordon Hake, 59, 288, 297, 307; preface by Alice Meynell, 100; exported to U.S.A., 312; production costs, 316, 320

Hales, Samuel: friendship with Le Gallienne, 14; Le Gallienne's letters to, 15–29 *passim;* bookshop of, 16–17; as "Samuel Dale" in *Book-Bills,* 17–18

Hallam, Arthur Henry: *The Poems of,* 72, 103, 286, 311, 316, 320

Hamilton, Ian: *The Ballad of Hádji,* 79, 285, 297, 313, 314

Hardy, Thomas: *Tess of the D'Urbervilles,* 41; *The Trumpet-Major,* 61

Harland, Henry, 69, 159, 232, 288; and genesis of *Yellow Book,* 298–299

Hart-Davis, Rupert, 19, 290

Hawker, Rev. Robert Stephen: assists John Lane, 5

Hayes, Alfred: "From Midland Meadows," *see* Hayes, Alfred, et al.: *A Fellowship in Song*

Hayes, Alfred, Richard Le Gallienne, Norman Gale: *A Fellowship in Song,* 56, 286

Hazell, Watson and Viney (Aylesbury Press), 284

Hazlitt, William: *Liber Amoris,* 72, 100, 286; interest in Jacobean drama, 222

Hazlitt, W. Carew: and editing of *Liber Amoris,* 100

Hegel, Georg Wilhelm, 224; aesthetics of, 228

Henley, William Ernest, 115, 122, 146, 263, 309; *Lyra Heroica,* 37, 88; *The Song of the Sword,* 88, 153; *A Book of Verse,* 153; *In Hospital,* 153; decadent-modern elements in poetry of, 153; *London Voluntaries,* 153, 186; influence on Symons, 187; Kenneth Grahame's mentor, 247; review of Le Gallienne's *Religion of a Literary Man,* 259–260

Hentschel, Carl, 69

Hickey, Emily: *Verse-Tales,* 13, 284

Hill, A. Fraser, *Land and Wealth of New South Wales,* 289, 312

Hillier, Arthur C., 161, 168, 170

Hind, C. Lewis: description of Rhymers' Club meeting, 159–160; *Naphtali,* 159

Hinkson, Katharine Tynan, 162, 166, 211, 288, 303; on Bodley Head books, 84–85
  Cuckoo Songs, 47, 288, 296; title page, 65; exported to U.S.A., 312; production costs, 320

Hobby Horse, the, 66, 70, 274, 277, 278, 286, 300, 302–303, 306, 307, 309, 314; Dowson's verse in, 173, 177; aims and purposes of, 302; Bodley Head publication of, 303; production costs, 324

Hogg, Warrington: Bodley Head art work of, 296

Horne, Herbert, 120, 151, 157, 160, 168, 245, 273, 275, 277, 278, 286, 302, 303, 306; *Diversi Colores,* 57, 278, 296, 306–307, 314; and the Century Guild, 66; opposition to ideas, 153–154; on Rhymers' Club meeting, 161; title page for *Silhouettes,* 188; Bodley Head art work of, 296

Housman, Laurence, 60, 290; Bodley Head books designed by, 47; and typographical revival of nineties, 47; influences on art of, 47, 73, 337n48; title pages designed by, 64–65; binding designs of, 75, 76; Bodley Head art work of, 296; work on title page of *Random Itinerary,* 340n118

Howe, Ellic: on cost of typesetting, 85

Hutchins, Patricia, 327n4

Hutton, Richard Holt: review of De Tabley's *Poems*, 148; and Laureateship battle, 220

Huysmans, Joris Karl: *A rebours*, 210, 218

Ibbett, William Joseph (Antaeus): *The Backslider and Other Poems*, 86, 284, 315

Ibsen, Henrik, 224; *A Doll's House*, 221; influence on theater of nineties, 221–222; *Ghosts*, 222; plays attacked and defended, 223; *Hedda Gabler*, 243

Igdrasil, 285, 304, 314

Image, Selwyn, 60, 72, 151, 157, 160, 167, 168, 302; title pages designed by, 51, 66–67; and Century Guild, 66; review of *Book of the Rhymers' Club*, 167; Bodley Head art work of, 296

Impressionism: in poetry of nineties, 153

Independent Theatre: performances of "Le Baiser," 199; and Bodley Head authors, 221; founding of, 222; production of *Question of Memory*, 234–235

Jackson, Holbrook, 17, 222

Jacobi, Charles, 24, 37, 60; as manager of Chiswick Press, 39–41; on book production and design, 40–41; on varieties of paper, 89–90; on methods of paying authors, 92; early life, 335n14

On the Making and Issuing of Books, 36, 40, 59, 90, 284, 315

James, Henry, 199, 298, 300

James, William P., 277

Romantic Professions, 65, 288, 296; exported to U.S.A., 103, 311; production costs, 316, 322

Jepson, Edgar: description of Rhymers' Club meeting, 161; on Ernest Dowson, 173, 174

Johnson, Effie: *In the Fire and Other Fancies*, 66, 285, 296

Johnson, Lionel, 13, 151, 157, 160, 162, 163, 166, 167, 168, 170, 171, 199, 212, 245, 273, 279, 303; on Mathews, 31; opposition to ideas, 153–154; on Rhymers' Club meetings, 160–161; role in publication of *Book of the Rhymers' Club*, 163; and the Catholic church, 177, 178; religious verse, 178; ascetic nature, 178–179; early years, 178–179; verse compared with Tennyson's, 182; John Gray as "Dorian," 199; as portrayed in Le Gallienne's

Young Lives, 213; opinion of Le Gallienne's poetry, 218

The Art of Thomas Hardy, 87, 262, 274, 289, 297; use of paper in, 90; production costs, 90, 317; exported to U.S.A., 312

Rhymers' Club verse, 178–183 *passim;* "By the Statue of King Charles at Charing Cross," 162, 168, 178, 180, 183; "Plato in London," 168, 178–180; "Mystic and Cavalier," 182–183

Kay, J. Illingworth, 60; title pages designed by, 65; binding design by, 76; Bodley Head art work of, 296

Keats, John, 21, 203, 217; *Three Essays by*, 86, 284, 315

Kegan Paul and Trench, 154, 155; financial troubles of, 79, 343n10; transfers to Bodley Head, 313, 314

Kelmscott Press, 37, 38, 41, 46, 51, 52, 71; and the Bodley Head book, 55, 58

Keynotes series, 265, 274, 277, 278; selling price of, 106, 108; genesis of, 262–263

Kimball, Hannibal Ingalls, 307

Kingsley, Charles, 259; *Westward Ho!*, 5

Kramer, Sidney, 306

Lamb, Charles, 21, 222

Lane, John, 53, 55, 57, 58, 64, 75, 79, 91, 96, 97, 101, 105, 114, 116, 117, 119, 134, 211, 246, 258, 264, 265, 274, 275, 276, 277, 279, 283, 290, 292, 295, 301, 303, 307, 309, 313; on founding of Bodley Head, 1, 7, 327n3, 328n32; and Mathews, 3, 4, 6, 8–10, 31–33, 266, 271, 273, 278, 329n35; clerk in Railway Clearing house, 4; antiquarian interests, 4–5; early years, 4–6; seeks Bodley Head premises, 4, 6–7; interest in rare books, 4, 5, 6, 9, 78; described, 5–6; as silent partner in Bodley Head, 12–13, 30, 31; and Le Gallienne, 14–15, 26, 31–34, 113, 120–121, 124; joins Bodley Head officially, 30, 34, 268; bibliography for Le Gallienne's *George Meredith*, 35, 111, 120–122, 123–125, 130–131, 284; knowledge of book design, 37; shrewd business head of, 84, 150, 328n29; negotiations with printers, 87–88; publication of *Yellow Book*, 103, 298, 299; negotiations with De Tabley for *Poems*, 136*ff.;* literary tastes of, 150, 215, 363n88; attention to decadent art, 150, 353n3; and philosophy of Bodley Head, 154; accepts *Silverpoints* for publication, 200; dismisses Beardsley, 211; as portrayed in Le Gallienne's *Young Lives*, 212–214; negotiations for John Davidson's *Plays*, 230–231; relations with Wilde, 236–237, 274, 366n48; row over *Salome* designs, 239; social milieu of, 266; tastes of, 266; characterized by J. Lewis May, 268; views on breakup, 271–272; takes sign of Bodley Head, 272; moves to Albany, 272, 370n25; relations with Bodley Head artists, 291; visits Rothenstein in Paris, 291; establishes branch in U.S.A., 306; conservative nature of, 328n23; buccaneering spirit of, 334n142

Lang, Andrew, 14, 22, 57, 78, 80, 122, 167, 184–185, 295

Leather, Robinson Kay, 28, 123, 314; friendship with Le Gallienne, 26–27. *See also* Leather, Robinson Kay and Richard Le Gallienne

Leather, Robinson Kay and Richard Le Gallienne: *The Student and the Body-Snatcher and Other Trifles*, 27–28, 30, 32, 111, 262, 284

Le Gallienne, Mildred (Mrs. Richard), 20, 21, 29, 123

Le Gallienne, Richard, 3, 13, 20, 56, 85, 133, 140, 157, 162, 163, 166, 168, 170, 268, 274, 277, 278, 286; *My Ladies' Sonnets*, 14, 15, 19, 22, 23, 24, 30, 37, 57, 79, 112, 119; Lane's discovery of, 14–15; youthful adulation of Wilde, 16*ff.*; *The Book-Bills of Narcissus*, 17–18, 26, 27, 111, 112, 314; early years in Liverpool, 17–26; *Young Lives*, 18, 25, 119, 212–214, 259; aesthetic influences on, 18–19; "Oblivion's Poppy," 20, 111; early reading, 20-21; literary secretary to Wilson Barrett, 22; antiquarian book interests, 22–23, 71; knowledge of book production, 23, 30, 37; begins career in London, 28; as "Logroller" for *Star*, 28–29; described and characterized, 29; attitude toward Mathews, 30; role in Bodley Head, 30; relationship with Lane, 31–34, 113, 120–121, 124; relationship with Mathews, 33, 112–113, 125–128, 279, 368n100; *The Romantic '90s*, 84; visits George Meredith, 112; Pater's influence on, 113–114, 260; defends George Meredith, 115; assists De Tabley, 134–137; reviews *Poems, Dramatic and Lyrical*, 148; opposition to

Decadents, 150, 212–219; and philosophy of Bodley Head, 154–156; as reader for Bodley Head, 155, 229, 255, 263, 333n134; hostility toward Francophiles, 119, 211–219 *passim*; traditionalist view of poetry, 212–219 *passim*; middle-class life of, 245–246; religious beliefs of, 258–259; *Retrospective Reviews*, 260; critical principles of, 260; decadent verse of, 353n1; rivalry with William Watson, 260, 363n90; "Nightingales" (*see* Hayes, Alfred, *et al.: A Fellowship in Song*); *The Student and the Body-Snatcher* (*see* Leather, Robinson Kay and Richard Le Gallienne)

Volumes in Folio, 3, 13, 37, 86, 87, 110, 111, 215, 283, 284; publication of, 22–23; format, 23; correpondence with Mathews about, 23–24; reviews of, 25; success of, 25; bears first Bodley Head imprint, 36; binding, 72; sales, 79; exported to U.S.A., 311; production costs, 315

George Meredith: Some Characteristics, 20, 27, 28, 30, 31, 32, 59, 260, 262, 284, 296, 306; contract signed for, 26, 111; payment for, 92, 94; history of publication of, 110–132; begins work on, 111; genesis of, 112; critical approach in, 113–115; plans for writing, 114–115; reviews of, 117, 129–131; controversy over title page of, 123–125; publication of, 125–129; second edition of, 130–131; exported to U.S.A., 311; production costs, 322

English Poems, 20, 35, 59, 87, 138, 285; reviews of, 55, 197, 211; binding, 71; production costs, 88, 316, 322; binding costs, 91; insular point of view in, 214; derivation of title, 215; various poetic modes in, 215; purpose of, 215, 217; traditional nature of, 215–217; discussed, 215–219; publication of, 219; success of, 219; exported to U.S.A., 311

Prose Fancies, 288, 297; payment for, 92; exported to U.S.A., 104–105, 311; production costs, 316–317, 322

Religion of a Literary Man, 59, 287; payment for, 92; exported to U.S.A., 104–105, 311; sales of, 107; genesis of, 256–257; success of, 256–257; controversy surrounding, 256–259; contract for, 258; contents of, 259; publication of, 259; reviews of, 259–260; production costs, 316, 322

Limited Editions, A Prose Fancy, 287; productions costs, 316

Legros, Alphonse: influence on Strang, 294; 200

Leighton, John ("Luke Limner"): binding designs of, 71

Leighton Son and Hodge, 73, 74; bindings for Bodley Head books, 91

Lippincott and Co.: exports to Bodley Head, 106, 312; Bodley Head exports to, 312

Liverpool, 14, 112; and Aesthetic Movement, 16–17; Le Gallienne's early years in, 17–26

London: lack of Bohemia in, 245

Longus: *Daphnis and Chloe, see* Ricketts and Shannon

Louÿs, Pierre, 199, 206, 236

"Luke Limner," *see* Leighton, John

Maas, Henry, 176

Mackail, J. W., *see* Beeching, H. C. *et al.*

Mackmurdo, Arthur, 66, 151, 160

McLean, Ruari, 39, 48, 52, 60, 61, 70–71

Macmillan, Alexander: correspondence with Pater, 49–50

Macmillan, Frederick, 102; rejects *Keynotes,* 103; rejects *Yellow Book,* 103

Macmillan, London: policy on Large-paper editions, 83

Macmillan, New York: Bodley Head exports to, 101–103, 311

Mallarmé, Stéphane, 213; influence on Symons, 188; Gray's translations of, 206–207

Marlowe, Christopher and George Chapman: *Hero and Leander, see* Ricketts and Shannon

Marston, Phillp Bourke: *A Last Harvest,* 87, 104, 285, 311; vogue of, 103–104; *Collected Poems,* 103–104

Martin, William Wilsey: *Quatrains, Life's Mystery and Other Poems,* 285

Marwick, William: editor of *Igdrasil,* 285, 304

Marzials, Theo: *The Gallery of Pigeons,* 185–186, 314

Mathews, Charles Elkin, *see* Mathews, Elkin

Mathews, Elkin, 23, 26, 27, 55, 57, 58, 77, 78, 79, 88, 91, 96, 97, 102, 104, 105, 106, 114, 116, 117, 119, 123, 125, 148, 149, 157, 159, 168, 211, 239, 274, 276, 277, 283, 292, 295, 299, 303, 304, 306, 307, 309, 313; patron saint of, 1, 33, 369n6; early life, 1–2; bookshop in Exeter, 1–4; described, 2, 12; interest in publishing, 2–3, 279; pre-Bodley Head publications, 3, 13, 283; and Lane, 4, 31–33, 266, 268, 271, 273, 277, 278; and founding of Bodley Head, 4–10; meets Le Gallienne, 16; attitude of Lane and Le Gallienne toward, 30, 31–32; characterized, 31–32, 268, 334n142; relationship with Le Gallienne, 33, 112–113, 368n100; role in Bodley Head, 87, 268; publication of *George Meredith,* 123–129; publication of *Poems, Dramatic and Lyrical,* 136ff.; literary tastes of, 150; and philosophy of Bodley Head, 154; publication of *Book of the Rhymers' Club,* 162–163; relations with Rhymers' Club, 166, 275, 370n42; home in Bedford Park, 229; publishes *Sicilian Idyll,* 229; friendship with Michael Field, 233; successes of, 264–265; and Keynotes series, 265; social milieu, 266–268, 369n6; on causes of breakup, 271, 300; offers Lane Bodley Head sign, 272; post Bodley Head business, 275; letter to TLS on breakup, 279; publishes Yeats, 279; service to poetry, 279; excluded from *Yellow Book* dinner, 300; Exeter Catalogs of, 327n1, 327n3; on move to London, 329n35; sisters of, 365n22

Mathews, Nest Elkin, 2, 327n4

Mathews, Thomas George: clerk in Railway Clearing house, 4; acquaintance with Lane, 4

May, J. Lewis, 5, 10, 12, 157, 270, 278; as Bodley Head stock boy, 29; describes Le Gallienne, 29; describes Mathews, 31; describes Bodley Head, 268

Meredith, George, 153, 233; *Rhonda Fleming,* 111; *Sandra Belloni,* 111, 122; Le Gallienne visits, 112; *The Egoist,* 112, 115, 116, 122; *Diana of the Crossways,* 115; *The Ordeal of Richard Feverel,* 116, 122; response to Lane's bibliography, 122; influence on Symons, 187

Meredith, W. Maxse: Bodley Head art work of, 120, 296

Meynell, Alice, 100, 151, 277, 288; disapproval of *Yellow Book,* 211, 301

Poems, 56, 87, 286; title page, 61; bindings costs, 91; production costs, 316, 322

Rhythm of Life and Other Essays, 59, 286; binding costs, 91; production costs, 316, 322

Miles, Alfred H., 134; preface to De Tabley's *Poems,* 133

Millais, John Everett: "Ophelia" and Gray's "On a Picture," 200

Miller, J. and Son, 87, 166, 284, 285, 286, 287, 288, 289

Milman, Lena, 94, 289. *See also* Dostoevski, Feodor

Milton, John, 21, 214

Mix, Katherine, 298

Monkhouse, Allan, 277
Books and Plays, 289; title page, 65; on Ibsen in, 223; exported to U.S.A., 312; production costs, 322

Monkhouse, [William] Cosmo, 15, 31; *Corn and Poppies,* 31, 56, 81, 87, 166, 186, 284, 297

Monroe, Lucy: on Bodley Head books, 309

Moore, George, 152, 199, 289; preface to *Poor Folk,* 100

Moore, T[homas] Sturge, 44; poetry in *Dial,* 304

Morris, William, 37, 41, 46, 58, 59, 134, 151, 195, 266, 302, 303; rivalry with Blaikie, 38; influence on Ricketts, 45; *The Roots of the Mountains,* 45, 51; *A Tale of the House of the Wolfings,* 45, 51; *The Defence of Guenevere,* 51; influence of Rossetti on, 51; *The Life and Death of Jason,* 51; *Love Is Enough,* 51; views on printing and typography, 53, 54; *Note on Aims,* 55; demand for first editions of, 80

Moulton, Louise Chandler, 285, 289; interest in P. B. Marston, 103; annual visit to England, 104; edits O'Shaughnessy's poetry, 185; reviewed Bodley Head books in U.S.A., 309

Muir, Percy, 12, 16, 31, 56, 77

Murray, Alma: roles of, 222–223; popularity of, 223. *See also Alma Murray as Beatrice Cenci*

Murray, Frank: transfers to Bodley Head, 314

National Observer, 247, 259, 309
National Review, 115, 260
Nettleship, John Trivett, 158, 168, 277
Robert Browning, 30, 60, 87, 262, 284;

agreement for publication, 94; exported to U.S.A., 312; production costs, 318

Nerval, Gérard de, 184–185

Nichol, J. B. B., *see* Beeching, H. C., *et al.*

Noble, James Ashcroft, 15, 277; reviewer for *Academy,* 14; edits *Liverpool Argus,* 17; reviews *Volumes in Folio,* 25; mentor to Le Gallienne and Watson, 363n90
The Sonnet in England and Other Essays, 262, 286, 297; payment for, 94; production costs, 318

Noel, Roden: *Poor People's Christmas,* 284
Nowell-Smith, Simon, 50
Nutt, David, 78

Oliver, Dr. George: *Lives of the Bishops of Exeter,* 3; *Monasticon Dioecesis Exoniensis,* 3. *See also* Attwood, J. S.

Orrock and Son: Bodley Head books bound by, 91

Osgood and McIlvaine, 41, 139; Ricketts' book designs for, 45

O'Shaughnessy, Arthur: interest in French literature, 185; Parnassian verse of, 185; *Arthur O'Shaughnessy, His Life and His Work,* 106, 185, 289, 312

Over, George E., 285, 286, 313. *See also* Rugby Press

Pall Mall Gazette, the: 82–83, 85, 130, 238
Pantazzi, Sybille, 71
Parnassians: doctrine of, 185; influence of Gautier, 185; poetry of, 185–187
Parnassiens: fixed verse forms of, 186
Pater, Walter, 53, 174, 215, 236, 242, 250; Le Gallienne's discipleship, 16, 20–21; influence, 16, 20–21, 153, 170–171, 173, 184, 190, 210, 339n94; *The Renaissance,* 21, 23, 49, 56–57, 184, 243; interest in book format, 49–50; Yeats's view of, 184; and decadent milieu, 188; Watson's attitude toward, 260–261; Rothenstein's portrait of, 292–293; opinion of Rossetti's poetry, 354n10
Appreciations: influence on Le Gallienne, 20–21, 113–114, 260; Watson's review of, 123, 260

Payne, John: *Songs of Life and Death,* 198
Pickering, William, 39, 48, 60, 61, 108
Pinkerton, Percy: review of *Silhouettes,* 197; *Galeazzo,* 314
Pioneer, the, 284, 304–305
Pissarro, Lucien, 44; art work in *Dial,* 304

Plant, Marjorie, 84

Plarr, Victor, 157, 160, 161, 167, 168, 170, 275, 279; Rhymers' Club verse of, 183

Poet Laureateship: battle for (1892–1895), 220

Poets and the Poetry of the Century, The: De Tabley's poems in, 133, 134. *See also* Miles, Alfred H.

Pollard, Alfred: essay on title pages, 70

Pound, Ezra, 13, 220, 279

Powell, York, 246, 273, 287, 290

Pre-Raphaelites, 17, 19, 47, 66, 151, 266, 267, 302, 306

Pritchard, Dr. Owen, 4, 9, 15, 245, 328n20

Publishers' Circular, the, 25, 34, 131, 276, 279, 283; on demand for first editions, 79–80; Bodley Head ads in, 81; *George Meredith* announced in, 125

Publishers' Weekly, 306, 307

Putnam's Sons, G. P., 88; and faulty shells for *Prose Fancies,* 104–105; Bodley Head exports to, 104–105, 311

Radford, Dollie, 275, 277; *A Light Load,* 285, 296

Radford, Ernest, 28, 157, 160, 163, 166, 168, 272, 273, 275–278

    Chambers Twain, 56, 284, 296; title page, 66; sheets required for, 86; Parnassian verse in, 186–187; production costs, 315

Raffalovich, Mark André, 239; friendship with John Gray, 198–199

Reade, Brian, 67–69, 73, 232, 239, 242, 263

Reading Guild Handbook, the, 284

Revival of Printing, the: 36–37, 47, 48, 51, 53, 58

Rhys, Ernst, 12, 84, 151, 163, 167, 168, 211, 245, 267, 277, 299; describes Le Gallienne, 29; co-founder of Rhymers' Club, 157; describes Rhymers' Club meeting, 158–159; on the *Hobby Horse,* 302; essay on artists in London, 367n75

    A London Rose, 51, 288, 296; title page, 66; binding, 76; exported to U.S.A., 312; production costs, 316, 320

Rhymers' Club, the, 279; aesthetic views of, 151; members, 151, 157–158, 168; genesis, 151, 157–160; antipathy to ideas, 153–154; books of characterized, 155–156; Yeats's description of, 156–157; Yeats on founding of, 157–158; meetings, 158–163, 267, 370n42; Mathews chosen as publisher for, 166; Bodley Head authors in, 166, 168; third book planned, 168, 276; poets of, 170–183, verse of, 183; support for Mathews among, 275–276; Irish origin, 355n32; lack of organization, 355n43. *See also Book of the Rhymers' Club* and *Second Book of the Rhymers' Club*

Ricketts, Charles de Sousy, 35, 36, 37, 60, 64, 67, 72, 95, 144, 233, 286, 295; as designer of books, 40–47; books designed for Wilde, 41; early career, 41–46; Bodley Head books designed by, 44–46; on design of *The Sphinx,* 45; views on book design, 46–47; influence on Housman, 47; book designs of, 57–58; title pages designed by, 69–70; influence of Rossetti, 73–75, 141, 207; binding designs, 73–75, 141, 207; contract for illustrating *The Sphinx,* 96–97; payment for *The Sphinx,* 99; illustrations for De Tabley's *Poems,* 137–138, 139, 145, 146, 148; De Tabley's hostility toward, 145; Bodley Head art work of, 296–297; edits the *Dial,* 303; early work, 335n21. *See also* Hacon and Ricketts; Ricketts and Shannon; Vale Press

Ricketts and Shannon, 96, 151, 245, 288, 304, 313; and the *Dial,* 44–45; influence of work, 47; Bodley Head art work of, 297

    Daphnis and Chloe, 44, 45, 47, 55, 58, 98, 290, 293, 297; subcription list for, 82; price, 108

    Hero and Leander, 44, 45, 55, 58, 76, 288, 290, 293, 297, 307; use of colophon in, 70; contract for, 98–99; price of, 108; exported to U.S.A., 311; production costs, 320

Robb, John, 23, 27, 28, 30, 32, 123, 132, 284; and printing of *George Meredith,* 117–119, 125–129, 131; Le Gallienne's devotion to, 119; Lane's anger toward, 128

Roberts Bros. (Boston), 94; publish *Keynotes* in U.S.A., 101; negotiations with Mathews, 104; Bodley Head exports to, 311

Roberts, W.: essay on first editions mania, 80, 81, 82

Rolleston, T. W., 157, 158, 161, 163, 168, 170

Roman Catholic church: and poets of nineties, 177–178; attitude of Decadents toward, 359n116

Ross, Robert, 239, 242, 298
Rossetti, Dante Gabriel, 18, 19, 27, 47, 53, 180, 182, 184, 213, 215, 268, 306; Le Gallienne's devotion to, 16; re-discovers Blake, 48; binding designs of, 51, 73–74; influence of, 51, 73–74, 187, 191, 210, 341n142; Bodley Head art work of, 297; Pater's critique of, 354n10
    Poems (1870): interest in format of, 50–51; binding design of, 73–74
Rossetti, Christina, 303; *The Prince's Progress*, 51; *Goblin Market*, 73
Rothenstein, Sir John, 293
Rothenstein, William, 44, 151, 245, 246, 273, 298; on Michael Field, 233–234; early life, 290; relations with Lane, 291; described by Beerbohm, 291–292; portrait of Pater, 292–293; Bodley Head art work of, 297
    Oxford Characters, 287, 297; contract, 99; genesis, 290; stir caused at Oxford, 291–292; controversy over, 291–293; original concept of, 293; production costs, 324
Royal Geographic Society: negotiations with for Bodley Head premises, 7, 8, 10, 329n34
Rugby Press, 56, 285, 286. *See also* Over, George E.
Ruskin, John, 17, 151, 264, 302, 303, 304
Ruskin Reading Guild: publications of, 304. *See also Reading Guild Handbook*

St. James's Gazette, the, 129, 130, 247, 279
Saintsbury, George: Watson critical of, 260–261
Saturday Review, the: review of *Poems, Dramatic and Lyrical* in, 148
Savoy, the, 151, 152
Schaff, Philip: *Literature and Poetry*, 13, 106, 284, 312
Scott, Temple, 17, 24, 112
Scott, William Bell, 79, 144, 297; *A Poet's Harvest Home*, 60, 286
Scribner's Sons, Charles, 24, 82, 106, 284; Bodley Head exports to, 311; Bodley Head imports from, 312
Second Book of the Rhymers' Club, The, 276, 289; contributions to solicited, 168–169; publication, 168, 169–170; format, 169; Yeats's opinion of, 170; reviews of, 170–171; verse of characterized, 170–183; disposition of at breakup, 275; ex-

ported to U.S.A., 312; production costs, 318
Sewell, Brocard, 198, 361n55
Shakespeare, William, 21, 223, 224
Shannon, Charles Hazlewood, 233, 286, 302; meets Ricketts, 41; early career, 41–47; binding designs of, 73; influence of Rossetti on, 73; designs for Wilde's plays, 97, 244; Bodley Head art work of, 297. *See also* Ricketts and Shannon
Sharp, William (Fiona MacLeod), 120, 122
Shelley, Edward, 96
Shelley, Percy B., 121, 172, 213; production of *The Cenci*, 222–223
Sketch, the: *Yellow Book* interview in, 299–300
Smith, George Dyke, 284, 304
Smithers, Leonard, 200
Spectator, the, 148, 220; Bodley Head ads in, 81
Spenser, Edmund: influence on Davidson, 229
Spirit Lamp, the: review of *Silhouettes* in, 197
Star, the, 211, 245, 307; Le Gallienne as "Logroller" for, 28–29; and "Dorian" controversy, 199
Stedman, Edmund Clarence: correspondence with Rhys, 158–159
Steer, Philip Wilson, 298; Bodley Head art work of, 295, 297
Stevenson, Robert Louis, 80, 122, 247, 255
Stoddard, Richard Henry: *The Lion's Cub with Other Verse*, 106, 285, 312
Stone and Kimball, 94, 289; Bodley Head imports from, 106, 312; influence of Bodley Head on, 306–307; Bodley Head exports to, 306–312 *passim*; credo, 307
Strang, William, 30–31, 79, 81, 295; Binyon on art of, 294; influence of Legros on, 294; Bodley Head art work of, 297
    The Earth Fiend, 35, 48, 60, 285, 290; production costs, 88, 316; etchings in, 294; publication, 294
Street, G[eorge] S[lythe], 263, 277
    Autobiography of a Boy, 262, 263–264, 288, 296; binding costs, 91; hero of, 263; Le Gallienne's report on, 263; as satire on aesthetes, 263; exported to U.S.A., 312; production costs, 316, 320
Studio, the, 47, 67; review of *Salome* in, 242

Sutton, Denys: on Ricketts and Shannon, 45

Swinburne, Algernon Charles, 121–122, 134, 201, 222; interest in French art, 184; influence of, 187, 197, 210

Symbolists, 202, 206, 207, 214, 250; influence on English poetry, 187, 188, 194; John Gray's knowledge of, 199

Symonds, John Addington, 277, 278, 286, 296; early life, 249; homosexual tendencies, 249–250; Italian travels, 250, 253–254

    In the Key of Blue, 45, 46, 57, 59, 60, 256, 309; binding design, 55, 74–75, 91; title page, 69; exported to U.S.A., 102, 311; bohemianism in, 246, 250, 253–254; poetry in, 250–253; impressionistic elements in, 250–253; Whistlerian effects in, 253; production costs, 320

Symons, A. J. A., 47, 52, 57, 67, 300; on Ricketts' book designs, 46; on books of nineties, 58; on Arthur Symons' poetry, 195; critique of Beardsley, 293–294

Symons, Arthur, 4, 117, 130, 150, 157, 161, 162, 163, 167, 168, 171, 210, 220, 245, 246, 275, 279; orientation of poetry, 151; broad aesthetic aims, 152–153; on Henley's verse, 153; on modernity in verse, 153, 195; on the Decadent Movement, 153, 212; on Dowson, 173, 174; Rhymers' Club verse of, 183; early life, 187; influence on Yeats, 187; influences on poetry of, 187–188, 360n11; meets Verlaine, 187–188; decadent nature of, 188–189, 191

    Silhouettes, 31, 35, 285, 296; reviews of, 55, 197–198, 211; "Javanese Dancers," 183, 192–194; French influence on, 187–198 *passim;* format, 188; publication, 188; impressionist elements in, 188–190, 192, 196, 197; analysis of poetry of, 188–197; preface, 195; poetry of the city in, 195–197; influences on poetry of, 196, 197, 198; public attitude toward, 211; and modern poetic tradition, 220; bohemian aspects of, 246

Taylor, John Russell, 64, 69; on the *art nouveau* book, 52, 55–56

Temple, Ruth Z., 187

Tennyson, Alfred, Lord, 134, 143, 212, 219, 220, 228; *Poems, Chiefly Lyrical,* 140; verse compared with Johnson's, 182; attitude toward French poetry, 184

Thompson, D'Arcy Wentworth: essay on Blaikie quoted, 37, 38

Thompson, Francis, 157, 160, 168, 245, 277; *Poems,* 47, 59, 287, 296, 306, 309; title page, 64; binding design, 75; sales, 107; exported to U.S.A., 311; production costs, 320

Times, the (London), 129, 301; review of *Salome* in, 236

Todhunter, John, 157, 161, 162, 163, 166, 168, 222, 225, 233, 267, 274, 275, 277, 279; Rhymers' meeting at home of, 159–160; influence of Hegel, 228; neighbor of Mathews, 229; home described, 355n40

    A Sicilian Idyll, 56, 66, 87, 221, 232, 266, 284, 295; production costs, 86, 315; reviews of, 224, 228; genesis of, 224–226 *passim;* analysis of, 224–228; Yeats's approval of, 226, 228; produced at Bedford Park, 228–229; decorated by Crane, 229; publication of, 229

Townsend, J. Benjamin, 229, 254

Tree, Herbert Beerbohm: *The Imaginative Faculty,* 54, 72, 98, 109, 287, 296, 316

Tynan, Katharine, *see* Hinkson, Katharine Tynan

Unwin, T. Fisher: books transferred to Bodley Head from, 314

Vale, The, 47, 151; described, 44; gatherings at, 44

Vale Press, the, 44, 45, 46, 244, 313

Van Dyke, Henry: *The Poetry of Tennyson,* 13, 54, 87, 106, 107, 262, 277, 284, 312, 320

Verlaine, Paul, 290; definition of poetry, 153; influence on Symons, 187–188, 196, 198; John Gray's translations of, 206; visit to England, 246

Vigo Cabinet series, 329n34

Vigo Street: Dunthorne's shop in, 7; Bodley Head premises in, 7–12 *passim;* history of, 10, 12, 329n43

Walker, Emery: lecture on printing, 40, 51, 53–54, 59, 89–90

Walton, Izaak: Mathews' patron saint, 1; Mathews' celebration of, 267; Le Gallienne's essay on, 368n100

Warren, John Leicester, *see* De Tabley, Lord

Watson, William, 17, 120, 150, 151, 157, 168, 222, 277; demand for first editions of, 80; mental illness, 97; contract negotiations with, 97–98; criticism of Meredith, 115; role in *Yellow Book* crisis, 211, 301; traditionalist literary position, 215–216; hostility to French influence, 216; on Ibsen's dramas, 223; attitude toward Wilde, 238; literary criticism of, 260–261; attitude toward Pater, 260–261; on "Beardsley Period," 301–302; popularity in U.S.A., 308, 310; rivalry with Le Gallienne, 260, 363n90

  The Prince's Quest, 75, 79, 285, 313, 314

  The Prince's Quest (2nd ed.) 75, 85, 94, 97, 98, 211, 285 314, 316, 320

  The Eloping Angels, 90–91, 94, 98, 107, 286, 296, 309, 316, 320

  Excursions in Criticism: 97, 102–103, 107, 260–261, 262, 286, 311, 320

Watts, Theodore (Watts-Dunton), 117, 122; urges De Tabley to publish poems, 133–134; characterizes De Tabley, 135; review of *Poems, Dramatic and Lyrical*, 147–148

Watts-Dunton, Theodore, *see* Watts, Theodore

Wedmore, Frederick: *Renunciations*, 15, 56, 59, 273, 277, 286; *Pastorals of France; Renunciations*, 287, 296, 311, 320

Welch, Jimmy, 22, 28; friendship with Le Gallienne, 17

Whistler, James McNeill, 44, 82, 151, 153, 253, 293; *The Gentle Art*, 21, 52; influence of, 51–52, 69, 73, 196, 197, 210; title pages designed by, 69

White, Gleeson, 15, 47; Bodley Head art work of, 297; *Letters to Living Artists*, 262, 285, 315

Wicksteed, Philip Henry: *Dante: Six Sermons*, 13, 54, 91, 107, 109, 320

Wilde, Oscar, 18, 22, 44, 56, 57, 69, 150, 151, 158, 160, 168, 212, 232, 263, 264, 267, 274, 303; Le Gallienne's adulation of, 16, 19–20, 130–131; interest in book design, 41, 53, 72–73; *Dorian Gray*, 41, 58, 199; visits to The Vale, 44; offers to finance *Silverpoints*, 95; contracts negotiated with Bodley Head, 95–97; *A Woman of No Importance*, 97, 222, 245; *The Duchess of Padua*, 97, 245, 274; en-

livens the Rhymers, 161; friendship with John Gray, 199, 206; influence of French writers on, 210; opinion of French art, 210–211; arrest and trial of, 211, 343n16; advice on *Question of Memory*, 234, 235; relations with Lane, 237, 274, 366n48; Watson's poem about, 238; rift with Beardsley, 239; *The Importance of Being Earnest*, 244, 274; praises *Dial*, 304

  The Sphinx, 46, 58, 60, 76, 275, 288, 297, 307; Ricketts' designs for, 45; title page, 70; binding designs, 73, 91; contract, 96–97; price, 105, 108; French influence on, 207; publication, 210; production costs, 322; exported to U.S.A., 311

  Salome, A Tragedy in One Act, 87, 99, 201, 275, 288, 295, 306, 307, 308, 309; Wilde's dislike of binding, 53; title page, 69, 242; binding design, 73; contract, 97; prices, 105–106, 108–109; heroine of, 235–236; reviews of, 236, 242; characterized, 236, 242–243, 244; publication, 238, 242; Beardsley's illustrations for, 238–239, 242; row over illustrations, 239; relation of text to illustrations, 242; decadent elements in, 242–243; exported to U.S.A., 311; production costs, 316, 322

  Lady Windermere's Fan, 87, 221, 287, 297; binding, 73; contract, 97; discussed, 243–244; produced, 244; published, 245; production costs, 316

  Poems (1892), 35, 41, 45, 285, 296; sheets bought from Bogue, 79; binding costs, 91; contract, 95–96; French influence on, 207–210, influence of Whistler on, 210

  Salomé, drame en un acte, 286; cover described, 236; publication, 236; refused license, 236, 237–238; reaction to censorship, 237–238

  plays: designed by Charles Shannon, 244; contract for, 244; discussed, 235–245, 309

  "The Portrait of Mr. W. H.," 46, 57, 245; negotiations for publication of, 274–275

Wordsworth, William, 133, 248

World Literature, 285, 304

Wratislaw, Theodore: *Love's Memorial*, 211–212

Wynne, Frances: *Whisper!*, 79, 288, 313, 314, 322

Ye Sette of Odd Volumes, 124, 129, 151, 353n5

Yeats, Jack, 266, 267, 369n6

Yeats, William Butler, 13, 159, 160, 161, 163, 167, 168, 184, 187, 192, 199, 213, 220, 273, 275, 278, 279, 290; describes Rhymers, 153–154, 156–157; on founding of Rhymers' Club, 157–158; "Lake Isle of Innisfree," 162, 172, 183, 358n99; on *Second Book of the Rhymers' Club*, 170; Rhymers' Club verse of, 171–173, 183; early years, 171–172; interest in Irish legend, 171–173; hostility to Parnassians, 185; concept of poetic drama, 225–226; describes Bedford Park, 266–267

Yellow Book, the, 12, 151, 159, 232, 265, 271, 273, 274, 277, 278, 288, 295; published in U.S.A. by Copeland and Day, 103, 307, 311; *succès de scandale* of, 107, 300–301; sales, 108; crisis, 211, 268; Beardsley's art work in, 266, 300; genesis, 298; aims, 299–300; distinctive features, 300; format, 300; publication dinner, 300; parodies of, 301; reviews of, 301; popularity in U.S.A., 308, 310; production costs, 322

Young, Austin: Bodley Head art work of, 297

Zola, Émile, 222, 264